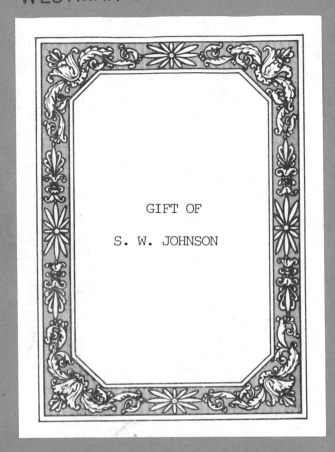

Theories of Personality

LAWRENCE S. WRIGHTSMAN
Consulting Editor

The Environment and Social Behavior:
Privacy, Personal Space, Territory and Crowding
Irwin Altman, The University of Utah

Contemporary Issues in Social Psychology, 3rd Edition
John C. Brigham, Florida State University
Lawrence S. Wrightsman, University of Kansas

The Behavior of Women and Men
Kay Deaux, Purdue University

Research Projects in Social Psychology:
An Introduction to Methods
Michael King, California State University, Chico
Michael Ziegler, York University

Moving Bodies: Nonverbal Communication in Social Relations
Marianne LaFrance, Boston College
Clara Mayo, Boston University

Evaluating Research in Social Psychology:
A Guide for the Consumer
Clara Mayo, Boston University
Marianne LaFrance, Boston College

Toward Understanding Women
Virginia E. O'Leary, Oakland University

Three Views of Man: Perspectives from Sigmund Freud,
B. F. Skinner, and Carl Rogers
Robert D. Nye, State University of New York, College at New Paltz

Theories of Personality
Duane Schultz, The American University

Dictionary of Social Behavior and Social Research Methods
David J. Stang
Lawrence S. Wrightsman, University of Kansas

Interpersonal Behavior
Harry C. Triandis, University of Illinois at Urbana-Champaign

Social Psychology, Second Edition
Lawrence S. Wrightsman, University of Kansas

Theories of Personality

Duane Schultz
The American University

Brooks/Cole Publishing Company
Monterey, California

A Division of Wadsworth Publishing Company, Inc.

ISBN: 0-8185-0179-0
L.C. Catalog Card No.: 75-32953
Printed in the United States of America

10   9   8

Production Editor: *Valerie Daigen*
Interior & Cover Design: *John Edeen*
Illustrations: *Reed Sanger*
Typesetting: *Continental Graphics, Los Angeles, California*

To Sydney Ellen

Preface

This text is written expressly for the undergraduate student with no previous exposure to personality theories. My purpose is to inform and interest people who know little of the topic, and, if the style of writing is clear and, on occasion, even engaging, then I hope their difficult task has been made a bit easier. I have not written for instructors or researchers in the field. Rather, I have tried to offer the general outline and flavor of various theories—a clear map or picture of the forest, not an exhaustive analysis of every tree.

The theories are discussed as objectively and fairly as possible. The book is not an indoctrination to any one point of view but an introduction to diverse points of view. The students may well form their own biases, but they shouldn't feel compelled to accept mine.

I believe the beginning undergraduate student must be aware of the diversity of approaches to the understanding of personality, and I have therefore included theorists representing psychoanalytic, neoanalytic, self, developmental, cognitive, trait, stimulus-response, and social-learning approaches, as well as both clinical and laboratory approaches to the field. The last chapter deals with several theorists who approach personality in limited-domain fashion by focusing on only one personality construct rather than attempting to account for the total personality. I have included an appendix dealing with current developments in German-language personology in order to expose the student to still other ways of studying personality.

Where biographical data are sufficient, I have speculated on how the development of various theories might have been influenced by specific events and experiences in the theorists' personal and/or professional lives. Students are often surprised and fascinated by how closely a theoretical position seems to reflect early experiences in the life of a theorist. This apparent correspondence may suggest that the development of science through theory construction is not always objective and rational but rather can be influenced by personal experiences that are refined and extended by more rational processes.

Each theory is discussed as a unity. While I recognize the value of an "issues" or "problems" approach that contrasts and compares a number of theories on specific points, I think its usefulness is greater with more advanced students. The issues-oriented book may not allow the beginning student to unite the many facets of a theory in order to gain an understanding of its essence or flavor. In this book, each theory is organized and presented in the way that seems clearest for that theory; I have not attempted to force the divergent points of view into a standard format. However, the last three sections in the discussion of each theory are: techniques of inquiry, the image of human nature provided by the theory, and an evaluative comment.

Except for placing Freud first, in recognition of his chronological priority, I have not arranged the theorists in any order of perceived importance. Nor should any suggestion of relative significance be inferred from the varying lengths of the chapters.

Suggested readings are offered at the end of each chapter, and an instructor's manual is available.

I am grateful to Professor Lewis W. Brandt of the University of Regina (Canada) for pointing out the importance of current work in German-language personology and for writing the appendix. Professor George Windholz read several chapters of the book and offered valuable comments. I would also like to thank the following reviewers for their helpful comments: Dr. Desmond Cartwright, University of Colorado, Dr. Bruce R. Fretz, University of Maryland, Dr. Jaques Kaswan, Ohio State University, Dr. Rhoda Lindner, California State University, Long Beach, Dr. John McGuire, Florida Technological University, Dr. Robert C. Nicolay, Loyola University, Dr. David A. Sachs, New Mexico State University, Dr. David Sue, California State University, Chico, Dr. Richard G. Weigel, Colorado State University, and Consulting Editor Dr. Lawrence S. Wrightsman, George Peabody College for Teachers.

My wife, Sydney Ellen, deserves my greatest thanks. When I needed a source, no matter how obscure, it magically appeared on my desk, along with criticisms where warranted and advice and encouragement where needed. From research to final editing, her influence is present on every page.

Duane Schultz

Contents

The Study of Personality Theories 1

Many students begin the study of psychology excited at the prospect of learning all about personality—their own or someone else's. It is often with disappointment that the introductory psychology student discovers that personality is only one part of psychology, and a rather small part at that.

In the standard thick and heavy introductory textbook, perhaps only two or three chapters out of 20 or so are devoted to the topic that first sparked the students' interest in the field. They find themselves reading instead about the nervous system, drives, perception, learning, thinking, and statistics. If my own experience in teaching the first course in psychology is any indication, many students feel almost cheated, as though they had signed up for one course and were given something else instead.

Now you are beginning a course devoted entirely to theories that have been devised to explain the nature of personality. Lest you experience another disappointment, there is one point on which you should be warned. Reflected in the title of this book, *Theories of Personality*, is the fact that there are a plurality of ways of looking at the topic. There is not one single theory, not even the best known (Freud's), that you can turn to with absolute assurance of finding the ultimate answer to the riddle of personality.

You will find, in the pages to follow, a lack of consensus among psychologists regarding the nature of personality. There is no single conception of the subject on which all, or even most, psychologists agree. Indeed, it is even difficult to find agreement on the definition of personality, much less on its nature and characteristics. Instead, diverse definitions and theories of personality are developed, expounded, and defended with equal passion and conviction.

Be warned, therefore, not to look for one answer to the question "What is personality?" There is no neat or simple answer—at least not yet. The complexity of the subject matter is evident in the diversity of the attempts to come to grips with it. What you will find in this book is a discussion of some of the answers thus far offered. As to which, if any, of these theories is the best or perhaps ultimate answer, who is to say? Only those persons already committed, intellectually and emotionally, to one position can answer that question with certainty.

This is not to suggest that one of these theories may turn out to be correct and all the others wrong. It is not so simple as that. That the theories conflict with one another does not necessarily indicate that they are misguided and destined to fall into disrepute. Any one theory may be partly correct or all theories may be partly correct, and the final answer may involve the combination of part-truths into yet another theory. Thus, although it may eventually transpire that none of these theories will suffice as the complete explanation, for now they represent the level of development of that part of psychology that attempts to understand the human personality.

Why Study Theories of Personality?

Since psychology is not yet in a position to agree on a common definition and theory of the nature of personality, why, you may ask, should you expend the effort and time demanded by this course? Of what value is the study of personality theories to you, or to society?

The lack of agreement among theorists does not necessarily imply that the various theories are not useful. Psychologists do not agree on a single definition of intelligence, but that has not prevented them from using the concept of intelligence in a variety of ways to understand and predict human behavior.

Each of the personality theories offers tantalizing insights into human nature—conclusions based, for the most part, on years of patient probing, questioning, and listening to what people have to say. These theories are the work of highly perceptive and intelligent individuals, each of whom has looked closely at mankind through the uniquely ground lens of his or her theoretical viewpoint.

The theorists have something important, impressive, and provocative to say about the nature of human beings. If they do not always agree, we must look to three factors to explain the dissension: (1) the complexity of the subject matter, (2) the differing historical and personal contexts in which each theory was formulated, and (3) the fact that psychology is such a young discipline, a recent entry in the catalog of sciences.

Indeed, the very facts of its newness and complexity make personality a fascinating subject for study. It is not a closed or finished subject in which one simply learns the rules and definitions and then moves on to something else. On the contrary, the study of personality is still evolving, and, for those who like the challenge and excitement of exploring areas not yet fully mapped, there could be no more appropriate or useful study than personality.

There is also a personal reason for this course of study: natural curiosity about our own behavior. Why do we act and think and feel as we do? Why do you respond to a certain event in one way and your friend in another way?

Why is one person aggressive and another inhibited, one courageous and another fearful, one sociable and another shy? What makes us the way we are and our brother or sister—reared in the same house—totally different? Why do some people seem so successful at life in terms of their friendships, careers, and marriages, while others, perhaps with equal potential, move from one failure to another?

Surely the need to understand ourselves, the curiosity about our motives and fears, is strong in most of us. Through the examination of these various approaches to personality, you may achieve at least a modest beginning to the difficult and usually lifelong task of knowing yourself.

There is one additional reason for the study of personality—perhaps the most vital and compelling reason of all. When we examine the multitude of crises and problems confronting us in the closing decades of the 20th century, we see one root cause: human beings themselves.

Consider some of the problems that we face today: threat of war, depletion of natural resources, rape of the environment, overpopulation, prejudice, rampant crime, injustice, exploitation, epidemic starvation, emotional sickness. The human misery these problems provoke and reflect is evident all around us.

These conditions can be ameliorated through a more fully developed understanding of human nature. Abraham Maslow, a contemporary theorist, wrote: "If we improve human nature we improve all, for we remove the principal causes of world disorder."[1] Through a truer under-

---

[1]A. H. Maslow. A philosophy of psychology: The need for a mature science of human nature. *Main Currents In Modern Thought*, 1957, 13, 27–32.

standing of ourselves and those around us, we can better cope with the problems of modern life. This is probably more important than achieving a higher standard of living and certainly more vital than new weapons or technological breakthroughs. History has shown repeatedly that advances in technology have disastrous consequences when put to use by greedy, selfish, fearful, or hate-filled people. Thus, because humanity's greatest hope may lie in an improved understanding of itself, the study of personality may well be psychology's most important endeavor.

The Place of Personality in Psychology

Because of the importance of the study of personality, and of its primary role in the understanding of behavior, it seems quite natural to assume that the field of personality has occupied a prominent position in psychology throughout the history of the field. Indeed, it might reasonably be assumed that personality is what psychology is all about. This is not the case, however. Personality is not the dominant emphasis in psychology today; for more than half of psychology's history as a science, it paid relatively little attention to personality.

Psychology emerged as an independent and primarily experimental science out of an amalgamation of certain trends in philosophy and physiology. The birth of the new discipline took place more than a century ago in Germany and was primarily the work of Wilhelm Wundt, who began psychology's first laboratory in the 1870s.

The new science of psychology was directed toward the analysis of conscious experience into its elemental components, and its method was strongly modeled after the approach taken by the natural sciences. Physics and chemistry were, so it seemed, unlocking all the secrets of the physical universe by reducing the material world to its basic elements and studying each of those elements. If, it was argued, the material world could be understood by the method of reduction—breaking it down into elements—why couldn't the mental universe, the mind, be studied in the same way?

The method by which physics and chemistry pursue their work is the experimental method. So convinced was Wundt of the efficacy of this approach that he studied only those psychological processes that could be investigated by the experimental method—for example, reaction time, the time taken for various conscious processes to occur. Thus, Wundt and others of his time who were concerned with studying human nature were greatly affected by the example of the natural-science approach.

In this way, researchers proceeded to study the mind. Since they felt they could use only the experimental method, they were limited to those mental processes that could be affected by some external stimulus capable of being manipulated and controlled by the experimenter. In practice, that constraint restricted them to the study of sensory-perceptual processes and of other experience of quite limited dimensions. There was little room in this approach for consideration of a multidimensional construct such as personality. The topic, complex and vague, was not compatible with either the subject matter or the methodology of the new science of psychology.

In the early decades of this century, a revolution occurred in American psychology, directed against the work of Wilhelm Wundt. The new movement, behaviorism—led by the psychologist John B. Watson—opposed Wundt's focus on conscious experience.[2] Even more devoted to a natural-science approach than Wundt, Watson argued that psychology, if it was to become a science, must focus only on the tangible aspects of human beings: that which can be seen, heard, recorded, and measured. In short, only overt behavior could be the legitimate topic of psychology. Watson's revolution was highly successful; his definition of psychology as the "science of behavior" is the one we find in most introductory psychology texts today.

Consciousness, Watson said, cannot be seen or experimented upon, and so, like the older concept of soul, it is meaningless for science. The psychologist must deal only with what he or she can see and manipulate and measure, and that means only the external stimulus and the subject's response to it. According to Watson, whatever happens inside the organism after the stimulus is presented and before the response is made cannot be seen or experimented upon and is, as a result, sheer speculation of no scientific interest.

Behaviorism presents a mechanistic image of human beings, who are seen as well-ordered machines responding automatically to external stimuli. It has been said that behaviorists depict a person as a vending machine. Stimuli are fed in to him or her (or it), and appropriate conditioned responses (learned from past experiences) spill out. Personality, in this view, is nothing more than the accumulation of learned responses, or "habit systems." Personality is reduced to what can be seen and observed objectively.

Where, you may ask, are all those notions, feelings, and confusions that come to mind when you use the word *personality*? Where is the consciousness that you experience every moment you are awake? Where are those unconscious forces that sometimes seem to move you in mysterious ways and over which you feel no sense of control?

---

[2]At approximately the same time, a German movement, Gestalt psychology, was also revolting against the Wundtian approach. Our focus, however, is on behaviorism and the uniquely American form of psychology that it shaped.

These problems were dealt with in another area of inquiry, one that began independently of Wundt and experimental psychology. They were investigated by Sigmund Freud and what he called *psychoanalysis.* There seems no doubt that much of contemporary personality theory has been influenced more by Freud than by any psychologist. Notice that I did not say any *other* psychologist.

Psychoanalysis and psychology are not synonymous or interchangeable terms. Freud was not a psychologist by training. He was a physician in private practice, working with persons suffering emotional disturbances. Though trained as a scientist, he did not use psychology's method of experimentation in his work. Instead, he developed his theory of personality on the basis of *clinical observation* of his patients. That is, through a lengthy series of psychoanalytic sessions, Freud applied his creative interpretation to what the patients told him of their feelings and past experiences, both actual and fantasized. While his work can certainly be considered scientific (in the broad sense of the term), it was far removed from the rigorous experimental laboratory investigation of the elements of behavior, whether defined in Wundtian or in behavioristic terms.

Under the impetus of Freud's work, the first small group of personality theorists, outside the mainstream of academic experimental psychology, developed unique conceptions of human nature. These theorists focused on the whole person as he or she functions (or tries to function) in the real world, rather than on elements of behavior (stimulus-response units) as studied in the laboratory. Further, these early personality theorists assumed or accepted the existence of both conscious and unconscious forces. Such assumptions were anathema to the behaviorists, who accepted the existence of nothing they could not see. As a result of their emphases and methods, these initial personality theorists had to be speculative in their work, relying more on inference based on observations of patients' behavior than on the quantitative and experimental operations dictated by experimental psychology.

Thus, we see that psychology and the study of personality began in two entirely separate traditions, using different methods and pursuing different aims.

This is not to suggest that experimental psychology in its early years totally ignored personality. Aspects of personality were being studied (primarily in the area of individual differences), but there did not exist a psychology of personality as an area of specialization. Personality did not have a separate identity as did child psychology or social psychology.

It was not until the mid-1930s that the study of personality became formalized and systematized in American psychology. Professional books appeared, universities offered courses, research was begun, and there was a growing recognition that psychoanalysis—or at least some aspects of it—could be incorporated into psychology to form the basis of a scientific study of personality.

Experimental psychology has made increasing use of certain concepts from Freudian theory and its derivatives, and psychoanalysis is more and more aware of the benefits of the experimental method, but there has not been a full merging of or agreement between the two approaches. They began as separate traditions and so, for the most part, they remain. We shall see examples of both approaches in the theories to follow. Each approach offers advantages and one of the basic issues in psychology today is the question of which approach may ultimately prove to be of greater value. Each has a definite contribution to make, and both must be given an open and impartial hearing.

The Definition of Personality

The lack of agreement about the nature of personality and which approach is most effective to study it is reflected by an equal amount of disagreement with regard to the word itself. In his classic study of personality, Gordon Allport[3] discussed some 50 definitions of *personality*. It is a word that we all use, however loosely or inaccurately, and that we all feel we know the meaning of. And perhaps we do.

One psychologist[4] suggested that we can get a fairly good idea of the meaning of the word *personality* if we closely examine what we intend and encompass every time we use the word *I*. When you say *I*, you are, in effect, summing up everything about yourself—your likes and dislikes, preferences and penchants, fears and loathings, virtues and weaknesses. The word *I* is what defines you as an individual, as a person separate and apart from all the other individuals in the world.

We could, in our effort to define the word more precisely, look to its source. *Personality* derives from the Latin word *persona*, which refers to the masks used by actors in the Greek theater. It is easy to see how the word *persona* came to refer to an outward appearance, a public face that individuals display to those around them.

Based on its derivation, then, we might conclude that personality refers to those external and visible aspects of a person that other people can see. Thus, a person's personality would be defined in terms of the impression that he or she makes on others—that is, what the person appears to be. The first definition of personality in a standard college dictionary is in accord with that derivation: the visible aspect of one's character as it impresses others.

[3]Gordon Allport. *Personality: A Psychological Interpretation.* (New York: Holt, Rinehart and Winston, 1937.)

[4]D. Adams. *The Anatomy of Personality.* (Garden City, N.Y.: Doubleday, 1954.)

But is that all we mean when we use the word *personality*? Are we talking only about what we can actually see, what a person displays to us? Does personality refer solely to the facade, the mask, the role that we play for other people? Most of us, I think, mean more than that when we use the term. We are usually referring to many attributes of an individual—a sum total or constellation of various characteristics including more than just surface appearances. We refer to a host of subjective or internal characteristics as well, ones that we may not be able to see directly or that a person may try to hide from us—and that we may try to hide from others.

We may also, in our use of the word *personality*, refer to enduring characteristics. We assume a degree of stability and predictability in a person's personality. However, while we recognize that a friend may be calm much of the time, we know that he or she can also be excited, nervous, or even on the verge of panic at other times. Personality, therefore, is not rigid and unchanging, yet we do recognize that for many situations the attributes that distinguish an individual are reasonably consistent.

We may also feel that personality is unique to each of us. While we recognize similarities among people, we sense that individuals possess special properties or combinations of properties that distinguish them from one another. Thus, in everyday life, we tend to think of personality as an enduring and unique cluster of characteristics.

But this is not a definition on which all psychologists would agree. To achieve any degree of precision in defining the concept, we will have to understand what each theorist means by his or her own use of the term. Each theorist offers a unique version—a personal vision of the nature of personality—and that view becomes a definition of the term. And that is what this course is all about: to reach an understanding of these different versions of the concept of personality and to examine the various ways of defining *I*.

The Role of Theory

The notion of a theory is often described in contemptuous or derogatory terms, as exemplified by the comment "Well, it's only a theory." Many people feel that a theory is always vague, abstract, speculative—really no more than a hunch or a guess and quite the opposite of a fact.

It is true that a theory without evidence to support it is speculation. It seems equally true, however, that a mass of research data can be meaningless unless it is organized into some sort of explanatory framework or context. A theory provides this framework for simplifying and describing empirical data in a meaningful way. A theory can be considered a kind of map that represents the data in their relationships with one another. It attempts to bring data into some kind of order, to fit them into an overall structure in which each datum is an integral part.

Theories are not restricted to science; we all use personal theories in our everyday interactions with others. As discussed earlier, we all have some idea of the concept of personality, and we all make certain suppositions about the personalities of those with whom we interact. Further, many of us speculate about human nature in general. We may believe, for example, that "all people are basically decent" or that "people care only about themselves."

These suppositions are theories. They are frameworks within which we place the data of our commonplace observations of other people. We usually form these personal theories on the basis of data derived from our perception of the behavior of those around us. In that respect—the fact that our theories derive from our observations—personal theories are similar to formal theories in psychology.

However, this is the only point of similarity. Personal theories have several major weaknesses compared to the more fully developed scientific variety. In the first place, we usually derive our personal theories on the basis of a limited number and type of people. In contrast, a psychologist developing a theory systematically observes many more people, and usually of more diverse natures, than are generally found among an individual's circle of friends and acquaintances. Thus, the personality theorist draws on a much broader range of data to support his or her theory.

Also, our own theorizing is based on observation of ourselves as much as of others. We tend to interpret the actions of other people in terms of our own thoughts and feelings, evaluating their reactions on the basis of our own feelings or behavior in similar situations. In other words, we view others in highly subjective and personal terms. Ideally, scientists are able to observe more objectively, without being biased in what they see by their own needs, fears, desires, and values.

A third weakness of personal theories is that we tend to persist in our beliefs even in the face of contradictory evidence. Once we have developed a theory about people in general, or one person in particular, we tend to see only those behaviors that confirm our theory and fail to see those that refute it.

Ideally, psychological theorists are not blinded by their theories;[5] they are able to observe reality as it is and not as they want or need it to be. They are not committed to only one point of view but are capable

---

[5]Unfortunately, there are many examples in the history of science and psychology of individuals who were biased or prejudiced by their theory. Some scientists become so thoroughly committed, intellectually and emotionally, to their theoretical positions that their objectivity is compromised. Still, the ideal of objectivity remains the goal toward which all scientists strive.

of seeing and accepting data that do not support their theories. Further, the psychologist should be able to change and even reject his or her theory if sufficient new evidence against it is found.

Formal theories are tested repeatedly against reality, often by scientists other than the one who proposed the theory. Our personal theories are not so tested, either by ourselves or by a neutral party.

While we all use personal theories in our everyday interactions with other people, our theories differ in several ways from formal theories of personality.The personality theories discussed in this book were systematically developed and formulated and attempt to be comprehensive and complete in accounting for the complex behavior of the whole person functioning in the real world. They are supported to various degrees by empirical research.

One should not get the impression, however, that theories or conjectures about personality are the sole approach to understanding human nature. Research is constantly being conducted on various aspects of personality: motives, drives, personality types or traits, the influence of childhood experiences on personality development, and so on. In addition, much research is aimed at devising ways of assessing or measuring personality. Indeed, the development and use of personality tests constitute significant portions of American psychology. This research has been performed on animals and humans in psychological laboratories and on patients in institutions and in the offices of psychologists in private practice. Personality research has been so extensive and broad that a whole course could easily be devoted to its methods and findings.

However, that is not our purpose. We shall focus on theories, those frameworks that seek to incorporate and describe research data and that depend on data for their form and validity. As we discuss each theory, we shall examine the techniques of inquiry used by the individual theorist—the methods by which the supporting data were gathered. And we shall also note the kind of data on which each theory is based.

One final word about the interrelationship of data and theories: not only is a theory formed on the basis of empirical data, but in turn the theory generates new research inquiries that further investigate certain of its aspects, as well as new techniques of assessment and therapy. Thus, a theory both incorporates research data and leads to the search for new data. Ideally, the theory is reshaped, modified, and elaborated—or discarded—on the basis of the research it has generated.

Issues in Personality Theory

There are a number of fundamental questions that people have asked, and are still asking, about their own nature—questions that go to the very core of what it means to be a human being. Poets, philosophers, and artists continually rephrase these questions, and we see their widely varying attempts at answers in our great books and paintings.

Personality theorists too have addressed themselves to these thorny questions and have reached no greater consensus than have painters or writers. Not every theorist has grappled with each of the issues, but, by the time you complete this book, you will have seen diverse points of view on each question.

The first of these basic issues concerns the perennial controversy between *free will* and *determinism*. Do we consciously direct the course of our own actions? Can we spontaneously choose the direction of our thoughts and behavior, rationally selecting from among alternatives? Do we, in other words, have a conscious awareness and control of ourselves? Are we free to choose, to be masters of our own fates, or are we simply victims of past experiences? Are we prisoners of what happened to us as children? Have these early experiences so firmly shaped our personalities that we are capable only of behaving in accordance with our pasts?

We will see personality theorists taking both extremes on this issue and some, taking more moderate positions, arguing that some behavior is determined by past events while other actions can be spontaneously chosen and directed.

The second issue has to do with the *nature-nurture* controversy. Which is the more important influence on behavior: inherited attributes or the features of the individual's environment? Is our nature—our personality—determined solely by the abilities, temperaments, or predispositions that we may inherit, or are we shaped more strongly by the environments in which we live? Controversy rages on the topic of intelligence: is it influenced more by genetic endowment or by the quality and amount of stimulation available in the home and school? The same question is asked about personality.

As is the case with the first issue, the alternatives are not limited to extreme positions. A number of theorists assume that personality is shaped by both sets of forces. To some, one type of influence is predominant and the other of minor importance, although both are believed to be determinants of personality.

A third issue involves the relative importance of *childhood experiences* as compared with experiences that occur later in life. Which set of experiences is the more powerful in shaping personality? If we assume, as some theorists do, that what happens to us in infancy and childhood is critical to personality formation, we must consequently believe that the later development of the individual is little more than an elaboration of basic themes laid down in the early years of life. Our personalities, so this line of thought goes, are rather firmly fixed by the age of 5 or so and subject to little change over the rest of our lives. The personality of the adult, then, is determined by the nature of these early experiences.

The opposite position on this issue considers personality to be more independent of the past, capable of being influenced by events and experiences in the person's present and even by his or her future aspirations and goals. Of course, an intermediate position is also available. One could assume that early experiences do indeed shape personality, but not rigidly or permanently. In this view, later experience may function to reinforce or alter earlier personality growth.

How truly *unique* is each individual? This is another issue that often divides personality theorists. A person's personality may be viewed as being so individual that each act, each utterance, has no counterpart or equivalent in any other person. This obviously makes comparison of one person with another absolutely meaningless. Other positions allow for uniqueness but interpret this characteristic within overall patterns of behavior accepted as more or less universal, at least within a given culture.

A fifth issue revolves around what might be called the *ultimate and necessary goals* of human beings. Theorists differ in opinion on what constitutes a person's major motivation. Are we each simply a sort of self-regulating mechanism, content as long as our basic physiological requirements are satisfied? Do we function solely to obtain pleasure and avoid pain? Is our happiness dependent only on keeping tensions at a minimum?

Some theorists view humans as more than tension-reducing, pleasure-grabbing animals. They consider individuals to be motivated primarily by the need to actualize or realize their full potentials, to stretch themselves, to reach for ever-higher levels of self-expression and development.

There is one additional issue that you may have already decided for yourself: are human beings basically *good or evil*, kind or cruel, compassionate or merciless? Here we are dealing with a question of morality, a value judgment, which supposedly has no place in the objective and dispassionate world of science. The question, however, has been dealt with, at least implicitly, by some of our theorists. Some views of personality are clearly more optimistic and hopeful than others, depicting mankind as humanitarian, altruistic, and socially conscious. Others see few, if any, of these qualities in humans—individually or collectively.

The important point about these issues is that there are diverse ways of looking at the development and growth of the human personality. Perhaps one or more of these theories (or parts of all of them) will be congenial to you, or perhaps they will clash with your personal views. It is a study few of us can approach with an absence of prejudice, for it is the study of ourselves.

Suggested Readings

Carlson, R. Personality. *Annual Review of Psychology,* 1975, *26,* 393–414.

Edwards, A. L., & Abbott, R. D. Measurement of personality traits: Theory and technique. *Annual Review of Psychology,* 1973, *24,* 241–278.

Holzman, P. S. Personality. *Annual Review of Psychology,* 1974, *25,* 247–276.

Rosenthal, R. Training students in personality theory. *American Psychologist,* 1958, *13,* 605–606.

Sanford, N. Personality: Its place in psychology. In S. Koch (Ed.), *Psychology: A study of a science* (Vol. 5). New York: McGraw-Hill, 1963. Pp. 488–579.

Singer, J. L., & Singer, D. G. Personality. *Annual Review of Psychology,* 1972, *23,* 375–412.

Sigmund Freud
Psychoanalysis

2

*Man's chief enemy and danger is his own unruly
nature and the dark forces pent up within him.*

—Ernest Jones

Contemporary personality theory in general has been influenced
more by Sigmund Freud than by any other single individual. His system
of psychoanalysis was the first formal theory of personality and to this
day remains the best known of any personality theory. Indeed, the term
psychoanalysis has become virtually a household word, known and recognized by most of the literate peoples of the world. Not only did Freud
greatly influence psychological and psychiatric work on personality, but
his work also had a tremendous effect on our view of ourselves and
our world. It can be argued that few ideas in the history of civilization
have had such a broad and profound influence.

Many of the subsequently developed personality theories are, as
we shall see, derivatives of or elaborations on Freud's basic work; others
owe their impetus and direction in great part to their opposition to psychoanalysis. It would be extremely difficult to comprehend and assess

more recent efforts to deal with personality without first understanding Freud's system.

For psychoanalysis was *his* system, and his alone. On that point he was most adamant. "Psychoanalysis is my creation," he wrote. "No one can know better than I do what psychoanalysis is." Those who disagreed with his views were excommunicated from the official psychoanalytic community, as we shall see in later chapters.

An understanding of Freud is essential not only for the historical reasons discussed, but also because of his continuing influence. Though his loyal followers have revised and modified the system since his death in 1939, it remains in widespread use in both academic and mental-health settings. For these reasons, it would be difficult to justify any other starting point for a discussion of contemporary theories of personality.

The Life of Freud (1856-1939)

Freud was born in 1856 in what is now Czechoslovakia and moved with his family to Vienna four years later. His father was a never-too-successful wool merchant, and Freud's youth and adolescence could hardly be described as affluent.

It is interesting to speculate on how Freud's childhood experiences might have helped shape his theory of personality. If early experiences do influence personality development (as Freud stated), which then determines how we view the world, then, it might be suggested, these experiences will also influence whatever theory we might devise about the nature of personality.

When Freud was born, his father was 40 years old. His mother (the elder Freud's second wife) was only 20. The father was somewhat strict and authoritarian, and there is evidence that the young Freud felt a mixture of fear and love toward him. Freud's mother, on the other hand, was very protective and loving, and he felt a passionate, even sensuous, attachment to her; perhaps this situation set the stage for the development of the concept of the Oedipus complex, an important part of Freud's system.

His mother took great pride in her firstborn, convinced that an old woman's prophecy—that he would be a great man in the world—would come true. One of Freud's lifelong characteristics was his high degree of self-confidence. Again reflecting the impact of early experiences, Freud wrote: "A man who has been the indisputable favorite of his mother keeps for life the feeling of a conqueror, that confidence of success that often induces real success."

There were eight children in the family, two of them grown half brothers with children of their own. Freud's closest companion in child-hood was his nephew, who was only a year older. So strong an influence did this nephew have on Freud that he later described him as the source of all his (Freud's) friendships and hatreds. The young Freud evidently experienced much rivalry with and resentment toward all the children in his family, and was jealous and angry when new rivals for his mother's affection were born. Perhaps as a result, he became highly competitive.

We can see preludes to Freud's theory of the nature of human beings in the experiences and insecurities of his own childhood. "The child," the poet Wordsworth wrote, "is father of the man," and perhaps too the father of the theory of mankind one formulates in adulthood.

From a very early age, Freud evidenced an extremely high intelligence, which his parents helped to foster in every way possible. His sisters, for example, were not allowed to study the piano lest the noise disturb Freud's studies. He was given a tiny room to himself—so small it was called a cabinet—containing little more than a narrow bed, a desk, and chairs. Here he spent most of his time; he even took his meals there so as not to waste time. The room was the only one in the apartment to contain a prized oil lamp; the rest of the family had to use candles.

Freud entered high school a year earlier than was usual and was at the head of his class most of the time. In addition to Hebrew and German, the young Freud mastered Latin, Greek, French, and English and taught himself Italian and Spanish. He particularly enjoyed English; he had been reading Shakespeare since the age of 8.

Freud had many interests, including military history, but, when it came time to choose a career (from among the few professions open to a Jew at that time in Vienna), he settled on medicine. It was not that he had a desire to practice medicine, but he thought that medical study could lead to a career in scientific research, which was then his goal. While completing his medical degree at the University of Vienna, he conducted intensive physiological research into such areas as the spinal cord of fish and the testes of the eel, making very respectable contributions to the field.

Freud was discouraged from his intended career in scientific research by a professor, who convinced him that it would be many years before he could support himself financially in the university system of the day. Since he lacked an independent income, Freud decided to enter into private practice upon completing his training. A further impetus toward private practice was his engagement to Martha Bernays, which lasted four years before he could afford to marry. (Even then, he had to borrow money and pawn his watch.) Thus, Freud established a practice as a clinical neurologist in 1881 and began his exploration into the personalities of those suffering emotional disturbances.

He studied for a time in Paris with the psychiatrist Jean Charcot, from whom he learned a great deal about the use of hypnosis. Another significant influence on Freud and the system he was to develop was his friendship with Josef Breuer, a Viennese physician who had achieved some success in working with disturbed patients by encouraging them to talk freely about their symptoms. Freud, who grew dissatisfied with hypnosis (he was not a good hypnotist), turned to Breuer's "talking-cure" method and found it most effective. It was to form the basis of Freud's chief method of inquiring into the unconscious. Breuer was later to disappear from the arena of the development of psychoanalysis because of his disagreement with Freud's view of the central role of sexual energy in emotional disturbance.

Freud worked long hours, saw many patients, and gradually, on the basis of what they told him—particularly about their childhood experiences—fashioned a coherent picture, as he saw it, of the development of the individual personality and its processes and functions.

As his work became known through books and papers, Freud attracted a group of young student-disciples (most of whom were physicians) who met with him weekly to learn about his new psychoanalysis. Some of them (several of whom will be discussed in the chapters to follow) later broke away from Freud and developed their own theories.

Freud's private practice grew, as more and more people began to pay respectful attention to his work. In 1909 he received his first recognition on an international scale: he was invited to the United States to give a series of lectures at Clark University in Massachusetts.

As his fame grew, however, so did the spirited opposition. Never really accepted by organized medicine and psychiatry, Freud faced increasingly virulent hostility and abuse, which surfaced in clashes at scientific meetings as well as in private. He was loathed by many who considered psychoanalysis to be pornographic and who argued that its practitioners should be locked away in prison. Freud made no effort to reply to his critics; he preferred to spend his time refining his theory.

During the 1920s and 1930s, Freud reached the pinnacle of his success, but, unfortunately, at the same time his health began to deteriorate. From 1923 until his death 16 years later, he underwent 33 operations for cancer of the mouth. (He smoked 20 large cigars every day.) Portions of his palate and upper jaw were removed, and he suffered almost continuous pain.

When the Nazis came to power in Germany in 1933, they expressed their feelings about Freud by publicly burning all of his books, along with those of other "enemies of the state," including Einstein and many other Jewish intellectuals. In 1938 the Nazis occupied Austria, but despite the urgings of his friends Freud refused to leave Vienna. Finally, after his home was repeatedly invaded by gangs of Nazis and his daughter Anna arrested, Freud left for London, where he died in 1939, having continued to work almost to the end.

The Nature and Importance of Instincts

Freud interpreted the functioning of the human organism in physiological terms. From his medical training he knew that the human body operates by creating and expending a kind of physical energy. Food is transformed in the body into a form of energy that is used to fuel such functions as breathing, blood circulation, and muscular and glandular activity.

The mind also performs certain functions. It perceives the external world; it thinks, imagines, remembers. Using the analogy with the body, Freud assumed that the mind also carries out its functions through the use of energy—psychic energy—which differs in form but not kind from the body's physical energy. He further assumed, based on the principle of the conservation of energy, that the body energy could be transformed into psychic energy, and vice versa. The energy of the body therefore influences the mind. The link between these two forms of energy, the "frontier" between the psychic and the somatic, lies in Freud's concept of *instinct.*

Briefly defined, an instinct is the representation in the mind of stimuli that originate within the body. The instinct became Freud's basic element or unit of the personality. It is the motivating, propelling force of personality that not only drives behavior but also determines its direction. Freud's term in German for this concept is *Trieb,* which is best translated as *a driving force.* Instincts are a form of energy—transformed physiological energy—that serves to connect or bridge the body's needs to the mind's wishes.

The stimuli for instincts are internal, such as the tissue deficit of hunger. These instinctual stimuli arise within the body and can best be described as *needs.* When a need such as hunger is aroused, it generates a state of physiological excitation in the body—a physiological energy. This somatic energy, or need, is transformed in the mind into a *wish.* It is the wish—the mental representation of the body need—that is the instinct or driving force that motivates the person to behave so as to satisfy the body need; for example, the person may look for food. Thus, the instinct is not the body state—the tissue deficit of hunger—but rather is the transformation of that body need into a mental representation, a wish.

We can see that, to Freud, the processes and functions of the mind—such as perception, thinking, remembering—depend upon activities of the body; indeed, they are manifestations of body processes.

When the body is in a state of need, the person experiences a condition of tension or pressure. The aim of an instinct in every case is to satisfy the need and thereby reduce the state of tension. Thus, Freud's theory is essentially a homeostatic approach. We are motivated continually to restore and maintain the equilibrium of the body, to eliminate the tension and keep the body tension free.

Freud believed that there is always a certain amount of instinctual tension or pressure that we must constantly operate to reduce. It is not possible to escape these bodily needs, as one might escape an annoying external stimulus; they are always present. This means that instincts influence our behavior as long as we live, in a continuing cycle of bodily need leading to reduction of need.

While the goal of every instinct remains constant, the individual may take different paths to achieve the goal. For example, the sexual drive or need may be satisfied in a variety of ways—heterosexually, homosexually, autosexually—or the need may be channeled into some other form of activity.

Freud thought that psychic energy may be displaced to substitute objects, and this energy displacement he considered of prime importance in determining an individual's personality. While instincts remain the exclusive source of energy for behavior, the energy can be displaced in a variety of ways. And it is this variation that explains the diversity we see in human behavior. All of the assorted interests, preferences, and attitudes that we display as adults were seen by Freud to be displacements of energy from the original objects that satisfied the instinctual needs. Instincts, then, as noted earlier, are the basic motivating forces of all human behavior.

Having determined what instincts are, the next question we must ask is: how many of them exist? Freud said there are as many instincts as there are bodily needs to give rise to them. How many bodily needs are there? This question Freud did not answer. He felt that we did not yet know enough about bodily states and that their investigation was within the province of physiology, not psychology.

However, Freud said that an exact knowledge of these body needs was not necessary; the important point is how they affect behavior, and that effect can be observed in the aims of the instincts. So, to Freud, it was not important to know how many instincts there are. Regardless of their number, the instincts can be grouped into two categories: the life instincts (Eros) and the death instincts (Thanatos).

The *life instincts* serve the purpose of survival of both the individual and the species by seeking to satisfy the needs for food, water, air, and sex. The life instincts are oriented toward growth and development. The form of psychic energy manifested by the life instincts is the *libido*. The libido can be attached to or invested in objects, a concept that Freud called *cathexis*. For example, if you like a particular person, Freud would say that your libido is cathected to that person.

The life instinct that Freud considered the most important to personality is sex, which he defined in very broad terms. He did not refer solely to the erotic but included almost all pleasurable behaviors and thoughts. Freud stressed sex as our primary motivation. Regarding the erotic component, Freud was quite specific. Erotic wishes arise from the erogenous zones of the body: the mouth, anus, and sex organs.

Freud viewed human beings as predominantly pleasure seeking, and much of his personality theory revolves around the way in which we cope with our sexual needs in a society that continually tries to thwart their expression. We must remember the time period in which Freud generated his theory—an era when sexual expression was severely suppressed by society. A theory, like a person, reflects the climate of opinion and values of the era in which it develops. A personality theorist today operates in an entirely different climate of thought.

Freud postulated, in opposition to the life instincts, the destructive or *death instincts*. Drawing from biology, Freud stated the obvious fact that all living things decay and die, returning to their original inanimate state. In line with this, he assumed that people have an unconscious wish to die. The death instincts were not developed as fully by Freud as were the life instincts, for Freud felt they were difficult to study; they operate internally and silently. Neither did Freud discuss a separate energy by which the death instincts operate.

A vitally important component of the death instincts is the *aggressive drive*, which is the wish to die turned against objects other than the self. The aggressive drive compels us to destroy, conquer, and kill. Eventually, Freud came to consider aggression to be as important a part of human nature as sex.

It is interesting that Freud developed the notion of the death instincts late in life. As the physiological and psychological debilitations of age began to affect him, as his cancer worsened, and as he witnessed the carnage of World War I, death and aggression became major themes in his theory. Not so incidentally, Freud in his later years greatly dreaded his own death and exhibited hostility and aggression toward colleagues and disciples who broke away from his theoretical viewpoint.

There is one important point to reiterate about instincts: all the psychic energy needed by the personality is derived directly from them.

They provide energy, motivation, and direction for all facets of the individual's personality.

The Structure of Personality

Freud's original conception divided personality into three levels of consciousness: the conscious, the preconscious, and the unconscious.

The *conscious*, as Freud defined and used the term, corresponds closely to its ordinary everyday meaning. It includes all the sensations and experiences of which we are aware at any given moment. As I write these words, for example, I am conscious of the feel of my pen, the sight of the page, the idea that I'm trying to express, and a dog barking in the distance.

Freud considered the conscious to be a small and limited aspect of our personality, because only a small proportion of our thoughts, sensations, and memories exists in conscious awareness at any one time. Freud likened the mind to an iceberg. The conscious is the portion above the surface of the water—merely the tip of the iceberg.

What is much more important, according to Freud, is the larger, invisible portion below the surface: the *unconscious*. This is the focus of psychoanalytic theory. Its vast dark depths contain the instincts, wishes, and desires that direct and determine our behavior. The unconscious, then, contains the major driving power behind our behavior and is the repository of forces we cannot see or control.

Between these two levels of consciousness, Freud posited the *preconscious* (or foreconscious). This is the storehouse of all memories, perceptions, thoughts, and the like of which we are not consciously aware at the moment but which we can easily bring into consciousness.

For example, in the unlikely event that your mind strayed from this page, and you began to think about someone else or what you did last night, you would be summoning material up from your preconscious into your conscious. There is a great deal of two-way traffic between these two levels, and we often find our attention shifting back and forth suddenly from experiences of the moment—this page or a lecture or a television program—to events from the preconscious.

In later years, Freud revised this theory and introduced three basic structures in the anatomy of the personality: the id, the ego, and the superego.

The *id*, the original or oldest system of the personality, corresponds closely to Freud's earlier notion of the unconscious (though there are unconscious aspects of the ego and superego as well). The id is the storehouse or reservoir for all the instincts. It also contains the total psychic energy—libido. The id is thus a powerful structure in the personality; indeed, it supplies all the power for the other two structures.

Because the id is the reservoir of the instincts, it is vitally and directly related to the satisfaction of bodily needs. As we discussed earlier, a tension or pressure is produced when the body is in a state of need, and the organism then acts to reduce this tension by satisfying the need.

The id operates in accordance with what Freud called the *pleasure principle;* that is, it functions to avoid pain and increase pleasure, through its concern with tension reduction. There is one important point about the id's tension-reduction function: it strives for immediate satisfaction of its needs. It does not tolerate delay or postponement of satisfaction for any reason, be it manners or morals or some other dictate of everyday reality. The id—that "cauldron full of seething excitations"—knows only one thing: instant satisfaction. The id drives people to want what they want when they want it, without regard to what anyone else may want or need. It is a purely selfish, pleasure-seeking structure—primitive, amoral, insistent, and rash.

Further, the id has no perception of reality. If we may oversimplify a bit, we might compare the id to a newborn infant. It screams and claws frantically when its needs are not satisfied, but it has no knowledge of how to bring about such satisfaction. The hungry infant cannot find food for itself. The only ways the id is able even to attempt to satisfy these needs are through *reflex action* and through wish-fulfilling hallucinatory or fantasy experience—what Freud called *primary-process* thought. Left to its own devices, the newborn would die, since it knows nothing of the external world. As the infant grows, it learns about objects in the environment that can satisfy its needs—where these objects are, which behaviors are appropriate to obtain them, and so on.

For example, most children learn that they cannot take food from other people unless they are willing to face certain consequences, that they must postpone the pleasure obtained from relieving anal tensions until they get to a bathroom, and that they cannot indiscriminately give vent to sexual and aggressive longings. In short, the growing child must learn to deal intelligently and rationally with the outside world and must develop the powers of perception, recognition, judgment, and memory that an adult uses to satisfy his or her needs. Freud called these processes *secondary-process* thought.

These abilities, perhaps best known simply as reason or rationality are subsumed under Freud's second structure of personality, the *ego.* The ego possesses an awareness of reality. It is capable of perceiving and manipulating the individual's environment in a practical manner and operates according to what Freud called the *reality principle.*

We might refer to the ego as the rational master of the personality.

Its purpose is not to thwart the impulses of the id but rather to help the id in obtaining its necessary tension reduction. The ego, since it is aware of reality, decides when and in what manner the instincts can best be satisfied. It determines appropriate and socially acceptable times, places, and objects that will satisfy the id impulses. While the ego does not prevent id satisfaction, it does try to postpone or delay or redirect it in accordance with the demands of reality.

Freud compared the relation of the ego to the id with that of a rider to a horse. The raw brute power of the horse must be guided, checked, and reined in by the rider; otherwise the horse may bolt and run, throwing the rider to the ground.

The ego serves two masters—the id and reality—and it is constantly mediating and striking compromises between their often conflicting demands. (It serves a third master as well, as we shall see shortly.) Also, the ego is, in a sense, never independent of the id. It is always responsive to the demands of the id and derives all its power or energy from it.

It is the ego, this rational master, that keeps you working at a job you may dislike (if the alternative is an inability to provide food and shelter for your family) or tolerating people you may not care for, because reality demands such behavior as an appropriate way of satisfying the incessant demands of the id. The controlling, postponing function of the ego must be continuously exercised, or the impulses of the id would dominate and overthrow the rational ego. Individuals must constantly protect themselves from being controlled by the id, and Freud postulated a variety of mechanisms (to be discussed later) by which people may defend their egos.

Thus far we have a picture of the individual in battle, trying to restrain the id while at the same time serving it, perceiving and manipulating reality so as to relieve the tensions of the id impulses. Human beings are driven by their biological instinctual forces, which they are continually trying to guide—walking the tightrope between the demands of reality and those of the id, both of which require constant attention.

But that is not Freud's complete picture of human nature. There is a third set of forces—a powerful and largely unconscious set of dictates or beliefs—which the individual learns in childhood: his or her ideas of right and wrong. In everyday language we call this internal morality a "conscience." Freud called it the *superego*. This moral side of the personality is learned, usually by the age of 5 or 6, and consists initially of the rules of conduct set down by the parents. Through punishment, praise, and example, the child learns which behaviors the parents consider wrong or bad. Those behaviors for which the child is admonished or punished become part of the *conscience*, which is one part of the superego. The other part is the *ego-ideal* and consists of good or correct behaviors.

The child thus learns a series of rules—"Thou shalts" and "Thou shalt nots"—that earn acceptance or rejection from the parents. In time, the child internalizes these teachings, and the rewards and punishments are then self-administered. Parental control is replaced by self-control. The parents' rules and commands have influenced the child, who lives in at least partial conformity with these now largely unconscious moral guidelines. As a result of this internalization, the child (and later the adult) experiences guilt whenever he or she performs—or even thinks of performing—some action that is contrary to this moral code.

The superego, as the arbiter of morality, is relentless—even cruel—in its constant quest for moral perfection. In terms of intensity, irrationality, and blind, determined insistence on obedience, it is not unlike the id. Its purpose is not to postpone the pleasure-seeking demands of the id but rather to inhibit them—particularly, in Western society, those concerned with sex and aggression. The superego strives neither for pleasure (as does the id) nor for the attainment of realistic goals (as does the ego). It strives solely for moral perfection. The id is pressing for satisfaction, the ego is trying to delay it, and the superego urges morality above all. Like the id, the superego admits no compromise with its demands.

As you can see, the ego is very much caught in the middle, pressured by these insistent opposing forces. The superego, then, is the ego's third master. To paraphrase Freud, the poor ego has a hard time of it, pressured on three sides, threatened by three different dangers—the id, reality, and the superego.

Thus, we see continual conflict within the human personality. The British psychologist D. Bannister[1] describes Freud's human being as "basically a battlefield. He is a dark cellar in which a well-bred spinster lady [the superego] and a sex-crazed monkey [the id] are forever engaged in mortal combat, the struggle being refereed by a rather nervous bank clerk [the ego]." The inevitable result of this friction, when the ego is too severely pressed, is the development of anxiety.

Anxiety

We all have a general idea of what the word *anxiety* means and of how we feel when we say we are anxious. We can agree to some extent on the internal experiences associated with such feelings. We know that anxiety is a feeling not unlike fear. We feel frightened, but we do not know of what. Anxiety has been defined as an objectless fear; we cannot point to its source, to an object that induces it.

[1]D. Bannister. Psychology as an exercise in paradox. *Bulletin of the British Psychological Society*, 1966, 19, 21-26.

Freud made anxiety an important part of his system of personality, asserting that it is fundamental and central to the development of neurotic and psychotic behavior. He suggested that the prototype of all anxiety is the trauma of birth (a notion elaborated upon by a disciple, Otto Rank).

The fetus in its mother's womb is in the most stable and secure of worlds, where every need is satisfied without delay. Suddenly, at birth, the organism finds itself thrust into a hostile environment. It must at once begin to adapt to reality, since its instinctual demands may not always be immediately met. The newborn's nervous system, immature and ill prepared, is suddenly bombarded with intense and diverse sensory stimuli. Consequently, the infant engages in massive motor movements, heightened breathing, and increased heart rate.

The birth trauma, then, with its tension and fear that the id instincts won't be satisfied, is the individual's first experience with fear and anxiety. Out of this experience is created the pattern of reactions and feeling states that will occur whenever the individual is exposed to danger in the future.

When an individual is unable to cope with his or her anxiety, when he or she is in danger of being overwhelmed by it, the anxiety is said to be *traumatic*. What Freud meant by this is that the person, regardless of age, is reduced to a state of total helplessness like that experienced in infancy. In adult life, infantile helplessness is reenacted, to some degree, whenever the ego is threatened.

Freud posited three types of anxiety, which vary as a function of the kind of situation that produces them. The types of anxiety differ in terms of their seriousness or potential harm to the individual.

The first type of anxiety, from which the other two are derived, is *reality* or *objective anxiety*. As the name indicates, it involves a fear of tangible dangers in the real world. Most of us fear—justifiably—fires, tornadoes, earthquakes, and similar dangers. We run from a wild animal, get out of the way of a speeding car, flee a burning building. Reality anxiety, then, serves the very positive purpose of guiding our behavior with regard to actual dangers. Our fear subsides when the threat is no longer present.

These reality-based fears can be carried to an extreme, however, and can become harmful. The person who won't leave home for fear of being hit by a car, or won't light a match for fear of fire, is carrying reality-based fears beyond the point of normality.

The other two kinds of anxiety are much more consistently troublesome to an individual's mental health.

Neurotic anxiety has its basis in childhood, in a conflict between instinctual gratification and reality. Most children suffer at least some punishment from parents for impulsively satisfying the demands of the id, particularly those of a sexual or aggressive nature.

The child is often punished for overtly expressing sexual or aggressive impulses. Anxiety or fear is therefore generated by the wish to gratify certain id impulses. This anxiety is at first conscious but is later transformed into an unconscious threat—a province of the ego. The neurotic anxiety that emerges is a fear of being punished for impulsively displaying id-dominated behavior. Notice that the fear is not of the instincts themselves but rather of what may happen as a result of gratifying the instincts. The conflict becomes one between the id and the ego, and its origin, as noted, has some basis in reality.

Moral anxiety is the third type, and it results from a conflict between the id and the superego. Basically, it is a fear of one's own conscience. When you are motivated to express an instinctual impulse that is contrary to your moral code, your superego retaliates by causing you to feel shame or guilt. In everyday terms, you might describe yourself as "conscience stricken."

Moral anxiety is obviously a function of how well developed the superego is. A person with a strong, puritanical, inhibiting conscience will experience much greater conflict than someone with a less "virtuous" set of moral guidelines. Like neurotic anxiety, moral anxiety has some basis in reality. Children are punished for violating their parents' moral codes and adults are punished for violating society's moral code. The shame and guilt feelings in moral anxiety are, however, from within. It is the person's own conscience that causes the fear and the anxiety, and Freud believed that the superego can exact a terrible retribution for violation of its tenets.

Whatever the type, anxiety serves as a warning signal to the person that all is not as it should be. It induces tension in the organism and so becomes a drive—much like hunger or thirst—that the individual is motivated to satisfy. The tension must be reduced.

Anxiety alerts the individual that the ego is being threatened and that, unless action is taken, the ego might be overthrown altogether. What can be done? How can the ego protect or defend itself? There are a number of options: the person may try to run away from the threatening situation, may try to inhibit the impulsive need that is the source of danger, or may try to follow the dictates of the conscience. But if none of these rational techniques work, the person may resort to nonrational mechanisms to defend the ego.

The Defense Mechanisms

Anxiety functions as a signal that impending danger, a threat to the ego, must be counteracted or avoided. The ego must reduce the conflict between the demands of the id and the strictures of society or of the superego. This conflict is ever present in the "dark cellar" that is human nature, according to Freud, because the instincts are always pressing for some degree of satisfaction, and the taboos and mores of society tend to limit such satisfaction. Freud felt, therefore, that the *defenses* must always be in operation to some extent. Just as all behavior is motivated by instincts, so too all behavior is defensive in nature, in the sense of defending against anxiety. The intensity of the battle within the personality may fluctuate, but it invariably continues.

Freud postulated a number of specific defense mechanisms but noted that an individual rarely uses just one. We typically defend ourselves against anxiety by using a variety of the mechanisms at the same time. Also, there is quite a bit of overlap in these mechanisms. Although varying in their specifics, the defense mechanisms share two very important characteristics. First, they are denials or *distortions of reality*—necessary ones, but distortions nonetheless. Second, the defense mechanisms operate *unconsciously*. Individuals are unaware of them, which means they have distorted or unreal images of themselves and their environments on the conscious level. After we discuss several specific mechanisms, we will return to this important point.

Repression

Repression is a word we use quite frequently in everyday conversation. When we say "I've repressed that," we usually mean we have put it out of our conscious awareness, deliberately and consciously suppressed something we no longer wanted to think about. This is not the sense in which Freud used the term. Repression, as explained by Freud, is an *involuntary* removal of something from consciousness. It is, in essence, an unconscious denial of the existence of something that brings us discomfort or pain.

At first glance, there might seem to be a contradiction here. The defense mechanisms are operated by the ego, which, as we have seen, functions in accordance with the reality principle. Is it not unrealistic to omit or deny segments of reality, as happens with repression?

To answer that, we must recall the primary function of the ego: to aid the id in bringing about pleasure and avoiding pain. Of course, the pressing of certain id impulses for satisfaction leads to anxiety when these impulses are contrary to one's moral teachings or to the demands of reality. By repressing the source of the anxiety, the organism relieves the tension the anxiety induces. It does so by denying the existence of the original wish. The immediate danger to the ego of being overpowered by the id is thus reduced. Of course, anxiety remains in the unconscious, where it may wreak all sorts of havoc, but the conscious conflict is no longer present. In a sense, a false reality (although true as the individual perceives it) is established within which the individual can function.

Repression can operate on memories of situations or people, on our perception of the present (so that we may fail to comprehend some disturbing event that is in open view), and even on the physiological functioning of the body. For example, sexual drives can be so strongly inhibited that the person becomes impotent.

Once a repression is in use, it is extremely difficult to get rid of. After all, we are using it to protect ourselves from some danger, and we would have to know that the idea or memory is no longer dangerous in order to remove the repression. But how can we find out that the danger no longer exists unless we release the repression? A vicious circle!

The concept of repression is basic to much of Freud's system of personality and is involved in all neurotic behavior.

Reaction Formation

One defense against a disturbing impulse is to actively express the opposite impulse. A person who is strongly driven by, let us say, sexual impulses that are threatening may repress those impulses and replace them with more socially acceptable behavior. For example, a person who is threatened by his or her sexual longings may reverse them and become an active crusader against pornography. Another person, disturbed by extreme aggressive impulses, may become overly solicitous and friendly. Thus, lust becomes virtue, and hatred becomes love.

This does not mean that everyone who is especially considerate, or concerned about X-rated movies, is masking deep feelings of hostility or sexual longings. What distinguishes behavior arising from true convictions from that which results from reaction formation is the intensity and extremity of the behavior. A person who crusades against "loose morals," "free love," "dirty movies," and the like, to a degree out of proportion to their actual incidence, may well be reflecting reaction formation.

Projection

One way of defending oneself against disturbing impulses is to attribute them to someone else. Thus, lustful, aggressive, or other unacceptable impulses are seen as being possessed by others, not by oneself.

The person says, in effect, "I don't hate him—he hates me." A middle-aged mother may ascribe her troublesome sexual drive to her adolescent daughter. The impulse is still being manifested but in a way that is more acceptable to the individual.

Regression

In this mode of defense, the individual retreats or regresses to an earlier period in life that was more pleasant and free of the frustration and anxiety he or she now faces. Regression usually involves a return to one of the psychosexual stages of development (discussed later in this chapter). The person returns to this more secure time of life by manifesting behaviors that he or she displayed at that time, such as childish and dependent behavior.

Rationalization

This is another defense mechanism that many of us use from time to time. It involves a reinterpretation of our own behavior to make it seem more rational and acceptable to us. We excuse or justify a thought or act that is threatening to us by convincing ourselves that there is a rational explanation for that thought or act.

The person who is fired from his or her job may rationalize by saying that the job wasn't a good one anyway. The loved one who turns you down suddenly has many faults. If you miss a ball in tennis, you may glare angrily at the racket or throw it to the ground. There is something wrong with the racket, you are saying, and not with your playing.

It is less threatening to blame someone or something else for our failures instead of ourselves. It is perhaps a point to remember when you next blame your instructor for your failing an exam (unless, of course, your instructor is disguising his or her aggression by projecting it onto you, but it is probably not a good idea to ask if that is the case).

Displacement

If, for some reason, an object that satisfies an id impulse is not available, the person may shift or displace the impulse to another object. For example, if a child hates his or her father or an adult hates his or her boss, but is afraid to express this hostility toward the father or boss for fear of punishment, he or she may displace the aggression onto someone else. The child may hit a younger brother or the adult may shout at his or her children.

In these examples, the original object of the impulse has been replaced by one that is not a threat. Of course, the substitute object will not be as good a source of tension reduction as the original object. If the person is involved in a number of displacements, a reservoir of undischarged tension accumulates. As a result, the person is increasingly driven to find new ways of reducing the tension.

Sublimation

While displacement involves finding a substitute object to satisfy id impulses, sublimation involves an altering or displacing of the id impulses themselves. The instinctual energy is diverted into other channels of expression—ones that society considers not only acceptable but admirable. Sexual energy, for example, is diverted or sublimated into artistically creative behaviors. Freud believed that a great variety of human activities, particularly those of an artistic nature, are manifestations of id impulses that have been redirected into socially acceptable outlets.

As with displacement (of which sublimation is a form), sublimation is a compromise. As such, it does not bring total satisfaction but leads to a buildup of undischarged tension.

As we noted earlier, Freud said that all defenses are denials or distortions of reality. Further, all the defenses are unconscious. We are, in essence, lying to ourselves when we use these defenses but are not aware of doing so. Indeed, if we knew we were lying to ourselves, the defenses would not be effective. If they are working well, defenses keep threatening material out of our conscious awareness. As a result, we do not know the truth about ourselves. We have a distorted picture of our needs, fears, longings, and so on.

It follows that such rational processes as problem solving, decision making, and logical thinking are not based on an accurate picture of the individual. In short, according to Freud, we are driven and controlled by internal and external forces of which we are unaware and over which we can exercise little rational control.

There are, however, certain situations in which the truth about ourselves does emerge—that is, when the defenses break down and fail to protect us. This can happen in times of great stress and when a person is under psychoanalysis. When the defenses fail, we are stricken with overwhelming guilt or anxiety. We feel worthless, dismal, and depressed —a situation we cannot long endure.

Unless the defenses are put back into operation, or new ones are formed to take their place, the individual is very likely to become neurotic or psychotic. The defense mechanisms, then, are vital and necessary. We could not survive long without them.

Psychosexual Stages of Development

We have seen that all behavior is defensive but that not everyone uses the same defenses in the same way. We are all driven by the same id impulses, but there is not the same universality in the nature of the ego and the superego. While they perform the same functions for everyone, their specific content or nature varies from one person to the next. They differ because they are formed through experience, and no two people have precisely the same experiences, not even siblings raised in the same home. Thus, a part of our personality may be said to be formed on the basis of the unique set of relationships we each have as children with a variety of people and objects. We develop a personal set of character attributes, a consistent pattern of behavior that defines us as individuals.

Freud felt that a person's unique character type develops in childhood from the nature of the parent-child interaction. The child tries to maximize its pleasure by satisfying the id demands, while its parents (as representatives of society) try to impose the demands of reality and the strictures of morality. So important did Freud consider childhood experience that he believed the adult personality was shaped and solidly crystallized by the fifth year of life. What convinced him of the importance of these early years were the memories revealed by his adult patients. Invariably, as they lay on Freud's psychoanalytic couch, they reached far back into childhood. Increasingly he saw that the adult neurosis had been formed in the early years of life.

Freud sensed strong conflicts of a sexual nature in the infant and young child—conflicts that seemed to revolve around specific regions of the body. Further, he believed that each body region assumes a greater importance (is the center of conflict) at a different age. And so he formulated the theory of psychosexual development, in which the infant passes through a series of stages, each defined by an erogenous zone of the body. (An erogenous zone is a body region that is sensitive to stimulation. It feels good when rubbed or massaged or stimulated in certain ways.) In each stage of development there is a conflict that must be satisfactorily resolved before the infant or child can move on to the next stage.

Sometimes an individual is reluctant or unable to move from one stage to the next because the conflict has not been resolved or because the needs have been so supremely satisfied that he or she doesn't want to move on. In either case, the individual is said to be *fixated* at this stage of development. In fixation, a portion of libido (psychic energy) remains invested in that stage of development, leaving less energy for the next stages.

Central to these psychosexual stages of development is the infant's sex drive. Freud shocked colleagues and the public alike when he argued that babies are motivated by sexual impulses. However, as we have noted, Freud did not define sex solely in the narrow sense in which we usually think of it. The infant is driven to obtain a very diffuse form of bodily pleasure, which Freud said derived from the mouth, the anus, and the genitals—the erogenous zones that define the stages of development during the first five years of life.

The Oral Stage

The first stage of psychosexual development lasts from birth to some time in the second year of life. During this period, the principal source of pleasure for the infant is the mouth. Pleasure is derived from sucking, biting, and swallowing, with the attendant sensations of the lips, tongue, and cheeks. Obviously, the mouth is used for sheer survival—for food and water—but Freud placed a much greater emphasis on the erotic and sexual (broadly defined) satisfactions derived from oral activity.

The infant, at this time, is in a state of complete dependence on the mother, who becomes the primary object of the child's libido. In more familiar terms, we might say that the infant is learning, in a very primitive way (because it is functioning at a primitive level), to love the mother. How the mother responds to the infant's demands (the id demands) totally determines the nature of the baby's small world. The infant learns from the mother, during the oral stage, to perceive the world as good or bad, satisfying or frustrating, safe or perilous.

There are two modes of activity during this stage: oral incorporative behavior and oral aggressive or sadistic behavior.

The *oral incorporative* mode occurs first and involves the pleasurable stimulation of the mouth by other people and by food. An adult fixated at the oral incorporative stage is excessively concerned with oral activities—eating, drinking, smoking, kissing, and the like. If, as an infant, the person was excessively gratified, his or her adult oral personality will be predisposed to excessive optimism and dependency.

The second oral phase—*oral aggressive*—occurs during the painful and frustrating eruption of teeth. As a result of this experience, the infant for the first time views the mother with hatred as well as love. A person fixated at this phase is prone to excessive pessimism, hostility, and aggression. He or she is likely to be argumentative and sarcastic, making "biting" remarks. The oral stage ends at the time of weaning (although some libido may remain if fixation has occurred), and the infant's focus shifts to the other end.

The Anal Stage

For the most part, society, in the form of parents, has deferred to the infant's needs during the first year, adjusting to its demands and expecting relatively little adjustment in return. This state of affairs changes around age 2, when a demand is made on the child—namely, toilet training. Freud saw the experience of toilet training as crucial to personality development.

Elimination of feces produces pleasure for the child, but, with the onset of toilet training, he or she must learn to postpone or delay this pleasure. For the first time, the gratification of an instinctual impulse is interfered with as parents attempt to regulate the time and place of defecation.

As any parent can attest, this is a time of trauma and conflict for all parties. The child learns that he or she has (or is) a weapon that can be used against the parents. For the first time, the child has control over something and can choose to comply or not with the parents' demands.

If the toilet training is not going well—if the child has difficulty learning or the parents are excessively harsh and demanding—the child reacts in one of two ways to this frustration. One way is to defecate when and where it is forbidden by the parents to do so, thus defying the parents' attempts at regulation. If the child finds this a satisfactory technique for reducing frustration and uses it frequently, he or she is on the way to developing what Freud called an *anal aggressive* personality. This is the basis for all forms of hostile and sadistic behaviors in adult life, including cruelty, destructiveness, and temper tantrums.

A second way the child may react to these parental demands is to hold back or retain the feces. This also produces a feeling of pleasure (derived from a full lower intestine) and can be another successful technique for manipulating the parents. They may become overly concerned if the child doesn't defecate for long periods of time. Thus, the child has discovered a new method of securing attention and affection from them.

This behavior is the basis for the development of an *anal retentive* personality, described as being stubborn and stingy. Such a person hoards or retains because his or her security depends on what is saved and possessed and on the careful order in which possessions and life are maintained. The person is likely to be rigid and compulsively neat.

The Phallic Stage

Assuming the parents and child have survived the combats and conflicts of the child's first two stages of development, they face a new set of problems around the fourth to fifth year. The focus of pleasure shifts at this time from the anus to the genitals. Again the child faces a battle between an id impulse and the demands of society as reflected in the parents' expectations.

Children at this age seem to spend a good deal of time exploring and manipulating the genitals—their own and others'. Pleasure is derived from the genital region, not only through behaviors such as masturbation but also through fantasies. The child becomes curious about birth and about why a sister or brother is different in the genital area; he or she talks about marrying the parent of the opposite sex.

Phallic conflicts constitute the last of the so-called pregenital or childhood stages of development and are the most complex ones to resolve. In addition, they are difficult for people to accept because they involve the notion of incest, a strict taboo in the Western world. Between incestuous desires and masturbation we can see the seeds of potential shock, anger, and suppression being sown in the parents of the 4-year-old. Reality and morality come to grips with the evil id once again.

The basic conflict of the phallic stage centers around the unconscious incestuous desire of the child for the parent of the opposite sex. Accompanying this desire is the unconscious desire of the child to replace, or even destroy, the parent of the same sex. (Small wonder that people at the turn of the century considered Freud a pervert and a pornographer.)

Out of this conflict appears one of Freud's best-known concepts: the *Oedipus complex.* Its name is taken from the Greek myth described in the play *Oedipus Rex* (written by Sophocles in the fifth century B.C.). In this story, young Oedipus kills his father and marries his mother, not knowing who they are at the time.

The Oedipus complex operates differently for the boy than for the girl, and I will describe the male part first—not out of male chauvinism, but because it is the more fully developed concept of the two.

As we have stated, the mother becomes a love object for the boy. Through both fantasy and overt behavior, he exhibits his sexual longings for her. However, the boy sees an obstacle in his path—the father—whom he comes to look upon as a rival and a threat. He perceives that the father has a special kind of relationship with the mother in which he, the boy, is not allowed to participate. As a result, he becomes jealous and hostile toward his father. Along with the desire to replace his father is the fear that his father will retaliate and harm him. At the same time, his mother may be reacting to his sexual "advances" with punishment and threats of withholding her love. Freud saw this as a time for great anxiety for the young boy.

To make matters worse, the boy develops a specific fear about his penis. He interprets his fear of his father in genital terms; in other words, he fears that his father will cut off the offending organ—the source of his pleasure and sexual longings. And so *castration anxiety,* as Freud called it, comes to play a significant role in the boy's life. So great is his fear of castration that he is forced to repress his sexual desire for his mother.

This is what Freud termed the resolution of the Oedipal conflict. It involves replacing the sexual longing for the mother with a more acceptable affection and developing a strong identification with the father.

By identifying with his father, the boy is able to experience a degree of vicarious sexual satisfaction. To further the identification, he attempts to become more like his father, adopting many of his mannerisms, behaviors, and attitudes. One of the results of the resolution of the Oedipus complex is the development of the superego. The boy adopts his father's superego standards, which prompted Freud to say that the superego is the "heir of the Oedipus complex."

Freud was less clear about the *Electra complex*, the female version of these phallic conflicts. In Greek mythology, Electra cajoled her brother into killing their mother and the mother's lover, both of whom had earlier killed Electra's father—another warm and happy mythical family.

The girl's first object of love, like the boy's, is her mother, for she is the primary source of food, affection, and security in infancy. During the phallic stage, however, the father becomes the girl's new love object.

Why does this shift from mother to father take place? Freud explained it in terms of the girl's reaction to her discovery that boys have a protruding sex organ and girls do not. The girl blames her mother for her "castrated" condition and therefore loves her mother less. Indeed, she may even hate her mother for what she imagines the mother did to her. She transfers her love to her father because he possesses the highly valued organ. However, as much as she loves her father for this possession, she also envies him. And so what Freud called *penis envy* develops in the girl as the counterpart to the boy's castration anxiety. She feels she has lost her penis; he is afraid he is going to lose his.

Freud was not specific about the resolution of the Electra complex, although he did believe it could never be totally resolved. He thought that an adult woman's love of men was always tinged with some degree of penis envy. Of course, there is less need for the girl to resolve her phallic conflict than for the boy; she is not threatened with castration. As a means of resolving the complex, the girl does come to identify with her mother and to repress her love for her father.

The Oedipus complex (using the term now to include both sexes) and the degree of its resolution are paramount in determining adult relations with and attitudes toward the opposite sex. Poorly or insufficiently resolved Oedipal conflicts may cause lingering forms of castration anxiety and penis envy in the adult. The so-called *phallic* character or personality evidences strong narcissism and, although continually trying to attract the opposite sex, has difficulty in establishing mature heterosexual relationships. Such persons need continual recognition and appreciation of their attractive and unique qualities. As long as they receive such support, they seem to function well, but, when it is lacking, they are gripped by feelings of inadequacy and inferiority.

The male phallic personality is seen to be self-assured, displaying a kind of "devil-may-care" attitude. The female phallic personality exaggerates her femininity and uses her talents and charms to overwhelm and conquer men.

The tense drama that marks the phallic period is repressed in all of us. Its effects operate in the adult at the unconscious level, but we recall little, if any, of the conflict.

The Latency Period

The storms and stresses of the oral, anal, and phallic stages of psychosexual development are the amalgam out of which most of the adult personality is shaped. The three major structures of personality—id, ego, and superego—have now largely been formed, and the important relationships among them are being crystallized.

Fortunately—for the child certainly could use some rest—the next five or six years represent a quiet period. This period is not a psychosexual stage of development; the sex instinct is largely dormant during this time, apparently temporarily sublimated in school activities, hobbies, and sports and in developing friendships with members of the same sex. Freud has been criticized for his lack of interest in this time of life. Other psychoanalysts consider this period to have its own problems and conflicts, which involve getting along with peers and learning to adjust to an ever-widening world.

The Genital Stage

The fourth and final psychosexual stage of development begins at the time of puberty. The body is becoming physiologically mature, and, if there have been no major fixations at any of the earlier stages of development, the individual may be able to lead a non-neurotic life with normal heterosexual relationships.

There is conflict during this period but less than in the earlier stages. There are still many societal sanctions and taboos concerning sexual expression to which the adolescent must conform, but conflict is minimized through the use of sublimation. The sexual energy pressing for expression can be at least partly satisfied through the pursuit of socially acceptable substitute outlets.

Freud strongly emphasized the importance of the early years of childhood in determining the adult personality. The first five years are the crucial ones. Later childhood and adolescence received less attention in his personality theory, and he was little concerned with personality formation in adulthood. What we are as adults, how we behave and think and feel, is determined by the complex of conflicts to which we are exposed and with which we must cope before many of us have even learned to read.

Techniques of Inquiry

This section is concerned with the techniques or methods of inquiry by which Freud gathered the data that form the basis of his theory. If we were to define the word *research* very broadly, as meaning a critical and exhaustive investigation, then this section could be labeled *methods of research*. It is purposely not called that, because *research* in psychology has come to refer almost exclusively to controlled experimental laboratory research, in which one variable is isolated for study and manipulated to determine its effects on behavior.

Neither Freud nor most of the other personality theorists covered in this book conducted their inquiries or research in this manner. The techniques they developed are quite different in nature and usually serve two purposes: (1) to gather data about human nature on which to formulate and develop a theory of personality and (2) to serve as a technique of therapy designed to aid disturbed individuals. Our discussion focuses primarily on the first purpose.

As you now know, Freud considered the unconscious to be the major motivating force in our lives. All of our childhood conflicts are repressed out of conscious awareness. Freud believed that the goal of psychoanalysis was to bring these repressed memories, fears, and thoughts back to the level of conscious awareness.

But how can one probe this invisible portion of the mind, this dark arena that is not even accessible to ourselves? Over the course of his work with many patients, Freud developed two basic methods of inquiry: *free association* and *dream analysis.*

Free Association

Freud developed this basic technique, the "fundamental rule of psychoanalysis," over a number of years of working with his patients. Its origin owes a great deal to Josef Breuer, the Viennese physician mentioned earlier, who befriended Freud during Freud's early years in private practice. Breuer found, in treating a young female hysteric, that placing her under hypnosis enabled her to recall repressed experiences and events. Recalling the events—reliving the experience, in a sense—brought about relief of the disturbing symptom.

Freud used this technique himself with some success and applied the term *catharsis* (from the Greek word meaning *purification*) to the process. After a while he gave up hypnosis, in part because of his difficulty in hypnotizing some people, and he developed a new method for helping patients to recall repressed material. In this method, the patient lies on a couch and is encouraged to relax as much as possible and to concentrate on events in the past. The patient engages in a kind of daydreaming out loud, saying whatever comes to mind. He or she is instructed to express spontaneously every idea and image exactly as it occurs, no matter how trivial, embarrassing, or even painful the thought or memory might be. There must not be any omitting, rearranging, or restructuring of the memories.

Freud found, in the course of using free association, that it sometimes did not operate very freely. Some experiences or memories were evidently too painful to talk about, and the patient would refuse to disclose them. Freud called these moments *resistances,* and he felt that they were of great significance, indicating proximity to the source of the patient's problems. Resistance is a sign that the treatment is going in the right direction and that it should continue to probe more deeply in that area. Part of the task of psychoanalysis is to break down or overcome resistances so that the patient can face the repressed experience.

Freud found that a patient's memories inevitably were of childhood experiences, either real or fantasied, which were most often of a sexual nature. It was due, for the most part, to his patients' fascination with and concentration on childhood experiences that Freud came to emphasize the early years as the source of all later neuroses.

Dream Analysis

Some patients, in the course of free association, told Freud their dreams, and he began to use these dreams as a basis for further associations, asking the patient to free-associate to specific features or events that appeared in a dream. He found that dreams often revealed important repressed memories.

Freud also used this technique to conduct his own analysis. On awakening each morning, he would write down his dreams of the previous night and then free-associate to them. So necessary did Freud consider this method that he continued it for self-analysis all his life.

Freud believed that dreams represent, in disguised or symbolic form, repressed desires, fears, and conflicts. So strongly have these feelings been repressed that they can surface only in disguised fashion during sleep. Thus, Freud distinguished two aspects of the content of dreams: the actual events in the dream (the *manifest content*) and the hidden symbolic meaning of those events (the *latent content*).

Over the course of his work with many patients, Freud found consistent symbols in dreams—events that signified the same thing for nearly every patient. For example, he said that steps, ladders, and staircases represented sexual intercourse; candles, snakes, and tree trunks stood for the penis; and boxes, balconies, and doors signified the female body. However, Freud warned that, in spite of this apparent universality of certain symbols, they still have to be interpreted within the context of the individual conflict. Further, many symbols are specific to the patient at hand and could have a vastly different meaning for another patient.

An additional characteristic of dreams is that they reveal conflicts only in a condensed and intensified form. Further, Freud felt that any single event in a dream has many sources; dream events rarely result from a single cause.

It is important to note that Freud believed that dreams could also have mundane origins; they are not all necessarily caused by conflicts. Physical stimuli such as the temperature of the room, or contact with one's partner can cause dreams of a particular nature. Dreams can also be caused by an internal stimulus, such as an upset stomach.

Both techniques—free association and dream analysis—reveal to the therapist a great deal of repressed material, but all of it is in disguised or symbolic form. The therapist then has the difficult task of interpreting or translating the material for the patient. Freud compared this process with the task of an archeologist in reconstructing a building or community that has been destroyed and buried under the accumulation of more recent years. Just as the archeologist reconstructs a building from the broken fragments, so a psychoanalyst reconstructs an experience from fragmented, buried memories. Thus, much depends on the skill, training, and experience of the psychoanalyst.

In formulating his theory of personality, Freud depended on his own skill in observing and interpreting the evidence. He modified his theory when new evidence—or a new interpretation of old evidence—warranted, but he remained the sole judge of the soundness of the data and of the validity of the theory he constructed from them.

Freud's Image of Human Nature

Freud did not present us with a flattering or optimistic picture of human nature—indeed, quite the opposite. The individual is a "dark cellar" in which conflict continually rages. We are depicted in pessimistic terms, condemned to this struggle with our own inner forces—a struggle we are almost always doomed to lose. All people are doomed to anxiety, to the thwarting of at least some of the constantly driving impulses. Tension and conflict are always present, and we are endlessly defending ourselves against the forces of the id, which stand ever alert to topple us.

Freud held a deterministic view of human beings. Everything we do and think (and even dream) has been predetermined by inaccessible and invisible forces within us. We are perpetually in the grip of the life and death instincts. Our adult personality is fully determined by interactions that took place before we were 5, at a time when we had only limited control over our lives. We are doomed by these early experiences, which forever cast a pall over us, determining our every move.

And what of human intellect and the powers of reason and logic—the abilities that supposedly raise us above the level of the lower animals? Cannot these powers of thought and reason release us from the dark cellar? No, not according to Freud. The idea of a rational person in control of his or her destiny, spontaneously acting on the basis of reason and logic, crumbles under the heavy weight of the id. It is the id, not the intellect, that is our master. Thought and reason are mere servants, operating only to serve our primal desires—a full-time job in itself.

In performing this task, the ego, operating through the defense mechanisms, must often distort or conceal the truth. How, then, in the absence of a realistic and accurate self-perception, can logical thinking or other forms of rationality be of any value?

It is interesting to ask if Freud's picture of human nature, painted in these dark hues, reflected his personal view. In the beginning of this chapter we discussed the possibility that a theorist's childhood experiences could influence his or her theory of personality, just as they influence his or her personality. Freud once described himself as a "cheerful pessimist." What this apparently meant was that Freud felt differently toward the individuals he met than toward humanity as a whole. Toward individuals he expressed a benevolent and optimistic attitude (unless they disagreed with his point of view), but for people in general his judgment was harsh. He viewed them as worthless riffraff, stating that "most of them are trash." This stern judgment seems to be reflected in his theory of human nature.

A Final Commentary

Freud's theory has had a phenomenal impact on psychology and psychiatry, on humanity's self-image, and on the understanding of human personality. Some consider him one of the great contributors to civilization and speak of him as of Karl Marx, Albert Einstein, or Jesus Christ. Whether we agree or disagree with his theory, there is simply no denying Freud's importance. We see daily evidence of it in the fact that so many people in so many walks of life know his name, if not the details of his theory. He is honored the world over, at least by the fact of recognition. That alone makes him a candidate for the small roster of individuals who have been pivotal in the history of civilization.

We shall see further evidence of Freud's importance as we discuss other personality theorists. A great many psychologists and psychiatrists continue to use Freud's work, either as a starting point or as a base of opposition against which to develop their own theories. Great ideas inspire, not only by being perceived as valid and true, but also by being perceived as incorrect and thus stimulating the development of another viewpoint.

There is no need to expound further on Freud's greatness. What is important before we leave Sigmund Freud is to attempt to place his work within the context of legitimate criticism. An exhaustive criticism of Freud—or of any of these theorists—is not intended. Rather, in keeping with the intent of this book, which is to introduce you to the general outline and flavor of the theories, I shall do no more than introduce you to the criticisms.[2]

Much criticism has been offered by experimental psychologists, who argue that psychoanalysis (along with most of the other personality theories) is weak from the standpoint of scientific methodology and theory construction. These critics point out that the psychoanalytic data were not obtained in controlled, systematic (laboratory) fashion and that the various hypotheses that make up the theory were not derived from the data in an orderly or empirically verifiable manner.

These arguments are certainly valid, but, as noted in Chapter 1, there are large and important differences between the behavioristically oriented experimental approach to human behavior and the approach taken by most personality theorists. These two approaches can perhaps be viewed as two distinct disciplines, with different languages, methods, goals and subject matters. If the spirit of behaviorism is taken as the one and only standard for studying people, then most of the current approaches to personality will fall far short. While behaviorism has made impressive contributions to the understanding of human nature, it does not hold exclusive rights to that study. Psychoanalysis has a totally different set of assumptions, methods, and aims, and the fact of this overwhelming difference precludes, in my opinion, judging it by the standards of behaviorism.

There are substantial criticisms and questions from other personality theorists, many of which we will discuss in the chapters to follow. Other

---

[2] An entire book could easily be devoted to criticisms of Freud, but being exhaustive can be exhausting—a condition best saved for graduate school.

individuals have developed their own theories of personality to counteract what they perceive to be weaknesses and errors in Freud's formulations.

Many people argue that Freud placed too great an emphasis on biological forces as shapers of personality. Some critics take emphatic issue with Freud's emphasis on sex and aggression and feel that we are shaped more by social experiences than by sexual ones. Other critics disagree with Freud's deterministic picture of us as passive victims of our instincts and conflicts. They believe that we have more free will than Freud granted and that we can choose to act and grow spontaneously, having at least partial control of our fate. Another criticism has focused on Freud's emphasis on past behavior to the exclusion of future aspirations. These critics argue that we are shaped as much by the future as by the past, by what we hope for and plan to do as much or more than by what we experienced before the age of 5. Still other personality theorists feel that Freud placed too much emphasis on the emotionally crippled, the immature, and the disturbed, to the exclusion of the healthy and mature individual. If we are interested in developing a theory of human personality, these critics argue, we should study the best and the healthiest individuals, not the disturbed ones—the positive human emotions rather than only the negative ones.

The ambiguous definitions of certain of Freud's concepts have been questioned. Critics point to what they see as confusion, and even contradiction, in such terms as id, ego, and superego. Are they physical structures or levels in the brain? Are they fluid processes and functions? Are they even sharply separated from one another? It is interesting to note that in his later writings Freud himself spoke of difficulties and ambiguities in these and other concepts.

Evidence from anthropological studies of various cultures seems to contradict Freud's basic assumption that the biological basis of personality is universal. So much diversity in human behavior has been found across cultures that the assumption of an instinctual commonality is subject to question. The evidence suggests that child-rearing practices are more important in personality formation than are inborn biological forces. For example, cultures exist in which there is no taboo against incestuous sexual relations and in which no evidence of Oedipal conflict—castration anxiety or penis envy—can be found.

There are theorists who remain faithful, in large part, to Freud's basic assumptions and overall point of view although they challenge certain of his premises. A major change introduced into psychoanalysis by these loyalists is an expanded emphasis on the ego. Rather than being the servant of the id, the ego, in this new conception, is seen as being more independent of the id, possessing its own energy not derived from the id, and having its own functions separate from the id. Another change introduced by the loyalists is the de-emphasis of biological forces as influences on personality in favor of social and psychological forces.

From this brief overview of the criticisms, questions, and contemporary modifications of Freud's system, we can see that his original formulations may not be as appropriate in the closing decades of the 20th century as they might have been when the century began. As times change, we must continually seek new and better ways of looking at ourselves.

This book is a history of modern insights into human nature. We are, in our personal and social growth, never free of the past, nor should we want to be. It offers the foundation on which to build, as later personality theorists have done on Freud's work.

If Freud's theory has served no other purpose than that—an inspiration for others, a framework within which to develop new insights—then his importance to the world of ideas is secure. Every structure is dependent upon the soundness and integrity of its foundation. Freud gave personality theory a solid and challenging base on which to build.

Suggested Readings

Freud, S. *The standard edition of the complete psychological works of Sigmund Freud* (24 vols.). (J. Strachey, Ed. and trans.). London: Hogarth Press. This is considered the definitive reference source for Freud's writings.

Grotjahn, M. Psychoanalysis twenty-five years after the death of Sigmund Freud. *Psychological Reports,* 1965, *16,* 965–968.

Hale, N. *Freud and the Americans: The beginnings of psychoanalysis in the United States, 1876–1917.* New York: Oxford University Press, 1971.

Hall, C. S. *A primer of Freudian psychology.* New York: World, 1954.

Jones, E. *The life and work of Sigmund Freud* (3 vols.). New York: Basic Books, 1953–1957.

McGuire, W. (Ed.). *The Freud/Jung letters.* Princeton, N.J.: Princeton University Press, 1974.

Roazen, P. *Freud and his followers.* New York: Knopf, 1975.

Alfred Adler
Individual Psychology

3

*Man is not bad by nature; whatever his faults
have been, faults due to an erroneous
conception of life, he must not be oppressed by
them. He can change. The past is dead. He is
free to be happy.*

—Alfred Adler

     The work of Alfred Adler represented the first major defection from
the still-developing psychoanalysis. You can see quite readily from the
opening quotation why Freud and Adler had to part company. Adler
fashioned an understanding of human nature that did not depict us as
victimized by instincts and conflict and doomed by biological forces and
childhood experiences. He called his new approach *individual psychology*
because it focused on the uniqueness of each person, denying the universality of biological motives and goals ascribed to us by Freud.

Each person, in Adler's opinion, is primarily a social, not a biological, being. Our personalities are shaped by our individual social environments and interactions, not by biological needs and our continual efforts to satisfy them. Sex, of primary importance to Freud, is greatly minimized by Adler as a determining factor in personality. Finally, the conscious rather than the unconscious is at the core of personality. Far from being driven by forces we cannot see and control, we actively direct and create our own growth, our own future.

We have, then, two vastly different theories created by two men raised in the same city in the same era and educated as physicians at the same university. There was only a 14-year difference in their ages. As we shall see, certain elements in Adler's childhood (which was quite different from Freud's) may have presaged his way of looking at human nature, yet he fashioned a theory holding that we are not bound by the past. Ironically, this notion may also have had its roots in childhood experiences.

The Life of Adler (1870–1937)

The second of six children, Alfred Adler was born on February 7, 1870 and raised in a suburb of Vienna. Adler's father, like Freud's, was a merchant, though apparently a more successful one. While Freud was raised in a Jewish ghetto and was conscious of his minority-group status all his life, Adler knew only a few Jewish children and so was influenced more by Viennese than by Jewish culture.

Adler's early childhood was not a happy one. It was marked by sickness, an awareness of death, unhappiness, and jealousy. He suffered from rickets, which kept him from running and playing with other children. At the age of 3, he witnessed the death of a younger brother in the next bed; at 4, Adler himself was close to death from pneumonia. It was then—when he heard the doctor tell his father "Your boy is lost"—that he decided to become a doctor himself. (He was also run over twice.)

A sickly child during the first two years of his life, he was pampered by his mother, only to be dethroned by the arrival of a new brother. There is some suggestion of rejection on the part of his mother, but Adler was clearly his father's favorite.

As he grew older and his health improved a bit, he began to spend more time outdoors, primarily because he was not happy at home. In spite of his clumsiness and unattractiveness, he worked hard to become popular with his playmates and found a sense of acceptance and self-esteem that he had not found at home. As a result, he developed a great fondness for the company of other people, a characteristic he retained all his life.

In school he was unhappy and was only a mediocre student. In fact, one of his teachers advised his father to apprentice him to a shoemaker; the teacher felt that the young Adler was unfit for anything else. He was particularly bad in mathematics, but through persistence and hard work he rose from a failing student to the best in the class.

In many ways, his childhood reads like a tragedy; it also reads like a textbook example of Adler's later theory of overcoming childhood weaknesses and inferiorities and shaping one's destiny instead of being shaped by it. The man who would give the world the notion of inferiority feelings certainly spoke from the depths of his own early experiences.

Fulfilling his childhood ambition, he studied medicine at the University of Vienna. He entered private practice as an ophthalmologist but shifted after a few years to general medicine. He was particularly interested in incurable diseases but was so distressed at his helplessness to prevent death, particularly in younger patients, that he soon abandoned general medicine for neurology and psychiatry.

Adler's nine-year association with Freud began in 1902, when Freud invited him (and three others) to meet once a week at Freud's home to discuss his newly developing psychoanalysis. The two men worked closely together, although the relationship was never an intimate one. It is important to note that Adler was never a student or disciple of Freud's and was never psychoanalyzed by him.

By 1910, although Adler was president of what was then called the Vienna Psychoanalytical Society and co-editor of its new journal, he was also an increasingly vocal critic of Freudian theory. "I am having an atrocious time with Adler," Freud wrote. In 1911, Adler severed all connection with psychoanalysis and went on to develop his own system. Freud remained hostile and bitter toward Adler for the rest of his life. He called Adler a pigmy, saying "I made a pigmy great." Adler shot back that a pigmy standing on the shoulders of a giant can see farther than the giant can. That may be true of a pigmy, Freud replied, but not of a louse in the giant's hair! In 1912, Adler founded the Society for Individual Psychology.

After serving in the Austrian army during World War I, Adler was asked to organize government-sponsored child-counseling clinics in Vienna. These clinics soon grew rapidly in number and popularity. In 1926, Adler made the first of an increasingly frequent series of visits to the United States, where he taught and made highly successful lecture tours. Before long he was spending more time in the United States than in Vienna; by 1936 he no longer maintained a home there. In 1937, on a strenuous 56-lecture tour, he suffered a heart attack and died in Scotland.

Inferiority Feelings

Inferiority feelings is another of those many terms from psychology that have come into everyday use in the English language. It derives from Adler's approach to personality; indeed, it is at the core of his approach. A general feeling of inferiority, Adler believed, is everpresent and vital as a determining force in behavior. "To be a human being," he wrote, "means to feel oneself inferior." Thus, it is a condition common to all people and, as such, is not a sign of weakness or abnormality.

In fact, Adler believed the opposite: inferiority feelings are the source of all human striving. All individual progress, growth, and development result from the attempt to *compensate* for one's inferiorities, be they imagined or real. Throughout an individual's life, he or she is motivated by the need to overcome this sense of inferiority and to strive for ever-higher levels of development.

The process begins in infancy, according to Adler. The infant is small and helpless, totally dependent upon adults. Adler felt that the infant is aware of the relatively greater power and strength of its parents; it is aware of the hopelessness of trying to resist or challenge that power. As a result, the infant develops feelings of inferiority relative to the larger, stronger people in the environment.

This initial experience of inferiority happens to everyone in infancy but is not genetically determined. Rather, it is a function of the environment, which, for the infant, is the same everywhere: helplessness and dependency relative to adults.

It is important to understand that inferiority feelings are inescapable, but—even more important—they are necessary. Again, they provide the major motivation to strive, to grow, to progress, to succeed. All forward and upward movement results from the attempt to compensate for these inferiority feelings. They are, therefore, beneficial and useful. They motivate us to solve the problems of adjustment and growth.

But suppose an individual does not grow and develop? What happens when a child is unable to compensate for his or her inferiority feelings? As you might imagine, an inability to overcome inferiority feelings heightens and intensifies these feelings and leads to the development of an *inferiority complex*. Adler defined this condition as "an inability to solve life's problems," and he found such a complex in the childhoods of many adults who came to him for treatment. An inferiority complex can originate in three ways in childhood: through organic inferiority, through spoiling, and through neglect.

The investigation of *organic inferiority* was Adler's first major effort, carried out while he was still associated with Freud (who, incidentally, approved of the notion). Adler stated that defective parts or organs of the body affected personality development through the person's efforts to compensate for the defect or weakness.

For example, a child who is physically weak might concentrate on that weakness and work to develop superior athletic ability. History records many examples of such compensation: the stutterer Demosthenes became a great orator, and the weak and sickly Theodore Roosevelt became a specimen of physical fitness as an adult. Thus, organic inferiority can lead to striking artistic, athletic, and social accomplishments. But it can also lead to an inferiority complex if the attempts at compensation are unsuccessful.

Spoiling or pampering a child can also lead to an inferiority complex. The spoiled child is, of course, the center of attention in the home, where every need and whim is satisfied and little is denied. Under the circumstances the child quite naturally develops the idea that he or she is the most important person in any situation and that others should always defer to him or her. The first experience at school—where the child is no longer the center of all attention—comes as a rude shock for which the child is not equipped to cope.

Spoiled children have little, if any, social feeling and are exceedingly impatient with others. They have never learned to wait for what they want. Neither have such children learned to overcome difficulties or to adjust to others. When confronted with obstacles in the path to gratification, they come to believe that it is their own lack of ability that is thwarting them. Hence, an inferiority complex develops.

It is easy to understand how the *neglected* child—the one who is unwanted and rejected—can develop an inferiority complex. His or her infancy and childhood are characterized by a lack of love and security, because of indifferent or even hostile parents. As a result, the child may develop feelings of worthlessness—even anger—and look upon everyone with distrust.

Whatever the source of inferiority feelings, a person may tend to overcompensate and so develop what has been called a *superiority complex*. This involves, as you might guess, an exaggerated opinion of one's own abilities and accomplishments. A person may feel superior inwardly and not manifest a need to demonstrate it with accomplishments. Or, the person may feel such a need and so become extremely successful in some pursuit. In either case, the individual's behavior is characterized by boasting, extreme vanity and self-centeredness, and a tendency to denigrate others. I'm sure you recognize the type.

You can see, then, how vitally important inferiority feelings are to personality formation. A requisite for all positive growth and development, they can also cripple such development.

Inferiority feelings are what push us forward, but to what end? What is the ultimate goal for which we strive? Is it simply to be rid of inferiority feelings? No, Adler viewed humans as striving for something more.

His thinking with regard to our ultimate goal changed over the years. Initially he identified inferiority feelings with a general feeling of weakness or femininity and spoke of compensation for this weakness as "masculine protest." The goal of the compensation was a will to power in which aggression played a large part. Later, he rejected the notion of equating inferiority feelings with femininity and the striving for power and developed instead a much broader viewpoint in which we strive for *superiority*, a condition quite different from the superiority complex.

Striving for Superiority

The "fundamental fact of our life" was how Adler described his notion of *striving for superiority*. It is the ultimate goal toward which all people strive, but it does not mean superiority in the usual sense of the word.

By *striving for superiority*, Adler did not mean that each of us strives to be above everyone else in position or prestige. Nor does the phrase, in his usage, refer to an arrogant, domineering tendency. What he meant is best indicated by the word he often used synonymously with superiority: *perfection*. People strive for perfection, which is, as Adler variously described it, an overcoming, an upward striving, an increase, an urge from below to above, or the impetus from minus to plus.

This great upward drive parallels physical growth and is a necessary part of life. Everything we do follows the impetus and direction of this striving, which is constantly in operation. We are never free of it because it is life itself. Everything is marked by this striving for superiority, for perfection. Drawing upon Darwin and the notion of evolution, Adler said that all life expresses itself as constant movement toward the goal of the preservation and improvement of the individual and the species. And this goal is attained by adapting to and mastering that environment.

The various species, including humans, have evolved to their present level through this continuing adaptation. The necessity for better and more complete adaptation always exists. It cannot end; the striving to adapt, the striving for perfection, is innate. It must be innate, Adler argued, or no form of life could survive.

This ultimate and overall goal—the great upward drive—is, of course, oriented toward the future. Whereas Freud saw human behavior as rigidly determined by physiological forces (the instincts) and experiences of childhood, Adler saw our motivation in terms of expectations for the future. He argued that we cannot appeal to instincts or impulses as explanatory principles. Only the final goal of superiority or perfection can explain our motivation.

Thus, all psychological processes and phenomena can be explained by Adler's concept of *finalism*—the idea that we have an ultimate goal, a final state of being, and an ever-present tendency or necessity to move in that direction. There is an important aspect to this notion of finalism. The goals for which we as individuals reach do not exist as actualities, but rather as potentialities. We strive for ideals that exist in us subjectively.

Adler believed that our overall goals are fictional ideals that cannot be tested against reality. He added that we live our lives around such fictions. We may believe that all people are created equal or that all people are basically good, and such ideals influence the way we perceive and interact with those around us. The person who believes that he or she will be rewarded in heaven for a certain way of behaving lives in accordance with such a belief. Confidence in the existence of heaven is not a reality-based belief, yet it is quite real to the person who subscribes to the view.

Thus, we have Adler's concept of *fictional finalism*—the idea that fictional ideas guide our behavior. There are a great many such fictions by which we direct the course of our lives, but the most general one is the ideal of perfection. The best conception of this ideal so far developed by human beings is the concept of God, which represents what Adler described as "the concrete formulation of the goal of perfection."

There are two additional points about the striving for superiority. First, it functions to increase rather than lessen tension. In opposition to Freud, Adler did not see our sole motivation as the reduction of tension and the maintenance of a neutral or tension-free state. The striving for perfection, with its correlate notions of upward, forward, more, and increase, calls for great expenditures of energy and effort. Adler felt that human beings want quite the opposite of stability and quiet.

Second, the striving for superiority is manifested both by the individual and by society. Adler considered people very much social beings. We strive for superiority or perfection not only as individuals but also as members of a society; we strive for perfection of our culture. Adler viewed individuals and society as closely interrelated and interdependent, so that people must function constructively with others for the good of all. Contrary to Freud, Adler considered the individual not to be in conflict with his or her culture but rather to be totally compatible with it.

Thus, we have a picture of humanity perpetually striving for the fictional, ideal goal of perfection. How, in our daily lives, do we go about trying to attain this goal? This question Adler answered with his concept of style of life.

Style of Life

Mankind has only one ultimate goal—superiority or perfection—but there are a great many specific behaviors by which individuals strive for that goal. We each express our striving for superiority in a different way. Each of us develops a unique pattern of characteristics, behaviors, and habits by which we reach for the goal. In other words, every person develops a distinctive *life style.*

To understand how the style of life develops we must return to the concepts of inferiority feelings and compensation, for they form the basis of our life style. As we have seen, all infants are afflicted with inferiority feelings that motivate them to compensate in some way. In these attempts at compensation, the child acquires a set of characteristic ways of behaving. To repeat an earlier example, a sickly or weak boy may strive to increase his strength and physical prowess. This behavior becomes his style of life—a set of behaviors designed to compensate for an inferiority.

Everything we do is shaped and defined by our unique life style; it determines which aspects of our total environment we will attend to or ignore and what attitudes we will hold. The life style is learned from the parent-child interactions that take place in the early years of life. According to Adler, the life style is so firmly crystallized by the age of 4 or 5 that it is difficult to change thereafter.

The life style so formed becomes the guiding framework for later behavior. The nature of the life style will depend on the nature of the relationship between parent and child as the child works to find a way to compensate for his or her sense of inferiority. For example, a girl who has been neglected may feel inferior in coping with the demands of life. The neglect on the part of her parents may cause her to feel distrustful and hostile toward the world at large. Her style of life, then, may involve seeking revenge, resenting the success of others, and taking whatever she feels is due her. We might subsume all such behaviors under the term *character,* which is essentially what Adler meant by style of life.

You may have spotted the apparent inconsistency between this notion of life style and our earlier comments about Adler's theory. We noted that Adler's approach was a more optimistic and less deterministic view than Freud's. People are in control of their fate, Adler said, not victims of it. But now we find that the style of life is fully fixed by the parent-child relationship in the first five years of life and subject to little change after that. This would seem to be almost as deterministic as Freud; both stressed the importance of the early years in the formation of the adult personality. The notion of life style is not as deterministic as it may seem, however, as Adler later clarified with a concept known as the *creative self*.

In his various writings, Adler used several terms as equivalents for style of life: *personality, individuality,* and *the self.* But whatever terms used, he expressed in his later writings the belief that the style of life (the self) is created by the individual. People create their selves rather than being passively shaped by childhood experiences. The experiences themselves are not so important as the person's attitude toward them. Adler wrote that the person "does not relate himself to the outside world in a predetermined manner . . . . He relates himself always according to his own interpretation of himself." He argued that neither heredity nor environment determines personality. Instead, the way we experience these influences ("the interpretation he makes of these experiences") provides the basis for the creative construction of our attitude toward life.

In other words, Adler is arguing for the existence of individual free will that allows each of us to create our own most appropriate life style out of the abilities and experiences given us by heredity and environment. Although not very clear on precisely how this creative self operates, Adler insisted that our life style is not determined for us; we are free to choose and create our own selves. Once created, the life style remains constant throughout life and constitutes our basic character, which defines our attitudes and behavior toward outside problems.

Adler placed great importance on the problems in life that every individual must solve, and he grouped them into three categories: problems involving behavior toward others, problems of occupation, and problems of love. He posited the existence of four basic life styles adopted by people for dealing with these problems.

The first type shows a *dominant* or *ruling* attitude, with little, if any, social awareness or interest. Such a person is likely to behave without regard for others. The more virulent of this type directly attack others and become sadists, delinquents, and tyrants. The less virulent become alcoholics, drug addicts, and suicides. Adler argued that through such behavior they are attacking others indirectly. In other words, they see themselves as hurting others by attacking themselves.

The second type of life style—the *getting* type—which Adler considered the most common, expects to get everything from other people and so becomes dependent on them.

The *avoiding* type, as the name suggests, makes no attempt to face or struggle with life's problems. By avoiding the problems, such a person avoids any possibility of defeat.

As you can see, these three types are not prepared to face or cope with the everyday problems of life. They are unable to cooperate with other people, and the clash between their life styles and the real world is sufficient to result in abnormal behavior as manifested in neuroses and psychoses. All three types lack what Adler called *social interest*.

The fourth type—the *socially useful* type—is able to cooperate with others and to act in accordance with their needs. Such a person copes with life's problems within a well-developed framework of social interest.[1]

Social interest came to form a major part of Adler's system. He believed that getting along with others is the first task we encounter in life and that our subsequent social adjustment (part of our life style) influences our approach to all of life's later problems.

Social Interest

Adler viewed human beings as influenced much more strongly by social than by biological forces. However, he did consider the potential for social interest to be innate. In that sense, then, Adler's approach does have a biological element to it. But the extent to which the innate potential for social feeling is realized depends on the nature of the child's early social experiences. No person can detach himself or herself entirely from other people, Adler felt, or from obligations toward them. From earliest times, people have congregated with other people—in families, tribes, and nations. Such communities are indispensable to humans for protection and for the attainment of survival goals. Thus, it has always been necessary for people to cooperate, and this cooperation is what Adler meant by social interest. The individual must cooperate with and contribute to society in order to realize both his or her own and society's goals.

Beginning at birth, the newborn finds itself in a situation requiring cooperation from others—initially the mother, then other family members, and finally those beyond the home. In infancy, we cannot function very well in isolation and must develop social interest. Everything we do for the rest of our lives takes place within a framework of other people. All aspects of our character or style of life reveal the extent of the development of our social feeling.

Adler noted the important influence of the mother as the first person with whom the baby comes in contact. She can, through her behavior toward the infant, foster and develop social interest, or she can distort or thwart its development. (Of course, this influence depends, Adler

---

[1]It should be noted that Adler was opposed to typing or classifying human beings in any manner. He proposed these four general types only, as he put it, "for teaching purposes." He noted that in clinical work one should never make the mistake of classifying people into mutually exclusive categories.

noted, on how the child interprets the mother's behavior. The creative self forms the baby's character on the basis of this interpretation.)

The mother must teach the child cooperation, comradeship, and courage, concepts Adler considered to be very closely related. Only if a person feels united with all others, Adler said, can he or she act with courage in attempting to master life's problems. The child (and later the adult) who looks upon others with hostility and suspicion will approach life's problems with the same attitude. Those with no feeling of social interest will become socially undesirable people—neurotics, criminals, despots, and the like.

Obviously, there can be a wide latitude in social feelings. One could devote all one's time and energy to others or live an entirely selfish existence and make no sacrifice for the community. Of course, one could also sacrifice excessively for some group and yet have no social interest on the individual level—for example, for a member of one's own family. Adler was not arguing in favor of a blind subordination of oneself to the wants and needs of others. Rather, he urged a coordination or cooperation in which the individual best develops his or her own abilities in concert with efforts to improve society.

We saw, in the biographical sketch at the beginning of this chapter, that Adler as a boy enjoyed the company of other children; he developed a high degree of social interest, which characterized him all his life. It is interesting that early in his career Adler viewed people as driven by a lust for power and a need to dominate. This was during the time when Adler himself was struggling to establish his own point of view within the Freudian circle. Later in life, after he broke with Freud, achieved recognition on his own, and became aware of the human wreckage of World War I, he came to feel that people are strongly motivated by social interest. It is speculation, of course, to attribute such changes in the theory to changes within the theorist; but Adler was almost 50 years old when the war ended—an age when many individuals reassess themselves and their world.

Freud's biographer, Ernest Jones, commented that, when Adler was a part of Freud's circle, he was cantankerous and contentious and seemed very ambitious as he quarreled over the priority of some of his ideas. Years later, Jones observed, Adler's "success had brought him a certain benignity."[2] At any rate, Adler's system changed, as perhaps he did, from emphasizing power and dominance as motivating forces to stressing the more benign force of social interest.

[2]Ernest Jones. *The Life and Work of Sigmund Freud* (Vol. 2). (New York: Basic Books, 1955), p. 130.

Order of Birth

Adler posited birth order as one of the major social influences in childhood from which the individual creates a style of life. Even though siblings have the same parents and live in the same house, they do not have identical social environments. The facts of being older or younger than one's siblings and of being exposed to parental attitudes that have changed as a result of the arrival of more children create different conditions of childhood that greatly influence one's personality. Adler would often amaze lecture audiences and dinner guests by telling accurately what a person's order of birth was on the basis of his or her behavior. He focused on three different positions: the firstborn child, the second born, and the youngest.

The first child finds itself in a unique and in many ways enviable situation. Usually the parents are extremely happy at the birth of their first child and devote a great deal of time and attention to the new baby. The firstborn thus receives the full and undivided attention of the parents.

As a result, the firstborn often has a happy, secure existence—until the second child appears. What a shock it must be! No longer the focus of instant and constant attention, no longer receiving the undivided love and care of its parents, the child is, in Adler's terms, "dethroned" at this time. The constant love the firstborn received for the period of its reign must now be shared. The child must often submit to the outrage of waiting until after the newborn has been attended to and must be quiet at times so as not to awaken the new baby.

No one could expect the firstborn to suffer such a drastic displacement without putting up a fight. He or she must try to recapture his or her former position of power. All firstborns feel the shock of their changed position in the family, but those who have been excessively pampered will, of course, feel a greater loss. Also, the extent of the loss depends on the age of the firstborn at the time the rival appears.

The battle to retain his or her former supremacy is lost from the beginning; things will never be as they once were, no matter how hard the firstborn tries. But the child tries anyway and becomes, for a time, a behavior problem, breaking rules and objects, being stubborn, or refusing to eat or to go to bed. He or she is striking out in anger. Of course, the parents will probably strike back, and their weapons are far more powerful. When the firstborn is punished for the new, troublesome behavior, he or she interprets the punishment as more evidence of a changed position and may easily grow to hate the new child. The newborn is, after all, the cause of the problem.

"How could such a situation not affect one's outlook on life?" Adler asked. He found that oldest children are often oriented toward the past, locked in nostalgia, and pessimistic about the future. Having learned the advantages of power at one time, they remain concerned with it all their lives. To some degree, they can exercise power over the younger siblings. At the same time, however, they are usually more subject to the power of the parents than are the younger children; that is, more is expected of them.

As a result of all this, firstborns take an interest in the maintenance of order and authority. Adler found that they become very good organizers, conscientious and scrupulous as to detail and authoritarian and conservative in attitude. Incidentally—or perhaps not so incidentally—Freud was a firstborn. In fact, Adler referred to him as a "typical eldest son." The firstborn may also grow up to feel very insecure and hostile toward others. Adler found that perverts, criminals, and neurotics were often firstborns.

What lies in store for the second born, the one who's caused such a commotion? This child too has a unique situation. For one thing, he or she never experiences the powerful and focal position once occupied by the firstborn. Even if a younger sibling should appear, the second born does not experience the keen sense of dethronement felt by the firstborn. Furthermore, the parents may have changed by the time the second child arrives. A second baby is not the novelty the first was, and the parents may be less concerned and anxious about their behavior in rearing the second one; they may take a more relaxed approach to the second child.

The second born has, from the very beginning, a pacesetter in the older sibling. The second child is not alone as a child but always has the example of the older sibling's behavior as a model or a threat. This spurs on the second born, often stimulating a faster development than the firstborn exhibited. The second child is motivated to catch up and surpass the older sibling, a goal that usually speeds language and motor development. For example, the second child usually begins speaking at an earlier age than the older child did.

Not having experienced power, the second born is not as concerned with it as the firstborn is and is more optimistic about the future. The second child is likely to be highly competitive and ambitious. Adler was a second born.

However, there are a number of other outcomes that may arise from the relationship between the first and second born. Suppose, for example, the older sibling excels in sports or in scholarship—or in everything. The second born may sense that he or she can never surpass the older one and so may give up trying. In this case, competitiveness would not become part of his or her style of life. Of course, as they grow older, it might turn out that the younger child is smarter, better looking, or superior in some other way to the first, who then may again become a behavior problem.

The youngest or last-born child never faces the shock of dethronement by another child and often becomes the pet or baby of the whole family, particularly if the siblings are more than a few years older. Spurred on by the need to surpass older siblings, the youngest child often develops at a remarkably fast rate. As a result, last borns are often high achievers in whatever work they undertake as adults.

But quite the opposite may take place if the youngest child is spoiled and pampered by the rest of the family to the point where he or she needn't learn to do anything for himself or herself. As the individual grows older, he or she may retain the helplessness and dependency that marked his or her childhood. Unaccustomed to striving and struggling, used to being cared for by others, the person will find it difficult to cope with the problems and adjustments of adulthood.

What about the only child? In essence, he or she is the firstborn who never loses the position of primacy and power—at least not in childhood. The child continues to be the focus and center of family attention. Spending more time in the company of adults than a child with siblings does, the only child often matures very early and achieves adult-like behaviors and attitudes sooner.

The only child is likely to experience a severe shock as he or she grows older and finds that in areas of life outside the home (such as school) he or she is not the center of attention. The only child has learned neither to share nor to compete for the center stage. If the child's abilities do not bring sufficient recognition and attention, he or she is likely to feel keenly disappointed.

Adler was not laying down firm rules of development. As noted, a child will not automatically acquire one and only one kind of character as a result of order of birth. What he was suggesting was the likelihood of certain life styles developing as a function of one's position within the family. The individual must always be studied in his or her relationships with others, for these early social relationships are used by the creative self in constructing the life style.

Techniques of Inquiry

Like Freud, Adler developed his theory through observation of his patients—what they told him and how they behaved during treatment sessions. Adler's approach to his patients was more relaxed and informal than Freud's. Whereas Freud's patients lay on a couch while he sat behind them, Adler and his patients faced each other, seated in comfortable chairs. The sessions were more like chats between two friends than like the formal relationships maintained by Freud.

Adler obtained information about his patients by observing everything about them: the way they walked and sat, their manner of shaking hands—even their choice of which chair to sit in. He believed that the manner in which we use our bodies indicates something of our life style. Even the way in which we sleep was revealing to Adler. A person who sleeps flat on his or her back is seen as wanting to seem bigger than he or she is. Sleeping on one's stomach reveals a stubborn and negative personality.

The three major sources of information—the "three entrance gates to mental life," as Adler called them—are order of birth, first memories, and dreams. These were his primary tools.

We have already discussed how one's position in the family—*order of birth*—influences personality in the Adlerian view.

A patient's *first memory* is, according to Adler, an excellent guide to uncovering his or her life style. As we have seen, the life style develops (is created) in the first four or five years, and Adler felt that the earliest memory from this period would indicate the life style that continues to characterize the adult. Adler found that it made little difference whether the first memory was of a real event or was a fantasy. In either case, the primary interest of the person's life revolves around the remembered incident.

As one test of his theory, Adler asked more than 100 physicians for their first memories. He found that a majority of these memories were concerned with either illness or a death in the family, which apparently led them into a career of combating sickness.

While Adler felt that each first memory must be interpreted within the context of the individual patient, he found some commonalities among them. For example, memories involving danger or punishment indicate a tendency toward hostility. Those concerning the birth of a sibling indicate a continued sense of dethronement. Memories that focus on only one parent show a preference for that parent. Memories of improper behavior indicate an attempt to avoid repeating the behavior.

Adler's own first memories revealed his physical weakness, a rivalry with his older brother, a preference for his father over his mother, ambition, and the overcoming of his childhood fear of death—all quite characteristic of the young Adler.

Adler agreed with Freud on the great value of *dreams* in understanding personality but disagreed on the manner in which dreams should be interpreted. Adler did not believe that dreams fulfill wishes or reveal deeply hidden conflicts. Rather, dreams involve a person's feelings about a current life problem and what he or she intends or would like to do about it.

Adler felt that dreams engender feeling tones. As proof of this, he pointed to the fact that we very often cannot recall the specific events of a dream, but we do remember its mood; we remember whether it was frightening or beautiful without being able to recall in any detail the story of the dream. The moods evoked by a dream deceive the person, weakening his or her common sense and logic. In the fantasies that are dreams (both night and daydreams) we can surmount the most difficult obstacle, simplify the most complex problem. And that is the fundamental purpose of dreams: to help the individual solve present problems. Dreams are oriented toward the present and future—toward goals and not toward conflicts of the past.

Adler argued that dreams should never be interpreted by themselves—that is, without knowledge of the person and his or her situation. The dream is a manifestation of a person's life style and so is unique to the individual.

However, as with first memories, Adler did find common interpretations for some dreams. For example, he found, as did Freud, that many people have dreams of falling or flying. Freud interpreted such dreams in sexual terms. To Adler, a dream of falling indicates that one's emotional view is from above to below. The person might, for example, be afraid of losing self-esteem. The viewpoint in a flying dream is just the opposite and may indicate an upward striving, an ambitious life style in which the person wants to be above others. Some dreams combine both flying and falling, which Adler interpreted as a fear of being too ambitious and then failing. A dream of being chased by someone (or something) suggests a feeling of weakness in relation to others. Dreaming that one is unclothed indicates a fear of giving oneself away.

By whatever technique, the purpose of inquiry into an individual's personality is to discover his or her life style and to determine if it is the most appropriate one for that person.

Adler's Image of Human Nature

We noted in the beginning of this chapter how different Adler's image of human nature was from that of Freud. Adler's system provides an optimistic—even flattering—picture of us that many consider a welcome antidote to Freud's dreary picture. Certainly it is more satisfying to our sense of self-worth to consider ourselves capable of consciously shaping our own development and destiny rather than being dominated by sexual forces and childhood experiences. Adler's image of us might be said to be hopeful rather than hopeless. We are not driven by forces that we cannot see or control; we shape the forces ourselves and use them in our own creative way to construct a unique style of life. This uniqueness is another part of Adler's flattering picture. Many saw in Freud's system a depressing sameness in human beings.

Not only did Adler see each person as unique and highly conscious, but he also viewed humanity as a whole in the same terms. Adler was very optimistic about social progress. From childhood on, he was concerned with societal betterment. This persistent belief that we can change ourselves and our society was a hallmark of Adlerian theory. He was attracted to socialism and was very much involved in school guidance clinics and penal reform, illustrating his belief in the creative power of the individual.

His concept of social interest reflected the belief that people are capable of cooperating to bring about a morally desirable and healthy society. By portraying us as capable of feeling and expressing sympathy, affection, and identification with one another, Adler offered a picture of human nature that many feel is in keeping with the highest teachings of religion and ethics.

A Final Commentary

Adler's theory of personality, so warmly received by many who were repelled by Freud's dreary picture of humanity, has also been subject to a number of criticisms. These critical questions have come from those who take the orthodox Freudian point of view as well as from Freud's opponents.

One charge leveled against Adler by Freud himself was that individual psychology was oversimplified. Freud wrote that Adler's theory would be very appealing to many people: "A theory like this must be exceedingly welcome, which takes no complications into account, which introduces no new and difficult concepts, which knows nothing of the unconscious, which removes at a single blow the problem of sexuality . . . ."

Freud is not alone in making this charge. It is true that Adler's theory seems simpler than some others (certainly simpler than Freud's), but that was Adler's deliberate intention. "I have taken forty years to make my psychology simple," he wrote. One point that may reinforce the charge of oversimplification is that his books are much easier to read than those of many other theorists, perhaps in part because he intended most of them for the lay public and also because some were compiled from popular lectures.

A related charge is that Adler's theories rely too heavily on com-mon-sense observations from everyday life. Whether that is a valid criti-cism is debatable, since some of his observations appear to be insightful and useful.

Some critics allege that Adler was not always consistent or system-atic in his thinking—that there are gaps and unanswered questions in his theory. Are inferiority feelings the only problem people have to cope with in life? Do all people strive solely, or even primarily, for superiority or perfection? Is it possible that some people might become reconciled to a certain degree of inferiority and no longer be concerned with attempts to compensate for it? How important, specifically, are heredity and envi-ronment in influencing one's life style? These and many other questions have been asked, and they are not adequately answered in Adler's system. Of course, many theories leave us with a set of unanswered questions.

A problem that concerns many people—even some of Adler's fol-lowers—is the sticky question of determinism and free will. At the begin-ning of his career, he did not oppose the notion of determinism. It was, after all, strongly accepted in science at the time and certainly charac-terized Freud's position. Later, however, Adler felt the need to grant more autonomy to the self, and his final position was one that, as we have seen, rejected determinism. His doctrine of the creative self states that, before the age of 5, we each create our own life style out of the materials provided by our heredity and environment. It is not clear, however, just how the child is able to make such momentous decisions.

We know that Adler came out strongly in favor of free will and against the idea that a person is merely a victim of heredity and past environment. The position is clear, but the specifics of the forming of a life style are not.

While not denying the importance of these criticisms, there is also no denying Adler's influence, and we shall see examples of that influence in several of the theories to follow. His emphasis on social forces in personality development will be seen in the work of Erich Fromm, Karen Horney, and Harry Stack Sullivan, all of whom might be described as being as much neo-Adlerian as neo-Freudian. Even in the later develop-ment of psychoanalysis itself, Adler's influence is felt in the increased emphasis on consciousness and on motivating forces other than sex. His focus on the unity of personality and the whole person can be seen in the later work of Gordon Allport.

Adler's stress on the creative power of the person in shaping his or her own life and his insistence that future goals are more important than past events influenced the most recent work of Abraham Maslow. Maslow commented: "Alfred Adler becomes more correct year by year."

Adler's initial work on organ inferiority has been influential in the study of psychosomatic medicine, and the concepts of inferiority complex, compensation, and order of birth are still central in the study of personality. Curiously, although his ideas are widespread, Adler's personal recognition declined after his death in 1937, and he has received relatively little praise for his contributions. Many concepts have been borrowed from his system and put to use without proper acknowledgment of their origin.

Adler's loyal followers claim that individual psychology is growing today. The *Journal of Individual Psychology* is quite active, and individual-psychology associations exist throughout the Western world. The Alfred Adler Mental Hygiene Clinic, under the direction of his daughter Alexandra, is located in New York, a city that claims some 250 practicing Adlerian analysts. Thus, Alfred Adler's approach to personality is of more than historical interest.

Suggested Readings

Adler, A. Individual psychology. In C. Murchison (Ed.), *Psychologies of 1930.* Worcester, Mass.: Clark University Press, 1930. Pp. 395–405.

American Society for Adlerian Psychology & Mosak, H. (Eds.). *Alfred Adler: His influence on psychology today.* Park Ridge, N.J.: Noyes Press, 1973.

Ansbacher, H. L., & Ansbacher, R. R. (Eds.). *The individual psychology of Alfred Adler: A systematic presentation in selections from his writings.* New York: Basic Books, 1956.

Ansbacher, H. L., & Ansbacher, R. R. (Eds.). *Superiority and social interest: A collection of later writings by Alfred Adler.* New York: Viking Press, 1973.

Dreikurs, R. Adler's contribution to medicine, psychology, education. *American Journal of Individual Psychology,* 1952–1953, *10,* 83–86.

Dreikurs, R. What is psychotherapy?: The Adlerian viewpoint. *American Psychotherapy Monographs,* 1959, No. 1, 16–22.

Orgler, H. *Alfred Adler: The man and his work.* New York: New American Library, 1972.

Sperber, M. *Masks of loneliness: Alfred Adler in perspective.* New York: Macmillan, 1974.

Karen Horney

4

Man has the capacity as well as the desire to develop his potentialities and become a decent human being . . . . I believe that man can change and go on changing as long as he lives.

—Karen Horney

It is obvious from our opening quote that Karen Danielson Horney must be considered another defector from the orthodox Freudian point of view. While not a direct disciple or colleague of Freud's, Horney was nevertheless trained in the official psychoanalytic mode by one of Freud's most trusted students. She did not, however, remain long in the Freudian camp.

Horney began her divergence from Freud's doctrines by taking issue with his psychological portrayal of women. An early feminist, she argued that psychoanalysis focused more on the development of men than of women. Countering Freud's contention that women are driven by penis envy, Horney commented that, in her observation, men are envious of women for their ability to carry and give birth to children. "I know just as many men," she said, "with womb envy as women with penis envy." Although originally moved to depart from Freud on the issue of female psychology, Horney later broadened her attack on Freud and elaborated her own position, so that there came to be little in common between them.

Horney's theory was influenced, in part, by her sex but perhaps even more by the social and cultural forces to which she was exposed. She worked several decades after Freud's major developments appeared, and she formulated the essential lines of her theory in a culture radically different from Freud's—the United States. By the 1930s and 1940s, major changes had taken place in popular attitudes about sex and the roles of the sexes. These changes were noticeable in Europe but were even more visible in the United States. Social attitudes too, were different in the United States.

Horney found that her American patients were so unlike her previous German ones, both in their neuroses and in their more normal personalities, that only the differences in social forces could adequately account for the differences in their personalities. Personality, she therefore argued, cannot depend wholly on invariant biological forces, as Freud had proposed. If it did, we would not see such important differences in personality from one culture to another.

Thus, Horney became, like Adler, a social-psychological theorist, placing heavy emphasis on social relationships rather than on physiological forces as pivotal factors in personality formation. She argued that sex is not the governing factor, as Freud had claimed, and also took issue with his concepts of the Oedipus complex, the libido, and the structure of personality.

The center of personality, Horney theorized, is not sex or aggression but the need for and the efforts to obtain security. Like Adler, Horney's view of human nature is flattering and optimistic: we can overcome our anxieties and can grow and develop to the fullest use of our potential.

The Life of Horney (1885–1952)

Karen Danielson was born in a small village not far from Hamburg, in northern Germany. Her father was a ship captain of Norwegian background, and her mother was Dutch. Mrs. Danielson was 17 years younger than her husband and differed sharply from him in temperament.While the father was a devout Bible reader, morose and silent, the mother was attractive, vivacious, and a freethinker. The father was away at sea for long periods, and, when he was home, the opposing natures of the parents often led to arguments.

As with Adler and Freud, one can see how her future personality theory might have originated in Karen Danielson's childhood. Although she admired her father, she long remembered his stern manner, "frightening gaze," and disparaging comments about her appearance and intelligence—comments that hurt the young girl deeply. There is some hint of rejection by her mother as well, who seemed to favor her older brother. Nevertheless, she became very much the "adoring daughter" to her mother, apparently as a way of getting attention and security. As we shall see, Horney later discussed the role that lack of love in childhood plays in fostering basic anxiety, and she realized how much hostility had developed in her own childhood.

At the age of 12, after receiving very kind treatment from a doctor for an illness, she decided to seek a medical career. In spite of spirited opposition from her father and her own strong feelings of worthlessness and despair, Horney worked hard in high school to prepare herself for medical school. So strongly did her father resist the idea that, when she began her studies at the University of Freiburg, her mother left him and moved nearby.

At the age of 24, in 1909, she married Oscar Horney, a Berlin lawyer, and in due course had three children and entered into psychoanalytic training. She received her own analysis from a devoted disciple of Freud's, who mentioned her in glowing terms to the master.

In 1926, she and her husband separated, and six years later she emigrated to the United States, working first in Chicago and then settling permanently in New York. During these years she developed most of her theory. Toward the end of her life, she became interested in Zen Buddhism, and she visited a number of Zen monasteries in Japan the year before she died.

Safety and Satisfaction

Horney agreed with Freud, in principle, about the vital importance of the early years of childhood in shaping the adult personality, However, they differed on the specifics of how the personality is formed. Horney felt that it is social forces in childhood, not biological forces, that influence personality development. There are neither universal stages of development nor inevitable childhood conflicts. Rather, the social relationship between the child and the parents is the key factor.

Horney believed that childhood is characterized by two needs: the needs for *safety* and for *satisfaction*. They are drives of a universal nature and are both extremely important. However, in Horney's theory safety assumes a much greater importance than satisfaction. The latter, simpler need includes certain of our basic physiological needs. Humans require certain amounts of food, water, sexual activity, sleep, and so on. Obviously, neither the infant nor the adult could survive very long without at least a minimal level of satisfaction of most of these requirements, but they are not of fundamental importance in shaping personality.

What is primary, according to Horney—what is decisive in determining personality—is the need for safety, by which term she meant security and freedom from fear. Whether or not the infant experiences a feeling of security and an absence of fear determines the extent of the "normality" of its later personality growth.

The child's security depends entirely on the treatment he or she receives from the parents. In general, Horney felt, the major way in which parents can weaken or prevent security altogether is to display a lack of warmth and affection for the child. She believed that children can withstand much that is usually considered traumatic, such as occasional beatings, premature sexual experiences, or abrupt weaning, without ill effect, as long as they feel wanted and loved and are therefore secure.

Parents can, however, act in a variety of ways that undermine security and thereby induce hostility in the child. Some of these parental behaviors include: obvious preference for a sibling, unfair punishment, erratic behavior, unkept promises, ridicule, humiliation, and isolation of the child from others. Horney also believed that a child knows if the parents' love is genuine and is not easily fooled by false demonstrations and expressions of love. For several reasons, hostility thus engendered in the child may be repressed. These reasons include a sense of helplessness, fear of the parents, the need for expressions of love, and guilt feelings.

Horney placed a heavy emphasis on the helplessness of the infant. Unlike Adler, however, she did not believe that each infant necessarily feels helpless, although when this feeling does arise, it fulfills a primary condition for the development of neurotic behavior. Whether or not the child feels helpless depends on how the parents treat him or her. If the child is excessively sheltered, babied, and kept in a state of dependency, then helplessness will be encouraged. The more helpless the child feels, the less he or she will dare to oppose or rebel against the parents in any way. This means that any feelings of hostility will be repressed. As Horney noted, the child in this situation says, in effect: "I have to repress my hostility because I need you."

A child can easily be made to feel fearful of his or her parents through punishment, threats, or beatings. More indirect means of intimidation may also be used. The child can be made apprehensive and fearful about germs, moving cars, dogs, strangers, or other children by observing what the parents say and do in regard to these things. The more fearful the child becomes of these "dangers" in the world and of his or her parents, the more he or she will repress the felt hostility toward the parents. It is as though the child were saying: "I have to repress my hostility because I am afraid of you."

Paradoxically, love can be another reason for the child's feeling the need to repress feelings of hostility toward the parents. In this case Horney was referring to the situation in which the parents continually tell the child how much they love him or her and how much they are sacrificing for the child but do not feel genuine warmth and love. The child recognizes that these verbal expressions are substitutes for a deeper love. Yet they are all that the child has, and so he or she represses the hostility for fear of losing them.

These three factors—helplessness, fear, and love—can cause the child to repress his or her hostility in order to avoid damaging the relationship he or she has with the parents. The child either needs them or is afraid of them or fears losing whatever love they offer.

There is one final reason for repression of hostility. In our culture, children are often made to feel guilty about any expression of hostility or rebellion made against parents. The child is made to feel unworthy, wicked, or sinful for expressing or even harboring feelings of resentment. The more guilt the child feels, the more deeply he or she will repress the hostility.

For one or more of these reasons, then, the child holds in his or her hostility. Eventually, this repressed resentment manifests itself in the condition Horney called *basic anxiety.*

Basic Anxiety

Basic anxiety is the fundamental concept in Horney's theory of personality. She defined it as "an insidiously increasing, all-pervading feeling of being lonely and helpless in a hostile world." Basic anxiety is the foundation on which later neuroses develop, and it is inseparably tied to the feelings of hostility discussed in the previous section.

As the definition indicates, basic anxiety is all-pervading; it underlies all relationships the individual has or will have with other people. Horney drew an analogy between a person suffering basic anxiety and a nation undergoing political unrest. The anxiety and hostility within the individual are similar to the underground dissensions and protests against a government. In either case, the internal unrest may be manifested overtly—by strikes or riots in the nation or by neurotic symptoms in the individual.

Regardless of how the person manifests or expresses basic anxiety, Horney felt, the feeling state is more or less the same for everyone. The person feels "small, insignificant, helpless, deserted, endangered, in a world that is out to abuse, cheat, attack, humiliate, betray . . . ." Understandably, an individual, particularly in childhood, will try to protect himself or herself against these strong feelings of anxiety. Horney wrote that, in our culture, there are four such means of self-protection: gaining affection, being submissive, attaining power, and withdrawing.

By securing affection and love from other people, the person is saying, in effect: "If you love me, you will not hurt me." There are several ways in which the person may try to secure affection. He or she may, for example, try to do everything someone else wants or may try to bribe or even threaten others into giving the desired affection.

Submissiveness as a means of self-protection involves complying with the wishes of one particular person or of everybody. Such a person avoids doing anything that might antagonize others. The person dares not criticize or in any way give offense, must repress his or her own needs and desires, and cannot even defend himself or herself against abuse for fear that such defensive reactions might antagonize the abuser. Horney felt that most people who act in such a submissive manner believe that they are truly unselfish and self-sacrificing. Such a person seems to be saying: "If I give in, I won't be hurt."

Achieving power over others is the third self-protective mechanism. In this way, the person can compensate for his or her sense of helplessness and gain security through the achievement of success or through a sense of superiority over others. Such a person seems to believe: "If I have power, no one can hurt me."

These three self-protective devices have one aspect in common. By engaging in one of them, the person is attempting to cope with anxiety by interacting with other people. The final means of protecting oneself from basic anxiety is withdrawal from other people, not in a physical sense but in a psychological sense. The person attempts to become completely independent of others, not relying on anyone for the satisfaction of external or internal needs.

For example, if a man is able to obtain a great many material possessions, then he can rely on himself (or his things) for satisfaction of his external needs. Unfortunately, even when he has amassed a pile of possessions, he may be bound by too much anxiety to enjoy them. He must guard his possessions zealousy because they are his only safeguards against the constant threat of anxiety.

Independence with regard to one's psychological needs is achieved by becoming aloof and detached from others, no longer depending on them for satisfaction of emotional needs. Actually, it involves more than that; it involves a blunting, a minimizing, of one's emotional needs. By withdrawing from emotional contact and renouncing one's emotional needs, one protects oneself from being hurt by other people.

These four self-protective mechanisms have one goal: defense against anxiety. They are oriented toward gaining security and reassurance, not happiness or pleasure. In other words, they are a defense against pain, not a positive pursuit of well-being.

Another common characteristic of these protective devices is their power and intensity. Horney believed they can be even stronger compelling forces than sexual or other physiological needs. And these devices can work. They can perform their mission of reducing anxiety, but the cost to the individual is usually an impoverished personality and conflict with his or her environment.

Very often, the neurotic will pursue his or her search for security using more than one of these devices, and their incompatibility can lay the groundwork for further conflicts. For example, a person may be driven at the same time by the needs to dominate others and also to be loved by them. Or he or she may want to be submissive to others while simultaneously desiring power over them. Such incompatibilities cannot be resolved. Thus, attempts to combat basic anxiety can form the basis of deep conflicts.

Horney felt that any of these protective mechanisms can become so permanent a part of the personality that it assumes the characteristics of a drive or need in determining the individual's behavior. At one time, Horney listed ten such needs, which she defined as neurotic because she thought them to be irrational solutions to the person's problems. The ten *neurotic needs* are the following:

1. affection and approval
2. a dominant partner in life
3. narrow and constricted limits to life
4. power
5. exploitation
6. prestige
7. personal admiration
8. personal achievement or ambition
9. self-sufficiency and independence
10. perfection and unassailability

Horney noted that everyone has these needs to some degree. All of us are aware that at one time or another we have felt the need to exploit others or to be independent of them, the need for affection and approval, and so on. None of these needs is abnormal or neurotic in its everyday, transient appearance.

What makes them neurotic is the intensive and compulsive pursuit of their satisfaction as the only means of resolving basic anxiety. In this case, their satisfaction will not help the individual achieve security but will serve only to help him or her to escape from the pain of anxiety. Also, when pursuing gratification of these needs only to escape anxiety, the person tends to focus on only one need and to compulsively seek its satisfaction in any and all situations.

In her later work, Horney became dissatisfied with these ten needs, or at least with presenting them individually. She came to realize that they could be grouped into three clusters, each of which represents a person's attitudes toward himself or herself and others. Specifically, she said that each of the ten needs involves one of the following: movement toward other people, movement against other people, or movement away from other people. For example, needs (1) and (2)—for affection/approval and for a dominant partner—involve movement toward other people. Moving against other people includes the power, exploitation, prestige, admiration, and ambition needs. The needs for self-sufficiency, for perfection, and for narrow limits to life involve moving away from people. Horney called these three categories of directional movement *neurotic trends.*

Neurotic Trends

Because these neurotic trends evolve from the protective mechanisms discussed above, we shall see similarities among them. In a sense, we can say that the neurotic trends are elaborations of the protective devices.

These behavioral and attitudinal trends are compulsive; that is, the neurotic individual is compelled to behave in accordance with at least one of them. They are also displayed indiscriminately in any and all situations, including interactions with other people. Each of these neurotic trends leads to a certain type of behavior. The types are: moving toward people (the compliant type), moving against people (the aggressive type), and moving away from people (the detached type).

Moving toward People

The compliant type of personality is characterized by an intense and continuous need for affection and approval—a need to be loved, wanted, needed, and protected. These people display these needs toward all others, but they usually have a need for one person—a friend or a marriage partner, for instance—who will take charge of their lives and offer protection and guidance.

These people manipulate other people, particularly their one partner, in order to achieve their ends. In these manipulations they often behave in ways that others find attractive or endearing. For example, the compliant personality is often unusually sensitive and responsive to the needs of other people, particularly to their needs for sympathy and understanding. Since these people are so concerned with living up to the perceived ideals and expectations of others, they often behave in ways that others perceive as unselfish, including being considerate, appreciative, and generous to an exceptional degree.

In their dealings with others, compliant personalities are conciliatory, subordinating their own desires to those of other people. They are willing to take blame and to defer to others, never being assertive or critical or demanding of them. In short, they will do whatever the situation or another person requires (as they interpret it) to gain affection, approval, and love.

In addition to this consistent way of behaving toward others, compliant personalities display a consistent attitude toward themselves. Central to this attitude is a feeling of helplessness and weakness that they readily admit to themselves and to others, often in an appeal. They are saying, in effect: "Look at me. I am so weak and helpless that you must protect and love me."

As a result of this attitude toward themselves, they come to regard everyone else as better than they, superior in every way. Even in situations in which they are notably competent in comparison with others, they still regard themselves as vastly inferior to everyone else.

Because these people's security depends so totally on other people, on their attitudes and behavior toward them, they become excessively dependent on others. They constantly need approval and love; any sign of rejection—actual or imagined—is terrifying, leading to increased efforts to regain the affection of the person they believe has rejected them.

Bear in mind that the source of this behavior is the person's own repressed hostility. Horney found that compliant people have repressed (in the Freudian sense) strong feelings of defiance and vindictiveness, have a desire to control, exploit, and manipulate others, and have a lack of interest in others—quite the opposite of what their behaviors and attitudes express. The repressed impulses must be kept in check, and so compliant people become submissive and subservient, doing whatever anyone asks, always trying to please, and asking nothing for themselves.

Moving against People

As the label clearly indicates, aggressive personalities, in their constant movement against people, are the opposite of the compliant type. These people live in a world in which, as they see it, everyone is hostile and only the fittest and most cunning survive. The world is seen as a jungle in which supremacy, strength, and ferocity are the paramount virtues.

Although their motivation is the same as that of the compliant type—the alleviation of basic anxiety—aggressive personalities never display the same evident fear of rejection. These people act in a tough, domineering manner with no regard for others. To achieve the control and superiority so vital to them, they must constantly perform at a very high level. In excelling and receiving recognition, such people find the satisfaction of having their strength and superiority affirmed by others.

They must surpass others, and therefore they judge every person in terms of what benefit can arise from the relationship. There is no appeasement of others for those with aggressive personalities; they argue, criticize, demand, and manipulate—whatever is necessary to achieve and retain the feeling of superiority and power.

Since they drive themselves so hard to become the best and most competent, they may actually become highly successful in their work, although they will not get any intrinsic satisfaction from the work itself. Their work, like everything else in their lives, is a means to an end, not an end in itself.

People with aggressive personalities may appear to be supremely uninhibited in asserting and defending themselves and confident of their abilities. However, like the compliant personalities, they are driven by insecurity, anxiety, and hostility.

Moving away from People

People characterized by detached personalities are driven to maintain an emotional distance from all other people. They must not become involved with others in any way. They must not love, hate, or even cooperate with people. In order to achieve this total detachment, they strive to become extremely self-sufficient and resourceful. After all, if they are to function completely aloof and detached from others, they must rely only on their own resources, which must therefore be well developed.

Detached personalities have an almost desperate need for privacy. They need to spend as much time as possible alone, and it disturbs them to share even such an experience as listening to music. The need for independence causes them to be overly sensitive to anything that might represent an attempt to influence, coerce, or obligate them. Persons or situations that constrain them must be avoided, including timetables and schedules, long-term obligations such as mortgages or marriages, or even the pressure of a belt or necktie.

Detached people also experience the need to feel superior, but not

in the same sense as aggressive personalities do. The detached can't actively compete with others for superiority, so they feel that their greatness
should be recognized automatically, without any struggle or effort on
their part. One manifestation of this sense of superiority is the feeling
that one is a truly unique individual, different and apart from everyone
else.

As you might imagine, since detached persons don't want to be
involved in any way with other people, they suppress or deny all feelings
toward others, particularly love and hate. To grow close to others brings
one into conflict with them, and that must be avoided. Because of this
necessary constriction of their emotions, detached personalities place
great stress on the powers of reason, logic, and intelligence.

Horney found that, in the neurotic, one of these three trends is dominant, but the other two are also present in some degree. The person
who is predominantly aggressive, for example, also has some need for
compliance and for detachment. The dominant trend, of course, is the
one that determines the person's behavior and his or her attitudes toward
others. This is the mode of thinking and acting that best serves to keep
the basic anxiety at bay, and any deviation from it is threatening to the
neurotic. For that reason, the other two modes must be actively repressed.
But this repression only serves to make matters worse; the strength of
the repressed neurotic trends may be very great. Any indication that one
of the nondominant modes is pushing for expression causes severe conflict within the individual.

Conflict is thus defined as the basic incompatibility of the three
trends, and this conflict, according to Horney, is the core of neurosis.
All people, Horney said, whether neurotic or normal, suffer the same
kind of conflict among these basically incompatible modes. The difference between the normal person and the neurotic person is in the
intensity of the conflict; it is much more intense in the neurotic.

In the non-neurotic, all three modes are capable of being expressed.
That is, a person may sometimes be aggressive, sometimes compliant,
and sometimes detached, as circumstances require. The three trends are
not mutually exclusive categories in the normal person; rather, they complement one another and are integrated harmoniously in the personality.
The normal person is not fighting himself or herself as is the neurotic,
who must battle to keep the nondominant modes repressed.

Another way to characterize the difference between the normal and
the neurotic is in terms of flexibility in behavior and attitudes. The neurotic is rigid; he or she meets all situations with the same mode or trend
regardless of its appropriateness. The normal person is more flexible,
varying his or her behavior to adapt to various circumstances.

The Idealized Self-Image

Horney argued that all of us—normal or neurotic—construct a self-image, an idealized picture of ourselves that may or may not be based on reality. In the normal person, this self-image is built on a realistic appraisal of one's abilities, potentials, weaknesses, goals, and relations with other people. This image supplies a sense of unity and integration to the whole personality and is the frame of reference from which we approach ourselves and others. In order for us to achieve the ultimate goal of self-realization—the maximum development and fulfillment of our potentialities—our self-image must clearly reflect our real self.

What of the neurotic, who experiences conflict between basically incompatible modes of behaving? By virtue of this conflict, the self, the personality, is in disunity and disharmony. How can the individual integrate and unite these disparate demands?

The neurotic constructs an idealized self-image for the same purpose as the normal person does: to unify his or her personality. This attempt at unification is doomed to failure, however, because the model of the self developed by the neurotic does not coincide with reality. The image is an illusion, not an ideal that can be attained.

Although the neurotic's self-picture is far removed from reality, it is nevertheless real and accurate to him or her. Others can easily see through this false picture, but the neurotic cannot. The neurotic believes that the incomplete and misleading self-picture he or she holds is real. The neurotic's idealized self-image is a model of what he or she feels that he or she is, can be, or should be.

A realistic self-image is flexible and dynamic, changing as the individual changes. It reflects new strengths, new growth and awareness, and new goals. The realistic image is always, in part, a goal, something to strive for. Thus, it both reflects and leads the person.

The neurotic self-image, however, is static, inflexible, and unyielding. It is not a goal but a fixed idea, not an inducement or goad to growth but a hindrance to it. It becomes a dictator, demanding rigid adherence to its proscriptions.

The self-image of the neurotic serves as an unsatisfactory substitute for a reality-based sense of self-worth and self-confidence. The neurotic has little enough self-confidence because of his or her insecurity and anxiety, and his or her false self-image does not allow him or her to correct that deficiency. It provides only an illusory sense of pride and worth.

This self-image serves to alienate the neurotic even further from his or her true self. Developed to reconcile incompatible modes of behavior, the neurotic's self-image becomes just one more element in the basic conflict. Far from resolving the conflict, it only adds to it and to a growing sense of futility. The slightest crack or flaw in the neurotic's idealized self-picture threatens the superiority and security that the whole edifice was constructed to provide. It is a weak structure at best, built on false premises, with a shaky foundation in reality. Little is needed to topple it. Horney wrote that the neurotic self-image is "a treasure house loaded with dynamite."

Techniques of Inquiry

The methods that Horney used to inquire into the functioning of the human personality were essentially those favored by Freud—free association and dream analysis—although with certain modifications. Perhaps the most basic difference in technique between Freud and Horney was in the relationship between the analyst and the patient. Horney believed that Freud played too passive a role and was too distant and intellectual. She believed that analysis should be an "exquisitely co-operative enterprise" between patient and therapist, although the analyst quite deliberately conducts the proceedings.

Another major difference between Freud and Horney is the relative weight allotted to childhood material in the analysis. Instead of concentrating on early-childhood experiences and memories, Horney stressed the person's present situation. Childhood was not ignored in Horney's approach—indeed, she found that childhood material was almost invariably revealed—but her purpose was to explore the influence of the patient's neurotic trends on his or her present life.

Horney also used dream analysis in her work, believing that dreams reveal a person's true self. They represent attempts to solve conflicts, either in a constructive or in a neurotic way. They can indicate to a person a set of attitudes within himself or herself that may be quite different from the illusory world of his or her self-image. Along with Freud, Horney believed that the real meaning of a dream must be interpreted by the analyst. However, she did not offer a list of universal symbols. Each dream, she thought, must be interpreted within the context of the patient's problem.

While she used free association and dream analysis as important techniques of inquiry, Horney did not restrict herself to those methods. Believing that every person is unique and offers the analyst problems never before encountered, she was very flexible regarding how best to uncover the patient's problems. The analyst, she argued, must be adaptable enough to use whatever tools are best suited to each patient.

Horney's Image of Human Nature

As we saw in the beginning of this chapter, Horney's image of us, like Adler's, is considerably more optimistic than Freud's. Perhaps the most important reason for this optimism was her strong belief that we are not doomed by biological forces to conflict, anxiety, and neurosis. Neurotic behavior, of course, can and does appear, but, when it does, it is the result of social forces—the conditions that one faces in childhood. These conditions can either satisfy or frustrate the child's needs for safety and security. If they frustrate these needs, the result is neurotic behavior.

Thus, neuroses and conflict are not conditions that all people are fated to suffer. They can be avoided, Horney insisted, if the child is raised in a home offering security, trust, love, and genuine acceptance. Horney noted that the neurotic is "a stepchild of our culture."

Given the proper conditions of childhood, she believed, any child will grow and develop into a well-integrated and unified adult personality. Each person has the inborn potentiality for self-realization, the innate urge to grow. These intrinsic potentialities will blossom as inevitably and naturally as an acorn grows into an oak tree. The only thing that can obstruct the individual's development is the frustration of the basic need for security in childhood.

Horney also believed, somewhat in agreement with Adler, that we have the capacity to consciously shape and change our personality; individuals and societies can change for the better. Neuroses can be prevented by proper conditions in childhood. Human nature or personality, because it is flexible, is not bent into immutable shapes in childhood. Each person possesses the capacity to change in basic ways.

So confident was Horney of the self-growth capabilities of each individual that she emphasized self-analysis in her therapeutic work wherever possible. She wrote a book entitled *Self-Analysis,* which argues in favor of the individual's ability to help solve his or her own problems. Self-knowledge, she said, is a means of freeing our capability for spontaneous growth. The pursuit of self-knowledge is both a privilege and a responsibility. Each of us is capable of shaping our own life and achieving self-realization.

A Final Commentary

Although Horney was trained in orthodox Freudian theory and paid tribute to Freud for providing the foundation and tools to work with, her work deviated from psychoanalysis in a number of important respects. Because of this deviation, she was subject to a great deal of criticism from those who continued to adhere to Freud's position. We have only to look at the major points of difference to see why she was criticized. Denying the importance of biological instincts and placing less emphasis on childhood development, sexuality, aggression, and the unconscious were weaknesses in her theory, as the Freudians saw it. They were also highly critical of her concept of self-realization and argued that no real evidence for this force or ability was presented. To the Freudians, there was a mystical quality about it; they considered it an outgrowth more of wishful thinking than of sound scientific evidence.

Freudians and others argued that Horney's theory of personality is not developed as completely or consistently as Freud's. These critics charge that, because Freud's model was constructed so elegantly and precisely, it would have been better to reject it completely and start anew rather than attempt to refashion it along different lines.

Another criticism leveled against Horney is that her theory, while emphasizing so heavily the impact of social and cultural forces, makes little direct use of the research data from sociology and anthropology. Thus, it is said, she has not worked out the details of how social forces shape personality as precisely as she might have. A somewhat related charge is that her observations and interpretations are too greatly influenced by middle-class American culture. In her defense, it must be noted that all of us—including personality theorists—are products (or prisoners) of the class, culture, and time in which we live.

So much for criticisms. What has Karen Horney contributed? What is her place and stature in the study of personality? Professionally, she suffered one disadvantage that served to limit the spread of her viewpoint. She never formed a loyal band of disciples to disseminate and elaborate upon her theory. In part for that reason, there has been relatively little research on her theory. Unlike with Freud and Adler, there was no professional journal dedicated to examining and propounding her ideas.

On the other hand, her work drew a large public following. Her books are written for lay audiences, in a style readily understood by people without professional training. Her theory makes sense to many people and seems to be applicable to a person's own behavior (or that of an odd aunt or a weird friend). Primarily due to the heightened awareness of women's roles that began in the 1960s, Horney's books have enjoyed a recent renewed interest among members of both sexes.

Many feel that her ideas are more relevant to problems inherent to American culture than are those of Freud or Adler. In addition, certain of her concepts are considered important contributions to the understanding of personality. For example, many see value in her concept of neurotic trends as a means of categorizing deviant behavior. Others accept Horney's emphasis on self-esteem, the need for security, the role of anxiety, and the idealized self-image. The concept of the self-image is seen as being of particular importance.

That her position is still a viable one is evidenced by the establishment in 1955 of the Karen Horney Clinic in New York City. In more recent years, the Clinic has expanded to become a training center for analysts. While it does not adhere rigidly to every aspect of Horney's system, the Clinic operates under the philosophy of optimism that characterized her work—the idea that human beings "have the innate urge to grow, and are unhappy if they don't."

Suggested Readings

Brown, J. A. C. *Freud and the post-Freudians.* Baltimore, Md.: Penguin, 1961.

Horney, K. *Self-analysis.* New York: Norton, 1942.

Horney, K. *Are you considering psychoanalysis?* New York: Norton, 1962.

Kelman, N. Karen Horney, M.D., 1885–1952. *Psychoanalytic Review,* 1953, 40, 191–193.

Kelman, N. What is psychotherapy?: The viewpoint of the Karen Horney group. *American Psychotherapy Monographs,* 1959, No. 1, 37–43.

Wolman, B. Psychoanalysis without libido: An analysis of Karen Horney's contribution to psychoanalytic theory. *American Journal of Psychotherapy,* 1954, 8, 21–31.

Erich Fromm 5

*The most beautiful as well as the most ugly
inclinations of man are not part of a fixed and
biologically given human nature, but result from
the social processes which create man.*

—Erich Fromm

With Erich Fromm we meet a theorist who, along with Adler and Horney, is often referred to as a social-psychological theorist. As the opening quote indicates, Fromm shares with the aforementioned theorists a basic disagreement with Freud. Humanity, Fromm argues, is not inexorably driven or inevitably shaped by biological forces of an instinctive nature. Fromm also takes issue with Freud on the matter of sex; Fromm does not view it as a primary shaping force in either normal or neurotic behavior. Instead, Fromm sees our personality as influenced by social and cultural forces—both those that affect an individual within a culture and those universal forces that have influenced humanity throughout history. Thus, his stress on the social determinants of personality is broader than that of Adler or Horney. His goal is to develop "a theory of the various human passions as resulting from the conditions of the existence of man." Believing that an individual creates his or her own nature, Fromm feels that we must examine the history of mankind in order to understand that creation.

Note that Fromm says that people create their own natures. He rejects the notion that we are passively shaped by social forces, arguing that we shape the social forces ourselves. These forces act, in turn, to influence the personality.

We might say that Fromm takes a longer view of the development of the individual personality than other theorists do because of his concern with the history of mankind as well as the history of the individual. Because of our history, Fromm argues, modern people suffer from feelings of loneliness, isolation, and insignificance. Our basic needs, therefore, are to escape these feelings of isolation, to develop a sense of belonging, and to find meaning in life. Paradoxically, the increased freedom that mankind has achieved over the centuries—both from nature and from rigid social systems—has led to more intense feelings of loneliness and isolation. Too much freedom becomes a negative condition from which we attempt to flee.

Fromm believes that the kinds of conflicts that people suffer arise from the kind of society they have constructed. However, we are not irrevocably doomed to suffering. Quite the contrary is true; Fromm remains optimistic about our ability to solve our problems—problems that we ourselves have created.

While Fromm is a psychoanalyst (the first in our coverage without a medical degree), he is also a philosopher, a historian, and an anthropologist. He draws on data from many sources beyond the analytical couch, which makes it difficult to classify him neatly as a member of any single discipline.

The Life of Fromm (1900–   )

Fromm was born in Frankfurt, Germany, of a family deeply steeped in Orthodox Judaism. His father was a businessman, but his grandfather was a rabbi and his mother's uncle a well-known Talmudic scholar. As a child, Fromm was a devoted student of the Old Testament, the moral fervor of which influenced him greatly in his youth. Like Freud, the young Fromm was infused with the Jewish tradition of reason and intellectual activity and experienced the emotional impact of being a member of

a minority group. In later life, Fromm severed all connection with organized religion and became what he described as an "atheistic mystic,"
but there is no denying the influence of his early religious experiences.

Little has been written about Fromm's early childhood. He was an
only child (which should give pause to those of you who are enamored
of Adler's theory), and his early home life was described as tense. He
recalls that his father was given to moodiness and was highly anxious
and that his mother was prone to bouts of depression.

If we are searching for experiences and events that could have presaged his adult view of mankind, perhaps we should begin at a later
age with Fromm. For example, when he was 12, he was greatly upset
by the suicide of a family friend, a talented and beautiful woman. In
his adolescent years, he was confused and shocked by several such trage-
dies, both individual and societal, and particularly by the horrors of
World War I (which began when he was 14). It was not only the deaths
of millions (including friends and relatives) on the battlefields of Europe
that disturbed him but also the atmosphere of hate, hysteria, and fanati-
cism that pervaded Germany.

Fromm's growing interest in political theory was reinforced by the
chaotic social conditions in Germany following the war and, later, by
the rise of Nazism. He became a socialist in attitude (although he never
joined the party) and studied widely in the social sciences at Heidelberg.
He became quite knowledgeable in the works of Karl Marx, Max Weber,
Herbert Spencer, and other leading economic, social and political
theorists.

Seeking the answer to the riddle of human motivation, Fromm underwent psychoanalytic training in Munich and at the Psychoanalytic
Institute in Berlin, where he was trained along orthodox Freudian lines.
Still troubled by the suicide in his childhood, he felt that Freud's view
"seemed to be the answer to a puzzling and frightening experience."

This answer, however, did not satisfy him for very long. In the 1930s,
he began to write articles that were critical of Freud—particularly of
Freud's refusal to admit the impact of socioeconomic forces on personality. In 1934, he emigrated to the United States to escape the Nazi menace
and became associated with Karen Horney and Harry Stack Sullivan.

Fromm's theory has been presented—and, at this writing, is still
being presented—in a number of books offered in a popular style, more
for the public than for colleagues. Some of these books have been extremely popular, reaching best-seller status. Fromm has lectured at several
universities in the United States during his career and since 1951 has
made his home in Mexico City. He is a professor at the University of
Mexico and is director of the Mexican Psychoanalytic Institute.

Mankind's Basic Condition: Loneliness and Insignificance

The title of Fromm's first book, *Escape from Freedom*, provides us with an indication of his vision of the basic human condition. In the history of Western civilization, Fromm believes, as people have gained more freedom, they have come to feel more lonely, insignificant, and alienated from one another. Conversely, the less freedom people have had, the greater have been their feelings of belongingness and security. Thus, freedom would seem to be antithetical to our needs for security and identification. It is Fromm's contention that modern people, possessing greater freedom than has been offered in any other era, feel more lonely, alienated, and insignificant than people of ages past.

To fully understand what Fromm means by this apparent paradox, we must examine briefly the history of Western civilization, as Fromm interprets it. He begins by discussing our evolution from the lower animals and noting the basic distinction between animal nature and human nature: people are free of the instinctive biological mechanisms that guide the animal's every move. The lower an animal is on the phylogenetic scale, the more firmly fixed the pattern and form of its behavior. The higher the animal, the more flexible its behaviors. Human beings, as the highest animals, have the greatest flexibility of all. Our actions are the least tied to instinctive mechanisms.

But there is more to us than greater flexibility of behavior. We *know*; we are conscious and aware of ourselves and the world around us. Through learning, we accumulate a knowledge of the past. Through imagination we can go far beyond the present. Because we know, because we master nature, we are no longer at one with nature, as are the lower animals. As Fromm put it, we have transcended nature. As a result, while still a part of nature, in that we are subject to its physical laws (and can't change them), we are separate from nature—homeless, as it were.

Unlike the other animals, we realize how powerless we are ultimately; we know that we will die. And we know how different we are from the other animals. Looked at in one way, this knowledge of being separate and apart from the rest of nature is a kind of freedom. Our mind gives us infinite choice. But looked at in another way, this separateness spells alienation from the rest of nature. Human beings cannot revert to animal status; we cannot free ourselves of knowledge, of the mind. What, then, can we do? How can we escape the feelings of isolation and apartness?

Fromm said that early peoples tried to escape their state of alienation from nature by identifying fully with their tribes or clans. Sharing myths, religions, and tribal rites and customs, they obtained the security of belonging to a group. Membership in the group provided acceptance, affiliation, and a set of rules to follow. The religions that early peoples developed helped them, to some degree, to re-establish their link with nature. The focus of worship was on objects in nature: sun, moon, fire, animals, and plants.

But this tenuous security could not last. Human beings are striving creatures who develop and grow, and postprimitive people revolted against this subservience to the group. Indeed, each period of history, according to Fromm, has been characterized by increasing individuality (a process Fromm called *individuation*) as people have struggled toward ever-greater independence and freedom to grow, to develop, and to use all of their uniquely human abilities. The process of individuation reached its peak somewhere between the period of the Reformation and the present day—a time during which great alienation and aloneness have been matched by a high degree of freedom. (Actually, we should say *caused* by a high degree of freedom.)

Fromm designated the Middle Ages as the last era of stability, security, and belongingness. It was a time of little individual freedom, since the feudal system rigidly defined every person's place in society. One remained in the role and status to which one was born; there was no mobility, either social or geographic. The individual had little choice of occupation, social customs, habits of dress, and the like. Everything was determined by the class into which one was born and by the rigid rules of the Catholic Church.

Yet, although people were decidedly not free, they were not isolated, not alienated from others. The rigid social structure meant that the individual's place in society was clearly delineated. There was no doubt or indecision on anyone's part as to where or to whom one belonged.

Fromm argues that the social upheavals brought on by the Renaissance and the Protestant Reformation destroyed this stability and security by considerably enlarging people's freedom. People began to have more choice and power over their own lives. Of course, they achieved this greater freedom at the expense of the ties that had provided security and a sense of belonging. As a result, they became beset by doubts about the meaning of life and by feelings of personal insignificance.

Fromm characterizes the increasing freedom of Western people as a *freedom from* but not a *freedom to.* We have become *free from* slavery and bondage, but, because of the increased insecurity and alienation, we are not *free to* develop our full potentialities and enjoy this new freedom. Fromm has been especially critical of the American "marketplace" culture, in which we are quite free from many strictures but not free to develop the full essence of our selves. We find ourselves in quite a dilemma. How can we flee the sense of loneliness and insignificance? How can we escape from freedom?

Mechanisms of Escape

Fromm tells us that there are basically two approaches we can take in our attempts to find meaning and belongingness in life.

The first method, achieving *positive freedom*, involves the attempt to become reunited with other people without, at the same time, giving up one's freedom and integrity. In this optimistic and altruistic approach, Fromm sees us as relating to others through work and love—through the sincere and open expression of our emotional and intellectual abilities. In this kind of society, which Fromm calls a *humanistic* one, no one would feel lonely and insignificant, because all people would be brothers and sisters.

The other way to regain security is by *renouncing freedom* and surrendering completely our individuality and integrity. Obviously, such a solution will not lead to self-expression and personal development. It does, however, remove the anxiety of loneliness and insignificance and explain, according to Fromm, why so many people are willing to accept a *totalitarian* system such as the Nazi regime in the 1930s.

In addition to these general approaches to regaining lost security, Fromm posits specific mechanisms of escape—"psychic mechanisms"— which he feels are analogous to Horney's neurotic character traits.

The first mechanism, *authoritarianism*, manifests itself in either masochistic or sadistic strivings. Individuals described as *masochistic* feel themselves to be inferior and inadequate. While they may complain of these feelings and say that they would like to be rid of them, they actually feel a strong need for dependence, either on one person or on an institution. They willingly submit to the control of other people or of social forces and behave in a weak and helpless manner toward others. They gain security by these acts of submission and thus assuage their feelings of loneliness.

The *sadistic* striving, although the opposite of the masochistic, is found in the same kind of person, Fromm said. It represents, basically, a striving for power over others. There are three ways in which the sadistic striving may be expressed. In one way, the person makes others totally dependent on himself or herself so as to have absolute power over them. A second sadistic expression goes beyond ruling or dictating to others. It involves exploiting others by taking or using anything desirable that they possess—whether material things or intellectual or emotional qualities. The third form of sadistic expression involves the desire to see others suffer and to be the cause of that suffering. While the suffering may involve actual physical pain, it most often involves emotional suffering, such as humiliation or embarrassment.

The second escape mechanism Fromm calls *destructiveness*, which is the opposite of authoritarianism. While the first mechanism, in either the sadistic or the masochistic expression, involves some form of continuing interaction with an object, destructiveness aims at the elimination of the object. A destructive person says to himself or herself, in effect: "I can escape the feeling of my own powerlessness in comparison with the world outside myself by destroying that world." Fromm saw evidence of destructiveness, albeit disguised or rationalized, everywhere in the world. Indeed, he felt that virtually everything was used as a rationalization for destructiveness, including love, duty, conscience, and patriotism.

The third escape mechanism, described by Fromm as having the most important social significance, is *automation conformity.* Through this mechanism, a person eases his or her loneliness and isolation by erasing any and all differences between himself or herself and others. He or she accomplishes this by becoming just like everyone else, by conforming unconditionally to the rules that govern behavior. Fromm compared this mechanism with the protective coloring of certain animals. By being indistinguishable from their surroundings, the animals protect themselves. So it is with fully conforming human beings.

While such persons do temporarily gain the security and sense of belonging so desperately needed, it is at the price of the self. One who so totally conforms to others no longer has a self; there is no longer an "I," as distinct from "them." The person becomes "them," and a false self takes the place of the genuine self. And this loss of self, the surrender of "I," may leave the person in worse shape than he or she was in before. The individual is now beset by new insecurities and doubts. No longer having any identity of his or her own, no real self, the person is no more than a reflexive response to what others expect of him or her. The new identity, a false one, can be obtained and maintained only through constant conformity. There must be no relaxation, no slipups; approval and recognition from others would be lost if he or she did anything at variance with their norms and values.

We have seen so far the basic nature of human beings as viewed by Fromm. Historically and socially shaped, we must strike a balance between freedom and security so that we can form a self without experiencing loneliness and alienation. This ideal state has not yet been achieved.

But there is more to Fromm's personality theory than mechanisms of escape from freedom. There are additional aspects of personality that result from the social order in which we live and from our attempts to cope with it. To understand these factors, we must discuss the development of the individual, just as we discussed the historical development of mankind.

The Development of the Individual

Fromm believes that the development of the individual in childhood parallels the pattern of development of mankind. In a sense, the history of the species is repeated in the childhood of each individual, in that, as the child grows, he or she gains increasing independence and freedom. And the less dependent the child becomes on the primary ties with the mother, the less secure he or she feels. The infant knows virtually no freedom but is secure in its dependent relationship.

Fromm feels that some degree of isolation and helplessness always accompanies the maturation process and that the child will attempt to regain his or her former primary ties with security. In a very real sense, the child attempts to escape from his or her own growing freedom through several mechanisms similar to those described in the preceding section. Which mechanism the child uses is determined by the nature of the parent-child relationship. Fromm proposed three types of escape mechanisms: symbiotic relatedness, withdrawal-destructiveness, and love.

In *symbiotic relatedness*, the person never achieves a state of independence. Rather, he or she escapes aloneness and insecurity by becoming a part of someone else, either by "swallowing" or by being swallowed by that other person. Masochistic behavior arises from being swallowed. The child remains totally dependent on the parents and abnegates his or her self. Sadism arises from the reverse situation (swallowing) in which the parents give all authority to the child by submitting to his or her will on every issue. The child regains security by manipulating and exploiting the parents. Whether the child is doing the swallowing or being swallowed, the relationship is one of closeness and intimacy. The child really needs the parents for security.

The *withdrawal-destructiveness* interaction, in contrast, is characterized by a distance and separation from others. Fromm stated that withdrawal and destructiveness are simply the passive and active forms of the same type of relatedness with the parents. Which form the child's behavior takes depends on the behavior of the parents. For example, parents who act destructively toward the child, attempting to subordinate or subjugate him or her, cause the child to withdraw from them.

Love, the third form of interaction, is the most desirable form of parent-child relatedness. In this case, the parents provide the greatest opportunity for the child to develop his or her self by offering respect and a proper balance between security and responsibility. As a result, the child feels little need to escape his or her growing freedom and is able to love himself or herself and others.

Fromm agrees with Freud that the first five years of life are of extreme importance, but he does not believe that personality is firmly fixed by the age of 5. Later events, Fromm argues, can be just as effective in influencing personality as early events. He also agrees with Freud in viewing the family as the "psychic agency" or representative of society to the child. It is through interaction with the family that the child acquires his or her character and ways of adjusting to society. While there are differences in every family, Fromm felt that most people in a given culture have a common social character—a common set of mores and beliefs that define the proper way of behaving for that culture. The child develops this social character, as well as his or her own individual character, from the unique interactions with the parents plus his or her genetic endowment. This, Fromm feels, explains why different people react to the same environment in different ways.

Overall, it is the complex of social-environmental experiences—especially how the child is treated by the parents—that determines the nature of the adult personality, although not irrevocably so.

Human Needs

As living organisms, people have a number of basic physiological needs that must be satisfied in order to assure survival. These needs—for example, for food, water, and sex—are no different for us than for other animals in terms of their nature and origin. However, we differ from lower animals in two respects. In the first place, we do not satisfy these needs in "instinctive" fashion—that is, by following rigid behavior patterns. Our behavior is infinitely varied and flexible, since it is learned by each individual in his or her unique environment. The other difference is that we are motivated by a second set of needs—those of a psychological nature—which are socially created and vary greatly from one individual to another.

However, Fromm felt that the drive for security (to escape loneliness) and the conflicting drive for freedom (to create the self) are universal. The choice between regression to security on the one hand and progression to freedom on the other is inescapable. All human cravings are determined by this polarity. Fromm postulated the existence of five needs that result from this dichotomy: relatedness, transcendence, rootedness, identity, and frame of reference.

The need for *relatedness* arises from the disruption of our primary ties with nature. By virtue of the powers of reason and imagination, the individual is aware of his or her separation from nature, his or her powerlessness, and the arbitrary nature of birth and death. Because people have lost their former instinctive relationship with nature, they must use reason and imagination to create a new relatedness with fellow human beings. The ideal way of achieving this relatedness is through what Fromm calls *productive love,* which involves care, responsibility, respect, and knowledge. In loving, a person is concerned with another's growth and happiness, responds to the other's needs, and respects and knows the loved one as he or she really is.

Productive love can be directed toward the same sex (brotherly love), toward fusion and oneness with a member of the opposite sex (erotic love), or toward one's child (motherly love). In all three forms, the person's ultimate concern is with the development and growth of the other person's self.

Transcendence refers to the need to rise above the passive-animal state, with which people cannot be satisfied because of their reason and imagination. People must become creative and productive individuals. In the act of creation, whether of life (as in having children), of material objects, of art, or of ideas, we surpass the animal state and enter into a state of freedom and purposiveness. Fromm also indicates quite clearly that, if the creative need is blocked for any reason, people become destructive; that is the only alternative to creativeness. Destructiveness, like creativeness, is in our nature. Both tendencies satisfy the need for transcendence. Creativity, however, is the primary tendency.

The human need for *rootedness* also arises from the loss of our primary ties with nature. As a result of that loss, we stand detached and alone; we must establish new roots in our relationships with others to replace our previous roots in nature. Feelings of brotherliness with others, according to Fromm, are the most satisfying kind of new roots we can develop.

In addition to the needs for rootedness and relatedness, for a sense of belonging, people need a sense of *identity* as unique individuals. There are several ways of achieving this sense of identity. For example, a productive and creative person could develop his or her talents and abilities to the fullest, or he or she could identify himself or herself with a group—a religion, a union, or a nation—perhaps to the point of conformity.

The need for a *frame of reference* stems from our powers of reason and imagination, which require a framework for making sense of all the puzzling phenomena to which we are exposed. We must develop a consistent and coherent picture of the world by which we are able to perceive and understand all that is going on around us. This frame of reference may be based on rational or irrational considerations (or a combination of the two). The important thing is the consistency and coherence with which it is maintained.

The manner in which these five needs are manifested or satisfied depends on social conditions and opportunities afforded by the culture. Thus, the way in which a person copes with or adjusts to his or her society is a sort of compromise that the individual works out between these needs and the social conditions in which he or she lives. As a result of this compromise (or series of compromises), the person develops his or her personality structure—what Fromm called orientations or character traits.

Character Traits

Fromm proposed that the character traits underlie all behavior and are powerful forces by which a person relates or orients himself or herself to the world. He describes the traits in separate terms, but he is careful to note that the personality or character of an individual is a blend of some or all of these traits, although one usually plays a dominant role.

The traits are divided into nonproductive and productive types. Nonproductive traits include the receptive, exploitative, hoarding, and marketing orientations.

Individuals with *receptive orientations* expect to get whatever they want—be it love, knowledge, or pleasure—from some outside source—another person, an authority, or a system. They are receivers in their relations with others, needing to be loved rather than loving and taking rather than creating ideas or knowledge.

Obviously, such people are highly dependent on others and indeed feel quite paralyzed when left on their own; they feel incapable of doing anything without outside help. There is a similarity between this orientation and Freud's oral incorporative type, the receptive orientation also finding relief in eating and drinking. The kind of society that fosters this trait is one in which exploitation of one group by another (for example, slave by master) is practiced.

In the *exploitative orientation*, the person is also directed toward others for what he or she wants. However, instead of expecting to receive from others, these people take from them, either by force or by cunning. Indeed, if something is given to them, they see it as worthless. They want only what belongs to and is valued by others: wives or husbands, ideas, possessions, and so on. What has to be stolen or taken by force has much greater value than what is given freely. This trait is similar to Freud's oral aggressive type and can be seen in robber barons, fascist leaders, or domineering people in any setting.

As the name indicates, in the *hoarding orientation* the person derives his or her security from the amount he or she can hoard and save. This miserly behavior applies not only to money and material possessions but also to emotions and thoughts. In a sense, such people build walls around themselves and sit there, surrounded by all that they have hoarded, protecting it from outside intrusion and letting as little of it out as possible. There is an obvious parallel here with the Freudian anal retentive type.

Fromm said that this kind of orientation was particularly common in the 18th and 19th centuries in those countries that had stable middle-class economies characterized by the Puritan ethic of thrift, conservatism, and sober business practices.

The *marketing orientation* is a 20th-century phenomenon characteristic of capitalist societies, particularly the United States. In a commodity-based marketplace culture, Fromm argued, people's success or failure depends on how well they sell themselves. The set of values is the same for personalities as for commodities; indeed, one's personality becomes a commodity to be sold. Thus, it is not so much one's personal qualities, skills, knowledge, or integrity that counts but rather how nice a "package" one is.

Such an orientation cannot produce any feeling of security, because the person is left without genuine relatedness to others. Indeed, if the game is played long enough, there is no longer even a relatedness to or real awareness of one's self. The packaged role the individual is forced to play completely obscures his or her own genuine qualities and characteristics, not only from others but from the person himself or herself. As a result, such people find themselves in a state of total alienation, with no personal core or center and with no real relationship to those around them.

Fromm's fifth character type, the *productive orientation,* is the ideal and represents the ultimate goal in human development. Covering all aspects of human experience, this concept assumes our ability to use all of our capacities and to actualize or realize all of our potentials. Fromm does not define productivity as synonymous with creativity in an exclusively artistic sense. The productive orientation is an attitude that can be attained by every human being. It has as its most important object not the acquisition of material things but the development of our selves.

He believes that this orientation is the ideal condition for mankind, although it does not yet characterize any society. Actually, Fromm feels that it is not yet achieved totally by anyone. The best we can achieve—at least with our present social structure—is a combination of the productive and nonproductive orientations. The influence of the productive orientation can then transform the nonproductive traits. For example, guided by productivity, the aggressiveness of the exploitative type can become initiative, the miserliness of the hoarding type can become sound economy, and so on. Only through social change can the productive orientation become dominant in any culture.

In more recent years, Fromm introduced a pair of new orientations:

necrophilious and biophilious. The *necrophilious* character type is attracted to death—to corpses, decay, feces, and dirt. Such a person seems most alive when he or she is talking about death, burials, or sickness. This person dwells on the past, is enamored of force and power, and is attracted to darkness and to nighttime.

The opposite orientation, the *biophilious* type, is in love with life. He or she fights against death, darkness, and decay. This attitude is congruent with the productive orientation; such a person is concerned with growth and development of self and others.

As with the other orientations, pure forms of either of these traits are rare. Most personalities represent a blending of the two, with one orientation being dominant.

The Importance of Society

We have seen, throughout our discussion of Fromm, the prominent role he ascribes to culture in shaping the personality. He also notes that, in order for any kind of society to function well, it is imperative that the personalities or characters of all the people be shaped to satisfy the demands of that society. In other words, individuals must be trained in childhood to behave in ways that will fit the needs of the society. A feudal or fascist society must shape its people to be passive and submissive, for example. Those in a commodity-oriented capitalist society must be shaped to consume—to buy the goods and gadgets the society produces and to replace them with newer ones shortly thereafter.

All societies, throughout history, have frustrated people by placing demands on them that are antithetical to human nature. Fromm feels that any society that does not satisfy people's basic needs is sick and should be replaced, and he remains optimistic about the possibility of shaping a society that will allow people to fulfill themselves.

Fromm calls this ideal society *humanistic communitarian socialism* and describes it as a world in which love, brotherliness, and solidarity characterize all human relationships, in which the productive orientation is able to develop to its fullest, and in which all feelings of loneliness, insignificance, and alienation disappear. The future of civilization, Fromm pleads, depends on how well and how quickly we can develop such a society.

Techniques of Inquiry

Unfortunately, it is difficult to describe the methods Fromm used to develop and support his theories. The psychoanalysts we have discussed so far based their systems on the clinical data they obtained from their patients, and they were quite clear as to their precise methods of analysis. Relative to these earlier theorists, Fromm has written very little about his techniques of inquiry and therapy, and there seems to be no way of knowing on what data he based the theories. He occasionally refers to "psychoanalytic observations" but does not offer specific analytical findings or case studies. We do know that he uses a form of free association and that he considers dream analysis to be one of the most important therapeutic tools, although he does not describe his use of the techniques in much detail.

On what basis, then, did he develop his theories? For the most part, it seems that the theories are based on generalizations and speculations derived from his interpretations of historical changes and social-cultural forces.

It should be noted, however, that, in 1970, Fromm published a cross-disciplinary in-depth study, "Social Character in a Mexican Village," designed to test his theory of social character. Over a period of several years, psychologists, anthropologists, physicians, statisticians, and other specialists analyzed a Mexican village in terms of its history, economic and social structure, health, attitudes, and even dreams. The data support the social-character theory.

Fromm's Image of Human Nature

It should be clear by now that Fromm expresses a generally optimistic picture of human nature. Agreeing with Adler and Horney, he does not consider us doomed to conflict and anxiety by immutable biological forces.

It is true that he views us as shaped by social, political, and economic forces at work in the society in which we live. However, we are not infinitely malleable. A person is not simply a puppet reacting to the strings pulled by social forces, or "a blank sheet of paper on which culture can write its text." Thus, we are neither fixed by instincts nor totally commanded by social forces. On the contrary, we have an inherent nature, a set of psychological qualities by which we can shape our personalities and our societies. And this is where Fromm's optimism—or at least hope—enters the picture. He believes that we have an innate drive or tendency to grow, develop, and realize our potentialities. This, according to Fromm, is our major task in life—to become what we have the potential to become. The result of this inherent tendency in any individual is the personality. Fromm also believes that we possess an innate striving for justice and truth. Failure to realize all of our potentialities—failure to become productive—results in unhappiness and mental illness.

Fromm continues to believe that humanity can and will reach the state of realization of its potential for full and harmonious growth and integration, although he is saddened by our failure thus far. He does not believe that we are inherently either good or evil but rather that we become evil if we fail to develop and grow fully. The only way in which we can be at one with one another and with ourselves is by making full, productive use of our abilities. There is no other way to achieve true harmony.

Neither outcome—goodness or evil, fulfillment or frustration, harmony or chaos—is predetermined, either by society or by human nature. Only the potential for goodness and fulfillment exists; the rest is up to us. And it is Fromm's optimism that allows him to hope that we will make the right choice and allows him to say, at the age of 70, "Who can give up hope as long as there is life?"

A Final Commentary

Fromm's approach to personality is wide ranging in its perspectives and propositions. He is not exclusively a psychoanalyst but draws on information from other disciplines—notably, history, sociology, and anthropology. One result of this diversity is that a critic must be well versed in these areas in order to be able to attack Fromm's total system. Few people can do so; therefore, criticisms have often been directed against only one part or another of his theory. For example, a major criticism, as we have noted, is that there is no strong (or even visible) empirical support for his theory. Fromm does not supply any specific, factual supporting data. The Mexican-village study came considerably after the theory was proposed. One cannot find in his writings any data on which he based his theories (a criticism not unique to Fromm, however).

He has also been criticized for not keeping current with newer developments in psychoanalysis. His major reference has been the works of Freud, with occasional formulations from Jung, Horney, and Sullivan. More recent works—for example, those of the humanistic psychologists, who have reached some conclusions that parallel his own—are not recognized in his publications. Many readers see this as a serious omission.

Those knowledgeable about the history and social conditions of the Middle Ages challenge Fromm's allegation that humanity had attained security, identity, and belongingness during that period. These critics charge that Fromm has painted a highly idealized picture of that era and omitted the stark calamities that occurred—the religious persecutions, witch hunts, plagues, wars, and other physical and psychological hardships. If anything, they argue, the Middle Ages must have been a time of great insecurity and instability.

Such criticisms notwithstanding, Fromm's books have been tremendously popular, reaching audiences all over the world. He has deliberately written for the lay audience because he wants to reach the greatest number of people with his message about the kind of society we must develop in order to survive. Thus, his books are highly readable in style, with a bare minimum of technical jargon. This is not to say that the books are not challenging or provocative, but rather that the ideas are presented in highly engaging and interesting form.

Fromm has presented us with a unique interpretation of the interaction between humanity and society. Perhaps more than any other theorist, he has made us aware of the continuing and interrelated impact of social, economic, and psychological factors on human nature. Whether or not his specific interpretations turn out to be valid, he has shown us that a human being is not the exclusive product of a single set of forces but the result of an interplay of forces and events. He has challenged us to think beyond the boundaries of any one discipline and has consistently goaded us to evolve a newer and more humane society, pointing out the consequences of not doing so. Thus, his contribution, whatever its impact, has extended beyond psychoanalysis or psychology to include the broad spectrum of social problems that concern us all.

Suggested Readings

Brams, J. From Freud to Fromm. *Psychology Today*, 1968, *1*, 32–35; 64–65.

Brown, J. A. C. *Freud and the post-Freudians*. Baltimore, Md.: Penguin, 1961.

Evans, R. I. *Dialogue with Erich Fromm*. New York: Harper & Row, 1966.

Fromm, E. *Escape from freedom*. New York: Holt, Rinehart and Winston, 1941.

Fromm, E. *The sane society*. New York: Holt, Rinehart and Winston, 1955.

Fromm, E. *The anatomy of human destructiveness*. New York: Holt, Rinehart and Winston, 1973.

Fromm, E., & Maccoby, M. *Social character in a Mexican village*. Englewood Cliffs, N.J.: Prentice-Hall, 1970.

Schaar, J. H. *Escape from authority: The perspectives of Erich Fromm*. New York: Basic Books, 1961.

Harry Stack Sullivan
The Interpersonal Theory

Personality, I now define . . . as the relatively enduring pattern of recurrent interpersonal situations which characterize a human life.

—Harry Stack Sullivan

With Harry Stack Sullivan, we find yet another personality theorist who focuses on the cultural and social factors that influence the development of personality. Beyond that very general point, however, Sullivan's conception of personality differs greatly from those of the others we have discussed—Adler, Horney, and Fromm—who present social-psychological theories. Sullivan's approach represents a unique combination of psychiatry and social psychology; it is the study of interpersonal relations—the processes of interaction between people. He believed that the personality of an individual can never be studied in isolation, since it never exists in isolation—that is, separate and independent from other personalities.

Every aspect of a person's personality is a consequence of interpersonal relationships experienced by the person in his or her life, starting from the moment of birth. Personality is displayed or manifested only through a person's interactions with others; these others may be physically present or present in images, memories, or fantasies. Even the most isolated hermit has a personality defined by interactions with images and memories of others.

Sullivan considered tension to play a prominent role in personality. He believed that people continually strive to reduce tensions, which arise from two sources: biological needs and social insecurity. Therefore, the attainment of satisfaction and security becomes the goal of all behavior. Unrelieved tension leads to anxiety, which is a central concept in Sullivan's theory. Much of an individual's personality is thought to develop out of his or her attempt to deal with anxiety—to overcome it or to protect himself or herself from it.

Sullivan also placed great stress on the influence of early social relationships, in particular that between the infant and the mother, but he disagreed with Freud that personality was firmly fixed at the young age of 4 or 5. He felt that personality could change dramatically until as late as the adolescent years.

Sullivan's approach to personality has gained in popularity among professionals since his death. A blend of biology and sociology and of psychiatry and social psychology, his approach has been found to be useful in the treatment of emotional disturbances, particularly schizophrenia, a condition into which he had great insight.

The Life of Sullivan (1892–1949)

Sullivan spent his childhood on his parents' farm in Norwich, New York. His boyhood years were spent largely in isolation from others of his own age. He was the only child of his parents to survive and was one of very few Catholics in a small, predominantly Protestant community. His later phenomenal insight into the loneliness of schizophrenia may have stemmed from his own solitary years as a child. (He later commented that, as a result of his early isolation, he never developed a need to be liked by others. This attribute was a definite asset in one who became such a sharp and severe critic of others.)

Sullivan's childhood loneliness was compounded by his parents' behavior. His mother was apparently chronically dissatisfied, convinced that she had married beneath her class. His father was taciturn and withdrawn.

The young Sullivan received his M.D. in 1917 from the Chicago College of Medicine and Surgery. During his medical training, he studied psychoanalysis and entered into it as a patient. Following military service during World War I, he worked for the government until 1922, when he joined the staff of St. Elizabeth's Hospital, a federal hospital for the disturbed in Washington, D. C. The director of the hospital was a prominent psychiatrist, William Alanson White, who became something of a professional father figure to Sullivan. White stimulated Sullivan's interest in and criticism of Freud's domination of the field.

In 1923, Sullivan moved to the Sheppard and Enoch Pratt Hospital in Baltimore and joined the teaching staff of the University of Maryland Medical School. Over the next several years, he developed his techniques of interpersonal psychiatry, working primarily with schizophrenics, and came in contact with many of the leading social scientists of the day. He also received more than 300 hours of psychoanalysis during this period.

In 1929, Sullivan moved to New York City and established a private practice at a fashionable Park Avenue address. He continued to be very active in professional affairs. He was a founder and director of the Washington School of Psychiatry (a training institute), an editor of the journal *Psychiatry*, and a consultant to the Selective Service Board and to UNESCO, and he was instrumental in the establishment of the World Federation for Mental Health.

In 1947, he became severely ill. Apparently through the efforts of some of his students, who were able to obtain the new and scarce drug penicillin, Sullivan's life was saved. For the next two years, he was cared for by his students. He traveled to Paris in 1949 to attend a conference of the World Federation for Mental Health and died in a hotel room there.

The Nature of Personality

Sullivan believed that the nature of personality is determined by tensions that arise from both physiological and social-psychological sources. The primary aim of behavior is to minimize or reduce these tensions; this concept is similar to those expressed by other theorists, including Freud. However, by introducing socially derived tensions, Sullivan recognized—again, along with other theorists—the psychological as well as biological bases of personality. Specifically, the two sources of tension are physiological needs and social insecurity.

The *physiological needs* discussed by Sullivan are familiar: for food, water, rest, air, and sex. When any of these needs is in operation, the tension it generates brings about activity designed to achieve *satisfaction*, which in turn reduces the tension. This cycle of need-activity-satisfaction-relief continues throughout a person's life. The second source of tension, *social insecurity*, derives from cultural/interpersonal causes. The obvious aim of this source of tension is to achieve *security*.

Sullivan placed great emphasis on the relationship between an infant and its mother, who is, for a long time, the only source of satisfaction of the infant's physiological needs. The baby, after all, can do nothing for itself except communicate its needs to the mother through crying.

As long as its basic needs are being met, the infant is in a state that Sullivan calls *euphoria*, a blissful feeling of well-being. The infant's satisfaction and euphoria, then, depend on the nature of its first interpersonal relationship—that with its mother.

A person's feeling of security (or insecurity) also depends on the mother's behavior and attitudes toward the child. Sullivan believed that infants are extremely sensitive to the attitudes of others toward themselves. Through the process of empathy, which Sullivan described as a sort of "emotional contagion or communion," the child perceives and responds to the emotions of those around him or her.

Thus, if a mother is tense, angry, or unhappy at the moment she is satisfying the infant's physical needs, these feelings will be perceived by the child and translated as a threat to its security. The resulting feeling is a state of anxiety that Sullivan considered capable of reducing the child's competence or efficiency and of disturbing the very interpersonal relations needed to reduce the state of anxiety. Of course, anxiety can exist at various levels of intensity, from so extreme that it is paralyzing to relatively mild. Sullivan considered mild anxiety to be useful and educative.

It is important to note that the anxiety, although derived from the relationship with the mother, becomes attached to the larger world of the whole culture. This diffusion of the anxiety makes it harder to deal with; the anxiety has become unfocused and nonspecific.

The two overall aims, satisfaction and security, form much of the basis of personality and are common to all mankind. In infancy, satisfaction of the physical needs is the more persistent, driving force, but the later-developed need for security is the more important in terms of its total influence on personality. It is a more complex need, and more time and energy are expended in its pursuit.

Sullivan discusses two additional drives or needs that appear in infancy and that seem to derive from and be integral parts of the need for security. They are the power motive and the need for physical closeness.

One of the infant's earliest discoveries, according to Sullivan, is of its basic helplessness and powerlessness. There is virtually nothing the baby can do for itself until it is able to achieve some degree of power in its interpersonal relations. It cannot gain satisfaction or security without this power. How well this *power motive* is fulfilled helps determine the direction and form taken by the personality. The thwarting of the power motive can lead to insecurity.

The need for *physical closeness* to other human beings is considered by Sullivan to be inborn. This need is very much related to the need for security, for the prime result of frustration of this need is loneliness, a chief characteristic of insecurity (and of Sullivan as a child).

Aspects of Personality

According to Sullivan, there are three processes observable in the interpersonal interactions that define an individual's personality: dynamisms, personifications, and modes of experience.

Dynamisms

A dynamism is "a relatively enduring configuration of energy which manifests itself in characterizable processes in interpersonal relations." In less stilted terms, this means that any kind of behavior, either physical or mental (as in thinking), that lasts and recurs like a habit is a dynamism. Sullivan considered it to be the smallest element in studying or describing personality.

Dynamisms result from experiences with other people. They accumulate so that, the greater the amount and variety of experiences one has, the greater the number of dynamisms one exhibits. In a very broad sense, dynamisms are not unlike Adler's concept of style of life, in that they are "envelopes" (as Sullivan called them) of behaviors and attitudes that characterize one's interactions with other people.

For example, a person could have a malevolent dynamism, which means that he or she characteristically behaves in a hostile fashion toward certain people. There are, of course, a wide variety of dynamisms: aggressive, lustful, and friendly, to name just a few. Sullivan believed that all dynamisms can be categorized into two classes: zonal and interpersonal. *Zonal dynamisms* center around physical zones of the body, such as the mouth or genitals, and are concerned with physical activities such as eating, drinking, or sexual behavior. These dynamisms are innate, and they all serve physical needs, even though some dynamisms—like fear and rage—might seem only remotely connected with physical satisfactions. The *interpersonal dynamisms* are learned from experiences with other people. Both the innate and the learned dynamisms are pervasive attributes that significantly influence the nature of one's interpersonal relations.

The most important dynamism in the personality is the *self dynamism* (also known as the "self system" or, simply, the "self"). Essentially, it is a person's self-image, constructed on the basis of his or her interpersonal relationships. The self develops out of the anxiety generated in the original mother-infant relationship and is reinforced or compounded by subsequent threats to security. It is a system of protection derived from the infant's initial attempts to please the mother and thereby attain satisfactions and security. The infant conforms to the rules of society as represented by the mother and begins to distinguish a "good me" versus a "bad me"—one bringing praise, the other punishment.

Although absolutely necessary for protection, the self dynamism is in some ways counterproductive, in that it represents a system of conforming to the culture and, therefore, may not represent the true self. It is the way one ought to behave, which may not be the same as the way one wants to behave.

Since the self dynamism, if functioning properly, reduces anxiety, it becomes highly resistant to change, because any change may lead to anxiety. Therefore, its consistent maintenance is reinforced. The ideal situation is one in which the true self, to the extent it can become known, is aware of the machinations of the self dynamism. If the distance between the true self and the self system is too great, the person may become schizoid.

Personifications

This second aspect of personality refers simply to images one has of other people and of the self. They are not necessarily accurate representations, because, like all perceptions, they are strongly influenced by the nature of one's self system.

Like dynamisms, personifications begin in infancy and are concerned with protection from anxiety. By adopting a consistent perception of a certain class of people, the person is able to react to them in a consistent manner. If, for example, a child perceives his or her father as cruel and authoritarian, then he or she may come to perceive all older men in positions of power (policemen, bosses, and so on) in the same way and react to them, as an adult, with behavior similar to that which he or she once used to cope with the father.

Personifications that are believed by large numbers of people ("all Southerners are bigots," "all professors are absentminded") are known as *stereotypes*—prejudgments of a person's behavior and attitudes on the basis of his or her membership in a particular group. Categorizing and prejudging are what personifications are all about.

Modes of Experience

Sullivan wrote of three different ways of experiencing the world around us—three levels of thinking or cognition by which a person relates to others. They are called prototaxic, parataxic, and syntaxic experience.

The earliest and most primitive mode of experience, the *prototaxic,* occurs only during the first several months of infancy. It involves simply and directly perceiving sensations, thoughts, or feelings, immediately as they occur, without drawing any connections between them or interpreting them. The experiences are isolated and unrelated, random and unorganized, and usually quite brief, sensed for the moment and then buried under the impact of newer experiences.

As the infant grows older, it develops the ability to organize and draw some meaning from experiences. For example, the baby comes to learn that certain sights and sounds—the mother's face, her smile and tone of voice—are preludes to being fed or held. In this second mode of experience, the *parataxic,* the infant is beginning to make some sense out of the heretofore independent and meaningless stimulations of his or her world. The infant begins to understand causal relationships: B follows A; milk follows the sight of the bottle. Also, the infant begins to distinguish between "me" and "not me" and to use language to communicate, although still in a primitive way. For example, by making a certain sound, the baby can (sometimes) get someone to feed it. Another sound will get the infant picked up.

In the third and highest mode of experience, the *syntaxic,* the child learns the use of language—not just sounds, but symbols (words), the meanings of which are generally shared by all people in the culture. In this mode, the child learns logical relationships and is able to test his or her perceptions against those of others.

The Development of Personality

Sullivan considered the development of personality primarily in terms of the evolution of the self, which he said took shape over six stages or eras: infancy, childhood, the juvenile era, preadolescence, midadolescence, and late adolescence.

Infancy lasts from birth until the child begins to acquire the ability to communicate through speech. The mode of experiencing is primarily prototaxic, although toward the end of the period the child comes to recognize the distinction between the self and an objective world, learns to cope with some tensions associated with bodily needs, and begins to develop personifications based on the behavior of the mother. The all-important self dynamism begins its formation during this period.

Childhood begins with the development of language facility and lasts until age 5 or 6. The mode of experience is parataxic, shifting to syntaxic as the command of language increases. The child recognizes verbal manifestations of approval or disapproval of his or her behavior, and these verbalizations become extremely significant in the further determination of the self.

During this period, the circle of people who influence the child extends beyond the family to peers, and his or her ability to accurately perceive and manipulate people to enhance his or her security becomes more elaborate. If the child receives an excess of parental disapproval during this stage, he or she develops a "malevolent transformation," thus coming to view the whole world in negative and hostile terms. As a result, he or she will tend to perceive only the negative aspects of other people, becoming effectively blind to their virtues.

The *juvenile era* begins when the child first attends school and lasts for approximately five years. Now operating primarily in the syntaxic mode, the child has an even wider range of people—including teachers and perhaps other adults—from whom to receive appraisals that are incorporated into the still-developing self dynamism. In other words, children at this stage increasingly think of themselves as they feel others see them, and the opinions of others about them assume greater importance. The desire for social acceptance also becomes an influence. The juvenile era exposes the child to a much higher level of socialization, as he or she is increasingly engaged with others in both cooperative and competitive activities. The child also becomes subject to a greater number of adult authority figures than ever before.

The ages of 10 or 11 to 13 delimit *preadolescence,* during which there develops a very strong need for an intimate relationship with another person of the same age and sex. Sullivan considered this relationship ("chumship") to be extremely important, for it is the first reciprocal love relationship in life; that is, it is the first time that the security and satisfactions of someone else become at least as important as one's own. It is interesting that Sullivan's isolated boyhood did not include such a relationship. He described persons who have not had this relationship as having difficulty in later interpersonal relations, being relatively indifferent to public opinion, but standing well above average in achievement.

Midadolescence lasts to about the age of 17 and is the time when sexual desire appears. There is a strong—indeed, often overpowering—need for sexual affiliation. At the same time, there is the continuing and almost equally strong need for intimacy with someone of the same sex.

The most prevalent problem of this period, according to Sullivan, is the separation of the erotic need for someone of the opposite sex from the intimacy need for someone of the same sex. If these two needs become confused or united, a homosexual rather than heterosexual tendency can result.

The final period, *late adolescence,* lasts from 17 into the early 20s and involves the fusion of the intimacy and erotic needs into a focus on one person of the opposite sex. The self dynamism is totally developed and crystallized during this period (for better or for worse). It is the time—if all has gone well beforehand—of the development of a mature, socialized human being, one ready to take a place of responsibility as a full-fledged member of the society.

The Defenses of Personality

There are three ways in which the personality can defend itself against anxiety. In fact, Sullivan stated the importance of these defenses in more positive terms: they are the prime means for attaining and keeping security. If, beginning in childhood, an individual perceives himself or herself to be disapproved of, the person must protect himself or herself from evidence of this disapproval in order to keep the self dynamism intact. This image we have of ourselves must be maintained; anything that tends to undermine or conflict with this picture must not be allowed to intrude. Such an intrusion negates the seeking of security and, consequently, brings about anxiety. The three main defenses against anxiety are dissociation, parataxic distortion, and sublimation.

Very similar to Freud's concept of repression, *dissociation* involves excluding from conscious awareness anything (behaviors, attitudes, or desires) that is incompatible with the self dynamism. The mechanism of dissociation is always in operation, ceaselessly guarding against and ever alert to any threat to the self. As in repression, the person simply does not see or hear, or cannot recall, experiences that are socially unacceptable or repugnant. This selective inattention, omitting any and all aspects of reality that might induce anxiety, is, of course, a distortion of reality.

Parataxic distortion refers to the continuing use in adulthood of the childhood parataxic mode of experiencing. Parataxic experiencing is an unsophisticated level of functioning in which the child uses symbols (words) in an arbitrary and personal fashion. He or she has not yet learned the universally agreed-upon meanings of the words. In adulthood, parataxic distortion involves the person's changing (distorting) the meanings of events so that they do not threaten—and might even enhance—the self.

As with dissociation, reality is seen or interpreted not as it is but rather as the person needs it to be in order to prevent anxiety.

Sublimation, as used by Sullivan, seems identical to Freud's concept. Disturbing, threatening impulses (those antithetical to the self) are changed into more socially acceptable, self-enhancing impulses. While this defense, like the other two, distorts reality, Sullivan believed it to be a more "rational," mature defense because it allows for some expression of troublesome impulses, however disguised they may be.

Personality Types

As is the case with some other personality theorists, Sullivan was opposed, in principle, to typing personality, to rigidly assigning people to mutually exclusive categories. His conception of personality held that it is a fluid process, resisting static placement. Nevertheless, he did discuss a set of what he called *syndromes,* which he used to classify not individual personalities but interpersonal relations. These syndromes represent what might be called *styles of behavior,* which are manifested in interpersonal relations. They are patterns of behavior frequently encountered.

Sullivan's description of these syndromes was rather sketchy and vague, but the names themselves are indicative of their nature. The list includes the self-absorbed, incorrigible, negativistic, stammering, ambition-ridden, asocial, inadequate, homosexual, and chronically adolescent styles of behavior.

Sullivan apparently attached little importance to these syndromes. He outlined the concept only once and never expanded on what must be regarded as an incomplete formulation.

Techniques of Inquiry

Sullivan's primary method of securing data from his patients was the *interview,* although he also used dream analysis to some extent. His approach to the psychiatric interview has had a great influence on the practice of psychotherapy. The interview, as Sullivan saw it, is a significant interpersonal interaction in which the therapist must be both participant and observer.

As a *participant-observer,* the therapist must interact with the patient in the same way that any person interacts with another in a face-to-face situation. At the same time, he or she must view the situation and monitor the interaction from the standpoint of an impartial observer. Obviously, this is a difficult and challenging task. The therapeutic situation involves, of course, a lengthy series of interviews, which Sullivan believed proceeds through four distinct stages: inception, reconnaissance, detailed inquiry, and termination.

The *inception* stage includes the patient's introduction to the therapist and the interview situation and the therapist's introduction to the patient. The main intent during this stage is to determine the reason the patient is seeking psychiatric help and the nature of his or her problem.

In the *reconnaissance* stage, the therapist questions the patient in more detail, developing a case history of the patient's life. On the basis of the information obtained thus far, the therapist formulates a number of hypotheses about the person's disturbances and their origins.

In the third stage, *detailed inquiry,* the therapist tries to determine which of these hypotheses is the most valid and useful. The patient is questioned on past and present interpersonal relations in light of the hypothesis selected.

In the *termination* stage, the therapist summarizes and interprets for the patient the vast amount of material covered and sets out a prescription of behavior for the patient to follow.

In his dream analysis, Sullivan avoided any use of symbolism; he believed there are no hidden meanings in dreams. Rather, the dream must be taken as it is, as a picture of what we are not in our ordinary conscious life. Dreams, like waking activities, are interpersonal events, with the other person in the dream being a projection of certain impulses, either constructive or destructive. Dreams represent an attempt to gain certain satisfactions that the person cannot attain in waking life.

Sullivan's Image of Human Nature

While Sullivan does not present us with an excessively optimistic image of human beings, as do Adler, Fromm, and Horney, he nevertheless pictures us in fundamentally hopeful and positive terms. It is true that tension is an almost ever present condition of life, in Sullivan's view, and that anxiety is a continuing force that must be reckoned with. However, we are not in any sense doomed to suffer the pain of tension and anxiety without relief. We can protect ourselves from anxiety.

Further, we are capable of changing our own personality, of shaping its pattern of growth well beyond the age of 5—the time by which Freud believed it was formed. We are not destined for a certain kind or form of personality because of what happens to us in early childhood, the time of greatest dependence and least control. While these early experiences are important, they do not alone dictate later personality.

Just as we can change ourselves, so, Sullivan believes, we can change our society. He was a vociferous critic of contemporary Western culture and its deleterious effects on the human personality. But he did more than criticize; he devoted a great deal of time and energy to international affairs in the pursuit of world peace.

A Final Commentary

As mentioned at the beginning of this chapter, Sullivan's unique approach to the understanding of personality has gained increasing recognition among practitioners of psychiatry in the years since his death. His influence, however, on those who study personality, both empirically and theoretically, has been less broad and intensive. Also, his work has not developed a large popular following, or even interest. While many people have at least a passing acquaintance with Freud, Adler, Fromm, and Horney, such is not the case with Sullivan. He is much less well known outside psychology and psychiatry than are certain other theorists.

A possible reason for his relative neglect among those who study personality is the vague and, in some cases, almost casual manner in which he defined and used his concepts. It is often difficult, for example, to clearly distinguish between some personifications and dynamisms, two of the central concepts in his system. The ambiguity and sketchy character of his syndromes were mentioned earlier, and the same charge can be leveled against other aspects of his system.

His own presentation of his work is, for the most part, unsystematic, in that there is not a cohesive and testable set of hypotheses that derive from his theory (a charge, it should be noted, that can be directed with equal justification against a number of other personality theorists).

With the exception of one book, his works were published posthumously by his students as collections of papers and lectures. Lectures, often directed at audiences of quite diverse composition, are not the best medium for the presentation of a coherent system within the covers of a single book. Also, what he did write was not presented in a very engaging style.

Thus, we have a system that we can characterize as vague and ambiguous, that has not been clearly or effectively presented. It is understandable, then, that the theory has been unproductive of research and often neglected in the academic study of personality. So great has been the neglect in that sphere that we find a paucity of criticism of his system in the psychological literature. Perhaps ignoring Sullivan can be considered criticism enough.

Nevertheless, his influence is strong among those who are more concerned with treating individual personalities than with studying the concept of personality. His methods of treatment, particularly of schizo-phrenics, have a strong appeal, and his recognition of the importance of interpersonal relations is, to many, a welcome antidote for the heavy biological emphasis of Freud. There is a large and loyal group of Sullivan-ians who today carry on his work.

Suggested Readings

Brown, J. A. C. *Freud and the post-Freudians.* Baltimore, Md.: Penguin, 1961.

Carson, R. *Interaction concepts of personality.* Chicago: Aldine, 1969.

Chrzanowski, G. What is psychotherapy? The viewpoint of the Sullivanian school. *American Psychotherapy Monographs,* 1959, No. 1, 31–36.

Mullahy, P. (Ed.). *The contributions of Harry Stack Sullivan.* New York: Hermitage Press, 1952.

Munroe, R. L. *Schools of psychoanalytic thought.* New York: Holt, Rinehart and Winston, 1955.

Pearce, J., & Newton, S. *The conditions of human growth.* New York: Citadel Press, 1963.

Sullivan, H. S. *Conceptions of modern psychiatry.* New York: Norton, 1953.

Sullivan, H. S. *Interpersonal theory of psychiatry.* New York: Norton, 1953.

Sullivan, H. S. *The psychiatric interview.* New York: Norton, 1956.

Carl Jung
Analytical Psychology

7

My life is a story of the self-realization of the unconscious. Everything in the unconscious seeks outward manifestation, and the personality too desires to evolve out of its unconscious conditions . . . .

—Carl Jung

The theorists discussed in the four preceding chapters—Adler, Horney, Fromm, and Sullivan—had certain broad themes in common in their disaffection with and defection from orthodox Freudian psychoanalysis. They rejected Freud's emphasis on the biological determinants of personality and spoke instead of social-cultural determinants. They also placed considerably less emphasis on the ruling or controlling power of the unconscious, arguing that human beings are much more rational and self-conscious than Freud had allowed.

Carl Jung, the theorist to whom we now turn, was also a defector from Freud. However, this defection is all he shares with our last four theorists. Originally an intimate of Freud's, who considered him his spiritual heir, Jung went on to develop his own theory of personality, which differed dramatically from orthodox psychoanalysis.

Jung fashioned a new and elaborate theory of personality quite unlike any other theory that had been developed. To this day, his *analytical psychology* stands apart from all other approaches to personality in its complexity and unique emphases. And his theory continues to grow and strengthen in the 1970s—more than a decade after Jung's death—as increasing numbers of people find congenial or at least intriguing themes in his work.

The first point on which Jung came to disagree with Freud was the role of sexuality. In a sense, Jung broadened Freud's definition of libido by redefining it as a more generalized dynamic force of personality, a psychic energy that includes sex but is not restricted to it.

The second major difference is concerned with the direction of the forces that influence personality. While Freud viewed human beings as largely prisoners or victims of past events and processes, Jung argued that we are shaped by our future as well as by our past. A person is influenced not only by what happened to him or her as a child but also by what he or she aspires to do in the future.

The final major point of difference between Freud and Jung revolves around the unconscious. Rather than placing less emphasis than Freud did on the unconscious (as was the case with the dissenters discussed earlier), Jung placed a greater emphasis on the concept. He probed more deeply into the unconscious and added new dimensions to its composition: the inherited experiences of humans as a species and human beings' animal ancestry. While Freud had recognized this phylogenetic aspect of personality (the influence of inherited primal experiences), Jung made it the central point of his system of personality. As a result, history, mythology, primitive rituals and symbols, and religion all came to play a part in Jung's view of human nature.

The Life of Jung (1875–1961)

Black-frocked clergymen, deaths and funerals, neurotic parents in a failing marriage, a sexual assault by an adult he had worshiped, and a wooden mannequin for a companion marked Jung's early-childhood years. (A prophetic beginning for a personality theorist, judging by those discussed so far.)

Born in Switzerland into a family that included nine clergymen (eight uncles and his father), Jung was introduced at an early age not only to religion but to the classics as well. He was very close to his father, although he considered him weak and powerless. While generally kind and tolerant, his father often had periods of great moodiness and irritability.

His mother was the more powerful parent, although she had a number of emotional disorders that caused her behavior to be inconsistent. As a result, Jung came to distrust women, a suspicion that took many years to dispel. To escape his parents and their continuing marital problems, Jung spent many hours alone in the attic of his home, playing with and confiding in a figure he had carved out of wood.

During his childhood years, Jung recalled, he attended many funerals for fishermen who had drowned in a nearby waterfall. When he was 6 and living near Basel, he discovered the corpse of a man who had been killed in a flood, and once he nearly fell from a very high bridge. The notion of death, then, was no secret to the young boy.

Introverted and solitary, Jung disliked school, resenting the time he had to devote to his formal studies rather than to topics that truly interested him. To his delight, however, he was forced to miss six months of school as a result of a series of fainting spells. When he overheard his father lament to a friend "What will become of the boy if he cannot earn his living?" his "illness" disappeared, and he immediately returned to school to work harder than ever before.

He read a great deal, particularly on religious and philosophical topics, and was curious and confused about a great many of life's issues. In describing the loneliness that characterized his childhood, Jung wrote: "Thus the pattern of my relationship to the world was already prefigured; today as then I am a solitary."

He studied medicine at the University of Basel and decided, to the disappointment of his professors, to specialize in psychiatry, a field then held in low repute. Jung had long been interested in fantasies, dreams, the supernatural, and the occult, and he believed that psychiatry would give him the opportunity to explore these phenomena.

Beginning in 1900, he worked at a mental hospital in Zurich, under Eugen Bleuler, the famous psychiatrist who coined the term *schizophrenia*. During the following years, Jung lectured at the University of Zurich, developed a sizable private practice, and conducted research using a word-association test to investigate the emotional reactions of his patients.

Thus, when he became associated with Freud in 1907, it was as a professional with a well-established reputation, not as an unknown student. Freud and Jung began their relationship through correspondence, and, when they met for the first time, they were so congenial and had so much to share that they talked for 13 hours!

Jung remained in Zurich, but the two men met periodically, continued a voluminous correspondence, and journeyed together to the United States in 1909 to give a series of lectures at Clark University. Freud was grooming Jung to take over the presidency of the International Psychoanalytic Association. Concerned that psychoanalysis might come to be labeled a "Jewish science" (as it was called later, during the Nazi era), Freud wanted a non-Jew to assume titular leadership of the movement.

Their relationship was an intimate one. "I formally adopted you as an eldest son," Freud once wrote to Jung, "anointing you as my successor and crown prince." Jung apparently considered Freud a father figure: "I was overjoyed by your letter," he wrote, "being, as you know, very receptive to any recognition the father sees fit to bestow."

Contrary to what Freud had hoped, Jung was not a totally uncritical disciple. He had his own ideas, his own view of the human personality (which differed from Freud's view), and, when he began to express these unorthodox notions, it became inevitable that they would part company.

They severed their relationship in 1913, a circumstance described as distressful for Freud and shattering for Jung. At the same time, Jung, then almost 40, experienced what has come to be called the crisis of middle age. He described it as a "state of disorientation" and suspected a severe emotional disturbance in himself. So disturbed was he that he resigned his lectureship at the university and was unable to read a scientific book for three years.

It was a difficult and fallow period, but Jung overcame it by confronting his unconscious—recording and analyzing his dreams and fantasies. The result was a new and deeper level of Jung's own personality development and new insights into human emotional life. Nearly two-thirds of Jung's patients during his crisis were at the same stage of development—middle age. Not surprisingly, the emotional change at midlife became part of his system of personality.

The rest of his long life was fruitful, both personally and professionally. His analytical psychology was attracting increasing numbers of followers, his books were popular, and he explored diverse cultures in America, Africa (he even learned Swahili), Egypt, India, and Ceylon in order to broaden his understanding of human nature. In later years, the University of Basel established a special professorship for him, and a group of his students organized a Jungian training institute that is still active in Zurich today.

Psychic Energy: Libido

One of the earliest and most important points on which Jung took issue with Freud concerned the nature of libido. Jung could not agree that libido was exclusively a sexual energy, and he argued instead that it was a broad and undifferentiated life energy.

Actually, Jung used the term *libido* in two different ways: first, as the diffuse, general life energy mentioned above and, second, as a narrower psychic energy that, in a sense, fuels the work of the *psyche*, his term for personality. It is through the psychic energy that psychological activities such as perceiving, thinking, feeling, and wishing are carried out.

When a great deal of psychic energy is invested in a particular idea or feeling, that idea is capable of strongly influencing a person. For example, if you are highly motivated to obtain power, then most of your psychic energy will be devoted to seeking power. The amount of energy so devoted or concentrated is called a *value* in Jung's system.

Psychic energy has its counterpart in the physical energy used by the body to carry out its physiological activities. Jung described a reciprocal relationship between these two forms of energy. The energy of the body can be transformed into the energy of the psyche, and the energy of the psyche can be transformed into the energy of the body. In other words, the body can affect the mind, and the mind can affect the body (as is the case, for example, with psychosomatic illness).

Jung drew rather heavily from physics to explain the functioning of psychic energy in his principles of opposites, equivalence, and entropy.

The *principle of opposites* is a major tenet of his theory of personality. "I see in all that happens the play of opposites," he wrote. He notes the existence of opposites or polarities in physical energy—heat versus cold, height versus depth, creation versus decay.

So it is with psychic energy; every wish or feeling has its opposite. There must be antithesis, Jung felt, or there would be no energy. Without polarities or extremes, there would be no process or tendency toward equalization, and that process of equalization is energy. The principle of opposites, this conflict between polarities, was considered by Jung to be the prime mover of behavior, the generator of all energy. Indeed, the sharper the conflict between polarities, the greater the energy produced.

The *principle of equivalence* is essentially the first law of thermodynamics in physics—the principle of conservation of energy—applied to psychic energy. It states that energy is not lost to the personality but rather is shifted from one part to another. If, for example, one's psychic value in a particular area weakens or disappears altogether, that energy is transferred elsewhere in the psyche. If we lose interest in a person or a hobby or a field of study, the psychic energy formerly invested in that area is shifted to a new area, or to several different areas. Also, the psychic energy in use for conscious activities while we are awake is shifted to dreaming when we are asleep.

The word *equivalence* means that the new area to which energy has shifted must be of an equally strong psychic value—that is, equally desirable or compelling or fascinating. If that is not the case, the excess energy will flow into the unconscious. In whatever direction and manner energy flows, the principle of equivalence means that there is a continuing redistribution of energy within the personality.

The second law of thermodynamics is represented in Jung's system by his *principle of entropy*. In physics, this principle refers to the equalization of energy differences. For example, if a hot object and a cold object are placed in direct contact with each other, heat will flow from the hotter to the colder object until they are in equilibrium at the same temperature. It is, in effect, an exchange of energy resulting in a kind of homeostatic balance between the objects.

The same thing occurs, in principle, with psychic energy, according to Jung. There is always a tendency toward a balance or equilibrium in the personality. For example, if two desires or beliefs differ greatly in psychic value or intensity, energy will flow from the more strongly held to the weaker. Ideally, the personality would have an equal distribution of psychic energy over all its systems and aspects (a condition known as *self* or *selfhood*), but this state is never achieved totally. Indeed, if such a perfect balance or equilibrium were achieved, then no psychic energy would be produced, for, as we have seen, energy requires conflict between opposites. Thus, complete entropy remains a state to be striven for but never realized.

Psychic energy, then, through the principles of opposition, equivalence, and entropy, provides the dynamic mechanisms and power for the operation of the personality.

The Systems of Personality

The total personality or psyche was viewed by Jung as composed of a variety of separate structures or systems that, while quite different from one another, are nevertheless capable of influencing one another. The major systems are the ego, the personal unconscious, and the collective unconscious.

The Ego

The ego is the conscious mind, that part of the psyche concerned with perceiving, thinking, feeling, and remembering. It is our awareness of ourselves and is responsible for carrying out the normal activities of waking life. The ego performs a selective function, admitting into conscious awareness only a portion of the stimuli to which we are constantly exposed. The ego also provides a sense of continuity, coherence, and identity—a stability in the way we perceive our world and ourselves.

Obviously, such functions are important to an individual, but Jung insisted that the ego, the conscious level of personality, is secondary in importance, in terms of its effect on thought and behavior, to the two unconscious levels. Consciousness forms only the uppermost level of the structure of the psyche. The unconscious, like the lower levels of a building, helps to provide support for the upper level. Thus, Jung is in basic agreement with Freud on the relatively greater role played by the unconscious. But the two men differed sharply in their views of its nature.

The Personal Unconscious

There are two levels to the unconscious in Jung's system—a higher, more superficial level and a deeper, more profoundly influencing level. The more superficial aspect is the personal unconscious, which is not unlike Freud's preconscious. The personal unconscious is, in essence, a reservoir of material that was once conscious but that has been forgotten or suppressed because it was either trivial or distressing.

As was the case with Freud's preconscious, there is a great deal of two-way traffic between the ego and the personal unconscious. Our attention can shift readily from this printed page to the memory of what we did last night. All manner of experience is stored in a sort of file cabinet of our personal unconscious, and little effort is required to take something out, examine it for a while, and then put it back, where it will remain until the next time we want it or are reminded of it.

As an individual files more and more experiences in the personal unconscious, he or she begins to categorize or group them into clusters that Jung called *complexes*. A complex is a core or pattern of emotions, memories, perceptions, and wishes clustering around a common theme. In everyday terms, we might say that a person has a complex about power or status, for example; he or she is preoccupied with that theme, and it influences his or her behavior. The person may try to become powerful personally or to identify or affiliate with power, perhaps driving a motorcycle or a powerful car. In a variety of ways, the power complex determines how the person perceives the world; it directs him or her. Jung noted: "A person does not have a complex; the complex has him."

Once a complex is formed, it is no longer under conscious control but can intrude upon and interfere with consciousness. The person with a complex is not aware of its guiding influence, although others may observe his or her constant focus on one theme.

While the majority of complexes with which Jung dealt are harmful—indeed, are at least partly responsible for the neurotic condition that drove the person to an analyst—complexes may also be extremely useful to a person. For example, a perfection or achievement complex may cause a person to work hard at developing a particular talent or skill.

As to the origin of complexes, Jung stated that they grow out of childhood, adult, or ancestral experiences, the last being the heritage of the species contained in the collective unconscious.

The Collective Unconscious

The deepest and most inaccessible level of the psyche, the collective or transpersonal unconscious, is the most unusual and controversial aspect of Jung's system; to some critics it is the most bizarre aspect.

Jung believed that, just as a person individually accumulates and files all of his or her past experiences, so does mankind collectively, as a species. In the personal unconscious, each of us stores our individually accumulated experiences. In the collective unconscious, mankind as a whole accumulates the experiences of the human and prehuman species and passes this wealth of experience on to each new generation. The collective unconscious, then, is a storehouse of all the experience of mankind transmitted to each of us. It contains the entire catalog of experiences that have marked human evolution, and it is repeated in the brain of every human being in every generation.

Whatever experiences are universal—that is, are repeated, relatively unchanged, by each generation—become a part of each individual's personality. Indeed, the primitive past of human beings becomes the primary base of a person's psyche, directing and influencing current behavior. To Jung, the collective unconscious was the "all-controlling deposit of ancestral experiences." There is, then, in Jung's view, a definite linking of a person's present personality with the past—with his or her own childhood and early years as well as with the history of the entire species.

It is important to note that we do not inherit these collective experiences directly. We do not, for example, inherit an actual fear of snakes. Rather, we inherit the potentiality or predisposition to fear snakes. We are predisposed to behave and feel in certain ways, the same ways in which people have always behaved and felt. Whether the predisposition becomes a reality depends on the specific experiences the individual encounters.

Jung believed that certain basic experiences have characterized every generation throughout the history of humanity. For example, people have always had a mother figure, experienced birth and death, faced unknown terrors in the dark, worshiped power or status or some sort of god figure, and feared an evil, Satan-like figure. The universality of these experiences over countless evolving generations leaves their imprint in each person at birth. Since all people face essentially the same experiences, these universal experiences determine how we will perceive and react to our own world. Jung said: "The form of the world into which [a person] is born is already inborn in him, as a virtual image."

Thus, a baby is born predisposed to perceive the mother in a certain manner. Assuming that she behaves as we have generally considered mothers should behave, then the baby's predisposition will correspond with its reality. Thus, the form of the infant's world "inborn in him" determines how it adapts and reacts to its world.

Because the collective unconscious is such an unorthodox concept, the reason Jung proposed it and the kind of evidence he thought supported it are important. In his voracious reading about ancient cultures, both mythical and real, Jung discovered that certain common themes and symbols appear in diverse parts of the world. As far as could be determined, these common themes had not been transmitted or communicated orally or in writing from one culture to another.

Further, Jung's patients, in their dreams and fantasies, recalled and described the same kinds of symbols he had found in ancient cultures. He could find no other explanation for these shared symbols and themes over such great geographical and temporal distances than that they were transmitted by and carried in each individual's collective unconscious.

It should be pointed out that Freud also believed that basic primal experiences are passed on to each individual as general tendencies. In 1911, two years before their split, Freud wrote in a letter to Jung that "phylogenetic memory . . . will soon prove to be so."

Archetypes.   The ancient experiences contained in the collective unconscious are manifested or expressed in the form of images that Jung called archetypes. These images or pictures of universal experiences form a vital part of Jung's theory of personality, and he devoted much of the last half of his life to their study.

There are a great many of these universal experiences, Jung wrote—as many as there are common human experiences. By being repeated countless times in the lives of countless people and generations, they have become imprinted on our psyche.

Archetypes are not actual, fully developed memories. We cannot see an archetype as we can clearly see a picture of some past event or person in our own lives. Rather, an archetype is a predisposition that awaits an actual experience in a person's life before its content becomes clear.

Some of the archetypes with which Jung was concerned are: magic, the hero, the child, God, death, power, and the wise old man. Several archetypes are more fully developed than others and therefore influence the psyche more consistently. These are the persona, the anima and animus, the shadow, and the self.

The *persona*, as we saw in Chapter 1, originally referred to a mask worn by an actor to display a different role or face to the audience. Jung used the term with basically the same meaning. The archetype persona is also a mask, a public face the person wears to present himself or herself as someone other than who he or she really is. The persona is necessary, Jung believed, because we are forced to play a variety of roles in life in order to succeed in our work and to get along with the diverse kinds of people with whom we are forced into contact—from professors to roommates.

While the persona can be very helpful to a person—and, indeed, necessary—it can also be quite harmful. A person may well come to believe that this persona really reflects his or her true nature and being. From playing a role, the person comes to be that role; as a result, other aspects of his or her personality are, in a sense, shunted aside and not allowed to develop. Jung described it this way: the ego comes to identify with the persona rather than with the person's true nature, and the resulting condition is known as *inflation of the persona*.

Both cases—simply playing a role and coming to believe the role—involve deception. In the former case, a person is deceiving others; in the latter, a person is deceiving himself or herself as well—obviously a dangerous situation.

The *anima* and *animus*, collectively, refer to Jung's recognition that humans are essentially bisexual animals. On the biological level, each sex secretes the hormones of the opposite sex as well as of its own sex. On the psychological level, each sex manifests characteristics, temperaments, and attitudes of the other sex by virtue of centuries of living together. Thus, the psyche of a woman contains masculine aspects (the archetype animus), and the psyche of a man contains feminine aspects (the archetype anima).

These opposite sex characteristics aid in the adjustment and survival of humanity, for they better enable the person to understand the nature of the opposite sex. The archetypes predispose one to like certain characteristics of the other sex and guide one's behavior with reference to the opposite sex.

Jung was quite insistent that these archetypes must be expressed; that is, a man must exhibit his feminine as well as his masculine characteristics, and a woman must likewise express her masculine characteristics along with her feminine ones. Otherwise, these necessary characteristics will lie dormant and undeveloped, leading to a one-sidedness of personality. A person in this condition cannot become fully human, because one aspect of his or her nature has been suppressed.

There are potential dangers associated with all the archetypes discussed thus far, but the most dangerous and powerful archetype of all is the one with the sinister and mysterious label of the *shadow*. When Jung spoke of the collective unconscious as the repository of all past experiences, he included our animal (prehuman) ancestry. For that reason, the shadow has the deepest roots of all the archetypes; it contains the basic, primitive animal instincts.

That which society usually considers evil and immoral resides in the shadow, and this "dark side of man" must be tamed if people hope to live in harmony with one another. These primitive impulses must be suppressed, overcome, or defended against by the individual. If they are not, society will very likely punish him or her.

But there is a dilemma here. Not only is the shadow the source of that which society considers bad; it is also the source of vitality, spontaneity, and creativity. Thus, if the shadow is totally and absolutely suppressed, the psyche becomes rather dull and lifeless. Jung stated that it is the function of the ego to direct the forces of the shadow, to repress the animal instincts enough so that the person is considered civilized, while allowing enough expression of the instincts to provide creativity and vigor.

Jung's most important archetype is the *self*. It represents the unity, wholeness, and integration of the total personality—or at least the striving toward such wholeness. The symbol representing this archetype, one found in diverse cultures, is the mandala, or so-called magic circle.

We have mentioned Jung's principle of opposites and the importance of polarities to the psyche. The self is a point of equilibrium, midway between the polarities of the conscious and the unconscious, that forms the center of the psyche. The full realization of the self seems always to lie in the future. Jung spoke of it as a goal—something to be striven for but rarely achieved. As such, the self serves as a motivating force, one that pulls the individual from ahead rather than pushes from behind (as is the case with past experience).

The self archetype cannot begin to emerge until all the other systems of the psyche have become fully developed. This occurs, as we shall see, around the years of middle age, a crucial period of transition in Jung's view. The full actualization of the self involves a future orientation—plans, goals, a purpose—and an accurate perception and knowledge of one's self. Self-realization is impossible without a full knowledge of self. This makes the process the most difficult one we face, requiring persistence, perceptiveness, and great wisdom.

The Development of Personality

We have seen that Jung's theory of personality is in part a forward-looking one. Achieving selfhood or self-actualization involves an orientation toward the future. Jung believed that an individual's present personality is determined both by what the person hopes to be and by what he or she has been. The system, then, is both *teleological*, in that it looks to the future, and *causal*, in that it looks to the past. Jung was highly critical of Freud for emphasizing only causal factors, or past events, as shapers of personality. Human beings, both individually and as a species, are constantly developing and growing, always moving toward a more complete or fully human level of development.

Personality development, therefore, is ideally marked by what Jung called *progression*. But he also pointed out that development can go backward as well as forward, and so he invoked the opposing principle of *regression* to help explain personality development.

In regression, the libido "flows backward," away from the external environment and inward to the unconscious. Regression does not necessarily mean a cessation of progression. Indeed, it may aid progression because, by delving into the past experiences of the personal and collective unconscious and by introspecting and reconciling these experiences, the person may be able to resolve the problem that led to the regression in the first place. Regression, then, can involve a quiet retreat into oneself in order to foster creative thought and revitalization. Jung also pointed out that dreaming is a regression into the unconscious.

Another principle in Jung's theory of development is *synchronicity*. The word derives from the adjective *synchronous*, which refers to events occuring together in time. Jung was concerned here with events bordering on the supernatural, such as clairvoyance. We have all read, for example, of someone having a vision or a dream in which a friend or relative has an accident or dies and, shortly thereafter, learning that the event in the dream actually occurred. Jung did not think that such "coincidences" are causal in nature; the death does not cause the dream, even though the events are synchronous. But he believed in the occurrence of such phenomena, and his principle of synchronicity is an attempt to account for them.

He explains such mystical events in mystical terms, saying that there is an unknown order or force in the world that is beyond causality. An archetype is able to synchronously manifest itself in someone's psyche and in the external world by a process not explained (and perhaps not capable of being explained). (Jung, as we have seen, was very much concerned with spiritual phenomena, a concern not shared by most of psychology.)

There are two additional principles to be mentioned in connection with personality development: individuation and transcendence. They are both inherent parts of psychological growth and are so vital that development cannot occur in their absence.

Individuation involves, simply, becoming an individual. In infancy, the psyche is undifferentiated, a diffuse whole manifesting very little conscious activity. As the infant grows older, the structures of the psyche develop; that is, they become more sharply differentiated from one another and within themselves. Each structure becomes more complex; the persona, the shadow, and the ego all develop and take on solid and unique form. They must individuate rather equally. All of the structures must grow. None must be stifled or suppressed, and none must be overdeveloped at the expense of others.

Individuation involves the fulfillment or realization of all one's capacities. The goal of individuation—a fully harmonious, integrated personality—is, of course, the self. Jung pointed out that the tendency toward individuation is an innate and therefore inevitable process. It will occur, but it can be helped or hindered by environmental factors such as the nature of the parent-child relationship and of the individual's education.

Once all of the psyche's structures are fully individuated, the next step in development, *transcendence,* occurs. Full individuation results in diversity within the psyche. Self-actualization requires that these diversities and opposites in the psyche be transcended or united and made whole. The tendency toward individuation and transcendence in each of us is natural and inevitable.

As with individuation, environmental factors such as a poor marriage or supremely frustrating work can inhibit the process of transcendence. Self, you remember, is a goal not reached by everyone, and any factor that stifles individuation and transcendence delays or may totally prevent the achievement of self.

Levels of Development

Ideally, development of the psyche never stops, regardless of age. Thus, Jung took a longer view of personality development than did Freud, who concentrated on the early years of life and foresaw little development after the age of 5 or so. Jung also differs from Freud's approach to development in not spelling out the sequential stages of growth in as much detail. Nevertheless, he did speak of specific levels or periods in the overall process of individuation and transcendence.

Jung had relatively little to say about childhood and considered the early years to be not very decisive in laying down a fixed personality pattern. Initially, the child is governed primarily by physical instincts, and the ego begins to form only when the child is able to distinguish between himself or herself and other objects. Consciousness begins to form when the child is able to say "I."

It is not until the advent of puberty that the psyche begins to assume a definite form and content. This period, which Jung refers to as the *psychic birth* of an individual, is marked by a great many problems and the necessity of making a number of adaptations. Childhood fantasies must now end as the demands of reality confront the adolescent.

From the teen-age years through young adulthood, the person is deeply concerned with preparatory activities—completing education, beginning a career, getting married, and starting a family. The primary attitude during these years is that of *extraversion;* the focus is external.

Major changes occur when the second half of life begins at middle age, between 35 and 40. As we noted earlier, this period was a time of intense crisis for Jung himself. By middle age, the adaptational problems of life have usually been resolved. The 40-year-old is established in his or her job, community, and marriage. All the energy that had been invested in becoming so established must now be rechanneled. The first half of life was devoted to activities of consciousness; the second half must be directed toward the unconscious, which has been neglected until now.

The vitally important aspects of a person in the personal and collective unconscious must now be allowed expression. Thus, the person must turn away from an exclusive focus on the conscious and must confront his or her unconscious. The individual turns inward, becoming more introspective and *introverted.*

Jung said that at this time of life spiritual interests (broadly defined) must replace the materialistic considerations that defined the first half of life. This is the age at which the self may finally emerge. To Jung, middle age is much more crucial in the development of personality than childhood.

Additional Aspects of the Psyche: Attitudes and Functions

During Jung's 20-year search for a way to classify or type personalities—a search in what he called the "domain of practical psychology" —he found two basic *attitudes* of the psyche. In keeping with his insistence on the necessity for opposites, these two attitudes represent totally different directions the libido can take with reference to the outside world.

The libido can be channeled externally, toward the outside world, or internally, toward the self. These two attitudes—*extraversion* and *intro-*

version—are probably the best-known parts of Jung's system; the terms and concepts have come into general prominence. We discussed these opposing attitudes briefly in the previous section, in our consideration of personality development before and after middle age.

We all have a good idea of what these terms mean. When we say people are introverted, we mean that they are somewhat withdrawn, often shy, and focusing on self. Extraverts, on the other hand, are much more open, sociable, and socially aggressive. Everyone, according to Jung, has the capability for either attitude, but one becomes dominant (for reasons he did not make clear). Once an attitude has become the dominant one, the person's behavior and consciousness are largely ruled by it.

However, the nondominant attitude remains; it has not disappeared. It becomes part of the personal unconscious, where it is still capable of influencing behavior. For example, an introverted person may on occasion (or consistently in certain situations) display characteristics of extraversion, or he or she may wish to be more outgoing or may be very attracted to someone who is extraverted. The nondominant attitude, then, is everpresent, so that a person is not exclusively or totally an extravert or an introvert. The person carries both attitudes within.

Shortly after he developed the concepts of extraversion and introversion, Jung came to realize that his task of finding psychological types was not yet complete. This pair of opposites did not, as he had thought for a time, fully explain all the differences found among people.

He began to see that there were different kinds of introverts and extraverts, and so he developed another level of categorization dealing with what he called the *psychological functions*. The functions refer to different ways in which we perceive or apprehend both the external world of reality and the inner world of subjectivity. Jung posited four functions of the psyche: thinking, feeling, sensing, and intuiting.

Thinking and *feeling* are grouped together as *rational* functions. They involve making judgments and evaluations about experiences. While feeling is a function totally different from thinking, Jung believed that both are concerned with the ability to organize and categorize experience. Nevertheless, he did say that they were opposite functions. The kind of evaluation made by the feeling function is in terms of liked or disliked, pleasant or unpleasant, stimulating or dull. The thinking function involves a conscious judgment of whether an experience is true or false.

The second pair of opposing functions—*sensing* and *intuiting*—are called *irrational* functions because they make no use of the process of reason. These functions do not evaluate experiences; they simply experience them. Sensing reproduces an experience accurately through the senses in the way that a photograph copies an object. Intuiting does not arise directly from a stimulus in the external world. A person who believes someone else is with him or her in a darkened room may not do so on the basis of actual sensory experience but rather on the basis of intuition or a hunch.

Just as everyone has the capacity for the attitudes of extraversion and introversion, so everyone has the capacity for all four of these functions. However, just as one attitude is dominant, so only one function is dominant. The other three are submerged in the personal unconscious. Only one of the two paired functions can be dominant—either the rational or the irrational. Their incompatibility prevents equal status or power. And within each pair only one of the functions can be dominant, for again they are contradictory. A person cannot have both thinking and feeling modes or both sensing and intuiting modes dominant.

However, Jung stated that one representative of each pair of functions (rational and irrational) can be observed in the dominant or superior mode. For example, sensing and thinking may both be represented, or feeling and intuiting. Nevertheless, only one function remains exclusively dominant. The other serves as an auxiliary function.

There is still more to Jung's approach to categorizing personalities. The two attitudes and four functions can interact to form eight *psychological types*. An introverted person can be of the thinking, feeling, sensing, or intuiting type. Similarly, an extravert can be of any of the four types.

To fully determine the nature of an individual's personality, one must know which of the functions and attitudes are dominant—that is, which express themselves in consciousness and which have been relegated to the personal unconscious. Jung pointed out that pure types represent extreme cases and that there is a wide range of variation in any one type. Also, no single type is better or more preferred than any other.

Interactions among Parts of the Psyche

As we have seen, the personality is made up of a number of separate structures or aspects. While these structures are truly distinct, they are nevertheless capable of influencing one another. The interactions take place through the mechanisms of opposition, unity, and compensation.

Opposition has been mentioned frequently in this chapter as a sort of cornerstone of Jung's approach to personality. It exists everywhere within the psyche and is the source of psychic energy. The tensions that are created by polarization of opposing forces, while potentially harmful, are nonetheless necessary for the development of the psyche. Without them, there would be no psyche. There is conflict between the unconscious and the conscious and between the personal unconscious and the collective unconscious. Extraversion opposes introversion, the rational functions oppose the irrational functions, the anima opposes the animus, sensing opposes intuiting, and so it goes. If the conflicts are too harsh or severe, they may shatter the psyche. The result is neurotic or psychotic behavior.

Alternatively, and much more desirably, opposites can *unite* to form a synthesis or wholeness in which they come to complement one another. It is through this kind of balancing of opposites, the leveling or reducing of the conflicts, that the personality becomes fully integrated in the state, now familiar to you, known as the self. The principle of transcendence, discussed earlier, brings about this integration and balancing of opposites.

The third mechanism of interaction among the structures of the psyche is *compensation*, by means of which one structure can act to overcome the weakness of another structure. For example, if you are highly extraverted, your unconscious will act to develop your suppressed introversion. Themes of introversion may appear in your dreams. If, for some reason, circumstances interfere with the expression of your extraversion, the attitude of introversion will then be expressed.

If it were not for compensation, there would be a dangerously lopsided quality to your personality—excessive extraversion, or sensing, or intuiting, for example. Such overemphasis on one function, attitude, or structure leads to maladjustment.

Through opposition, unity, and compensation, the systems of the psyche seek balance and equilibrium, striving toward the fullest, most complete stage of development—the self.

Techniques of Inquiry

Jung's techniques for inquiring into the functioning of the psyche involve both science and what some call the supernatural, both an experimental and a mystical approach. He investigated a variety of cultures and eras, noting their symbols, myths, religions, and rituals. Through the fantasies and dreams of his patients and through explorations ranging from Sanskrit to alchemy, clairvoyance to astrology, he formed the basis of his unique theory of personality. And yet, the work that first brought Jung to the attention of American psychology involved experimental, quantitative, and physiological research. His techniques were an unorthodox blend of opposites, perhaps appropriate for his polarity-based theory. Basically, Jung used four techniques: word association, symptom analysis, life-history reconstruction, and dream analysis.

The *word-association* test, in which a subject responds to a stimulus word with whatever word comes immediately to mind, has become a standard laboratory and clinical tool in psychology. In the early 1900s,

Jung first used this technique with a list of 100 words he selected that were capable of eliciting emotions. Jung measured the time it took for a patient to respond to each word. He also measured physiological reactions to each word, thus determining the emotional effects of the stimuli.

He used this technique to uncover complexes in his patients. A variety of response factors were indicative of complexes, according to Jung, including the physiological responses mentioned. For example, delays in responding to particular words, making the same response to widely differing words, or failing to respond to any words can all indicate the existence of a complex.

The second technique, *symptom analysis*, focuses on the symptoms being experienced by the patient and is based on the person's free associations to a symptom. It is similar to Freud's cathartic method. Between the patient's associations to his or her symptoms and the analyst's interpretation of them, the symptoms will often be relieved and sometimes disappear altogether.

Life-history reconstruction, the extensive recollection of a person's past experiences, often provides a picture of certain developmental patterns that may have led to the present neurotic condition.

The final technique involves the *analysis of dreams*, which Jung, agreeing with Freud, considered to be the "royal road" into the unconscious. Jung's approach to dream analysis differed from Freud's in that Jung was concerned with more than the causal factors of dreams. He believed that dreams were more than unconscious wishes and saw in them two functions or purposes. First, dreams are *prospective;* that is, they help an individual prepare himself or herself for the experiences and events he or she anticipates in the immediate future. Second, dreams serve a *compensatory* function, in that they help bring about a balance between opposites in the psyche by compensating for the overdevelopment of any single psychic structure.

Whatever specific technique Jung used, the resulting data were then subjected to some of the most unusual interpretations to be found in any personality theory. As we saw earlier, Jung studied a variety of cultures and explored other approaches to understanding. On the basis of his massive knowledge of the ritualistic and symbolistic history of mankind, he interpreted the data he collected from his patients.

He found strong similarities between the fantasies and dreams of his patients and the archetypes, the ancient universal symbols and themes everpresent in the psyche. The ritualistic and mythological history of the species is acted out again in the life of every individual. Thus, to inquire into the psyche of an individual is to inquire into the psyche of all humanity.

Jung's Image of Human Nature

While perhaps not so optimistic about human nature as the social-psychological theorists, Jung nevertheless presented us with a more positive and hopeful image than Freud's. His air of optimism about human nature is apparent in his view of personality development. The individual is constantly trying to grow, to develop and expand, to improve and move forward. Human beings, individually and collectively, are forward looking and forward moving. Development, change, and progress do not stop in childhood, as Freud had assumed, but are never-ending processes. Thus, a person always has the hope of being better or more than he or she is at the moment.

The human species continues to improve, Jung argued. We 20th-century people, for all our faults, represent a significant step forward from our primitive ancestors. And Jung saw reason to hope that the 21st-century person would be an even more improved model. Jung's view is clearly forward, ahead, upward, and he applauds our psyche by calling it a "supreme realization," "an act of high courage," "the absolute affirmation of all that constitutes the individual."

Nevertheless, despite his basic optimism, Jung was concerned about a danger facing Western culture—the "sickness of dissociation" he called it. By placing too much emphasis on materialism, reason, and empirical science, we are losing sight of the unconscious. We must not abandon confidence and trust in the universal thought forms (archetypes) that form our heritage. We are, Jung feared, too one-sided.

Thus, his hopefulness is of a watchful, warning kind. "The world," he cautioned, "hangs on a thin thread, and that thread is the psyche of man . . . ."

A Final Commentary

Jung's highly complex, vastly unorthodox approach to the understanding of personality continues to draw a great deal of interest, or at least curiosity. He has written many books, received honorary degrees from Harvard and Oxford Universities, and is acknowledged as a potent influence on the work of historian Arnold Toynbee, social critic Philip Wylie, and others.

Yet, despite the honors and recognition heaped upon him by the intellectual community at large, his work has been, for the most part, either ignored or rejected by psychology. While it is true that the word-association test and the concepts of introversion-extraversion have been accepted, and his notion of self-realization is used (although in different ways) by other personality theorists, the bulk of Jung's work has not met with approval or endorsement.

Perhaps one reason for psychology's ignoring Jung has to do with the sheer difficulty of reading and understanding his concepts. Freud, Adler, and Fromm wrote with a clarity and smoothness of style that allow their books to be widely read. That is decidedly not the case with Jung, who did not write for the general public. It is often frustrating to read Jung, so beset are his books by apparent inconsistencies and contradictions. Jung himself once said of one of his books that it had been written "at top speed . . . without regard to time or method. I had to fling my material hastily together . . . . There was no opportunity to let my thoughts mature." How descriptive that may be of some of his other books is not known, but it helps explain how difficult it is to understand his writings.

Another criticism of Jung refers to the lack of systematization in his theory. It is difficult to focus on an overall and consistent system to evaluate. As mentioned, there are inconsistencies and contradictions in his work. Jung was quite clear on the matter of systematization; he was strongly against it and very distrustful of setting up an orthodoxy, an approved path to truth. "Thank God," he once wrote, "I am Jung and not a Jungian."

Jung's consistent appeal to the occult, the supernatural, mysticism, and religion is probably the source of most of the criticism directed at his theory. Evidence from mythology and alchemy is certainly not in favor in an era that argues that reason and science are the only legitimate approaches to knowledge and understanding. Critics charge that Jung accepted mythical and mystical occurrences in the reports of his patients as scientific evidence. Primarily for this reason, psychology has ignored his theory, rarely going beyond that charge to criticize his approach in more detail.

However, despite the mystical-religious content of his theory (indeed, perhaps because of it), Jungian analytical psychology has enjoyed a burst of growth, vitality, and acceptance in the United States in recent years. Many young people have found Jung highly congenial with their own interests in Eastern religions, existentialism, and mysticism, and their growing disaffection with materialism. Since the 1960s, formal training in Jungian analysis has been available in New York, San Francisco, and Los Angeles, and the number of applicants to these centers increases every year. Sales of Jung's books, particularly in college bookstores, are rising, and student interest has forced professors and writers in psychology and psychiatry to re-examine this novel theory of personality. Jung's views may be more relevant to these changing times than the ideas of others with whom we have dealt.

Such a resurgence of interest is strong praise for a man who began his professional work over seven decades ago.

Suggested Readings

Evans, R. I. *Conversations with Carl Jung and reactions from Ernest Jones.* Princeton, N.J.: Van Nostrand, 1964.

Fordham, F. *An introduction to Jung's psychology.* Baltimore, Md.: Penguin, 1953.

Jung, C. G. *Modern man in search of a soul.* New York: Harcourt Brace Jovanovich, 1933.

Jung, C. G. *Psychological types.* New York: Harcourt Brace Jovanovich, 1933.

Jung, C. G. *Memories, dreams, reflections.* New York: Pantheon, 1961.

McGuire, W. (Ed.). *The Freud/Jung letters.* Princeton, N.J.: Princeton University Press, 1974.

Marshall, I. N. The four functions: A conceptual analysis. *Journal of Analytical Psychology,* 1968, *13,* 1–32.

Read, H., Fordham, M., & Adler, G. *The collected works of C. G. Jung.* Princeton, N.J.: Princeton University Press, Bollingen series, 1953 to date. This is considered the definitive reference source for Jung's writings.

Selesnick, S. T.   C. G. Jung's contribution to psychoanalysis. *American Journal of Psychiatry,* 1963, *120,* 350–356.

Toynbee, A. The value of C. G. Jung's work for historians. *Journal of Analytical Psychology,* 1956, *1,* 193–194.

Henry A. Murray
Personology

8

For me, personality is an African jungle without boundaries.

—Henry A. Murray

Within the framework of what he called the *personological system,* Henry Murray has designed an approach to personality that is both eclectic and original. It contains partial and modified reflections of Freudian theory as well as highly original concepts and methods, drawn together effectively so as to be highly stimulating to others in the field of personality.

His formulations incorporate and develop his own diverse experiences in biochemistry and medicine, in psychoanalytic research and practice, and in his intensive study of literature, particularly of the writings of Herman Melville. As a result, his theory takes into account the unconscious as well as the conscious, mankind's past as well as present, and the influences of physiological as well as sociological forces.

The system places great emphasis on physiological functioning as it dictates to and directs the personality. As the center or seat of the personality, the brain functions to bring unity and coherence to behavior. Murray's interest in physiology is also evident in his concern (shared with Freud, among others) with tension reduction as a major force in behavior. Both on biological and psychological levels, he invokes the concept of tension reduction as a primary law of human functioning, although he elaborates on this basic and much-used notion.

The influence of Freudian psychoanalysis is seen in Murray's system in the importance of unconscious forces, the effect on adult behavior of experiences in infancy and childhood, and his incorporation of the notions of id, ego, and superego. However, while the imprint of Freud is clear, it is equally clear that Murray has given his unique interpretation to these psychological phenomena. Indeed, his deviations from classical psychoanalysis are so wide that his system must be classified with the neo-Freudians rather than with Freud.

Perhaps the two most distinctive features of his system are the highly sophisticated approach to human needs and the source of the data on which he constructed his theory. His carefully determined list of human needs, highly specific and differentiated, has been put to large-scale use in research, in the measurement or assessment of personality, and in clinical treatment. As for the source of his data, Murray, unlike any of the theorists discussed so far, studied not so much patients undergoing psychotherapy as presumably normal individuals (undergraduates at Harvard). Also, much of the data was derived from what could be considered the more empirically sound procedures of the laboratory rather than from case histories of people suffering (or enjoying) neuroses.

Because of his long affiliation with a major university (instead of relative isolation in a clinic or private practice), and because of certain appealing qualities of the man and his system, Murray gathered and trained a large number of psychologists, many of whom have since gained prominence in their own right and who have carried on at least some of his teachings. This extension and follow-through of his work is a gratification often denied to other theorists.

The Life of Murray (1893–   )

Neither poverty nor neurotic parents marked the childhood of Henry Murray. However, there were elements of Adlerian compensation for a physical defect, a supernormal sensitivity to the sufferings of other people, and a hint of rejection from his mother to ensure that his childhood would not be intolerably dull.

At any rate, Murray was certainly born to great wealth. He spent his childhood in a house in New York City on what is now the site of Rockefeller Center. Summers were spent on a Long Island beach. While still a child, he accompanied his parents on four long trips to Europe.

For the Adlerians among you, Murray's first memory is an interesting one. He calls it "the marrow-of-my-being memory." At about 4 years of age, he was looking at a picture of a sad-faced Queen sitting next to her equally sad-faced son. His mother told him that "it is the prospect of death that has made them sad." (It was the same kind of gloomy picture he later used in his famous Thematic Apperception Test).

Murray interpreted the memory as indicating the severance of emotional ties between himself and his mother, because she had abruptly weaned him when he was 2 months old and because she spent more time with his sister and brother. Thus, Murray was left with what he called "a limited, third-best portion" of his mother's affection.

Also at an early age, he became highly sensitized to the emotional problems and sufferings of others, due to his exposure to two neurotic aunts, one of whom was a hysteric while the other suffered intense bouts of depression.

As a child, Murray was afflicted with internal strabismus (crossed eyes). At the age of 9, in the dining room of his home, he was operated on to correct the condition. As a result, he no longer had internal strabismus; it was now external strabismus, thanks to a slip by the surgeon, and Murray was left without stereoscopic vision. After his surgery, no matter how hard he tried he was never able to play well at tennis, baseball, or any such game, because he could not focus both eyes on the ball. It was at that time that he began to stutter. He remained unaware of the visual defect until he was in medical school, when a physician asked him if he had had trouble playing games as a child.

These two defects—stuttering and ineptness at sports—created a need to compensate. When he played football, it had to be as quarterback (and he never stuttered when giving signals); he also took up boxing in school.

After Groton prep school, Murray went to Harvard. He majored in history and got mediocre grades because he devoted so much time to athletics. His career then followed a devious route to the study of personality. In 1919, he graduated from Columbia University Medical School as the top-ranking member of his class. Following that, he received an M. A. in biology from Columbia, then taught physiology for a short time at Harvard.

After serving a two-year internship in surgery at a New York hospital, he conducted biochemical research in embryology at the Rockefeller Institute for another two years. Then he went to England for further study and in 1927 received his Ph.D. in biochemistry from Cambridge University.

How, you may well wonder, did this circuitous educational path ever lead to psychology, particularly since he disliked the few psychology courses he had taken in college and medical school? Indeed, by the second lecture in his first psychology course, he had begun "looking for the nearest exit."

Murray's sensitivity to the sufferings of others has been noted. This was reinforced, during his internship, when he began to search for psychogenic factors in the backgrounds of his patients. Then, in 1923, he was greatly influenced by Jung's book *Psychological Types.* In 1927, he spent three weeks with Jung at his home in Switzerland. The two men spent every day together and, Murray wrote, "the great floodgates of the wonder-world swung open."

After another year at the Rockefeller Institute, Murray, in 1927, was offered an appointment by psychologist Morton Prince as an assistant in founding the Harvard Psychological Clinic, which was set up expressly to study personality. As a part of his own training, Murray underwent psychoanalysis and reported that one of his analysts became bored at the phlegmatic nature of his childhood and his lack of complexes.

In the late 1930s, Murray developed the well-known Thematic Apperception Test, one of the most widely used projective measures of personality in both research and treatment settings.[1] During World War II, he joined the army and became Director of Assessment for the Office of Strategic Services, screening candidates for the dangerous assignments of that "cloak-and-dagger" organization. In addition, for some 25 years Murray investigated the work of author Herman Melville, and in 1951 he published an analysis of the psychological meaning of the novel *Moby Dick.*

Murray stayed at Harvard until his retirement in 1962, conducting research, formulating his theory of personality, and training a large number of psychologists, many of whom achieved fame themselves in the study of personality. Well respected and recognized in psychology today, Murray has been awarded the Gold Medal Award of the American Psychological Foundation and the Distinguished Scientific Contribution Award from the American Psychological Association.

The Nature of Personality

Murray is careful to point out that his theory of *personology* (his term for the study of personality) is a tentative one, not intended to be a final, all-embracing formulation. Personology, he argues, is much too complex

[1]The test was published by Harvard University Press in 1943.

and new to allow for finality at this stage in our understanding. Rather, he views his theoretical and empirical work as "preparations for the scaffold of a comprehensive system." Nevertheless, there are certain basic principles that he apparently sees as solid foundation material for the scaffolding of his system.

The major principle in all of his work is the firm commitment to the notion that *psychological processes depend on physiological processes.* His pithy comment, "no brain, no personality," sums up this viewpoint nicely. Personality is rooted in the brain, for it is the individual's cerebral physiology that guides and governs the personality. For a simple example: a stroke or certain kinds of drugs can alter the functioning of the brain, and so the personality.

Everything on which the personality depends exists in the brain—feeling states, conscious and unconscious memories, and all of our beliefs, attitudes, fears, and values. The seat, therefore, of every aspect of personality is the brain. So important does Murray consider these controlling brain processes that he calls them *regnant* or ruling processes.

A second basic principle in Murray's system—he calls it an "all-embracing principle"—involves the importance to personality of altering the level of *need-induced tension* in the organism. Other theorists, as we have seen, also invoke the notion of tension reduction, but Murray goes a step beyond that in his formulation. It is true, he argues, that people try to reduce tension, whether of a physiological or psychological nature. However, Murray believes that it is not a completely tension-free state for which we strive. It is the process of reducing tension that is satisfying, rather than the condition of no tension.

Indeed, a tensionless state is a source of great distress, in Murray's view. Human beings have a constant need for excitement, activity, progress, movement, and zest—all of which involve increasing rather than decreasing tension. Thus, we generate tension in order to have the satisfaction of reducing it. Again, it is the act of reducing tensions that is most satisfying; Murray believes that a person's ideal state involves always having a certain level of tension to reduce.

A third general principle of Murray's system is the *longitudinal* nature of personality. The personality is always developing over time. "The history of the organism *is* the organism." Personality is, in a sense, constructed out of all the events occurring over the course of an individual's life. Therefore, the study of past events is of major importance in personality, and, in order to study those events, Murray introduced the notions of *serials* and *proceedings*. These are, in essence, the units of data used by the personologists and will be discussed in the "Techniques of Inquiry" section of this chapter.

There are additional elements and principles in Murray's view of the nature of personality. Personality is ever changing and progressing, not static or fixed; therefore, it cannot really be described. Something in such a constant state of flux cannot be pinned down sufficiently for description.

Murray also focuses on the uniqueness of each individual personality, while nonetheless recognizing certain similarities among all personalities. As he sees it, an individual human being is like every other person, like some other people, and like no other person.

The Divisions of Personality

As noted earlier, Murray's system is at least in part drawn from Freud's. Murray's analytic training was conducted along Freudian lines, and his own analysis was conducted by orthodox Freudians. The imprint of Freud is, therefore, visible in Murray's formulations, but he changed some of the Freudian teachings in the act of incorporating them into his own point of view.

When dealing with the basic divisions (a term he uses in place of *structure*) of the personality, Murray uses the Freudian terms id, superego, and ego, but his concepts are not what Freud had in mind.

Id

Like Freud, Murray believes that the id is the repository of all the innate impulsive tendencies. As such, the id provides both the energy for and the direction of behavior. Thus, the id is basically concerned with the motivational forces of the personality.

Murray's conception of the id is that it contains all the primitive, amoral, and lustful impulses that Freud described but that it also contains innate impulses that society considers acceptable and even desirable. For example, the id contains the tendencies to empathy, imitation and identification, forms of love other than lustful ones, and the tendency to master one's environment.

Virtually every aspect of the personality—what society considers good as well as what it considers evil—arises out of the id, which therefore provides all the energy, emotions, and needs to the individual. Murray also suggests that the strength or intensity of the id varies among individuals. Thus, one person can be seen to possess a much greater degree of zest and more intense appetites and emotions than someone else. Therefore, the problem of controlling and directing the id forces is not the same for all people; some have greater id energy to cope with.

Superego

Murray places great stress on the influencing force of the social environment, generally spoken of as culture, on personality. Agreeing with Freud, he defines the superego as the internalization of the culture's values, norms, and mores, by which rules the individual comes to evaluate and judge his or her own behavior and that of others. The form and substance of the superego are imposed on the child at an early age by parents and other authority figures, as Freud proposed.

However, Murray feels that other factors also shape the superego. He includes among them peer groups and the literature and mythology of the culture. He thus allows for influences beyond those of childhood experiences. The superego, therefore, is not rigidly crystallized by age 5 or so. Rather, it continues to develop throughout life, reflecting the greater complexity and sophistication of the experiences to which a person is exposed as he or she grows older.

Since, in Murray's conception, the id contains both good and bad forces—some that don't have to be suppressed—the superego is not constantly in conflict with the id, as is the case in Freud's view. It is true that the superego must try to thwart the bad (socially unacceptable) id impulses, but it also functions to determine when, where, and how an acceptable need should be expressed and which environmental objects may best satisfy it.

While the superego is developing, so is the *ego-ideal*. This ideal provides the individual with long-range goals for which to strive. The ego-ideal "portrays the person 'at his future best.' " This ideal self contains the individual's ambitions and aspirations. It may be congruent with the values of the superego or in conflict with them. In the latter case, the person may aspire to excellence in a kind of behavior that violates his or her internalized cultural norms, as exemplified by a person who aspires to be a master criminal.

Ego

The ego is the rational governor of the personality, which, as in Freud's view, tries to modify or delay the unacceptable impulses of the id. However, Murray considers the ego to do much more than "police" the personality. In its role as the central organizer of all behavior, the ego also consciously decides and wills the direction of positive behavior.

The ego thus assumes a much more active role in determining behavior than Freud had accorded it. Not merely the servant of the id, the ego directly and consciously plans courses of action; it seeks and makes opportunities for the gratifications that ensue from satisfying the positive id impulses. The ego is the spontaneously choosing free-willing "I" of the personality and includes the intellectual and perceptual abilities of the individual. The ego functions, then, not only to suppress id pleasure but also to foster and produce pleasure by organizing and directing the expression of the acceptable id impulses.

The ego is the arbiter between the id and the superego. As such, it may favor one over the other. For example, if the ego favors the id over the superego, it may direct the personality toward a life of crime. It can, of course, integrate both aspects of personality so that what a person wants to do (id) is in harmony with what society feels he or she should do (superego).

As you can see, there is opportunity in Murray's system for conflict between the id and superego. A strong ego can mediate effectively between the two, but a weak ego can leave the personality a battleground. The basic difference between Murray and Freud on this point is that Murray does not believe that this conflict is inevitable.

Motivation in Personality: Needs

Murray's most important contribution to both theory and research in personality is his concept of *need* to explain the motivation and direction of behavior. His extensive work in motivation, which forms the essence or core of his theory of personality, has provided the most elaborate and probably the most carefully determined categorization of needs to be found anywhere in psychology. It is important to note that this need concept is derived not from his own introspection or from case studies of patients undergoing treatment but from the intensive study of normal subjects.

A need, in Murray's view, is a hypothetical construct, "the occurrence of which is imagined in order to account for certain objective and subjective facts." It is physiologically based, in that it involves a physico-chemical force in the brain that organizes and directs all the intellectual and perceptual abilities of the individual.

Needs may arise from internal activities or processes such as hunger or thirst or from events in the environment. From whatever source, the need arouses a tension level that the organism tries to reduce by satisfying the need. As noted, the need both energizes and directs behavior; it activates behavior in the proper direction to satisfy the need.

Murray's original, now classic, research led to a list of 20 needs. Since then, Murray and his colleagues and students have offered some modifications, but the original 20 still represent the major needs in his system. They are not listed in any order of priority or importance.

dominance (n Dom)
> To control one's human environment. To influence or direct the behavior of others by suggestion, seduction, persuasion, or command. To dissuade, restrain, or prohibit.

deference (n Def)
> To admire or support a superior other. To praise, honor, or eulogize. To emulate an exemplar. To conform to custom.

autonomy (n Auto)
> To resist coercion and restriction. To be independent and free to act according to impulse. To defy conventions. To avoid or quit activities prescribed by domineering authorities.

aggression (n Agg)
> To overcome opposition forcefully. To fight. To revenge an injury. To oppose forcefully or punish. To deprecate and slander and to belittle or ridicule maliciously.

abasement (n Aba)
> To submit passively to external force. To accept injury, blame, criticism, punishment. To surrender and to admit inferiority, error, wrongdoing, or defeat. To seek and enjoy pain, punishment, illness, and misfortune.

achievement (n Ach)
> To accomplish something difficult, overcome obstacles, and attain a high standard. To rival and surpass others and to master, manipulate, or organize physical objects, human beings, or ideas.

sentience (n Sen)
> To seek and enjoy sensuous impressions.

exhibition (n Exh)
> To make an impression. To be seen and heard. To excite, amaze, fascinate, entertain, shock, intrigue, amuse, or entice.

play (n Play)
> To act for fun without further purpose. To laugh and make a joke of everything. To devote free time to sports, dancing, drinking, parties, cards.

affiliation (n Aff)
> To draw near and enjoyably cooperate with an allied other—one who resembles the subject or who likes the subject. To please and win affection of a cathected other. To adhere and remain loyal to a friend.

rejection (n Rej)
> To separate oneself from a negatively cathected other. To exclude, abandon, expel, or remain indifferent to an inferior other.

succorance (n Suc)
> To have one's needs gratified by the sympathetic aid of an allied

other. To always have a supporter. To be nursed, supported,
sustained, surrounded, protected, indulged, forgiven, or consoled.

nurturance (n Nur)

To give sympathy and gratify the needs of a helpless other—an infant
or any object that is weak, disabled, tired, inexperienced, infirm,
defeated, humiliated, lonely, dejected, sick, or mentally confused. To
feed, help, support, console, protect, comfort, nurse, or heal.

infavoidance (n Inf)

To avoid humiliation. To quit embarrassing situations or to avoid
conditions which may lead to belittlement. To refrain from action
because of the fear of failure.

defendance (n Dfd)

To defend the self against assault, criticism, and blame. To conceal
or justify a misdeed, failure, or humiliation.

counteraction (n Cnt)

To master or make up for a failure by restriving. To obliterate a
humiliation by resumed action. To overcome a weakness, to repress
fear. To maintain self-respect and pride on a high level.

harmavoidance (n Harm)

To avoid pain, physical injury, illness, and death. To escape from
a dangerous situation. To take precautionary measures.

order (n Ord)

To put things in order. To achieve cleanliness, arrangement,
organization, balance, neatness, tidiness, and precision.

understanding (n Und)

To ask or to answer general questions. To be interested in theory,
to analyze events and generalize.

sex (n Sex)

To form and further an erotic relationship. To have sexual
intercourse.

(As you may have gathered, Murray liked to list things and to coin
new terms!)

Murray does not suggest that all these needs exist in everyone. There
are some people who may experience all of them, at least over the course
of a lifetime, but there are other people who never experience some of
the needs. Certain of these needs are supportive of or congruent with
others, while some are in opposition to other needs. In recognition of
this, Murray has pointed out that there are five ways of categorizing
needs.

Ways of Categorizing Needs

The first categorization of needs is the *primary* (or viscerogenic) and
secondary (or psychogenic) dichotomy. Primary needs arise from internal
body processes and include the needs for satisfactions vital to survival

—air, water, food, defecation, harmavoidance—as well as some needs that do not have to be satisfied for an individual's survival, such as sex and sentience.

The secondary or psychogenic needs arise indirectly from primary needs (in a way not made clear by Murray) but have no specifiable origins within the body. They are called secondary not because they are less important to the organism but because they develop after the primary needs. They are concerned with mental and emotional satisfactions and include most of the needs listed earlier, such as achievement, dominance, affiliation, and so on.

Another way of categorizing needs is in terms of *focal* versus *diffuse*. This distinction has to do with the number of objects that can serve to satisfy the need. A focal need can be satisfied by only one or at best a few goal objects, while a diffuse need can be satisfied by many objects.

The third categorization is into *proactive* and *reactive* types of needs. A reactive need involves a response to something specific in the environment, in that the need appears only when that object appears. Harmavoidance, for example, appears only when a threatening object is present. Ideally, it exists only when there is some harm to avoid.

Proactive needs, on the other hand, do not depend on the presence of any particular object in the environment. They are spontaneous needs that call forth appropriate behavior whenever they are aroused, independent of the environment. A person who is hungry, for example, looks for food. He or she does not simply wait to react when an appropriate stimulus, such as an ad for a hamburger, is presented.

Manifest and *latent* needs are the fourth type of classification. Manifest needs are expressed overtly because society approves of their expression and may even reward them. In our society, achievement is such a need; its expression brings social approval.

Other needs, however, can only be expressed covertly, in fantasies or dreams or through symbolism. Aggression, for example, in a society that represses its expression, can be displayed only covertly and so remains latent.

The fifth categorization involves the *effect, process,* and *modal-activity* types of needs. Effect needs lead to or cause an effect; that is, they lead directly and immediately to an object. The individual may derive a great deal of pleasure out of the various activities that go to make up the need-satisfying behavior. Murray calls this *sheer function pleasure* or process activity and defines it as the pleasure derived from doing something just for the sake of doing it.

Finally, there is often a need beyond sheer function pleasure. Not content with merely doing something, simply performing an act, there is pleasure to be derived from doing it extremely well. The behavior is now not satisfying when it is merely performed; it must be performed well. Murray calls this the modal need because pleasure derives from the mode of performance of some behavior.

Additional Aspects of Needs

Needs can differ greatly in terms of the urgency or insistence with which they impel behavior, a characteristic that Murray refers to as a need's *prepotency*. If, for example, the needs for air and water are not satisfied, they can become the most insistent of needs and totally dominate behavior. At other times, if the primary needs are satisfied, the need for aggression may be strongest.

Some needs, though not identical, may be complementary, so that they can be satisfied by one behavior or one set of behaviors. Murray calls this a *fusion* of needs. For example, by acquiring fame and wealth through one's work, the achievement, dominance, and autonomy needs may all be satisfied.

The concept of *subsidiation* refers to a situation in which one need is activated to aid in the satisfaction of another need. For example, to satisfy the affiliation need by joining and mixing with others, it may be necessary to act deferentially toward others (thus invoking the deference need). The deference need would thus be subsidiary to the affiliation need.

Murray recognized that environmental objects and events in childhood can strongly influence the development of specific needs and, later in life, can trigger or call forth these needs. He called this influence *press*, because the object or event presses or pressures the individual in a certain way.

Of course, as you know, we often perceive the world around us in subjective terms; that is, our image of objects and events does not always coincide with reality. Thus, the environmental influence of press may be perceived subjectively or objectively. Objectively perceived pressure—that which directly reflects reality—is called *alpha press*, while subjectively perceived and interpreted pressure is called *beta press*.

Press also has the power to attract or repel an individual; it can be either positive or negative in its emotional tone. Murray used Freud's term *cathexis* to describe this characteristic of press. Thus, if a person is attracted to money, he or she is said to be positively cathected to it.

Because of the ever-present possibility of interaction between need and press, Murray introduced still another concept: *thema*. The thema —"the dynamical structure of an event"—is an amalgamation of both press and need, combining the nature of the environment and of the person. Largely unconscious, the thema relates needs and presses into a single pattern, the function of which is to give coherence to an individual's behavior. The pattern of the thema is formed through early childhood experience and comes to be a powerful force in an individual's personality. The pattern brings unity and order to behavior and so is also called a *unity-thema.*

In his more recent work, Murray introduced another concept, *value-vector,* which is intended to substitute for his earlier concept of need. Vector refers to the direction shown by behavior and the intensity of the desire bringing about the behavior. Some of the vectors listed by Murray are acquisition, avoidance, construction, destruction, and expulsion.

Value refers to the ideals an individual holds, including intellectual, ideological, and aesthetic ideals. In working with an individual, Murray gathers information on what is worthwhile to that person (value) and how he or she behaves in relation to these values (vector) and plots them in the rows and columns of a matrix. The concept, still being developed, is intended to provide specific objective descriptions of behavior to replace the more vague theoretical descriptions arising from the use of the need and press concepts.

The Development of Personality

Murray takes a longitudinal approach to personality, emphasizing the developmental history of the individual. His approach to personality development draws upon the traditional Freudian view, which he elaborates and extends. Like Freud, he focuses on events and experiences of early childhood and the patterns of behavior that are formed during these crucial years. Murray divides childhood into five stages, each of which is characterized by a pleasurable condition that is inevitably terminated by the demands of society. Each of these stages leaves its mark on personality in the form of *complexes,* which are patterns, formed from the imprints of the various stages, which unconsciously direct the individual's later development.

Everyone develops these five complexes, according to Murray, because everyone passes through the same five stages of development. There is, therefore, nothing abnormal about them, except when they are carried to extreme. When they are manifested in the extreme, the person remains more or less fixated at one level of development. His or her personality then is unable to develop spontaneity and flexibility, and the formation of the ego and superego are interfered with.

The five pleasurable conditions or stages of childhood and their related complexes are:

1. the secure existence within the womb. . . . . .claustral complex
2. the sensuous enjoyment of sucking
   nourishment while being held . . . . .oral complex
3. the pleasure resulting from
   defecation . . . . .anal complex
4. the pleasure accompanying urination . . . . .urethral complex
5. genital pleasures. . . . . .castration complex

Claustral Complex

As you no doubt remember, life within the womb is secure, serene, and highly dependent, a condition that we may occasionally wish to be able to reinstate. In its simplest form, this complex may be manifested by a desire to be in small, warm, dark places that are safe and secluded. It may mean remaining under the bedcovers in the morning, having a soundproof den or secret hiding place, living in a monastary or on an island, or enjoying a boat or a limousine.

This wish to return to womblike conditions is, however, only one of three forms the claustral complex may take. The complex can also center on the feeling of helplessness and lack of support in the womb which may cause the person to fear open spaces, falling, drowning, fires, earthquakes, or any situation of change and novelty.

The third claustral complex is actually an anticlaustral complex centering around fear of suffocation and confinement. Murray calls it the *egression* complex; it manifests itself in a preference for wide open spaces and fresh air and for movement, change, and novelty. It may also manifest itself in claustrophobia.

Oral Complex

There are also three varieties of oral complex. The *oral succorance* complex is a combination of mouth activities, passive tendencies, and the need to be supported and protected. The behavioral manifestations of this complex include sucking, kissing, eating, drinking, and a "hunger" for affection, sympathy, protection, and love. The *oral aggression* complex combines oral and aggressive activities in the form of biting, spitting, or shouting, or in verbal aggression such as sarcasm. The behavior involved in the *oral rejection* complex includes vomiting, being picky about food, eating little, fearing oral contamination (as from kissing), and needing seclusion.

Anal Complex

There are two anal complexes, involving the only two forms of activity one can practice anally—rejecting or retaining. In the *anal ejection* complex there is a preoccupation with defecation, including anal humor, and an interest in feces or feces-like material (dirt, mud, plaster, or clay). Aggression often becomes a part of this complex and is manifested in dropping and throwing things, firing guns, or setting off explosives. This type of person is usually dirty and disorganized. The *anal retention* complex manifests itself in retentive kinds of behavior—accumulating, saving, and collecting things—and in cleanliness, neatness, and orderliness.

Urethral Complex

This complex is unique to Murray's system and is associated with excessive ambition, a distorted sense of self-esteem, a history of bedwetting, and a strong self-love. It is also called the Icarus complex, after the mythical Greek figure who flew so close to the sun that the wax holding his wings together melted. Like Icarus, the person with this complex aims too high, and his or her dreams are shattered by failure.

Castration Complex

Murray disagrees with Freud's contention that fear of castration is the core of much adult anxiety. He interprets the complex in narrower and more literal fashion as simply "the fantasy that the penis might be cut off." Murray believes such a fear grows out of childhood masturbation and the parental punishment that may have accompanied it.

Techniques of Inquiry

Murray's techniques of gathering data are unique relative to the other personality theorists discussed. Rather than studying the abnormal personality, using strictly therapeutic tools such as psychoanalysis, he studied the more normal personality, using a variety of techniques and devices.

His pioneering program of research, so unlike anything ever before conducted, collected great masses of data from 51 male Harvard undergraduates, who were studied intensively for a period of six months. The subjects were interviewed a number of times and given a variety of tests, questionnaires, and ratings on their behavior covering, among other things, childhood memories, family relations, sexual development, sensorimotor learning, ethical standards, and social interaction.

The subjects were tested, interviewed, and studied by a staff of 28 scientists, including psychiatrists, psychologists, and anthropologists. Thus, each person was observed by specialists with different trainings and backgrounds using different techniques, in much the same way, in principle, that a medical diagnosis is conducted.

Each observer made his own diagnosis of a subject. This was then presented to a committee, which Murray called the Diagnostic Council, for a final evaluation. The council consisted of the five most experienced staff members. It reviewed all the evidence on each subject to arrive at a final diagnosis by the standard committee procedure of discussion and vote. The final evaluation or diagnosis was reached by majority vote (though apparently Murray gave his own rating more weight).

So much data was collected on each subject's life that it was necessary to divide it into different time intervals or segments. The basic unit or temporal segment of behavior is the *proceeding*, a period of time in which an important pattern of behavior is carried through from beginning to end. A proceeding always involves some interaction between the person and other people or objects in the environment. However, this interaction may occur in fantasy as well as in reality. The imagined interaction is called an *internal* proceeding, while a real interaction is called an *external* proceeding.

Proceedings are often linked together, not necessarily in time but in function. For example, on Monday a man may meet a woman and ask her for a date (an external proceeding). He may daydream about her at varying periods through the week (an internal proceeding) and may get a haircut (if he's over 30) and wash his car or himself (external proceedings) in preparation for the date. Each of those acts, including the imaginary one, is a proceeding, but taken together—as they should be, since they are related to the same function or purpose—they are called a *serial*. To be more precise, a serial is "a directionally organized intermittent succession of proceedings."

Much more lasting and, in the long run, more important than the findings of Murray's research program are the methods of assessing personality that he developed. Certainly the best-known of these techniques is the Thematic Apperception Test (TAT), which has come to be almost as widely used as the Rorschach Inkblot Test, another of the projective techniques.

Figure 8.1 A picture from the Thematic Apperception Test. From *Thematic Apperception Test: Manual,* by H. A. Murray (Harvard University Press, 1943). Reprinted by permission of the President and Fellows of Harvard College.

The TAT has found enormous application in both research and diagnostic work. It is widely used in practice and has generated a great deal of research on virtually every aspect of human behavior, from the most esoteric academic inquiry to the assessment of the behavior of consumers in the marketplace. (Remember, however, that the success of this test does not automatically reflect success on his theory of personality. It is a technique of inquiry and not the essence of his theoretical position.)

One of Murray's needs—achievement (n Ach)—has been the subject of exhaustive research, primarily directed by David McClelland (see Chapter 17). The need for affiliation has also been a popular subject for study. Fifteen of Murray's needs have been incorporated in a well-known objective test of personality, the Edwards Personal Preference Schedule, used in a variety of settings.

Thus, it is clear that some aspects of Murray's work have been highly productive in stimulating research in personality assessment.

Murray's Image of Human Nature

Murray's view of human nature is fundamentally hopeful and positive. He has been vocal in his criticism of those parts of psychology that project a negative and demeaning image of human beings. He argues that, with our vast powers of creativity, imagination, and reason, we are capable of solving any problem facing us. In line with these beliefs, Murray has been much involved in efforts to ameliorate social and personal problems. He has been concerned with both the intimate two-person level (as in marriage) and the broad cultural level, and he has advocated the abolition of war and the creation of a unified global state.

Humanity's orientation, in Murray's view, is largely toward the future. While he recognizes the imprint of past experiences on present behavior, he does not envision us as wholly captives of our past. We have the continuing capability to grow and develop; indeed, such growth is a natural and inevitable concomitant of being a human being. We can change through our own rational and creative abilities, and if we as individuals can change, we collectively can change the social system in which we live.

A Final Commentary

Murray is careful to note that he considers his personological system to be still in the embryonic and evolving stages. It is not, in his view, a finished or complete system by any means. This aspect of his system—its still-developing nature—must be kept in mind when we consider the criticisms directed against it. We cannot altogether condemn a building as ugly or useless, or praise it as beautiful and functional, when only the scaffolding is in place.

One problem in both the development and evaluation of Murray's position is that only some portions of it have been published. His ingenuity and full range of thought, therefore, are revealed only in limited amounts for careful study. His influence apparently has been most keenly felt by those who have worked with him—by those who have had access to his wide-ranging speculations, which he revealed in almost casual conversation. While some, perhaps many, of these ideas have been followed up by his students and colleagues, others have been lost to public scrutiny.

There is also the fact that what he has published is difficult to read, the language being stiff, formal, and highly technical. Certainly this has restricted the dissemination of his ideas to the educated public and even to many professionals.

While his work has been inspirational of much research, that research has been conducted, for the most part, on limited aspects of the theory, such as the achievement and affiliation needs, and on techniques devised to assess personality. Thus, only certain aspects of his theory have been put to experimental test, not the theory as a whole. Of course, by now you will recognize that this criticism is not unique to Murray's theory.

Specific aspects of his work have been criticized, beginning with his method of research. It is argued that, while the Diagnostic Council is laudably democratic, it is hardly scientific. To reach a scientific conclusion by majority rule may not be the most objective procedure.

Other questions asked of his system relate to the concepts of proceedings and serials. It is argued that these temporal units are too vaguely defined to be identified or delimited precisely. Just what constitutes a "significant pattern of behavior"? What happens to those judged not significant? How long is a proceeding? These are some of the questions not yet satisfactorily answered.

It is argued by some that Murray's classification of needs is overly complex and that there is a great deal of overlap among the needs. It is also unclear how the needs relate to other aspects of the personality and how the needs develop within an individual.

However complex his classification of needs may be, there is no denying the considerable impact the concept has had on personality research, particularly that devoted to the construction of psychological tests. In more theoretical terms, his concept of need and the importance he placed on motivation have influenced greatly the study of personality.

Overall, it is perhaps safe to say that his innovations in technique (such as the TAT), his influence on methods of assessing personality, and the personal impact he made on at least two generations of personology researchers during their years at Harvard have had a more lasting effect than his theoretical system. Such points of influence are considerable, as evidenced by his awards, from both the American Psychological Association and the American Psychological Foundation, given in recognition of his important contributions to the study of personality.

Suggested Readings

Atkinson, J. W. (Ed.). *Motives in fantasy, action, and society.* Princeton, N. J.: Van Nostrand, 1958.

Hall, M. H. A conversation with Henry A. Murray. *Psychology Today,* 1968, 4, 56–63.

Maddi, S. R. Humanistic psychology: Allport and Murray. In J. Wepman & R. Heine (Eds.), *Concepts of personality*. Chicago: Aldine, 1963. Pp. 162–205.

Murray, H. A. *Explorations in personality*. New York: Oxford University Press, 1938.

Murray, H. A. Preparations for the scaffold of a comprehensive system. In S. Koch (Ed.), *Psychology: A study of a science* (Vol. 3). New York: McGraw-Hill, 1959. Pp. 7–54.

Murray, H. A. Autobiography. In E. G. Boring & G. Lindzey (Eds.), *History of psychology in autobiography* (Vol. 5). New York: Appleton-Century-Crofts, 1967. Pp. 283–310.

Murray, H. A. *Encounter with psychology*. San Francisco: Jossey-Bass, 1969.

Murray, H. A., & Kluckhohn, C. Outline of a conception of personality. In C. Kluckhohn, H. A. Murray, & D. M. Schneider (Eds.), *Personality in nature, society, and culture* (2nd ed.). New York: Knopf, 1953. Pp. 3–52.

Erik Erikson

The personality is engaged with the hazards of existence continuously, even as the body's metabolism copes with decay.

—Erik Erikson

The term *identity crisis* has come to be a widely used (and abused) concept familiar to the American public consciousness. The man who identified and refined the notion, and who built a personality theory at least partially around it, is considered by some to be among the most influential psychoanalysts today. His books sell hundreds of thousands of copies and, in 1970, his picture appeared on the covers of both *Newsweek* and *The New York Times Magazine*—a most unusual sign of recognition for a personality theorist. In the same year, his book on the origins of militant nonviolence (*Gandhi's Truth*) was awarded a Pulitzer Prize. It is interesting that he has achieved such prominence and influence without an M.D. or a Ph.D. in psychology; indeed, he has no university degree at all.

Erik Erikson, trained in the Freudian tradition (by Freud's daughter, Anna), has developed an approach to personality that moves considerably beyond Freud, while nevertheless maintaining much of the core of Freud's thought. He has been called a "nondogmatic emancipated Freudian" because of the significant innovations he has offered to psychoanalysis.

What Erikson has done in extending Freud's theory is basically twofold. First, he has elaborated upon Freud's stages of development. Where Freud emphasized childhood and said that the personality is firmly shaped by the age of 5 or so, Erikson believes that personality continues to develop throughout the life span, moving through a series of eight crucial developmental stages.

Each of these stages, from infancy to old age, constitutes a crisis that must be resolved. At each stage there is a conflict, centering around an adaptive and a maladaptive means of dealing with the problems of that period. Failure at any one stage can lead to stress and anxiety and can retard development at a later stage.

The second extension of Freudian doctrine is Erikson's recognition of the impact of culture, society, and history on the shaping of the personality. People are not ruled entirely by biological forces at work in childhood. While these forces are important, they are far from being the whole explanation of the development of personality.

Erikson's is a developmental theory of personality, and the search for an ego identity is its central theme.

The Life of Erikson (1902–   )

Not surprisingly, the man who gave us the concept of identity crisis went through several such crises, each quite intense, in his early years. Erikson was born in Frankfurt, Germany, to Danish parents. His father had left before the child was born, and the young Erikson moved with his mother to Karlsruhe, where, three years later, his mother married his pediatrician, Dr. Theodore Homburger. Erikson was given his stepfather's last name. He was not told for some years that Homburger was not really his father. Erikson later called this an act of "loving deceit."

Another crisis of identity began when he was old enough for school. He considered himself a German, despite his Danish parentage, but his German classmates rejected him because he was Jewish. At the same time, his Jewish peers rejected him because of his tall, blond, Aryan appearance. At the synagogue, he was called "the goy."

He did not do well in school, achieving only mediocre grades. He did, however, evidence some talent for art, and when he graduated from high school he used that ability as a vehicle to try to find himself—that is, to establish an identity.

He became a dropout from society for a while and wandered throughout Germany and Italy, reading, recording his thoughts in a notebook, and observing the life around him. He described himself during that time as being morbidly sensitive and hovering on the vague borderline between psychosis and neurosis. He studied for brief periods at two art schools and had an exhibition in Munich, but, each time, he left formal training to resume his wandering.

In 1927, at the age of 25, he was invited to come to Vienna to teach at a small school, established for the children of Sigmund Freud's patients and friends. (Many of Freud's patients came from other parts of the world and, being wealthy, settled in Vienna with their families for the duration of their analysis.)

It was then that Erikson's professional career began. During the next years, he received his training in psychoanalysis; his own analysis was conducted by Anna Freud. She had a special interest in psychoanalysis of children, and this became Erikson's specialty. In 1933, when he finished his training, he became a member of the famed Vienna Psychoanalytic Institute. He continued to teach during his analysis and also studied the Montessori method of teaching, in which he was certified.

During his years in Vienna, he married a Canadian woman and, recognizing the new Nazi menace from neighboring Germany, in 1933 they emigrated, first to Denmark for a brief period and then to the United States. They settled in Boston, where Erikson set up a private practice specializing in the treatment of children.

The years in Boston were very productive. Erikson served on the staff of Henry Murray's clinic at Harvard (in the study of normal undergraduates discussed in Chapter 8) and also worked in a guidance center for emotionally disturbed delinquents and in Massachusetts General Hospital. During those years, he was fortunate in having contact with anthropologists Ruth Benedict and Margaret Mead and Gestalt psychologist Kurt Lewin, in addition to Henry Murray.

He began to study for a Ph.D. in psychology at Harvard but quit after a few months because of disaffection with a formal program of academic study. In 1936, he was invited to the Institute of Human Relations at Yale, where he continued his work with both normal and troubled children and also taught at the medical school. Two years later, Erikson and a Yale anthropologist studied methods of child rearing among the Sioux Indians of South Dakota. This study marked his initial focus on the influence of culture on the events of childhood, a concern that was to influence much of his later professional work.

He moved to San Francisco in 1939 to establish another private practice and to study the development of normal children at the Institute of Child Welfare at Berkeley. Unlike most psychoanalysts, Erikson was much concerned that his experience not be limited to the emotionally disturbed or to children of only one culture. In 1943, he investigated the life of another Indian tribe, the Yurok of Northern California.

In his contact with these two American Indian tribes, Erikson began to notice symptoms that could not be explained by orthodox Freudian theory. The symptoms revolved around a sense of uprootedness from one's cultural traditions and resulted in the lack of a clear self-image or identity. This phenomenon, which he initially called *identity confusion*, was observed also in the emotionally disturbed veterans with whom Erikson worked during and after World War II. He became convinced that the men were not suffering from repressed conflicts but rather from confusion as a result of traumatic war experiences and of being uprooted from their culture. Again, Erikson observed a confusion of identity—a confusion on the part of the veterans about just who and what they were.

Erikson left Berkeley in 1950 because he refused to sign a state loyalty oath and moved to Stockbridge, Massachusetts. There he worked at the Austin Riggs Center, a treatment center for disturbed adolescents. In 1960, he returned to Harvard, where he taught a graduate seminar and an extremely popular undergraduate course, entitled "The Human Life Cycle," until his retirement in 1970.

His strong interest in the role of history as it affects youth—that is, the impact of the times on youth—has resulted in a number of psycho-historical studies, on such figures as Adolf Hitler, Maxim Gorky, and Martin Luther. His famous study of the great 20th-century leader of India, Mahatma Gandhi, dealing with nonviolence as a technique for bringing about social change, examined an identity crisis that occurred at a later stage in life.

At this writing, Erikson remains extremely productive. In 1973, he published *In Search of Common Ground*, a dialogue between himself and black activist Huey P. Newton. His primary activity now is continued psychohistorical analyses to demonstrate the role of identity confusion in the lives of influential people.

The Stages of Psychosocial Development

As noted earlier, Erikson has built upon and elaborated Freud's psychosexual stages of development and carried his own developmental theory through the entire life span of the individual. The growth of the personality is divided into eight stages or "ages of man," as he calls them. The first four are somewhat similar to Freud's oral, anal, phallic, and latency stages of growth, but Erikson focuses much more on the psychosocial correlates of these stages than on biological ones, as was the case with Freud.

Erikson sees human development in terms of a series of conflicts; the personality must cope with a particular conflict at each stage. Each conflict, existing potentially at birth, rises to prominence only at a definite stage in development, when the environment makes certain demands on the individual. Erikson calls this encounter or confrontation with the environment a *crisis*. The crisis involves a marked shift in perspective for the individual. It is a time of vulnerability as well as of new strengths, of a shifting of instinctual energy from one focus to another, and of new environmental demands.

Each stage of development, then, involves a turning point—a change in behavior and personality in which the individual is faced with a choice between two ways of coping: a maladaptive and negative way or an adaptive and positive way. Only as each crisis is positively resolved does the personality manifest a normal development with the strength to confront the next critical stage of development.

We shall discuss the nature of each of these eight ages of human beings, but, for the moment, let us take a brief overview of the entire developmental process. The left column below shows each stage, the middle column the approximate years in which it occurs, and the right column the contrasting ways of adapting. As you can see, the ages of the last three stages may vary considerably with the individual.

1. oral-sensory   birth–1 year   trust versus mistrust
2. muscular-anal   1–3 years   autonomy versus doubt, shame
3. locomotor-genital   3–5 years   initiative versus guilt
4. latency   6–11 years   industry versus inferiority
5. adolescence   12–18 years   identity versus role confusion
6. young adulthood   19–35 years   intimacy versus isolation
7. adulthood   35–50 years   generativity versus stagnation
8. maturity   50+ years   ego integrity versus despair

Since it is the ways of coping that are vital to the shaping of the personality, we shall use these as headings in discussing Erikson's developmental stages.

Trust versus Mistrust

The oral-sensory stage of development, paralleling Freud's oral stage, occurs at the time of greatest helplessness in the life of the individual. The infant is totally dependent on someone else for survival, security, and affection, and that someone else is usually the mother.

During this stage, the mouth is of vital importance. Erikson noted that the infant "lives through, and loves with, his mouth." The relationship between the infant and its world is not, however, exclusively a biological one. It is also very much a social relationship—an interaction between mother and infant—which will determine the infant's later outlook on all the world. Specifically, it will determine whether he or she will view the world with an attitude of trust or of mistrust.

If the mother is highly responsive to the baby's physical needs and is affectionate, providing ample love and security, then the infant will begin to trust the world around him or her. It has been, after all, good to the infant so far. The sense of basic trust that has thus arisen characterizes the baby's attitude toward himself or herself as well as toward others. As a result of the appropriate and affectionate responsiveness of the mother, the infant learns to expect a degree of "consistency, continuity, and sameness" from the world; this expectation provides at least the beginning of a sense of ego identity. Establishing lasting patterns for the solution of the basic trust versus mistrust conflict is the initial task of the ego. These patterns depend, as we have seen, on the quality (more than on the absolute quantity) of maternal care. From this beginning ego and sense of basic trust will later develop a sense of being "all right"—a contentment and security with being oneself and a trust of oneself and others.

If, on the other hand, the mother is rejecting, inattentive, or inconsistent in her behavior, the infant, quite understandably, develops an attitude of mistrust toward the world around him or her. The individual will be suspicious, fearful, and anxious in his or her later relations with everyone.

Thus, the pattern of trust or mistrust as a dimension of personality is set in infancy. However, the problem may appear again at a later stage in life. For example, an ideal mother-infant relationship may produce a high level of trust in a child, but this sense of trust may be destroyed if the mother suddenly leaves (through death or divorce). In that case, mistrust can develop, even though the earlier attitude was one of trust. Similarly, mistrust may be overcome later in life through the behavior of a very loving and patient teacher or friend.

You can see why this stage of development is called psychosocial: as with all the later stages, it depends on social relationships much more than on biological or instinctual drives.

Autonomy versus Doubt, Shame

During the second and third years of life (Freud's anal stage), children rapidly develop a variety of physical and mental abilities. For the first time, they are able to do many things for themselves; they begin to walk, climb, push, pull, hold on to an object or let it go, and communicate more effectively. Children take great pride in these newly developing skills and abilities and want to do as many things for themselves as possible.

Of all these new abilities, Erikson places particular stress on those involving holding on and letting go; he considers these behaviors prototypes of later conflicting behavior and attitudes. For example, holding on can be done in a loving and benign fashion or in a hostile and destructive way. Similarly, letting go can become a venting of destructive rage or it can become a relaxed passivity, as exemplified by the phrase "let it pass." The important point here is that the child, for the first time, is able to exercise some degree of choice.

Thus, children experience their "autonomous will." Although still dependent on their parents, they begin to see themselves as persons or forces in their own right. They want to exercise will, and the key question becomes this: to what extent will the world, in the form of the parents, allow them to do what they are now capable of doing at their own pace and time?

There is a clash of wills here between parent and child, and a major test is the matter of toilet training, the first instance of a societal regulation of an instinctive need. Do the parents let the child proceed at his or her own pace, or do they become impatient and usurp the child's free will by forcing the training and showing impatience and anger when the child doesn't behave "correctly"? This situation is illustrative of a number of such clashes of will at this time.

When children are not allowed to exercise their will, Erikson believes, they develop a feeling of shame in their relations with others and a sense of doubt about themselves. The *will to be oneself* has been frustrated and thwarted. Thus, while the anal region may be a focus of this stage, the form and structure of the potential conflict is not so much biological as psychosocial.

Initiative versus Guilt

The third stage of development, occurring in ages 3 to 5, is analogous to the phallic stage in Freud's system. The child's motor and mental abilities have become more fully developed. He or she is able to do more things and strongly wants to do so; his or her initiative has grown strong.

Another development at this stage—an initiative in fantasy form—is the child's desire to possess the parent of the opposite sex, with an attendant feeling of rivalry with the parent of the same sex.

The key question is the same as at the earlier stages: how will the parents react to these new self-initiated activities and fantasies? If they punish the child and otherwise inhibit these initiatives, if they cause him or her to feel that the new initiatives are "bad," the child will develop guilt feelings. The guilt will persist and color all self-initiated activities in later life.

With regard to the Oedipal relationship, the child must, of course, fail, but, if the parents guide this particular failure in initiative in a loving and understanding manner, the child will be able to acquire a moral sense of what is permissible behavior and what is not. His or her initiative can be guided or channeled toward more realistic and societally sanctioned goals. The child is then on the way to developing an adult sense of responsibility and morality—in other words, a superego.

Industry versus Inferiority

The fourth stage, corresponding to Freud's latency stage (a time of relative quiet), begins when the child starts school and continues through about age 11. The child's world is considerably broadened at this time, as he or she is exposed to new influences and pressures outside the home. This does not mean, however, that parental influences are suddenly diminished; far from it. The child's experiences at home can greatly color the experiences in his or her new environment. At home and at school, the child begins to learn to work—to be industrious.

In both the home and the school, the child's new powers of deductive reasoning and ability to play by rules (rather than at random), lead to the deliberate development and refinement of skills that are displayed in building things. Usually, the boy of this age makes tree houses or model airplanes and the girl cooks and sews—both serious efforts to complete a task through concentrated attention, diligence, and persistence. Erikson noted: "the *fundamentals of technology* are developed, as the child becomes ready to handle the utensils, the tools, and the weapons used by the big people."

How well children perceive themselves to be developing these new skills is determined in large part by the attitudes and behavior of their parents and teachers. If their efforts are ridiculed, scolded, or rejected, they are highly likely to develop feelings of inadequacy and inferiority. Constructive and instructive praise and reinforcement, on the other hand, foster childrens' feelings of competence in their industry, which encourages them to strive for further development.

These first four childhood stages are, as noted, psychosocial versions of Freud's psychosexual stages. There is another characteristic that these stages share. The outcome of each crisis is dependent more on other people than on oneself—a function more of what is done to the child than of what the child does. Although there certainly is increasing independence from birth to the age of 11, the nature of the child's development is still very much dependent upon the nature of parents and teachers. They are *significant others* over whom the child has no control or choice.

The last four stages of development differ from the previous stages in that the person is increasingly able to control his or her environment. The individual consciously chooses friends, career, a spouse, and so on. Of course, it must be remembered that these deliberate choices are strongly directed by the characteristics that have developed in the individual by the time he or she reaches adolescence. That is, whether the person is trusting, autonomous, industrious, and possessing initiative or mistrustful, doubting, guilt ridden, and feeling inferior will obviously influence the future course of his or her life, no matter how independent he or she may later become of the environment and of other people.

Identity versus Role Confusion

The stage of adolescence, ages 12 to 18, is believed by Erikson to be particularly crucial, for it is at this time that the question of one's basic identity is met and must be resolved. It is a time of interpretation and consolidation, in which everything the person feels and knows about himself or herself is fused into a whole. The person must form a self-image that makes sense and provides both a continuity with the past and an orientation toward the future. There is, then, an integration of the person's ideas of what others think of him or her and what he or she thinks of himself or herself, which, ideally, should provide a consistent and congruent picture. This image—the picture of oneself—forms one's identity.

The shaping and acceptance of one's identity is, Erikson feels, an extremely difficult and anxiety-filled task, in which the adolescent must experiment with or try on different roles and ideologies to determine the best fit. Erikson looks upon adolescence as a hiatus between childhood and adulthood—a psychological moratorium that is absolutely necessary in order to allow time and energy to be devoted to role and image experimentation.

Those who emerge from this difficult stage with a strong sense of identity are equipped to face coming adulthood with an expanded sense of self-certainty and confidence. Those who fail to achieve an identity, who experience an identity crisis, show what Erikson calls role confusion. They do not know who or what they are or where they belong. As a result, they may drop out of the normal life sequence—education, job, marriage—and seek a "negative" identity, one opposite to that prescribed by society. Such an adolescent may become a delinquent or withdraw in isolation to a drugged state. This type of role is still an identification, and even a negative one (as society defines it) is preferable to no identification of any kind, although it is not as satisfactory as a positive identification.

Intimacy versus Isolation

The sixth stage of development, young adulthood, is much longer than any of the earlier ones, extending from the end of adolescence to the beginning of middle age. During what is usually quite an exciting time, a person finally establishes independence from his or her parents and from parent-like (protective) institutions such as school and begins to function as a mature, responsible adult.

Not only does the person perform some kind of productive work, but he or she also establishes intimate relationships with others in the form of close friendships and sexual unions. (Thus, intimacy is not restricted to a sexual relationship.) It also means a sense of caring and commitment, openly displayed, without the use of any self-protective devices and without fear of losing one's sense of self-identity in the relationship.

People unable to establish such intimacy function in a state of isolation; they avoid close contacts with others and may even come to reject or aggress against those whom they see as threatening to their own selves. Such people prefer being alone, because they fear intimacy.

Generativity versus Stagnation

The seventh stage of development finds the individual in middle age—roughly the years from 35 to 50. It is at this stage of maturity, Erikson argues, that people need more than intimacy with others. They need to be actively and directly involved in teaching and guiding the next generation.

This need extends beyond one's immediate family, although it can include one's own children, of course. The concern is broader and more long-range, however, extending to future generations and to the kind of society in which they will live. One need not be a parent to display generativity, nor does having children automatically guarantee satisfaction of this need.

Erikson feels that all human institutions—whether business, military, or academic—reinforce and safeguard the expression of generativity, in that they all involve the establishment of a fund of knowledge and methods to provide guidance to each new generation. Thus, one can satisfy the need to guide the next generation in virtually any organization of which one is a part.

When such behavior is not displayed by the middle-aged individual, he or she is overwhelmed by a sense of "stagnation, boredom, and interpersonal impoverishment." The person regresses to a stage of pseudointimacy, in which he or she indulges himself or herself in a childlike way. The person may become a physical or psychological invalid because of a total absorption (or obsession) with his or her own needs and comforts.

Ego Integrity versus Despair

The final age of life finds the individual in a state of either ego integrity or despair, which governs the way the person looks upon the whole of his or her life. At this time, a person's major endeavors are at or nearing completion. It is a time of reflection—of looking back and examining one's life and taking its final measure.

If a person looks back upon life with a sense of fulfillment and satisfaction, if he or she has adjusted to life's victories and failures, then he or she possesses what Erikson calls ego integrity. Simply stated, it involves the acceptance of one's place and one's past.

If, on the other hand, an individual views his or her life with a sense of frustration or rancor, angry at missed opportunities and regretful of mistakes that cannot now be rectified, then he or she is in a state of despair. He or she is disgusted with life, contemptuous of others, and bitter over what might have been, "if only . . . ."

Basic Virtues

Each of the eight stages of life has its own identity crisis, and each offers new opportunities for particular strengths to develop. Erikson calls these strengths *basic virtues*. He believes they are common over all generations and grow out of the positive, adaptive ways of handling each stage of growth. These basic human strengths are evolutionary in nature, developing over the course of the life of an individual and over the history of humanity as a whole. Each virtue is a vital, animating force in life. The virtues are not innate but must be developed and then reaffirmed continuously throughout a person's life.

There are eight basic virtues, corresponding to the stages of development; each emerges (if it is going to) only when each crisis is met and resolved satisfactorily. The four virtues that may appear in childhood are hope, will, purpose, and competence. Fidelity arises in adolescence and love, care, and wisdom in adulthood. The virtues are very much interdependent; none can develop until the previous one is securely confirmed.

Hope, growing out of basic trust, is the persistent belief that desires can be satisfied. It is a sense of confidence that is maintained in spite of temporary setbacks or reverses. *Will*, developing out of autonomy, is an irrevocable determination to exercise both freedom of choice and self-restraint, and it forms the basis for the necessary acceptance of law. *Purpose*, deriving from initiative, involves a sense of courage to envision and to pursue important goals. *Competence*, deriving from industry, might be called a sense of craftsmanship and involves the exertion of skill and intelligence in the pursuit and completion of tasks.

Fidelity, which grows out of ego identity, involves the maintenance of basic loyalties, a sense of duty, sincerity, and genuineness in relations with others. *Love*, deriving from intimacy, is considered by Erikson to be the greatest of the virtues—indeed, the dominant one. He defines it as "the mutuality of mates and partners in a shared identity "—the finding and losing of oneself in another person. *Care*, emerging from generativity, is a broad concern or solicitude toward others. It manifests itself in the need to teach and guide, not only for the sake of those being taught but also to fulfill one's own identity. The final virtue, *wisdom*, arises out of ego integrity. It expresses itself in a detached concern with the whole of life and conveys to the next generation an integration of experience perhaps best described by the word *heritage*.

Techniques of Inquiry

Erikson does not specifically detail the techniques of inquiry he has used. They could perhaps best be described, in general terms, as a combination of observation of normal and neurotic individuals within a framework of Freudian, historical, social, and anthropological insights, stirred together by a fertile and creative imagination.

In gathering his data from patients undergoing treatment, Erikson seems to have used the traditional Freudian techniques, without, however, being rigidly bound by them. He strongly believes that no technique of inquiry can be applied in the same way to every subject; rather, the techniques must be selected, shaped, and modified to fit the unique requirements of the individual case.

In his therapy with disturbed children, as well as in his research on normal children and adolescents, Erikson uses a variety of toys and observes how the subjects play with them. He believes that the form and intensity of acts of play can reveal aspects of the personality that might not be revealed verbally, particularly since children have limited powers of expression.

Mention was made of his anthropological studies of Indian tribes. Living among the Indians as a participant-observer, Erikson watched behavior and interviewed the subjects at length, with particular reference to their child-rearing techniques.

Erikson's most unusual technique of inquiry—the one most often associated with his name—is the method of psychohistorical analysis. In these biographical studies, Erikson applies his theory of the human life cycle and its various crises to such people as Hitler, George Bernard Shaw, Mahatma Gandhi, Maxim Gorky, and Martin Luther. He invokes not only psychoanalytic principles but also his extensive knowledge of European literature and social and political history.

Each analysis centers around a crisis in the person's development—an episode that crystallized and represented the major theme of his life, uniting his past, present, and future activities. Using what he called *disciplined subjectivity*, Erikson attempted to take the person's point of view as his own and to look upon historical events that occurred during the individual's life through the eyes of that person.

Erikson's Image of Human Nature

A personality theorist who speaks of basic virtues as being attainable and who writes of our "lofty moralism" must certainly be described as presenting a positive and hopeful image of human nature. While it is true that not everyone is successful in attaining hope, will, purpose, wisdom, and the other virtues, everyone has the potential or the capability of reaching these goals. We are not, by our own nature, prevented from doing so. Nor must we inevitably suffer conflict, anxiety, and neurosis because of instinctive biological forces.

Erikson's theory allows for hope because each stage of growth, while stressful enough to be labeled a crisis, nevertheless holds the definite possibility of a positive outcome. A person may resolve each crisis in a way that is adaptive and strengthening. Further, even if a person should fail at one stage and be left with a maladaptive character response (for example, isolation instead of intimacy), there is still hope for later stages. A failure at one stage can be corrected by success at a later stage. Thus, there is hope for the future at all stages of growth.

Finally, we are capable of consciously directing our own growth;

we are not passive products of our childhood experiences. While we have little control over the first four stages of development, we have an increasing ability, beginning in adolescence, to chart our own course by choosing ways of responding to the crises of development we must face.

A Final Commentary

While it may be somewhat exaggerated to call Erikson "the outstanding psychoanalyst of them all," as *Newsweek* has done, it is certainly no exaggeration to state that he has been and continues to be an extremely important influence in the psychoanalytic world. In addition, his influence has spread to the fields of education and social work. In any area where people work with children and adolescents, his ideas have been put to use. As a result, many children, both normal and emotionally disturbed, have been raised, taught, and cared for in ways directly influenced by Erikson's concepts of the psychosocial levels of development and the identity crisis. Thus, his ideas have found widespread use and application.

However, despite its wide popularity, his theory has generated little in the way of empirical research. The primary reason for this lack of research is probably the fact that his theory attempts to encompass the full and seemingly infinite complexity of human personality at all ages.

Another reason for the scarcity of research interest shown in Erikson's work is that he does not sufficiently specify or detail the behavior characteristics with which he deals. Concepts such as fidelity and wisdom, for example, are not defined with the precision needed to work with them in the laboratory. Erikson's response to this criticism is to suggest that, if the methods of the laboratory do not work with his theory, one should not automatically blame the theory; perhaps the methods are at fault.

Other critics attack the validity of his identity-crisis formulation when applied to females. Some data have suggested that women may not form a strong ego identity until after marriage, considerably later than men would form their identity, although this criticism may be less valid today, in view of the growing emphasis on female consciousness and the recognition that women can form unique identities before or in the absence of marriage.

Still other critics say that, while Erikson's theory claims to deal with the total development of a human being, from infancy to old age, he has paid more attention to infancy and childhood and focused less comprehensively upon the postadolescent years.

Erikson has shown little interest in responding to his critics (and the amount of criticism has not been all that large) or in defending his view of personality. He recognizes that there are many ways of looking at the same object or process, depending on one's perspective, and that no single perspective is the "right" way. Therefore, one cannot accuse Erikson of being rigid and dogmatic about his work.

His influence continues to grow, through his books and through large numbers of primarily younger psychiatrists, psychologists, and teachers, who see in Erikson's work a useful way of viewing the development of the individual from infancy to old age.

In reviewing one of Erikson's books, the journal *Science* wrote that it was "a unique combination of imaginative clinical description, rigorous thinking, gentle humor, and deep humanity." This seems an apt description of the man and his work.

Suggested Readings

Erikson, E. H. *Childhood and society* (2nd ed.). New York: Norton, 1963.

Erikson, E. H. *Identity: Youth and crisis.* New York: Norton, 1968.

Erikson, E. H. *Dimensions of a new identity.* New York: Norton, 1974.

Erikson, E. H. *Life history and the historical moment.* New York: Norton, 1975.

Evans, R. I. *Dialogue with Erik Erikson.* New York: Harper & Row, 1967.

Murrac, J. B. The identity image of the college student. *Psychological Reports*, 1964, 14, 267–271.

Gordon Allport 10

As the individual matures, the bond with the past is broken.

—*Gordon Allport*

Over the course of a productive career that lasted for more than four decades, Gordon Allport became one of the most stimulating and provocative psychologists to study personality. Indeed, it was Allport, more than anyone else, who made the study of personality an academically respectable part of psychology. We noted in Chapter 1 that the study of personality did not become formalized and systematized in psychology until the 1930s. Psychoanalysis and those theories that were derived from it were not considered to be in the mainstream of scientific psychology. Indeed, the area of personality as a whole was not a major part of psychology until Allport published an important book, *Personality: A Psychological Interpretation*, in 1937.

Allport, therefore, served two very important purposes in the study of personality: he helped to bring it into the mainstream of scientific psychology, and he formulated his own controversial and useful theory of personality. In addition to making many original contributions, he incorporated insights and ideas from other approaches, to form a truly eclectic theory of personality that attempts to deal with the whole person as a unique and dynamic functioning individual.

Allport took issue with Freud on several crucial points. First, he argued that the role of the unconscious had been exaggerated. Allport did not believe that unconscious forces dominate or even play a major role in the personality of the normal, mature adult. Rather, he saw the healthy, normal individual as functioning in rational and conscious terms, aware of and controlling many of the forces that motivate him or her. The unconscious, according to Allport, is of importance in neurotic or disturbed functioning but not in the normal person.

A second point of disagreement with Freud was over the role of the past in controlling the present. In Allport's view, human beings are not prisoners of childhood conflicts and experiences. Rather, we are guided much more by the present—and our view toward the future—than by the past. His whole focus in the study of personality was on contemporary influences. For example, in his extensive work in the area of motivation, he looked not to the past but to the current self-image of a person. Similarly, he felt that a person's ego structure is based on current events and feelings.

Allport was much opposed to studying personality through data collected from pathological subjects. Unlike Freud, who posited a continuum between the normal and the abnormal, Allport saw a sharp break between the two, with the abnormal individual still functioning at the level of infantile complexes and experiences. He insisted that the only way to study personality is through healthy, normal, mature adults; other populations—neurotics, children, animals—cannot be compared to normal adults. There is no functional similarity in the area of personality between child and adult, abnormal and normal, or animal and human.

Perhaps the most distinctive feature of Allport's approach to personality is his strong insistence on the uniqueness of each individual personality. He was much opposed to the traditional scientific emphasis on forming general constructs or laws that can be applied to everyone. Personality, he argued, is not general or universal in nature. Rather, it is highly particular and specific to each individual.

In addition to formulating his theory, Allport, along with his students—many of whom became prominent themselves—performed important empirical research on a variety of aspects of personality. He also developed several tests for assessing personality that are still very much in use in both the clinic and the laboratory. Thus, Allport's influence has been keenly felt in psychology, and he has received nearly every honor the field has to offer.

The Life of Allport (1897–1967)

With the eight theorists covered so far, we have speculated about possible relationships between childhood experiences and the form of the personality theory later proposed. Disappointingly, it is difficult to offer a relationship between Allport's childhood and his theory, either because there is not one or because he has been less candid about his childhood than the other theorists. This apparent lack of correspondence is interesting in a theorist who believes that one's past has so little influence on one's present.

Born in Montezuma, Indiana, Allport was the youngest of four sons. His father had been a businessman who turned to medicine rather late in life, opening a private practice when Allport was born. In fact, Allport believed that his own delivery was his father's first case. As the youngest child, Allport seemed to go very much his own way; he was too young to be a playmate to his brothers.

Allport was apparently isolated from children outside the family as well. "I fashioned my own circle of activities. It was a select circle, for I never fitted the general boy assembly." He described himself as an isolate who was skillful with words but not at sports or games and who worked hard at being the center of attention of the few friends he did have.

Out of such isolation and the feelings of rejection that may accompany it, personality theories have been known to develop—but not, apparently, in this case. Allport's childhood and home environment were wholesome—full of hard work and Protestant piety, generously mixed with trust and affection. He noted no formative influence of any particular importance during his childhood years.

In spite of being "uninspired and uncurious," he stood in second place in his high school graduation class of 100. But he had no firm idea of what to do next. Finally, at the end of the summer of 1915, he applied to Harvard, at the urging of his brother Floyd, who had graduated from Harvard two years earlier. (Floyd Allport also became a noted psychologist.)

Having barely passed the entrance exam, Allport entered Harvard, where, he wrote, "almost overnight my world was remade." The next four years were a time of great adventure and excitement, as whole new worlds of intellect and culture opened up to him. He was shocked by the low grades he received on his first exams, and so he doubled his efforts and finished the year with straight As.

Allport's interest in social ethics and social service, acquired initially from his parents, was reinforced at Harvard, where he engaged in extensive volunteer work with a boy's club, with factory workers, and with foreign students. He was also a volunteer probation officer for a time. He found these social-service activities extremely satisfying, in part because he genuinely liked to help people but also because "it gave me a feeling of competence (to offset a generalized inferiority feeling)." He felt that this kind of service to others reflected his search for a personal identity.

He took a number of undergraduate courses in psychology but did not major in it or intend a career in the field. When he graduated from Harvard, he had no more definite idea of what he would do with his life than he had had four years earlier. In order to see if he liked teaching, he accepted an offer of a position at Robert College in Istanbul, Turkey. He enjoyed the year very much, decided that he liked teaching, and so accepted a fellowship offered him by Harvard for graduate study in psychology.

Traveling back to the United States, he stopped in Vienna to visit another brother. While there, he wrote to Freud and received an invitation to visit the great man. When Allport entered Freud's office, he found Freud sitting silently, waiting for the young American to tell him the purpose of his visit. The silence wore on, and suddenly Allport blurted out an incident that had taken place on the streetcar ride to Freud's office. He told of watching a small boy who had an obvious fear of dirt. Everything seemed dirty to the boy; he changed his seat and told his mother not to let a "dirty man" sit next to him.

When Allport finished the story, Freud looked at him and said "And was that little boy you?" Allport was shaken and managed to change the subject, but the incident left a deep impression on him. He began to suspect that psychoanalysis explored too deeply into the unconscious and to believe that it should pay more attention to visible or surface motives.

He completed his Ph.D. in 1922, after two years of graduate study, which, incidentally, he felt was "not nearly stiff enough." His thesis presaged his lifelong work on personality and was entitled "An Experimental Study of the Traits of Personality," a topic on which he was later to do much more work. The thesis was the very first study in America on personality traits.

After receiving his degree, Allport spent two years traveling in Europe on a fellowship. When he returned to Harvard to teach, he offered a course on the psychological and social aspects of personality, which he said was probably the first course ever given in personality in the United States. He stayed at Harvard for two years, during which time he married, and then accepted a position at Dartmouth College, where he remained for the next four years.

He taught, studied, and worked in social psychology as well as in personality and produced a number of important papers, articles, and psychological tests, including the famous "Allport-Vernon-Lindzey Study of Values" and the "A-S (ascendance-submission) Reaction Study." The rest of his career, from 1930 until his death in 1967, was spent at Harvard, where he influenced several generations of students through his popular undergraduate course and his graduate seminars.

He became an elder statesman in psychology, and his awards were many: the Gold Medal of the American Psychological Foundation, the Distinguished Scientific Contribution Award of the American Psychological Association, and the presidencies of the American Psychological Association, the regional Eastern Psychological Association, and the Society for the Psychological Study of Social Issues.

The Nature of Personality

Allport reviewed some 50 different ways of defining personality before offering his own definition: "Personality is the dynamic organization within the individual of those psychophysical systems that determine his characteristic behavior and thought." We can best analyze his definition by elaborating upon certain key concepts within it.

By *dynamic organization*, he means that while personality is constantly changing and growing (dynamic), it is nevertheless an organized growth. Also, the form of the organization changes, as well as do specific aspects of the personality.

Psychophysical means that personality is composed of a mind and a body acting in concert and as a unit. Personality is neither all mental nor all biological but a combination of the two. He believed that our knowledge of the mental side of personality was far advanced over our knowledge of its biological composition. As a result, a psychological approach to the study of personality may be much more fruitful than a biological approach, at least until such time as we know more about the functioning of the brain.

The third key term is *determine*, by which he meant that "personality *is* something and *does* something." All facets of personality, in other words, activate and/or direct highly specific behaviors and thoughts.

The phrase *characteristic behavior and thought* means that everything an individual does or thinks is characteristic of that person. Every person is thus an individual and like no other.

A major point of support offered by Allport for his stress on uniqueness is that we are so much the product of the laws and form of our heredity and environment. Heredity provides the personality with its raw materials, which are then shaped (stretched or limited) by the conditions of the person's environment. These raw materials, according to Allport, consist of physique, intelligence, and temperament. Temperament involves one's general emotional tone, including how susceptible one is to stimulation and the fluctuation and intensity of one's moods.

It is this genetic background and the raw material of the personality that it provides that is responsible for the major part of a person's uniqueness. There are, after all, an infinity of possible gene combinations, and the chance that one's genetic endowment would be exactly duplicated in someone else is simply too small to warrant consideration. This individual combination of genes then interacts with one's environment—and no two people, even siblings in the same house, have precisely the same environment—to produce the inevitable result: a unique individual.

In studying personality, therefore, psychology must deal with the individual case—an approach Allport called *idiographic*. The opposite of the idiographic or individual approach is the *nomothetic* approach, which studies large numbers of subjects, describes them in terms of averages, and offers laws that explain the behavior of all people. Other areas of psychology, Allport said, may legitimately use the nomothetic approach, but the only way to study personality is idiographically because each personality is unique and cannot be compared with any other.

But what of similarities? Surely there are certain broad similarities among those in the same culture or the same age group or, on a larger scale, in the same species? Allport, of course, agreed with this point; it would be difficult not to. However, he insisted that a person can be effectively described independently of forces such as society or culture. Culture certainly influences behavior, in that it sets the limits or ranges of one's activities, but there remains a great deal of latitude for individuality within those limits.

A final point to be made about Allport's view is that he considered personality to be discrete or discontinuous. Not only is each person set apart from every other, but he or she is also divorced from his or her own past. There is no continuum of personality between childhood and adulthood. The infant is driven by primitive drives and behaves primarily in terms of reflexes. The adult operates on an entirely different level, so that there are, in a sense, two different personalities. There is a world of childhood and a world of adulthood, one more biological in nature, the other more psychologically based. One does not grow out of the other. An adult's functioning is not constrained by his or her past.

We have, then, quite a distinctive picture of the nature of personality: an overall stress on the conscious as opposed to the unconscious, a stress on the present rather than the past, a focus on the individual case rather than on generalities and similarities over all people, and a focus on the normal rather than the abnormal. Let us now examine other, more specific features of the "dynamic organization within the individual" that is personality, in the view of Gordon Allport.

Motivation

Allport believed that the central problem in any theory of personality is how it handles motivation. Indeed, he felt that a personality theory could stand or fall on the adequacy of its treatment of what motivates the individual. However, he acknowledged that no approach to motivation then available was fully adequate, even his own. (Of course, he believed that his theory of motivation was more adequate than any of the others.)

Allport began his analysis of motivation by laying down four requirements that a theory of motivation should meet. First, the theory must focus on the *contemporaneity* of motivation. As we have seen, Allport stressed the present in his approach to the understanding of personality, and this emphasis on immediacy is a central part of his theory of motivation. It is the present state of the individual—not what happened during toilet training or at the time of weaning—that is central. Whatever happened in the past is exactly that: past. It is no longer active. A person's past motivation explains nothing, unless it exists as a present or current motivating force.

The second requirement for a motivational theory is that it be *pluralistic*, recognizing the existence of many different types of motives. Human motivation is so vastly complex, Allport argued, that it is oversimplifying to reduce it to only a few drives, such as pleasure seeking, tension reduction, or needs for power or security. There is such a diversity of motivating forces that it is difficult to find a common thread among them—an overall drive that can include all the individual ones. Some motives are temporary, appearing once and never again, others recur from time to time, and still others are persistent and always at work. Some are conscious, others unconscious, and so on. It is not possible, Allport insisted, to reduce this complexity to a simple model.

The third requirement of a motivational theory is that it consider the importance of *cognitive processes*—specifically, the individual's plans and intentions. Allport was sharply critical of approaches to personality that stressed irrational and unconscious aspects of motivation at the expense of the rational and conscious. Deliberate, conscious intention, he believed, is an essential aspect of human personality. What a person wants and is striving to accomplish is the most important key we have to understanding the person's present behavior. Thus, Allport explained the present in terms of the future (intentions), rather than in terms of the past.

The final requirement for a motivational theory is that it recognize the *concrete uniqueness* of motivating forces. A motive must be defined concretely rather than abstractly. An abstract view of motives deals with personality or motivation in general, not with the individual case. Allport offered the following example to show the difference between a concrete and an abstract motive.

Concrete: "Mary has a strong desire to become a professional nurse."
Abstract: "She is cathecting an aim-inhibited sexual wish."

The concrete description is tied directly to the individual case. The abstract motive in the example could be applied by a Freudian to any number of cases to explain any number of behaviors.

Not surprisingly, the four characteristics Allport considered necessary to a motivational theory are accounted for by his own concept of motivation, known as *functional autonomy*.

Functional Autonomy

Allport was careful to point out that the concept of functional autonomy does not explain all human motivation. However, he believed that it recognizes the true nature of adult motivation more effectively than other approaches do.

Functional autonomy is really a simple concept. It says that a motive, in the normal, mature adult, is not functionally related to past experiences in which it may have originally appeared. The motive has become autonomous, independent of its original circumstances. Put another way, the means used to achieve an earlier goal become an end in themselves.

The same thing happens, in principle, with motives as happens with a child as he or she gradually becomes independent of the parents. The child becomes self-determining—historically related to the parents but no longer functionally related, in that they no longer control or guide his or her life. To give another example from Allport: it is obvious that the growth and development of a tree can be traced back to its seed. Yet, when the tree is fully grown, the seed is no longer necessary as a source of nourishment. The tree is now self-determining—no longer functionally related to its seed.

And so it is with motives. Consider a young man embarking on a career in business. He is poor, and so he works very hard, investing all of his energy in his work. Thirty years later, the hard work has paid off. He is financially secure and has enough money to live comfortably for the rest of his life without working anymore. Yet he continues to work just as hard at 50 as he did at 20. Such behavior can no longer be for the same goal; that goal has long ago been reached and surpassed. The drive to work hard, once a means to a specific end (money), has now come to be an end in itself. The motivation is independent of its original source.

There are many other examples that could be given: a skilled crafts-woman who insists on doing the best job possible, even when her extra concern brings in no additional money, or a miser who continues to live in a slum while he hoards his vast pile of money. In all such cases, the original motive is transformed into something else. A behavior that once satisfied some specific drive or need now serves only itself.

The adult motive, then, cannot be understood by exploring the child-hood of the person. The only way to understand the motivation of the adult is to investigate why he or she *now* behaves in a certain way.

Some years after initially formulating the notion of functional au-tonomy, Allport elaborated upon his position somewhat and proposed two different levels of autonomy.

Levels of Autonomy

Allport called these two levels of autonomy *perseverative functional autonomy* and *propriate functional autonomy*. Perseverative autonomy is the more elementary and basic of the two types and is concerned with such behaviors as addictions and repeated physical movements—for instance, a child's performance of an act over and over again or an adult's routine and habitual way of performing everyday tasks. They are behaviors that once served a purpose but no longer do so and that are at too low a level to be considered an integral part of the personality itself.

Allport cited as supporting evidence for this kind of autonomy both human and animal examples. For instance, when a rat that is well trained to run a maze for food is given more than sufficient food, it may still run the maze, obviously for some purpose other than food. At the human level, he cited examples of our preference for the routine and the familiar. The behavior continues or perseveres on its own, without any external reinforcement.

Allport considered propriate functional autonomy to be by far the more important of the two and absolutely essential to the understanding of motivation in the mature adult. The word *propriate* derives from All-port's term for the ego or self: the *proprium* (to be discussed later in this chapter). Propriate autonomy, therefore, is directly and intimately related to the very core of the personality, and it describes the status of interests, sentiments, values, attitudes, intentions, and one's self-image and life style.

Propriate motives are specific to the individual, unique and highly necessary to the ego or proprium, which determines which motives are maintained and which are discarded. For example, those motives that enhance or enrich one's self-esteem or self-image are kept. Because of this, Allport noted, there is usually a direct relationship between a person's interests and his or her abilities; people enjoy doing what they do well.

He pointed out that the original motivation for learning a skill—say, playing the piano—may have nothing at all to do with the person's interests. As a child, a person may be forced, very much against his or her will, to practice. If, however, in spite of this initial resistance, the person becomes proficient at the piano, he or she may become totally committed to it. The original motive (perhaps fear of parental displeasure) has disappeared, and, once again, the means to an end has become an end in itself. Somehow, the behavior of playing the piano becomes necessary to the self-image, and so the behavior continues.

The propriate structure of a person—that is, our sense of ego or self—will determine how we perceive the world around us (what we will pick out to attend to), what we remember from our experience, and the tone and direction of our thought. In other words, all our perceptual and cognitive processes are highly selective, picking and choosing from the mass of stimulation available to us only that which is relevant to our interests and values. That we are perceptually selective is supported by a great deal of research in social psychology.

Propriate functional autonomy, then, is an organizing process that determines and maintains a person's sense of self. How it determines and organizes the personality is explained by Allport in three principles of propriate functional autonomy.

Principles of Propriate Autonomy

The first principle is that of *organizing the energy level*. While this principle does not explain how a motive develops (or, more correctly, how it is transformed from an earlier motive), it does try to account for the acquisition of new motives. New motives, or latent older motives, come to the surface out of necessity, to help consume excess energy that otherwise might be expressed in more destructive and harmful ways. For example, when a woman's children are grown and leave home for good, she may suddenly find herself with much extra time and energy, which must be channeled into new interests and motives.

The second principle, *mastery and competence*, refers to the high levels at which persons prefer to satisfy motives. It is not enough, Allport argued, to achieve at merely adequate levels. The normal, healthy adult is motivated to perform better and more efficiently—to increase his or her degree of competence and mastery.

The third principle of propriate autonomy is known as *propriate patterning,* which is basically a restatement of what was said in the previous section about propriate functional autonomy. Propriate motives are not all independent of one another; they are all dependent on the self structure, in which they are firmly anchored. Thus, as we noted, a person organizes or patterns his or her perceptual and cognitive processes around the self, keeping that which enhances the self and rejecting the rest. Propriate patterning is a striving for consistency and integration of the personality.

Non-Functionally Autonomous Behavior

It was noted that Allport did not believe that absolutely every behavior or motive could be explained by his theory of functional autonomy. He listed eight kinds of behaviors or attributes that are not under the control of functionally autonomous motives.

1. behavior arising from biological drives—for food, water, sleep, air, and so on
2. reflex actions—blinking, knee jerk, digestive processes, and so on
3. constitutional equipment—the fixed elements of body build, intelligence, temperament, and health
4. habits. While some habits are functionally autonomous, others have no motivational value at all.
5. behavior dependent upon primary reinforcement—behavior that is discontinued in the absence of reinforcement (for example, when a child no longer goes to visit a neighbor after the neighbor has stopped giving the child cookies)
6. infantilisms and fixations—when an adult continues to act out a childhood conflict
7. some neuroses—those tied to a repressed incident in childhood, when the revealing of the incident leads to a cessation of the behavior
8. sublimation—when the true motive is sublimated into another one

The Proprium

The *proprium* is Allport's term for the self or the ego, labels he rejected because of the wide diversity of meanings ascribed to them by other theorists. The proprium includes all those aspects of personality that are distinctive and vital to the emotional life of an individual. The aspects encompassed by the proprium are unique to the person, setting him or her apart from everybody else, and they unite his or her attitudes, perceptions, and intentions into a unified whole.

Allport discussed the nature and development of the proprium in terms of seven aspects or functions that develop gradually in stages until maturity is reached, at which time the proprium is fully developed.

Before the proprium begins to emerge, there is no sense or awareness of self. In very early infancy, there is not yet a separation of "me" from everything else—no sense of self-consciousness. The infant at this time simply receives sensory impressions from the external environment and reacts to them automatically and reflexively, with no sense of self to mediate between stimulation and response.

The first aspect of the proprium to develop is *bodily self*, when the infant begins to be aware of a "bodily me." For example, the infant begins to be able to distinguish between its fingers and an object they may be holding or manipulating.

Self-identity defines the second stage. It is marked by a sense of continuity of identity; that is, the child realizes that he or she remains the same person in spite of the great changes in growth and ability that are taking place. Greatly aiding the sense of self-identity is the child's learning his or her own name and gradually coming to see himself or herself as a distinct and continuous self.

Self-esteem refers to a growing sense of pride as the child learns that he or she is able to accomplish some things on his or her own.

The fourth stage is *extension of self*, which involves the child's growing awareness of other objects and people in the world and the identification of some of them as "belonging" to him or her. For instance, the child begins to speak of "my house," "my parents," "my school," and so on.

A *self-image* develops next, and it incorporates how the child sees and would like to see himself or herself. These actual and ideal images develop from interaction with the parents, who make the child aware of their expectations and of the extent to which the child's behavior is satisfying (or failing to satisfy) these expectations.

The sixth stage is the *self as a rational coper*. This occurs when the child realizes that he or she has a rational ability that can be applied to the solving of problems. The child begins to see that he or she can handle problems in a rational and logical manner.

Propriate striving is the name of the final stage, which occurs when the person realizes the existence in himself or herself of long-range purposes, goals, and intentions. The individual's view is clearly toward the future, for which he or she now begins to plan. Allport believed that until a person begins to plan ahead to long-range goals, the sense of self cannot be complete.

The development of the proprium through these seven stages is gradual and lasts from infancy until sometime during adolescence. The stages occur at approximately the following ages: the first three stages (bodily self, self-identity, and self-esteem) take place during the first three years of life, self-extension and self-image occur from ages 4 to 6, rational coping from 6 to 12, and propriate striving during adolescence. All of these aspects are united under the term *proprium*.

As the proprium and its propriate functions become more and more fully developed, there gradually emerges a set of characteristic traits that distinguish the behavior of each person from that of every other individual.

Traits

The study of personality traits was of long and abiding interest to Allport. His Ph.D. dissertation dealt with traits and was the first such study done anywhere in the United States. Early in his psychological career, he spoke of two categories of traits: *individual* and *common*. As you might suspect, individual traits are unique to the person and define the nature of his or her individual character. Common traits are those shared by a number of people, such as the members of a culture.

Common traits are abstractions, in that they reflect social mores and values and result from social pressure to behave in a certain way. Allport did not consider them to be basic traits, belonging to the individual. Rather, they are surface manifestations only. The individual is not deeply committed to the common traits; they do not define specifically one person's personality as opposed to another. Allport noted, as evidence for the ephemeral nature of common traits, the fact that they can and often do change, as social standards or mores change.

Because of the possible confusion that can result from calling both of these phenomena traits, Allport later revised his terminology and called common traits simply *traits* and individual traits *personal dispositions*. Both are still traits, of course. They are "neuropsychic structures," in Allport's words, and serve to initiate as well as guide behavior. The definitions he provided for traits and personal dispositions are almost identical, except that the phrase *peculiar to the individual* is added to the definition of personal dispositions.

Both traits and personal dispositions exist in, or as part of, the person, but they cannot be seen directly (any more than we can see intelligence or thought directly). However, the existence of traits and personal dispositions can be inferred by observing someone's behavior over a period of time and noting consistencies and regularities in the way the person responds to various stimuli.

Once an observer has inferred the existence of a trait, the label he or she attaches to it may be arbitrary, according to Allport, as long as it is not deliberately misleading. To help in the naming of traits, Allport presented a list of some 18,000 trait labels (for those at a loss for words). Some examples of Allport's traits are dominance, submission, neuroticism, authoritarianism, masculinity or femininity, and conformity.

Allport was careful to distinguish what he considered traits from other personal characteristics that are also capable of initiating and guiding behavior—specifically, habits, attitudes, and personality types.

Habits obviously have a determining influence on behavior. You have only to look at your own habits to see how they affect the way you behave. Habits, however, are much more narrow and limited influences than are traits. They are also inflexible, involving a specific response to a specific stimulus. A trait or personal disposition is much broader because it arises from the integration of a number of individual habits that have in common the performance of the same adaptive function for the person. A number of habits may thus blend or fuse to become a single trait.

Allport offered the example of a child learning to brush his or her teeth twice a day. After a while, the behavior becomes automatic (habitual). The child also learns to wash his or her hands after going to the toilet and before eating. These behaviors, and others serving the same function (cleanliness), become so many separate habits all directed toward the same purpose. All of them taken together form a trait of the person: cleanliness.

Allport noted that it is often more difficult to distinguish between a trait and an *attitude*. Consider, for example, patriotism. Is it a trait fostered by the mores of a culture, or is it an attitude directed toward one's country? Other terms, such as authoritarianism or extraversion, could also just as easily be called either traits or attitudes. Allport does not resolve the question, except by noting that in cases such as these it doesn't make any difference which label we apply to them; both are appropriate.

However, it is possible, in general, to distinguish between traits and attitudes in two ways. First, attitudes always have very specific objects of reference. A person has an attitude toward something: blond-haired people, or a particular teacher, or school, or pine trees. A trait is not so specifically directed to a single object or even to a class of objects. A man described as extremely shy (a personal disposition) would behave in the same way toward blonds, redheads, brunettes—and probably other men as well. Traits, then, are much broader in scope.

The second point of distinction between traits and attitudes is that attitudes are either for or against something—positive or negative. They lead a person to like or hate, accept or reject, or approach or avoid the object. An attitude involves an evaluation, pro or con, which a trait does not.

Allport also distinguished between traits and *personality types:* "A person *has* a trait but *fits* a type." A type, then, does not so much exist in a person as in the eye of someone who perceives the person. Traits, on the other hand, exist in the person, independently of how he or she is viewed by someone else.

Types of Traits

Not all traits are of the same intensity or significance in an individual. Some are more masterful, meaningful, or powerful than others. Allport posited three types: cardinal, central, and secondary traits.

A *cardinal* trait is one that is so pervasive, general, and extremely influential that every aspect of a person's life is touched by it. A cardinal trait is so powerful that a person is truly dominated by it; every act is influenced by it. Allport called such a trait a "ruling passion," "a master sentiment," and gave as examples sadism and chauvinism. Not everyone, of course, has such ruling passions.

Less general and pervasive are the *central* traits, which everyone possesses in small numbers—between five and ten in the average individual, according to Allport. Central traits are the kinds of characteristics one would mention in writing a letter of recommendation; they are the handful of "themes" that describe a person's behavior, such as aggressive, self-pitying, sentimental, or cynical.

The least important and least general kind of trait is the *secondary* trait, which is displayed less conspicuously and less consistently than the other types. Secondary traits may be so seldom displayed or so slightly revealed that only a very close friend might notice them.

The Development of Personality

In view of Allport's strong belief that there is a dichotomous rather than a functionally continuous relationship between the personality of the child and the adult—that the personality of the mature adult is more a function of the present and future than of the past—it is perhaps surprising to find any expression of interest on his part in childhood and the developmental aspects of personality. Yet, as we saw in the discussion of the proprium, Allport indicated recognizable changes in various aspects of personality as a function of the age of the individual. Further, one of his most important concepts—functional autonomy—involves a transformation of an original motive into an entirely new motive at a later time in life.

While Allport did discuss the development of personality, he did not do so in terms of a series of clearcut steps in growth, except for the seven aspects of the proprium, which occur at well-defined ages. Rather, he presented us with a broadly stroked picture of the changes that take place from infancy through adolescence.

He described the infant as a purely pleasure-seeking, destructive, "unsocialized horror," totally selfish, impatient, and dependent. The genetic raw materials of physique, temperament, and intelligence—bases of an eventual personality—are present, but there exists in infancy little of what could be called a personality. The infant operates in accord with drives and reflexes concerned with reducing tensions and pain and maximizing pleasures.

Of vital importance during this period is the attainment of adequate affection and security, primarily from the mother. If the child is successful in having these needs met, then positive psychological growth will follow, along the lines noted in the discussion of the proprium. Motivations are free to be transformed into autonomous propriate strivings, selfhood and the ego begin to differentiate and grow, a network or pattern of personal dispositions is formed, and a mature, normal adult is the inevitable result.

Under these conditions, the individual changes from a tension-reducing, biologically dominated organism to more of a psychological organism, in which motivations are divorced from those of childhood and become future oriented and in which the characteristics of maturity develop. In this sense, then, the adult personality is discontinuous with that of the child. It grows out of childhood, to be sure, but is no longer dictated to or dominated by the nature of childhood drives.

That is what happens in the development of the normal personality—one whose needs for affection and security were well met in infancy. Quite a different picture emerges, however, in the case where those needs are thwarted and frustrated. In that situation, the child becomes insecure, aggressive, demanding, jealous, and totally self-centered. As a result, psychological growth is stunted and the person continues to function at the level of infantile drives and conflicts. Motives do not become functionally autonomous but continue to be tied to their original conditions. The proprium does not develop, nor do unique traits, and the personality as a whole remains undifferentiated, as it was in infancy.

Such a person, as an adult, is considered by Allport to be mentally ill. In this case, there is not a dichotomy between the personalities of adulthood and childhood. They remain one and the same in form. Allport was much more interested in the positive growth of the normal, mature adult and had relatively little to say about the neurotic.

The final stage of normal development, the mature, healthy personality, is described in terms of six criteria.

1. extension of the sense of self
2. warm relating of the self to others (intimacy, compassion, tolerance)
3. emotional security (self-acceptance)
4. realistic perception, the development of skills, and commitment to some form of work
5. self-objectification (an understanding or insight into self and a sense of humor, which Allport considered the most striking correlate of insight)
6. a unifying philosophy of life

With the attainment of these criteria, the person has become autonomous of his or her infancy and childhood and is able to face the present and realistically plan for the future, without being victimized or imprisoned by the experiences of early years.

Techniques of Inquiry

Allport wrote much more about the specific methods or techniques appropriate to the study of personality than have most other personality theorists. In one of his most popular books (*Pattern and Growth in Personality*, 1961), he devoted three long chapters to the topic. He noted that, despite the existence of so many techniques, there is no one best method. Personality is so complex that any and all legitimate methods must be employed.

To provide a general framework within which to study personality, Allport described 11 different methods, all of which are subsumed under the basic method of all science: observation followed by interpretation. Allport used some of the 11 methods himself, suggesting that the others needed more careful study. The methods are:

1. constitutional and physiological diagnosis
2. socio-cultural setting, membership, role
3. personal documents and case studies
4. self-appraisal
5. conduct sampling
6. ratings
7. tests and scales
8. projective techniques
9. depth analysis
10. expressive behavior
11. synoptic procedures (combining information from a variety of sources in a synopsis)

One of the techniques used by Allport was the personal-document approach. As the name suggests, this technique involves the study of diaries, autobiographies, letters, literary compositions—any written or spoken record of a person. The most famous of these documents is a collection of 301 letters written by a middle-aged woman over a period of 12 years, published by Allport in 1965 (*Letters from Jenny*). This kind of material is analyzed to detemine the number and kinds of traits of the person in question.

The same sort of analysis can be performed with third-person material about an individual, such as that found in case histories and biographies. With both autobiographical and biographical material, it is a relatively simple procedure to have a group of judges read the material and note the number and kinds of traits they find in it. Given a reasonable degree of agreement among the judges, it is then possible to group individual judgments into a fairly small number of categories. Quite often in this approach, the agreement among judges is high, revealing a large element of consistency in their assessments. For example, in Allport's original research with the letters from Jenny, 36 judges yielded a total of almost 200 trait names. However, because so many of the trait terms given were synonymous, Allport was able to reduce that large number to only eight categories.

Allport made more extensive use of research into the nature of expressive behavior. The observation of expressive behavior is based on the premise that some behaviors will express a person's personality. He divided behavior into two types: coping and expressive. *Coping* behavior is oriented toward a specific purpose, consciously planned and formally carried out, determined by specific needs inspired by the situation, and ordinarily directed toward bringing about some change in the person's environment. *Expressive* behavior is quite the opposite. It is more spontaneous, reflects basic aspects of the personality, is very difficult to change, has no specific purpose, and is usually displayed without our being aware of it.

Allport offered the example of attending a lecture. The lecturer is actually communicating on two levels. The formal and planned level (coping behavior) includes the content of his or her lecture. The informal and unplanned level consists of the lecturer's movements and tone of voice (expressive behaviors), which you observe while attending to the content of the lecture. Perhaps he or she is perspiring and flushed, speaks quickly in a shaky voice, repeats himself or herself, fidgets with a tie or earring, or walks back and forth. All of these are spontaneous behaviors reflecting elements of the lecturer's personality.

By giving subjects a variety of tasks to perform, Allport was able to judge the consistency in their expressive movements over different situations. He found a high level of consistency in voice, handwriting, posture, and gestures and was able, on further analysis, to deduce the existence of certain traits, such as introversion-extraversion, from these expressive behaviors.

Other research on expressive behavior has shown that personality can be quite accurately judged on the basis of tape recordings and films of subjects and even, to some degree, handwriting. Our facial expressions, the tone of our voice, and our idiosyncratic gestures and mannerisms tend to give us away and communicate to a trained observer facets of our personality.

The essence of these and other techniques used by Allport is their idiographic nature. Consistent with his theoretical emphasis on the uniqueness of the individual is his methodological insistence on using techniques of inquiry that investigate the unique nature of each subject. The individual case, not the average performance of groups, is the basis of Allport's psychology.

It must be noted that Allport's work in developing psychological tests (the "A–S Reaction Study" and "A Study of Values") has presented us with additional techniques for inquiring into the nature of the individual personality.

Allport's Image of Human Nature

The quotation with which we opened this chapter—"As the individual matures, the bond with the past is broken"—tells us much about Allport's view of human beings. People (or at least normal, mature adults) are not inexorably tied to and irreversibly driven by the events of childhood. The neurotic, however, is very much a prisoner of early conflicts and experiences.

When we deal with the healthy adult, we find that Allport presented a positive and hopeful picture, a view that depicts people as being in conscious control of their own lives. We are able to rationally attend to the present and plan for the future and to fashion our own identity. Allport stated that human beings are always in the process of *becoming*, by which he meant that each person can creatively design and implement a satisfactory style of life for himself or herself. The basic urge to become, to grow, to seek unity, and to find meaning is a given in human nature; it is "a major facet." Within the framework of this inherent need for autonomy, individuality, and selfhood, we each grow and develop through our own conscious, deliberate efforts. Growth is a fundamental law of life. We continually move forward, toward integrity and fulfillment.

Allport's position was reflected in his personal liberal stance and his active campaigning for social reform. The humanistic attitude expressed in his work was reflected in his own nature. His intimates and students tell us that he genuinely liked people and cared about them and that these feelings were reciprocated by those who knew him.

A Final Commentary

Allport's theory and research, both so very influential in psychology, are the first in our series not strongly influenced by or growing out of psychoanalysis. Allport is also our first theorist who was not himself psychoanalyzed and who did not provide therapy for the emotionally disturbed. His system, then, does not derive from long therapeutic sessions with neurotics. Because of the origins of his theory in an academic rather than an analytic setting and because of the nature of the theory itself, it has received great interest among academic psychologists concerned with the study of personality.

In spite of this popularity, however, Allport's theory has not been very successful in stimulating research, for several reasons. His stress on idiographic research (studying the individual case) goes against the main current of thought of contemporary psychology, which dictates that the only valid approach is to study large numbers of subjects and describe them in group terms through sophisticated statistical analyses. Allport's insistence on studying only healthy adult subjects is also at variance with the majority position in research in clinical psychology, which emphasizes the study of the neurotic and psychotic.

Also, it must be said that it is extremely difficult to translate some of Allport's concepts into specific terms and operations suitable for study by the more traditional research methods. How, for example, can one observe functional autonomy under laboratory conditions? How can one manipulate it in the laboratory in order to observe its effects or the effects of other variables on it?

Aside from the difficulties of experimentation, there are other criticisms of Allport's system, particularly of the concept of functional autonomy. Allport did not make clear exactly how an original motive is transformed into an autonomous one. By what process is an initial motive to work hard for money, for example, changed into a motive to work hard for its own sake when the person later becomes wealthy? Since the mechanism of transformation is not known, how, critics ask, can one predict which motives in childhood will turn out to be autonomous motives in adulthood?

Allport's conceptual focus on uniqueness is also criticized, the argument being that his position is focused so extremely on the individual that it is impossible to generalize from one person to another. The traditional approach in science is to seek uniformities and generalities. This is impossible, critics charge, when one focuses exclusively on the individual case.

Many psychologists also find it hard to accept Allport's statement of a discontinuity between child and adult, animal and human, and abnormal and normal. They point out that research on children, animals, and the abnormal has yielded much knowledge about the functioning of the normal adult.

Finally, we noted with earlier theorists the emphasis on social and cultural determinants of behavior. Not only in personality theory but in much of academic experimental psychology as well, there is a strong insistence on the role of the social environment in influencing behavior. Critics feel that this influence is not adequately recognized in Allport's theory.

In spite of these points of criticism, Allport's theory has been well recognized and received. His work has not been ignored by those studying and writing about personality, as has been the case with other theorists.

His books are written in a highly readable style, the concepts presented in a manner that has a common-sense feel and appeal for many readers. His approach to the definition and assessment of traits has found wide acceptance among psychologists; indeed, many feel it is his greatest contribution to the study of personality.

The major themes of Allport's theory, while criticized by some, are seen by others as positive contributions. It is argued that his emphasis on rational and conscious determinants of behavior is a useful alternative to the position that we are irrationally and unconsciously driven by uncontrollable forces. In the same vein, his view that we are shaped more by future events than by those of the past is looked upon with favor by those who see human nature in hopeful and humanistic terms.

Suggested Readings

Allport, G. *Becoming: Basic considerations for a psychology of personality.* New Haven, Conn.: Yale University Press, 1955.

Allport, G. *Pattern and growth in personality.* New York: Holt, Rinehart and Winston, 1961.

Allport, G. Autobiography. In E. G. Boring & G. Lindzey (Eds.), *History of psychology in autobiography* (Vol. 5). New York: Appleton-Century-Crofts, 1967.

Allport, G. *The person in psychology.* Boston: Beacon Press, 1968.

Long, L. Alfred Adler & Gordon Allport: A comparison on certain topics in personality theory. *American Journal of Individual Psychology,* 1952–1953, *10,* 43–53.

Maddi, S. R. Humanistic psychology: Allport & Murray. In J. Wepman & R. Heine (Eds.), *Concepts of personality.* Chicago: Aldine, 1963.

O'Connell, D. C. Idiographic knowledge. *Journal of General Psychology,* 1958, *59,* 21–33.

Carl Rogers

11

*The organism has one basic tendency and
striving—to actualize, maintain, and enhance the
experiencing organism.*

—Carl Rogers

Carl Rogers is no doubt well known to you already as the originator
of an extremely popular approach to psychotherapy known as nondirective or client-centered (or, simply, Rogerian) therapy. This form of psychotherapy has generated an enormous amount of research and found
wide application in the treatment of the disturbed. Indeed, Rogerian therapy seems to be almost as popular as Freud's psychoanalysis as a method
of treatment.

As was the case with some of our earlier theorists, Rogers' theory
of personality derived directly from, and is continually being revised in
the light of, his experiences in working with patients, or *clients*, as he
prefers to call them. His formulations on the dynamics and structure
of personality are tied directly to his approach to therapy. Therefore,
his view of the therapeutic situation tells us a great deal about his view
of the nature of personality. Consider the name of his approach: client-

centered therapy. It is intended to suggest that individuals have the ability as well as the responsibility in themselves to change and improve their personality, with the therapist acting to facilitate rather than to direct such change.

Rogers sees people primarily as conscious and rational beings ruled by the conscious perception of their own selves and of their experiential world. There is little influence of the Freudian position to be found in his theory. Rogers does not ascribe a dominant influence to unconscious forces of which an individual has neither awareness nor control.

Rogers also rejects the notion that past events exert a controlling influence on present behavior. While he does recognize that past experiences, particularly those of childhood, can influence the way in which people perceive their world and themselves, he insists that one's present feelings and emotions are of greater importance in the dynamics of personality. Rogers' ultimate concern, both in theory and therapy, is with the change and growth in present personality, not with unconscious or past experiences that might have led to the present state of the personality.

Because of the importance of the conscious and the present, Rogers believes, a personality can only be understood from an individual's own point of view—that is, on the basis of his or her inner, subjective experiences. Rogers, therefore, takes a phenomenological approach to personality—one that deals with reality as it is perceived by the individual. This perception may or may not always coincide with objective reality.

Rogers believes that people have one overriding motivation, with which we come equipped at birth: a tendency to actualize, to develop all of our abilities and potentialities, from the strictly biological to the most sophisticated psychological aspects of our being. The ultimate goal is the actualization of the self—a concept of central importance in Rogers' system. To maintain and enhance the self, to become a "fully functioning person," is the goal toward which all of a person's being is directed.

Rogers' approach to both therapy and theory, and the optimistic and humanistic picture of human beings it provides, has met with an enthusiastic response and has been found to have wide relevance to psychology, education, and family-life research. He has also been one of the more positive (and sobering) influences in the recent upsurge of interest in sensitivity training and encounter groups.

The Life of Rogers (1902–   )

To try to relate Rogers' adult view of personality to his childhood experiences, we would have to look not for insecurity or rejection, conflict or hostility, but rather for signs of an autonomous self, a reliance on his own experience, an emphasis on developing and actualizing potentialities, and a belief that people can consciously change and improve them-selves. Not too surprisingly, that is what we find.

Rogers was born in 1902 in a suburb of Chicago; he was the fourth child in a family of six. His parents were extremely strict in their religious and ethical views, worked very hard, and instilled the "virtue of hard work" in their children. Work was believed to be the cure for almost everything and a kind of ultimate goal, to which everything else should be subordinated.

The parents were very devoted to their children and also very con-trolling in their influence. As Rogers later did in his nondirective counsel-ing, his parents promoted their influence in subtle and loving ways; he could not remember ever having been given a direct command. Yet it was clearly understood by all the children "that we did not dance, play cards, attend movies, smoke, drink, or show any sexual interest."

The family was very close—so much so that Rogers had virtually no social life outside his home. The children teased each other a great deal—"unmercifully," as he described it—and Rogers felt that his parents favored an older brother over himself. As a result, there was "much rivalry and hard feeling" between the brothers, but at the same time there was a great deal of companionship.

Rogers describes himself as having been a solitary boy, dreamy and lost in fantasy much of the time. He read incessantly, any book he could find, even the dictionary and encyclopedia. As a result of this solitude, he came to rely very much on his own experience and his own view of the world, a characteristic that has stayed with him all his life and that forms a part of his personality theory.

When Rogers was 12, the family moved to a farm 30 miles from Chicago, an experience that led to the awakening of Rogers' interest in science. This awakening came about in two ways. First, he became fas-cinated by a certain species of moth that he discovered in the woods. He did more than observe it; he captured some, bred and raised them over many months, and read everything he could find about moths.

The second impetus to his interest in science was farming, which his father insisted be as scientific and modern as possible. He read the books his father brought home about scientific farming, learning about hundreds of experiments and coming to appreciate the scientific method of control groups, isolation of a single variable for study, and statistical analyses of the results. It was an unusual understanding for a boy of 15.

When it came time for college, Rogers chose to study agriculture at the University of Wisconsin, which his parents, two older brothers, and a sister had attended. After his second year, his goal in life changed. As a result of the religious influences in his home and student religious conferences in college, he shifted from the study of scientific agriculture to preparation for the ministry.

During his junior year at Wisconsin, in 1922, Rogers was selected to attend the World Student Christian Federation Conference in Peking, China. During the six months of travel, he wrote to his parents of his changing views, from fundamentalist to liberal, and of his own philosophy and goals. He freed himself of his parents' way of thinking, a departure that grieved his parents but that gave him an emotional and intellectual independence. It was then that he formed the notion, which became the cornerstone of his personality theory, that the individual must rely on his or her own experience as the ultimate guide.

In 1924, Rogers graduated from Wisconsin, married a girl he had known since childhood, and began formal study for the ministry at the Union Theological Seminary in New York City. He stayed there for two years, then transferred across the street to Columbia University Teachers College to study clinical and educational psychology, in which he had developed a greater interest than he had in the ministry.

In 1931, he received his Ph.D., having served an internship in child guidance and done his dissertation on the measurement of personality adjustment in children. For 12 years, from 1928 to 1940, Rogers served on the staff of the Child Study Department of the Society for the Prevention of Cruelty to Children, in Rochester, New York. Most of that time was spent in the diagnosis and treatment of delinquent and underprivileged children, and, in 1939, when the agency was re-formed into the Rochester Guidance Center, he was made director.

In 1940, he moved from a clinical to an academic setting with an appointment as Professor of Psychology at Ohio State University. There, primarily in his work with bright graduate students, Rogers began to formulate and express his views on the counseling and treatment of the emotionally disturbed. He also became involved in professional affairs in psychology, helping to bring clinical psychology into the mainstream of contemporary psychological thought, as represented by the American Psychological Association.

He left Ohio for the University of Chicago in 1945, and went on to the University of Wisconsin in 1957. During these years he was very prolific, publishing a number of articles, papers, and books, which served to bring his method of therapy and view of personality before a wide and interested audience. In 1963, he moved to California, where he is now a Fellow at the Center for Studies of the Person in La Jolla.

Rogers was President of the American Psychological Association in 1946 and ten years later received that organization's Distinguished Scientific Contribution Award.

The Basic Striving: Actualization

As we saw in the opening quotation, Rogers views people as motivated by one overall basic tendency: the tendency to actualize, to maintain and enhance the experiencing organism, which is, of course, ourselves. This innate tendency is the "one fundamental need" of human beings, and it includes all the physiological and psychological needs; but it is, in reality, more oriented toward the biological than the psychological.

As our one fundamental need, the tendency toward actualization includes everything, even the simplest, most reflexive physiological needs, such as those for air, food, and water. It is by attending to these basic physiological needs and by defending the organism against attack that the actualization tendency serves to maintain the organism. That is, it provides for sustenance and for survival itself.

However, as we have seen, the actualization tendency does more than simply maintain the organism; it also facilitates and supports the growth and enhancement—the development—of the organism. It guides growth by providing for the development and differentiation of each and every organ and physiological function of the body. It is responsible for all those aspects of growth that are subsumed under the label *maturation*, which is the genetically determined development of the body's parts and processes, ranging from the growth of the fetus to the appearance of the secondary sex characteristics at the time of puberty.

All these changes, programmed or blueprinted in the person's genetic makeup, are brought to fruition and culmination, according to Rogers, by the actualizing tendency. Even though such changes are genetically determined (programmed in advance), the organism's progress toward full maturation is not an automatic and effortless progression of stages. Rather, Rogers describes the process as involving "struggle and pain," such as when the child takes its first steps. The child falls and is hurt, and it would be less painful to remain in the crawling stage. But no, the child persists. He or she falls and cries again but still continues. The child persists in spite of the pain, Rogers says, because the tendency to actualize, to move forward, to develop and grow is much stronger than any urge to regress brought on by the pains that accompany growth.

This actualizing tendency is seen not only in humans and animals but in all living things. In describing all life, Rogers uses such phrases as the "tenacity of life" and the "forward thrust of life," indicating his belief in the existence of virtually irresistible forces that cause an organism not only to survive, sometimes under extremely hostile conditions, but also to adapt and develop and grow.

There is, then, a very strong biological core to the actualization tendency. We shall see shortly that as the individual matures, this tendency takes on a psychological form as well.

The Frame of Reference: The Experiential Field

Rogers was very much concerned with the environment in which a person operates—the frame of reference or context of the individual, which so strongly influences that person. We are exposed to countless sources of stimulation in the world around us—some trivial and some important, some threatening and some rewarding. How do we perceive and react to this multifaceted environment?

Rogers answers this question very simply by saying that the reality of a person's environment is how he or she perceives that environment. And one's perception may not coincide with objective reality. We know that we may perceive some aspect of reality in a far different way than someone else does. You may see a long-haired college student in a dramatically different light than does your 80-year-old grandmother. Also, our perceptions can change with time and circumstances. Your own perception of a college student may have changed drastically by the time you are 80.

The notion that perception is highly subjective is an old one, certainly not unique or original with Rogers. The important aspect of it, in his view, is that the world of a person's reality is a strictly private affair. It can be known, in any complete sense, only to the individual.

A person's experiential world includes not only immediately present experiences of which the person is aware but also all the stimuli of which he or she is not aware (such as the pressure of the chair on your body as you read) and memories of past experiences, insofar as they are actively guiding the person's perceptions of the moment.

As the infant's actualizing tendency leads it on to ever-higher levels of development, its experiential world broadens. The baby is exposed to more and more sources of stimuli, and its behavior is always in reference to these stimuli as they are perceived.

Experiences combine to make up the experiential field, coalescing into one's own private view of the world. One's experiences, therefore, become of supreme importance. There is, after all, no other basis on which to make judgments and to behave. Rogers wrote: "Experience is, for me, the highest authority. The touchstone of validity is my own experience." Higher levels of development sharpen and define one's experiential world, and they also lead to the formation of what is a central aspect of Rogers' view of personality—the self.

The Self

As an infant develops a more complex experiential field, one part of his or her experience becomes differentiated from the rest. This new and separate part is defined by the words *I*, *me*, and *myself*. It is the self

or self-concept, and it involves distinguishing what is directly and immediately a part of oneself from what is external to oneself. The self-concept
is the person's picture or image of what he or she is, should be, and
might like to be.

There would seem to be room for inconsistencies here among these
three facets of the self-concept. However, Rogers argues that the self,
while fluid, is ideally a consistent pattern, an organized whole. Thus,
all possible aspects of the self strive toward consistency. For example,
someone who considers himself or herself to have absolutely no aggressive feelings toward others dares not express any need for aggression—at
least not in any obvious and direct manner. All behavior must be similarly
consistent with one's self-concept. (The consequences of inconsistency
or incongruity will be discussed later.)

As the self emerges, the infant also develops a need for what Rogers
calls *positive regard*. This need is probably learned, although Rogers believes that its source is irrelevant. Whether innate or learned, the need
for positive regard is pervasive and persistent and is found in all human
beings. As the name implies, positive regard includes acceptance, love,
and approval from other people, notably the mother during infancy. It
is satisfying to receive positive regard and frustrating not to receive it
or to have it withdrawn. Indeed, it is critical to the infant, whose behavior
is guided by the extent to which this affection and love are received.

If the mother does not bestow positive regard, the infant's tendency
toward actualization and enhancement of the self is hampered. The baby
perceives the mother's disapproval of his or her behavior as disapproval
of all aspects of himself or herself. If this occurs very frequently, the
infant ceases to strive to actualize the self and works instead to secure
positive regard. Ideally, the infant feels sufficient acceptance, love, and
approval overall, even though specific behaviors may be met with disapproval. This state or condition is called *unconditional positive regard*, imply-
ing that the mother's love for the child is not conditional upon how the
child behaves but is granted freely and fully to the child as a person.

An important aspect of the need for positive regard is its reciprocal
nature. When people perceive themselves to be satisfying someone else's
need for positive regard, they will, as a result, experience satisfaction
of the need themselves. Thus, it is rewarding to satisfy someone else's
need for positive regard.

Because of the importance of satisfying this need, particularly in
infancy, people become highly sensitive to the attitudes and behaviors
of others. In light of the feedback we receive from others (their approval
or disapproval), we develop and refine our own self-concept. As a part
of this self-concept, we begin to internalize the attitudes of others. As
a result, the positive regard gradually comes more from within ourselves

than from others, a condition Rogers calls *positive self-regard*. This becomes just as strong a need as was the need for positive regard from others, and what satisfies self-regard are the same conditions that brought regard from others. For example, infants who are rewarded by their mothers with affection, approval, and love when they are happy come to experience positive self-regard (on their own) whenever they are happy. They thus come to reward or punish themselves.

Out of this developmental sequence, from positive regard to positive self-regard, evolves the Rogerian version of Freud's superego—*conditions of worth*—which derives from *conditional positive regard*. We noted that unconditional positive regard involved love and acceptance for the infant without conditions—that is, independent of the baby's behavior. As you have probably guessed, conditional positive regard is quite the opposite.

Usually, and understandably, parents do not react to everything their baby does with positive regard. Some behaviors annoy or frighten or bore them, and for those behaviors they do not supply affection or approval. Indeed, they may supply just the opposite. And so the infant comes to learn that the affection and approval of the parents are dependent upon how he or she behaves. The baby comes to see that sometimes he or she is prized and sometimes not.

Out of this situation, infants develop conditions of worth, seeing themselves as worthy only under certain conditions. Having already internalized their parents' norms in their positive self-regard, infants now come to view themselves as worthy or unworthy, according to terms defined by the parents. Unless they abide by the terms of their conditions of worth, infants cannot look upon themselves in a positive manner.

Infants who have arrived at this point must begin to avoid certain behaviors and attitudes, regardless of how satisfying they might otherwise be. Therefore, they can no longer function in full freedom. They must judge and weigh their behavior closely, and so, according to Rogers, they are prevented from fully developing or actualizing their selves, because certain behaviors can no longer be expressed. In a sense, children may inhibit their own development by living within the confines of their conditions of worth.

Not only must the child inhibit certain behaviors; he or she must also deny the awareness of certain perceptions in his or her experiential field, or at least distort them so they will not be perceived accurately. Thus, there develops what Rogers calls *incongruence* between the self-concept and some aspects of an individual's experience. Those experiences that are incongruent with the self serve as a source of *threat* and usually are experienced as a form of anxiety.

As a result of closing oneself off to certain experiences, one is not true to—and may even become estranged from—oneself. Experiences are evaluated and either accepted or rejected, not in terms of how they could contribute to the full actualization of self but rather in terms of the positive regard they will bring.

The anxiety accompanying the threat must be defended against, and the only way one can accomplish this is, as we have seen, to deny or distort aspects of the perceptual field, closing off a portion of it. The result is a rigidity in one's perceptions.

According to Rogers, the level of a person's psychological adjustment, the degree of a person's "normality," is a function of how congruent or compatible the self is with experience. Psychologically healthy persons are able to perceive both themselves and their environments (including other people) much as they really are. They are freely open to all experience because none of it threatens their self-concept. No part of their experience has to be defended against by denial or distortion. Thus, they are free to utilize all experience, to develop all facets of the self, to fulfill all their potentialities. In other words, they are free to become self-actualizing—to proceed toward the goal of becoming fully functioning persons.

The Fully Functioning Person

The fully functioning person is the desired end product of psychological development and of social evolution, according to Rogers. Perhaps the primary characteristic of this self-actualizing person is *awareness of all experiences*. No experience is cut off, distorted, or denied in any way; all of it filters through to the self. There is no defensiveness involved, for there is nothing to defend against; there are no threats to the individual's self-concept. The person is free and open to everything—both to positive feelings, such as courage and tenderness, and to negative ones, such as fear and pain.

A second characteristic of the fully functioning person is the tendency or ability to *live fully and richly in each and every moment*. Each moment, and the experience it can bring, is fresh and new, or at least has the potential to be fresh and new. Hence, each moment cannot be predicted or anticipated. It is lived in fully, participated in rather than observed.

There can be no rigidity, no tight organization or structure imposed on one's experience. The structure, a fluid, ever-changing organization, emerges from the experience. In the nonhealthy person, all experience is organized and distorted to fit one's structured preconceptions.

The third characteristic of the healthy personality is the *trusting of one's own organism*. By that Rogers means trusting the "feel" of one's reaction rather than being guided solely by the judgments of others, or by a social code, or even by intellectual judgments. Rogers wrote: "I have learned that my total organism's sensing of a situation is more trustworthy than my intellect." Behaving in a way that "feels right," he said, is a trustworthy guide to truly satisfying behavior.

This is not to suggest that the self-actualizing person completely ignores data from his or her intellect or from others. Rather, it means that all such data (such experiences) are congruent with the person's self-concept. They are not threatening and can be perceived accurately and evaluated and weighed accordingly. The final decision regarding how to behave in a particular situation, therefore, results from a consideration of all experiential data. However, the person is unaware of undertaking such considerations (because of the congruence between self and experience), and so the decision seems to be intuitive. It seems more emotionally than intellectually based; again, it feels right.

A fourth characteristic is a *sense of freedom.* Healthy, self-actualizing persons feel genuinely free to move in any direction they wish—to be themselves or to hide behind a social role, to move forward or backward, or to behave in either self-enhancing or disabling ways. The point is that they do not feel compelled—either by others or by themselves—to behave in one and only one way. They are not driven along a single path.

Rogers also believes that the healthy personality is a very *creative* individual, living constructively and adaptively even as his or her environmental conditions may change. Allied with this creativity—indeed, very much a part of it—is a sense of spontaneity. The person can flexibly adapt to—and seek out—new experiences and challenges. He or she does not need predictability, security, or a tension-free state. In fact, those conditions are anathema to the fully functioning person.

Rogers does not feel that adjectives such as *happy, blissful,* or *contented* are appropriate to describe the self-actualizing person, though such a person would certainly have those feelings at certain times. More appropriate descriptive labels to apply to the healthy person's experience are *enriching, exciting, rewarding, challenging,* and *meaningful.*

Admittedly, it is difficult to be a self-actualizing person, for it involves continually testing, growing, stretching, and using all of one's potentialities. Put simply, "it involves the courage to be," and there is much complexity, trial, and challenge in that prescription.

There is one final point to be made about the self-actualizing person, and it is implicit in the ending of the word *actualizing.* Rogers never uses the word *actualized,* for that would imply a finished and static personality. That is decidedly not the case; the development of such a person is always in process. The self-actualizing person is continually changing and growing as he or she strives to actualize all of his or her potentialities. If such growth ceased, the person would lose the characteristics of spontaneity, flexibility, and openness to new experiences. The emphasis in Rogers' system is neatly captured in the title of one of his books: *On Becoming a Person.*

Techniques of Inquiry

Rogers believes that the only way to explore and understand personality is in terms of an individual's own subjective experiences—that is, through studying the individual's experiential field. The therapist, in Rogers' view, must see the client's world of experience (his or her reality) as much as possible through the client's own eyes. While Rogers considers this inquiry into a person's experiential field the only worthwhile approach to take, he is quick to point out that it is not infallible and that there are drawbacks to it.

For one thing, by focusing on subjective experiences, the therapist gains information only about those aspects of the experiential field that the individual consciously experiences. Experience not represented in conscious awareness is lost to view. There is also a danger in trying to infer too much about these nonconscious experiences. The inference may come to represent more the projections of the therapist than the experiences of the client.

Rogers recognizes that the amount that can be learned about a person's internal frame of reference depends heavily on the fidelity of the communications from the client. Noting that all forms of communication in all settings are "faulty and imperfect," Rogers argues that we see the client's world of experience imperfectly, not as a precise mirror image.

Within these limits, Rogers insists that his client-centered therapy provides the clearest view possible of a person's internal frame of reference. He maintains that other forms or approaches to therapy do not even attempt to explore the experiential field. One advantage he sees in his form of therapy is that it does not approach a client with a predetermined theoretical structure (Freudian or Adlerian, for instance) into which the patient must somehow be fit. The only predetermined belief of the nondirective therapist is in the inherent worth and value of the client with whom the therapist is working. Clients are accepted as they are and for what they are; in other words, they are given unconditional positive regard. No negative judgments are made of the clients' behavior, nor are clients given direction, guidance, or advice as to how they should behave or what they should do in their relations with themselves and others. As the name of the technique indicates, everything is centered in the client, including the responsibility and ability to change his or her own behavior.

Rogers is much opposed to the use of special techniques in therapy, such as free association, psychological testing, and even the taking of case histories. He believes that the use of such techniques is more harmful than helpful because it puts the client in a position of dependency relative to the therapist, who assumes an aura of expertise and authority. These techniques take away any sense of responsibility the clients would otherwise assume, by giving them the impression that the therapist knows everything about them as a result of the case history, tests, and free associations. The clients may then come to feel that the therapist must also have the answers to everything and that all they have to do is sit back and follow the expert's directions and prescriptions.

Rogers uses no such techniques. His therapy is characterized by the attitude that his clients have the ability to see to the roots of their own problems and to direct the future growth, enhancement, and actualization that was prevented by the incongruity that developed between themselves and their experience.

Rogers did introduce a radical innovation into psychotherapy, one that enabled researchers for the first time to fully investigate the nature of the client-therapist interaction. He did this by the simple and now rather widely used method of tape recording therapy sessions and sometimes filming them as well. Prior to that, the only data that proceeded from a therapeutic situation were in the form of the therapist's written reconstruction of what had been said. In addition to the vagaries and distortions of memory (for the therapy notes were usually made after the session had ended), such a written record misses the postural and gestural data. A facial expression or tone of voice can sometimes convey or reveal more than a patient's words.

With filmed and/or tape-recorded sessions, everything said and done during a session is available for study. Thus, much more actual data are available to Rogers than was the case for earlier theorists. It should be noted that Rogers always obtains the prior permission of a client to tape or film, and he has found that it does not seem to impede the course of therapy. In fact, clients quickly come to ignore the equipment and proceed as though it were not there.

While the bulk of the data from which Rogers' theory of personality is derived have come directly from therapy sessions, he and his associates have also conducted a large amount of research on the therapy process, the data from which have been used to further develop and support the theory. It is largely through Rogers' research that psychologists have been able to make at least a beginning in the understanding of the psychotherapeutic process.

In particular, this research focused on the self-concept and the various ways it may change during a course of therapy. Using both qualitative and quantitative techniques, Rogers and his associates analyzed various aspects of therapy sessions. Through the use of rating scales and content analysis of a client's verbalizations, it has been possible to investigate, in fairly precise terms, the nature of the changes in self-concept.

Rogers has also made great use of the "Q-Sort Technique," a procedure in which a client sorts a large number of statements that refer to self-concept (such as "I enjoy being alone") into categories that range from most descriptive of the person to least descriptive. It is a way of empirically defining the client's image or picture of himself or herself. There are a variety of Q-Sort procedures. For example, after sorting the statements in terms of the picture the person has of himself or herself, the client might be asked to sort the same statements in terms of his or her ideal self—that is, the kind of person he or she would like to be. Whatever specific procedure is used, the Q-Sort technique allows for the quantification of various aspects of a client's self-concept.

Rogers' Image of Human Nature

A personality theory that credits human beings with the ability, motivation, and responsibility to understand and improve themselves (with a therapist acting as facilitator instead of guide) obviously views people in a very optimistic and positive light. Rogers sees us as having a basically healthy nature; we have an innate tendency to grow and actualize all aspects of our being—to become all that we are capable of becoming.

Human beings are not, in Rogers' view, doomed to conflict with themselves or with their society, are not ruled by instinctive biological forces, and are not dictated to by events that occurred in the first five years of life. Our view is always forward, progressive rather than regressive, and oriented toward growth rather than stagnation. We experience our world fully and freely, not defensively, and seek new challenges and stimulation instead of hiding behind the security of the familiar.

To be sure, emotional disturbances do occur; stagnation and regression do take place, but they are the exception, not the rule. Further, people are able to overcome these regressions and disturbances (through nondirective therapy), using their own inner resources—their innate urge to grow and develop.

Since individuals are viewed in such positive terms, it follows that society is considered in the same light. After all, Rogers states, that which is compatible with enhancement and actualization of one individual is equally compatible with the growth of those with whom the individual interacts. The innate urge to fully develop one's potentialities, to become a fully functioning person, benefits not only the individual but society as well. Social enhancement follows the actualization of the individual members of a culture.

In summary, it is natural and inevitable for a human being to grow, to move forward, to be consciously aware of the self, and to facilitate and implement his or her own growth.

A Final Commentary

Rogers' client-centered approach to psychotherapy has been enormously popular among psychologists and has found wide application as a method of treating emotional disturbance. His theory of personality, while less influential than his form of psychotherapy, nevertheless has also received recognition and acceptance, particularly its stress on the importance of the self-concept. It must be noted that most of his writings have been directed toward his therapy. In contrast, he has written relatively little in the way of a formal statement of the full dimensions of his personality theory.

Criticisms of his theory have been directed primarily at two aspects of it. First, Rogers has been criticized for failing to state, in precise terms, what constitute the innate potentialities to enhancement and actualization that occupy such a central position in his theory. Critics ask whether this potential is primarily physiological or psychological and whether there are individual differences in it; that is, do some people have more of it than others? Nowhere in his writings does Rogers provide the answers to these and related questions about the exact nature of this potential. He describes it as a kind of "genetic blueprint," in accordance with which the organism will develop. But the way this mechanism operates, critics charge, has yet to be clarified.

The second major criticism refers to Rogers' insistence that the only way to explore personality is through the examination of a person's subjective experiences. Since he does this by listening to the client's self-reports, he is missing, critics allege, those forces and factors of which the client is not conscious, yet which can influence his or her behavior. Psychoanalysts, in particular, argue that patients may consciously or unconsciously distort their own subjective experiences, repressing some and elaborating on (or inventing) others, so as to conceal their true nature, to present an idealized picture of themselves.

On the positive side, Rogers' theory and his approach to therapy —and sometimes it becomes difficult to separate the two—have stimulated a wealth of research, performed by Rogers and his colleagues as well as by others moved by his formulations to take them into the laboratory. More than any theorist covered so far, he has been responsible for stimulating much valuable research on the nature of psychotherapy and the form and substance of the client-therapist interactions. Provoking even more research are his formulations on the self-concept. Probably no personality theorist has had a greater impact on both theoretical and empirical definitions of the self. If a theory is judged solely on the basis of its heuristic value—how much research it has provoked and generated— then the theory of Carl Rogers must be ranked very high indeed.

His background experience is a unique combination of clinic, lecture hall, and laboratory. Not confined to clinic or college, he has been able to draw on considerable experience in working with disturbed individuals as well as on the intellectual stimulation available to him during his years in academics. Further, he attracted large numbers of loyal Rogerian graduate students who continue to put his theory to the test in both the clinic and the laboratory.

Currently, Carl Rogers is actively exploring a relatively recent phenomenon in psychology: the great surge of interest in encounter groups, sensitivity training, T-groups, and related experiences that attempt to free human beings to become all they are capable of becoming.

Suggested Readings

Rogers, C. R. Some issues concerning the control of human behavior. *Science,* 1956, *124,* 1057–1066.

Rogers, C. R. *On becoming a person: A therapist's view of psychotherapy.* Boston: Houghton Mifflin, 1961.

Rogers, C. R. Toward a science of the person. *Journal of Humanistic Psychology,* 1963, *3,* 72–92.

Rogers, C. R. Autobiography. In E. G. Boring & G. Lindzey (Eds.), *History of psychology in autobiography* (Vol. 5). New York: Appleton-Century-Crofts, 1967. Pp. 341–384.

Rogers, C. R., & Dymond, R. F. *Psychotherapy and personality change.* Chicago: University of Chicago Press, 1954.

Smith, M. B. The phenomenological approach in personality theory: Some critical remarks. *Journal of Abnormal and Social Psychology,* 1950, *45,* 516–522.

Abraham Maslow

12

What a man can *be, he* must *be.*

—Abraham Maslow

Abraham Maslow is well known in contemporary psychology for the impetus he gave to a new direction, a new movement that has appeared in recent years: humanistic psychology. This so-called third force in psychology was mounted to combat what its proponents saw as weaknesses and failures on the part of the other two forces in contemporary psychology—behaviorism and psychoanalysis.

The humanist influence argues that a behavioristic approach to psychology (to be discussed in Chapters 15 and 16) studies people as if they were machines, reducing their complexity and richness to simple behaviors of the kind emitted by a rat in a maze. Human beings, Maslow argued, cannot be considered merely large rats or efficient computers.

Such conceptions dehumanize people—strip them of all the qualities that are associated with being human beings.

Maslow (and other third-force psychologists, among them Carl Rogers) was equally critical of the approach to understanding human beings taken by Sigmund Freud. By studying only the worst of humanity—that is, neurotics and psychotics—psychology ignores all the positive and beneficial human emotions, such as happiness, contentment, satisfaction, and peace of mind. One of Maslow's most frequently quoted statements is that "the study of the crippled, stunted, immature, and unhealthy specimens can yield only a cripple psychology . . . ."

We have underestimated human nature, Maslow charged, by not studying the best examples of humanity—the most creative, the healthiest, and the most mature. And this approach—studying what he calls the "growing tip" of mankind, the best representatives of the species—is one of the most distinctive features of Maslow's theory of the human personality. As he noted, when you want to determine how fast humans can run, you study not the average runner, and certainly not the crippled one, but the fastest runner you can find. Only in this way is it possible to determine the heights of human potential.

Maslow's theory of personality, therefore, does not derive from the emotionally disturbed or from the conflict or anxiety ridden but from the healthiest personalities. As a result of years of research on such people, a theory of personality has evolved that could just as easily be called a theory of motivation, for motivation is the core and foundation of his approach.

Using primarily case histories, Maslow intensively studied a small group of the healthiest and best personalities, living and dead. For example, using biographical material, he studied Thomas Jefferson, Abraham Lincoln, and other historical figures. From these investigations and those of living persons, he concluded that each person is born with certain *instinctoid* needs, which cause the person to choose to grow, develop, and actualize himself or herself—to fulfill all his or her potentialities.

Maslow posited a hierarchy of needs, a ladder of motivations; those needs on the bottom rung must be satisfied before the next rung assumes prominence. When the second-level need is satisfied, then the third-level need takes precedence, and so on. At the bottom level, the physiological needs are prominent. When they are satisfied, safety needs become paramount, then the needs for belongingness and love, followed by the need for esteem, and finally the need for self-actualization.

Maslow's approach to personality is highly controversial in psychology today, as is humanistic psychology in general. However, it is also very popular, particularly among younger psychologists and students, many of whom are carrying on Maslow's work.

The Life of Maslow (1908–1970)

It is perhaps understandable that Maslow, who rose out of a child-hood that today would be called disadvantaged to a position of respect and prominence, would believe in the tendency of the self to grow, develop, and actualize. It is also understandable that, coming from a background where food and shelter were important everyday concerns, Maslow would develop a system in which those needs assume a position of primacy until they are satisfied. Since as a child he felt lonely and isolated, it is not surprising that needs for belongingness, love, and esteem are important, in his theory, once physiological and safety needs are satisfied.

Maslow was born in 1908 in Brooklyn, New York. His parents were immigrants with little education and little prospect of rising above the marginal conditions under which they lived. As with so many immigrant parents, their hopes were for the next generation; they hoped that their children would rise to a higher station in life. Maslow's father, at the age of 14, had walked and hitchhiked from Russia across all of Western Europe, so great was his ambition to emigrate to America. This drive and motivation to succeed seems to have been instilled in the young Maslow.

Maslow's childhood was not an idyllic one. As the only Jewish boy in his neighborhood, he was very aware of his minority-group status. By his own description, he was isolated and unhappy, growing up without friends or companions. As so many others have done in similar situations of isolation and loneliness, Maslow turned to books for companionship. The library became the playground of his childhood and books and education the road out of the ghetto of poverty and loneliness.

At his father's insistence, Maslow began the study of law, but he decided after two weeks that he didn't like it. What he really wanted to do was study "everything," a desire his father found difficult to understand. His passion for learning was accompanied by a passion, at age 16, for the girl he would one day marry—another desire his father found hard to accept. Maslow left home, going first to Cornell and then to the University of Wisconsin, where his intended wife joined him.

They married—he at 20, she at 19—and it was a significant step for Maslow. The marriage seemed to provide him not only with a sense of belongingness and love but also with a purpose and direction. He said that life did not really begin for him until he got married and began his studies at Wisconsin. In addition to his wife, he discovered and was enraptured by the behavioristic psychology of John B. Watson, the prime mover in the revolution to make psychology a science of behavior. Maslow looked upon behaviorism, as so many people did in the early 1930s, as a panacea for all the world's problems. At Wisconsin he received solid training in experimental psychology of the behaviorist mode, working with monkeys under psychologist Harry Harlow. In addition to his professional training, Maslow received personal help and advice from his professors. They taught him the social amenities, including how to buy a suit.

It is a giant step from Maslow's graduate training and research in behaviorism to self-actualization, from monkeys to the growing tip of mankind. There were a number of influences that combined to bring about this profound shift—some intellectual and others highly personal and emotional. They ranged from exposure to Freud, Gestalt psychology, and the philosophies of Alfred North Whitehead and Henri Bergson to the birth of his first child. "That," he said, "was the thunderclap that settled things . . . . I was stunned by the mystery and by the sense of not really being in control. I felt small and weak and feeble before all this. I'd say anyone who had a baby couldn't be a behaviorist."

Maslow received his Ph.D. from Wisconsin in 1934 and returned to New York, first to Columbia University and then to Brooklyn College, where he remained until 1951. He was in New York at a most propitious time—the late 1930s and early 1940s—when the wave of emigrant intellectuals from Nazi Germany arrived. He eagerly met and learned from Erich Fromm, Karen Horney, Max Wertheimer (a leading Gestalt psychologist), and Alfred Adler. In addition, he was greatly influenced by the American anthropologist Ruth Benedict, whom he also met during this time. In fact, it was his awe of and admiration for Ruth Benedict and Max Wertheimer that led to his research on self-actualization and to the personality theory that derived from it.

During those early post-Ph.D. years, Maslow continued his Wisconsin research on sexual behavior but shifted from monkeys to humans. The research lasted until 1941, when his interests were changed by the beginning of World War II, an event that moved him deeply. From that time on, he devoted himself to research to improve the human personality and to demonstrate that we are capable of much higher and more noble behavior than hatred, war, and prejudice.

The beginning of the war was an intensely emotional experience. Maslow told of watching, with tears streaming down his face, a ragtag parade, shortly after the attack on Pearl Harbor. "I had a vision of a peace table, with people sitting around it, talking about human nature and hatred and war and peace and brotherhood."

The desire to humanize psychology and to understand humanity's loftiest potentials emerged from that experience and provided Maslow with a compelling sense of mission that never left him. In 1951, he went to Brandeis University, where he later became chairman of the psychology department. He remained at Brandeis, developing and refining his theory, until 1969, when he moved to California (under a foundation grant) to undertake the large-scale effort of formulating a philosophy of politics, economics, and ethics generated by a humanistic brand of psychology.

Toward the end of his life, he became an immensely popular figure, not only in psychology but among many segments of the general population as well. He was much involved with the sensitivity-group movement and was a strong supporter of the Esalen Institute in California. After he suffered a heart attack, he threw himself into his work more vigorously than ever and gave up favorite activities such as plays, poetry reading, and long walks in the woods. In one of his last interviews, he said, "How can I piddle around at these things when work has to be done, and mankind has to be helped."

During his lifetime, Maslow received a great many awards and honors, including election to the presidency of the American Psychological Association in 1967.

Motivation: The Hierarchy of Needs

Maslow's theory of motivation is very much at the heart of his approach to the understanding of personality. The basic idea of his motivational theory is straightforward. There are, Maslow wrote, a number of innate needs that activate and direct the behavior of every individual. The needs themselves are instinctoid; we come equipped with them at birth. The behaviors that we use to satisfy the needs, however, are not innate but learned and therefore subject to wide variation from one person to the next.

Another characteristic of these universal needs is their arrangement in a hierarchy of prepotency, as shown below.

5. the need for self-actualization
4. the need for esteem
3. the needs for belongingness and love
2. the need for safety
1. the physiological needs

The needs that stand at the bottom rung of the motivational ladder must be satisfied before those at the top can be satisfied. Indeed, the needs at the top will not even appear until the lower-order ones have been at least partially satisfied. For example, a person who is hungry and fears for his or her safety will feel no need whatsoever for belongingness or love. The individual is concerned (or perhaps obsessed) with bread, not love.

It is only when people have adequate food (and the rest of their physiological needs are satisfied) and when they feel safe that they come to feel the needs for belongingness and love. And when those needs are satisfied, people long for esteem. When they achieve that, they desire self-actualization. The important point is that people are not driven by all these needs at the same time. Only one need is dominant at a time; which one it will be depends on which of the others are satisfied or not satisfied.

A highly successful businesswoman is no longer driven by or even aware of the physiological needs; they are well taken care of. She may be driven now to seek esteem or self-actualization. However, the priority of the needs can be shifted or reversed. If a sudden economic recession grips the country and the businesswoman loses her job and uses up all of her savings, then the physiological needs can reassume priority, and she will forget all about esteem or self-actualization. A can of beans might then be more prized than an award from the Chamber of Commerce.

Higher versus Lower Needs

The lower the need is in the hierarchy, the greater its strength, potency, or priority. The higher needs are obviously weaker. Maslow made a number of other distinctions between higher and lower-order needs:

1. The higher needs appeared later in the evolutionary development of mankind. All living things need food and water, but only humans have a need to self-actualize and to know and understand. Therefore, the higher the need the more distinctly human it is.
2. Higher needs appear later in the development of an individual. Self-actualization, for example, may not appear until midlife, while the infant has physiological and safety needs.
3. Higher needs are less necessary for sheer survival, hence their gratification can be postponed longer. Failure to satisfy a higher need does not produce as much of an immediate emergency or crisis reaction as failure to satisfy a lower need. Thus, the lower needs are also called *deficit* or *deficiency needs* because failure to satisfy them produces some kind of deficiency in the individual.
4. While they are less necessary for survival, the higher needs nevertheless can contribute to survival and growth. Higher-level need satisfaction produces better health, longer life, and a generally enhanced biological efficiency. For this reason, the higher needs are also called *growth needs*.
5. Higher-need satisfaction is productive or beneficial not only biologically but psychologically as well, because it produces a deeper happiness, peace of mind, and fullness in one's inner life.

6. Higher-need gratification involves more preconditions and greater complexity than lower-need satisfaction. The search for self-actualization, for example, has the precondition that all the other needs have first been satisfied and involves more complicated and sophisticated behavior and goals than, say, the search for food.
7. Higher-need gratification requires better external conditions (social, economic, and political) than lower-need gratification. For example, greater freedom of expression and opportunity are required for self-actualization than for safety.

There is one additional point to be made before we discuss each of the specific needs in more detail. A need does not have to be absolutely and fully satisfied before the next one in the hierarchy emerges. Maslow spoke instead of partial satisfaction, of a declining percentage of satisfaction in each need as we go up the hierarchy. Using strictly hypothetical figures, he described a person who has satisfied, in turn, 85% of the physiological needs, 70% of the safety needs, 50% of the love and belongingness needs, 40% of the esteem need, and 10% of the self-actualization need.

The Basic Needs

Physiological Needs.   The obvious needs for food, water, air, sleep, and sex are, of course, the most basic and powerful of all the needs. They are capable of totally blocking out every other need. If you have ever had the experience of struggling for air while under water or going for days without food, you realize how trivial the needs for love or esteem or anything else become when a physiological need is not satisfied.

Maslow noted that a starving person thinks, dreams, and wants only food. But once the need is satisfied, the person is no longer aware of it, no longer driven by it. It ceases to direct or control the person's behavior or assume any importance to him or her. Such is the case for most people in an affluent, industrialized Western culture; physiological needs are usually more important as motivating forces in people for whom sheer survival is an everyday concern.

Safety Needs.   The need for safety is most important, Maslow believed, in infants and in neurotic adults. Healthy, normal adults generally have satisfied this need well. Its satisfaction requires security, stability, protection, structure, order, and freedom from fear and anxiety. In infants and young children, the safety needs can be seen most clearly, if for no other reason than that infants react more visibly and immediately to threats and fear than do adults, who have learned to inhibit their fear reactions to some degree.

Another visible indication of children's needs for safety is their preference for a structured routine—their need for a predictable and orderly world. Maslow felt that total permissiveness and freedom—a complete absence of structure and order—produces anxiety and insecurity in children because it is a threat to their security needs. Freedom must, of course, be granted to children, but only within the limits of what they can cope with. They must be given some guidance, for they are not yet capable of directing themselves.

A neurotic and insecure adult also needs a degree of structure and order in his or her environment because the safety need is still dominant. The neurotic compulsively avoids new, unexpected, or different experiences and orders his or her world so as to make it completely predictable. The person's entire life is constructed around a rigid set of routines—"At 9:00, I'll do this; at 10:00, I'll do that"—structuring every minute of the day and ordering every aspect of his or her world. Pencils must be kept in a certain place and clothes hung in a certain manner.

Maslow also pointed out that, although most normal adults have satisfied this need, they still require some degree of security. Most of us prefer predictability to the totally unknown, order to chaos, and so we save for the future, buy insurance, and remain in a safe job rather than take a chance on a new and unknown business venture. However, the need for this kind of security is not as compulsive or overwhelming in the normal adult as it is in the neurotic or the infant.

Belonging and Love Needs.   Once an individual's physiological and safety needs have been reasonably well satisfied, he or she develops the needs for belonging and love. These needs can be manifested in a variety of ways: through affectionate relations with other people in general, or through a relationship with a particular friend, lover, or mate, or through finding a place or position in a particular group and/or in society at large.

The need to belong, Maslow thought, is difficult to satisfy in an increasingly mobile society. Few people stay in the same neighborhood and keep the same friends all their lives, or even for more than a few years at a time. We change jobs, schools, and towns too frequently to put down roots, to develop a secure sense of belonging, and so we must seek to satisfy the need in other ways. Maslow suggested that the eager acceptance of sensitivity groups, personal-growth encounter sessions, and communes, which began in the late 1960s and early 1970s, demonstrates efforts to satisfy the feelings of loneliness and alienation that derive from failure to satisfy the need to belong.

The need for love, which involves the need to give love as well as receive it, can be satisfied in a warm relationship of intimacy with another person. Maslow did not equate love with sex (a purely physiological need) but recognized that sex is one way of expressing the love need. Failure to satisfy the need for love is, in Maslow's opinion, one of the fundamental causes of maladjustment in our culture. "Love hunger," he wrote, "is a deficiency disease."

Esteem Needs.   Once people feel loved and have a sense of belonging, they then develop the need for esteem. They now need respect both from themselves in the form of a feeling of self-worth, and from others, in the form of status, recognition, social success, fame, and the like. There are, then, two kinds of esteem needs: for self-esteem and for esteem granted by other people.

Satisfaction of the need for self-esteem allows a person to feel confident of his or her strength, worth, and adequacy. As a result of such feelings, the individual may become more competent and productive in all aspects of life. When there is a lack of self-esteem, on the other hand, the person feels inferior, helpless, and discouraged and lacks sufficient confidence to cope with problems. Maslow pointed out that self-esteem, if it is to be genuine, must be based on a realistic assessment of one's own abilities and competence and on truly deserved respect from others. It is vital that the status, prestige, and good reputation a person may be accorded by others not consist solely of unearned or undeserved praise but rather be earned recognition of real competence and adequacy.

Self-Actualization.   The person is now ready to move to the final stage of development, the realization and fulfillment of all his or her potentialities and capabilities. The person must become, and be, what he or she has the potential to be. Even though all four of the previous needs may be satisfied, the person who is not self-actualizing, not utilizing his or her potential, will be discontented and restless. The individual will be frustrated, as he or she would be at the failure to satisfy any other need.

Maslow wrote: "A musician must make music, an artist must paint, a poet must write, if he is to be ultimately at peace with himself." Self-actualizing can take many unique forms, not all of which result in some artistic product. Maslow pointed out that people in all walks of life—a woman raising children or driving a truck, or a man on an assembly line or employed as a cook—have the opportunity to fulfill their potential. .

There are a number of preconditions necessary for self-actualization. One is freedom from restraints imposed either by the culture or by one's own self. Another is that the person not be distracted by concerns for food or safety, be secure in his or her self-image and with family and other groups, and love and be loved in return. Above all, the person must know himself or herself—have a realistic knowledge of his or her strengths and weaknesses, vices and virtues, and skills and abilities. After all, how can a self be actualized if it is not known and understood?

Maslow's personality theory grew out of his research on self-actualizing people, and, as we shall see, he had much to say about the psychological composition of these people.

A Second Hierarchy of Needs

Maslow was quite definite about another set of human needs—the needs to know and understand—which he did not place in the hierarchy that we have been discussing so far. He posited curiosity, and the needs to know and to understand, as innate drives that push for satisfaction. He noted a number of lines of evidence that converge to support the existence of these needs.

1. Laboratory studies with animals show that they actively explore and manipulate their environments for no other apparent reason than curiosity.
2. There is much historical evidence of people seeking knowledge at the risk of their lives, thus putting this need ahead of even the safety needs.
3. There are many studies suggesting that healthy, mature adults are strongly attracted to the unknown and mysterious, the unorganized and unexplained.
4. In his clinical practice, Maslow described otherwise healthy people who suffered from boredom and a lack of zest or excitement in their lives. He referred to them as intelligent people leading "stupid lives in stupid jobs" and found that they improved when they involved themselves in some challenging cognitive activity.

Maslow believed that the needs to know and understand appear early in life—in late infancy and early childhood—and are expressed as a child's natural curiosity, which does not have to be taught, although schools and parents may teach a child to inhibit this spontaneous curiosity. Failure to satisfy these needs is harmful, as is failure to satisfy any of Maslow's needs, and can inhibit the development and full functioning of the personality.

There are several ways in which these needs are manifested. These include the need to analyze, to reduce things to their basic elemental parts, the need to experiment, to "see what will happen if I do this," and the need to explain, to construct a system or theory that will make sense out of the events and conditions of one's world.

While these needs are not, as noted, a part of the basic hierarchy of needs, Maslow suggested that they form a small, separate hierarchy of their own. The need to know is more potent than the need to understand. This hierarchy operates in the same way as the larger one; that is, the first need must be at least partially satisfied before the next is able to emerge.

Finally, Maslow pointed out that there is an inevitable overlap or interaction between the two need hierarchies. Knowing and understanding, finding a meaning in one's world, is basic to interacting with that environment in order to function properly and so gain love, esteem, and self-fulfillment.

Exceptions to the Hierarchy

While Maslow believed that the major need hierarchy is descriptive of most people, he pointed out that it does not apply to everyone. For example, throughout history, people especially dedicated to a cause or an ideal have willingly sacrificed everything, including their lives. People who fast until death, or set themselves on fire for a cause, are obviously denying their physiological and safety needs. Religious figures who abandon worldly goods to live a life of poverty and hardship may be expressing their fullest potential, in spite of the frustration of their deficiency or lower-order needs. The same may be said of artists who place their health and survival in danger for the sake of their work.

Maslow also pointed out a common reversal in the need hierarchy: some people place a greater importance on self-esteem than on love. Such individuals feel that they can satisfy the love and belonging needs only if they feel very self-confident and worthy.

Characteristics of Self-Actualizers

Maslow's research on the best and the healthiest people he could find—the growing tip of mankind—formed the basis for his personality theory. Although he did not find very many subjects who could be considered self-actualizing (he estimated that they constitute 1% or less of the population), he did study enough of them to show that they exhibit certain characteristics.

1. *A highly efficient perception of reality.* Self-actualizers are able to perceive the world around them, including other people, clearly and objectively. Their perception is not distorted by subjective factors such as fears and needs. They see reality exactly as it is, not as they might want or need it to be. Maslow called this highly objective, nonbiased kind of perception *Being Cognition* (or B Cognition). Self-actualizers are quite

accurate in their judgments of other people and are able to see through the false and the phony. In sum, they see the world as it is, unbiased by any prejudgment or preconception.

2. *An acceptance of themselves, of other people, and of nature in general.* Self-actualizers can accept their own natures—their weaknesses as well as strengths—without trying to falsify or distort their image and without feeling excessive shame or guilt about any failings (and they do have imperfections). They take the same attitude of acceptance toward the weaknesses and evils of other people and of mankind in general.

3. *A spontaneity, simplicity, and naturalness.* The behavior of self-actualizers is quite open, direct, and natural, not based on the facade of a social role. Ordinarily, self-actualizers do not hide their feelings or emotions or pretend to be something they are not, although they may do so if it would prevent hurting someone else. They are highly individualistic in their ideas and ideals but not necessarily unconventional in their behavior. Such persons are essentially themselves, without being aggressively rebellious about it.

4. *A focusing on problems rather than on self.* Self-actualizers ordinarily have a sense of mission in their lives—work outside of or beyond themselves to which they devote most of their energies. In fact, dedication to some work or duty or vocation—a sense of commitment—is one of the outstanding requirements for self-actualization, in Maslow's view. Because of this commitment, self-actualizers work very hard but find great pleasure and excitement in it.

Regardless of the specific direction in which they are committed, their lives are devoted to the search for what Maslow called *Being Values* (or B Values). These ultimate values include perfection, justice, beauty, goodness, playfulness, truth, and self-sufficiency, among others. B Values take on the characteristics of needs; Maslow called them *metaneeds*. As with other needs, their frustration produces a pathological condition (metapathology, in this case).

5. *A need for privacy and independence.* Not only are these extremely healthy people capable of withstanding isolation from others without harmful effects, but they also need solitude far more than the non-self-actualizing individual. They depend more upon themselves for their satisfactions and so do not need other people in the sense of being dependent upon them. Since they are so independent of others, even aloof, they are often considered unfriendly and cold, but this is not their intent or desire. They are simply more autonomous than most people and don't have to cling to or demand support or warmth from them.

6. *A continued freshness of appreciation.* Self-actualizers have the ability to continue to perceive and experience the world around them with freshness, wonder, and awe. While an experience may grow stale for the more

average person, the supremely healthy one will enjoy a sunset, a flower, or a symphony as though it were the first one ever experienced. Even mundane and trivial objects and experiences can be appreciated at a high level of delight, including possessions and accomplishments. Self-actualizers continue to freshly appreciate what they have, and they take nothing for granted.

7. *The mystical or "peak" experience.* Self-actualizers have moments of intense ecstasy, wonder, awe, and delight, not unlike deep religious experiences, during which the self is lost or transcended. During these experiences, the person feels all powerful—extremely confident and decisive. Experience is intensified, becoming orgasmic in strength; this can occur in the context of virtually any activity. Maslow said that "any experience of real excellence, of real perfection, of any moving toward the perfect justice or toward perfect values, tends to produce a peak experience." In his later work, he distinguished between two kinds of self-actualizers: peakers and nonpeakers. They share the same characteristics, except that the latter have few transcendent experiences. Maslow also suggested that some non-self-actualizers can have peak experiences, although not as many as self-actualizers.

8. *Social interest.* Maslow used Adler's term *Gemeinschaftsgefühl* to indicate the sympathy and empathy these extremely healthy people have for mankind in general. While they are often irritated or depressed by the behavior of individuals, they nevertheless feel a kinship with and an understanding of others. Borrowing from Adler, Maslow described the self-actualizer as having the attitude of an older brother toward other people.

9. *Interpersonal relations.* While their circle of close friends is not very large (there being so few other self-actualizing people), the friendships of self-actualizers are much more intense and profound than those of the average person. As you might imagine, they pick as close friends those who are healthier and more mature than most, just as we all choose friends whose characteristics are compatible with our own. Maslow also found that self-actualizers often attract admirers or disciples. Such relationships are usually one-sided, in that the admirer asks more of the self-actualizer than he or she is able (or willing) to give.

10. *Creativeness.* It is not surprising that those self-actualizing subjects in Maslow's research tended to be highly creative individuals, although they did not always produce artistic creations. That is, they were not all artists or writers, but they all exhibited inventiveness and originality in virtually every aspect of their lives.

In all their activities, self-actualizers are flexible, spontaneous, and willing to make mistakes. They are open and humble, in the same way that a child is before the world has taught it to be afraid of making mistakes or of doing something silly.

11. *A democratic character structure.* Self-actualizers, Maslow found, are very tolerant and accepting of everyone and display no racial, religious, or social prejudice. They are willing to listen to and learn from anyone who is able to teach them something. They do not act in a superior or condescending manner to those less educated or articulate than they but are able to relate to everyone openly and humbly.

12. *Resistance to enculturation.* These extremely healthy people are, as we have seen, autonomous, independent, and quite self-sufficient. As a result, they are free to resist social and cultural pressures to think and behave along certain lines. They do not openly rebel against cultural norms or deliberately flout social codes, but, on the other hand, they are governed by their own inner nature, not that of the culture.

This is truly an amazing set of characteristics. Self-actualizers seem almost saint-like; surely, you may protest, no one could be that perfect all the time. Rest easy. Self-actualizers do have imperfections and flaws. All is not constant goodness, truth, and beauty. After all, they are human. Maslow found that they could occasionally be rude and even extremely ruthless, displaying a "surgical coldness" toward others. They too have moments of doubt and fear, shame and guilt, and are sometimes gripped by conflict and tension. However, such imperfections are definitely the exception rather than the rule in their behavior and are less frequent and usually of shorter duration and lesser intensity than those of the average person.

Why Self-Actualization Is Not Universal

If, as Maslow suggested, the self-actualization need is innate (and so does not have to be learned), why isn't everyone self-actualizing? Why isn't the innate urge to actualize the self satisfied in all of us, just as the acorn naturally grows into an oak tree? Why has less than 1% of the population, according to Maslow, reached this stage of development?

One excellent reason is that the higher the need in the hierarchy, the less potent it is. Self-actualization, as the highest need of all, is therefore the weakest. Because it is not very strong to begin with, it is easily interfered with or inhibited by a poverty-stricken emotional environment that may make it difficult to satisfy love and esteem needs, by physical poverty that interferes with the satisfaction of the physiological and safety needs, and by inadequate education and poor child-rearing practices.

For instance, Maslow pointed to the sex-role training in our culture in which the little boy is taught to be manly, which usually means inhibiting such qualities as tenderness and sentimentality. One aspect of his nature is thus not allowed to develop fully. If a child is overly protected, not allowed to explore new behaviors or ideas, excessively taken care of so that he or she is not able to develop new skills and abilities, then he or she will be inhibited in exploring and growing as an adult—activities that are vital to self-actualization.

Another reason for the failure to self-actualize is what Maslow called the *Jonah* complex. This refers to our fears and doubts about our own abilities and potentialities. We are afraid of our highest possibilities and at the same time thrilled by them, but all too often the fear takes precedence.

A third reason that self-actualization is so seldom reached is that it takes a great deal of courage. Even when all the lower-order needs have been satisfied, one simply can't sit back and be passively swept along a royal road to self-actualization and fulfillment. Quite the contrary—it takes effort, discipline, self-control, and sheer hard work. Sometimes it is even painful. Therefore, it may well seem easier and safer to stay where one is (so to speak) than to grow, to deliberately seek out new challenges. The person who is self-actualizing is constantly testing and challenging himself or herself. It requires courage to give up safe, routine, well-practiced behaviors and attitudes.

It seems that childhood experiences are particularly crucial in allowing or inhibiting later growth toward self-actualization. As noted, excessive control and coddling may be harmful. Also, the opposite behavior —excessive permissiveness—may be equally harmful. Maslow warned that excessive freedom in childhood can lead to anxiety and insecurity, which can prevent further growth. The right mixture of permissiveness and regulation (giving the child what Maslow called "freedom within limits") is required.

Maslow stressed that sufficient love in childhood is vitally important as a prerequisite for self-actualization. He noted also the importance of satisfying the basic needs within the first two years of life. If a person is made to feel secure and strong in these early years, he or she will tend to remain so when faced with the problems of adulthood. Without adequate love, security, and feelings of esteem in childhood, it is extremely difficult for the self to grow in adulthood to the point of actualization and fulfillment.

Techniques of Inquiry

Maslow's study of self-actualization did not begin as a formal program of research. It started, as is the case with so much research, as an effort to satisfy his own curiosity about something—in this case, about two people who impressed him greatly. They were anthropologist Ruth

Benedict and Gestalt psychologist Max Wertheimer. Maslow loved and admired them, and he wanted to understand what it was about them that made them so different from others.

He felt that his training and experience in psychology was not sufficient for the task of understanding two such superior individuals. He observed them and made copious journal notes, finally concluding that they shared a common pattern of personal qualities. He found, to his great excitement, that they were the same kind of person, possessing characteristics that set them apart from the average individual.

Maslow then resolved to see if this same set of characteristics could be found in others. At first he turned to college students, an over-studied segment of the population, and found only one subject out of 3000 who could be considered self-actualizing. He concluded that the characteristics involved in self-actualization are not allowed the opportunity to develop in young people in our culture, and so he turned to the study of middle aged and older people. Even with these older subjects, however, only 1% of the population was capable of meeting his criteria for self-actualization.

The sample studied consisted of two dozen definite, partial, and potential cases of self-actualization, including creative people drawn from among Maslow's friends and great figures drawn from history. The latter category included Thomas Jefferson, Albert Einstein, Aldous Huxley, Eleanor Roosevelt, Pablo Casals, and William James, among others.

It is difficult to describe the specific techniques he used to study these people. As Maslow explained it, he used any technique that seemed appropriate to the problem at hand. In the case of the historical figures, he worked with biographical material, analyzing all the written records available on each person, searching for patterns of similarity among them.

With live subjects, Maslow relied heavily on in-depth interviews, free association, the Rorschach Inkblot Test, and Henry Murray's Thematic Apperception Test. Maslow found that many of his live subjects became self-conscious and, consequently, were difficult to probe. As a result, he said it became necessary to study them in an indirect and surreptitious manner, but he did not explain how that was carried out in practice. Since he could not release the names of his living subjects or the detailed information they provided, the original data are not available.

Maslow was the first to point out that his investigations leave much to be desired in the way of complying with the requirements for strict scientific research. In fact, he said, "By ordinary standards of laboratory research, i.e., of rigorous and controlled research, this simply was not research at all." However, he also noted that since the problem could not have been studied by rigorous scientific procedures, the only other alternative would have been not to study it at all.

Maslow's Image of Human Nature

We have already seen that Maslow's view of the human personality is a humanistic and optimistic one. His focus is on psychological health rather than malfunction, on growth and progress instead of stagnation, and on human virtues and potentials, not weaknesses and limitations. Basically, he had a strong sense of confidence, even trust, in our ability to shape our own positive and constructive growth and to shape a better society in the process. In fact, that trust remained the guiding credo for all of his work.

While he clearly stressed the importance of early childhood experiences in either facilitating or hampering later development, he did not believe that we are totally pawns or victims of these early experiences. People can take active roles in their own affairs. He believed that humanity has much more potential than it realizes and that we, as individuals and as societies, would be much more productive and happy if we could learn how to unleash that potential. His notion of self-actualization is a reflection of his belief that most people are capable of reaching a high level of functioning, given the proper conditions.

Maslow argued that our innate nature, the "character" with which we are born, is basically good, decent, and kind, but he did not deny the existence of evil in the world. However, evil and wickedness are not an inherent part of human nature but something thrust upon us by an inappropriate and inadequate environment. Self-actualization is, as we discussed, a relatively weak tendency or need. It always exists, but in the face of an inhibiting culture or repressive parents it has great difficulty being expressed.

Maslow cared deeply about people. His compassion is clear in his writings, and his hope for humanity is expressed in the firm belief that we can each fulfill our vast potential.

A Final Commentary

Perhaps in part because of the optimism and compassion Maslow expressed, his theory has become immensely popular and has a large following, particularly among the young. Arising from one of the prime movers of humanistic psychology, Maslow's work attracts admirers and disciples among students and professionals who have become disenchanted with the behavioristic and psychoanalytic approaches to personality and to psychology in general.

Just as humanistic psychology has met with criticism from representatives of those other approaches to psychology, so has Maslow's theory of personality. One target of this criticism is his method of research and the data that support his theory. It is charged that the sample from which the data were derived was too small. How, critics ask, can such generalizations be made on the basis of some two dozen subjects, fewer than half of whom were personally interviewed and tested (the rest analyzed from biographical material)?

Also, Maslow selected the subjects according to his own criteria of what constitutes a self-actualizing person. What criteria he used at the time were not made specific. Further, his description of the characteristics of self-actualizers derives from his own clinical interpretation of the data.

The charge that Maslow's research methods are weak from the standpoint of scientific rigor is valid. And, as noted, Maslow readily agreed with this criticism, which must be familiar to you by now; few personality theorists are immune to it.

Other criticisms are directed at the definitions of many of Maslow's concepts, including metaneeds, metapathology, peak experience, and, particularly, self-actualization. Critics point to inconsistencies or ambiguities in Maslow's use of these terms. Also, with reference to self-actualization, they ask on what basis this drive is assumed to be innate. Why, assuming such a need exists, could it not be learned behavior, the result of some unique combination of childhood experiences?

In Maslow's defense is his own estimate, shared by many others, that while his theory is not successful in the laboratory, it is highly successful in social, clinical, and personal terms. "It has fitted very well with the personal experience of most people, and has often given them a structured theory that has helped them to make better sense of their inner lives."

Maslow and his followers report empirical support for the theory, not from the laboratory but from industrial and organizational psychology. His need-hierarchy theory has been put to use in that environment, with some glowing reports of its verification. (Other reports, it should be noted, fail to confirm the theory.) The supportive studies have demonstrated, for example, that high-level executives, who presumably have satisfied all the lower-order needs, are more concerned with self-actualization than are lower-level employees. The latter are still working to satisfy lower-order needs. There are many other examples, and they led Maslow to conclude that his theory requires a real-life situation—such as people at work—for testing, rather than the artificial setting of a laboratory.

Maslow's theory, then, has generated much research and continues actively to do so some years after his death. One psychologist, Everett Shostrom, has developed a paper-and-pencil test—the *Personal Orientation Inventory*—that purports to measure variables related to self-actualization.

This test has furthered research interest in Maslow's theory. The concepts of need hierarchy and self-actualization are also proving useful in clinical work, where increasing emphasis is being placed on tapping and releasing a person's hidden potential instead of exploring inner childhood conflicts. A variety of growth-centered therapies, including sensitivity sessions and T-groups, are oriented in this direction.

The theory has been well received, and there is every indication that it is growing in popularity among psychologists and the educated public. It should also be added that a number of business leaders have embraced Maslow's concept of self-actualization as a way of improving the motivation, morale, and productivity of their employees. Maslow's election to the presidency of the American Psychological Association in 1967 suggests that his work is of great interest to psychologists.

Maslow issued a strong call to make psychology—at least humanistic psychology—relevant to the problems of modern people, arguing that the survival of civilization depends on our ability to understand ourselves and one another.

Suggested Readings

Goble, F. G. *The third force: The psychology of Abraham Maslow.* New York: Grossman, 1970.

Hall, M. H. Conversation with Abraham H. Maslow. *Psychology Today,* 1968, 2, 35–37; 54–57.

Maslow, A. H. (Ed.). *New knowledge in human values.* New York: Harper & Row, 1959.

Maslow, A. H. Eupsychia—the good society. *Journal of Humanistic Psychology,* 1961, 1, 1–11.

Maslow, A. H. *Toward a psychology of being.* (2nd ed.). Princeton, N.J.: Van Nostrand, 1968.

Maslow, A. H. *Motivation and personality.* (2nd ed.). New York: Harper & Row, 1970.

Maslow, A. H. *The farther reaches of human nature.* New York: Viking, 1971.

George Kelly
The Psychology of
Personal Constructs

13

*Each individual man formulates in his own way
constructs through which he views the world of
events.*[1]

—George Kelly

Kelly's personal-construct approach to personality is not only one
of the more recent theories to be proposed but is also clearly one of
the more original. Each of the theories previously discussed has distinctive
features and characteristic positions that set it apart from other theories.
There are certain similarities among the earlier theorists as well, however
—a focus on the conscious or the unconscious, for example, or on motivating forces that push the individual (as with instincts) or pull him or her
(as in a drive toward self-actualization).

[1]This and other quotations in this chapter are from *The Psychology of Personal Constructs*, Volume 1, by G. A. Kelly. Copyright © 1955 by George A. Kelly. Reprinted
by permission of W. W. Norton & Company, Inc.

Kelly's theory shares virtually nothing with the other approaches. He warned us that we will not find in it many of the familiar terms and concepts commonly found in personality theories. Having warned us, he then proceeds to shock us by pointing out how many of these terms are missing in his approach: unconscious, ego, need, drive, stimulus, response, reinforcement, and—most amazingly of all—motivation and emotion. How can one hope to understand the human personality without considering motivation and emotion?

The opening quotation provides some clue to how Kelly proposed to do that. All people, he said, are able to create and shape constructs about their own environment; that is, individuals interpret all the physical and social objects in their world to form a pattern. On the basis of this pattern, people make predictions about objects and about themselves and use the predictions to guide them in their actions. Thus, to understand individuals, one must understand their patterns—the way in which they personally construct their world. Therefore, it is the individual's interpretation of events, rather than the events themselves, that is of importance.

Kelly derived his theory of personality from his experience in working with troubled individuals, as is the case with most of our theorists. For several reasons, however—the kind of client with whom he dealt, his own scientific training, and his lack of a Freudian or other analytic bias—he interpreted this clinical experience in a vastly different manner.

The model of human nature that Kelly developed from his clinical work is unlike that of any other theorist in psychology: he viewed people as, in a sense, scientists. That is, he believed that people function in the same way that scientists do. "What does a scientist do?" Kelly asked. He or she constructs theories and hypotheses and then tests them against his or her form of reality, using experiments in the laboratory. If the theory is supported by the experiments, it is retained. If it is not supported, it is rejected or modified in some way and then retested.

This is, in essence, the way the psychologist who studies personality proceeds. Yet, Kelly noted, psychologists do not ascribe the same intellectual and rational facility to their subjects or patients that they do to themselves. "Why not?" Kelly asked. It is as if psychologists have two theories about human nature—one that applies to themselves and the way they look at the world and another that applies to the people they study. They see those they study not as capable of functioning in rational terms but rather as motivated by all manner of drives and subject to control by unconscious forces. The individual is believed to function on a purely emotional level, with little if any rational elements involved— quite unlike the way the psychologist functions.

Are psychologists superior beings? Contrary to what you might believe, no, they are not. They are really no different from the people they study. What works for one works for the other, Kelly said; what explains one explains the other. Both are concerned with predicting and controlling the events in their lives, which they are capable of doing on a rational basis.

Individuals, like scientists, construct their own theories, their own personal constructs, by which they are able to predict and exercise some control over events in their environments. The way to understand the individual, then, is through an examination of his or her personal constructs.

In the light of the emphases we have seen with other personality theories, it is not surprising that a theory that stresses human rationality instead of emotionality, and self-interpretations of experience instead of universal and instinctive drives, does not enjoy overwhelming popularity among traditional personality theorists. However, a large band of former students of Kelly actively pursue and defend this unique and provocative view of human functioning.

The Life of Kelly (1905–1967)

There is, unfortunately, little information available on the childhood and youth of George Kelly, so it is not possible to speculate on early experiences that may have influenced his theory of personality.

He was born on a farm in Kansas. An only child, he received a great deal of attention and affection from his parents, who were devoutly religious and firmly committed to helping the needy and the sick. His father had been trained as a Presbyterian minister but worked as a clergyman only sporadically. His parents worked hard on the farm and were fundamentalist in their religious beliefs and firmly opposed to frivolous entertainments such as dancing and card playing.

In 1909, when Kelly was 4 years old, the family traveled by covered wagon to Colorado to try farming there, but before long they returned to Kansas. Kelly's early education was irregular and conducted as much by his parents as by regular teachers. By the time he was 13, he was attending a high school in Wichita, and he seldom lived at home again.

In 1926, he received a B.A. in physics and mathematics from Park College. His future was uncertain since his interests were shifting from engineering and science to problems of a social nature. He worked briefly as an engineer and then switched to education, teaching at a labor college in Minneapolis, then working as an instructor for the American Banking Association, and even offering a course in citizenship to immigrants. During this time, he received a master's degree in educational sociology from the University of Kansas.

In 1928, he taught at a junior college in Iowa, where he also coached students in drama. There he met the woman he would later marry. Until this time his career had exhibited no firm direction toward psychology at all, but his professional training took a different turn when, in 1929, he was awarded a fellowship for study at the University of Edinburgh, Scotland. In a year there he earned a bachelor of education degree (credit having been given for his previous academic experience) and developed a strong interest in psychology.

He then undertook doctoral studies at the State University of Iowa, receiving a Ph.D. in 1931, two days before he married. His academic career began at Fort Hays Kansas State College, in the midst of the severe economic recession of the 1930s. There was not much opportunity to work in physiological psychology, the area that most interested him at the time, and so he changed to clinical psychology, for which there was a need.

He worked hard to develop a clinical-psychology service, both for the public school system and for the students at his college. He formed traveling clinics, which went from school to school and which gave him the opportunity to try out new approaches to clinical work. He began this work in the absence of a theoretical bias. That is, he was not already committed to a single approach to therapy or to one view of the nature of personality. Unlike so many personality theorists, he had not been psychoanalyzed as part of his training. (He noted that his first reaction to reading Freud was "incredulity that anyone could write such nonsense, much less publish it.") As a result, he felt free to experiment with existing methods as well as with new ones of his own design.

It was during his 13-year stay at Fort Hays Kansas State College that he developed his own approach. He offered the view that people can, on a rational and intellectual level, formulate their own personal construct about their world, which they use to predict and control the events of that world.

It is important to understand the kind of clinical experiences Kelly was exposed to, for they determined the nature of his theory. For the most part, the people he treated were not severely emotionally disturbed. They were not institutionalized psychotics or neurotics who sought out the services of a psychologist because they were having difficulty surviving emotionally. His counseling work was done with college and public-school students referred for counseling by their teachers for one reason or another.

Unlike the seriously maladjusted patients in a psychiatric ward or a psychoanalyst's office, Kelly's clients were perhaps capable of functioning, or at least of expressing their problems, in rational and intellectual terms—the terms in which most functioning occurs in an academic setting.

In the classroom, for example, one is taught to "intellectualize"—to discuss rationally the material being dealt with. Perhaps this intellectual context and attitude carried over from the classroom to the counseling situation, for it too took place in an academic setting. It is possible that, had circumstances placed Kelly during his formative professional years at work in the severely disturbed ward of a mental institution, his resulting theory would not have leaned so heavily on rational and intellectual abilities.

World War II interrupted Kelly's academic career, and he joined the Navy as a psychologist in the Bureau of Medicine and Surgery in Washington, D.C. When the war ended, in 1945, Kelly joined the faculty of the University of Maryland, where he stayed for a year before moving to Ohio State University. He spent 19 years there, during which time he further refined his theory of personality and, with the help of his students, conducted much research on various aspects of it.

Also during those years, he lectured at several universities in North and South America. In 1960, he traveled around the world, lecturing throughout Europe and Russia on the ways that his construct theory might be applied to resolving international problems. In 1965, he accepted a prestigious appointment to an endowed chair at Brandeis University, but he died shortly thereafter.

Kelly was a major force in developing the profession of clinical psychology, which was rapidly emerging during the years after World War II. He held several honored positions in the field, among them the presidencies of the Clinical and Consulting Divisions of the American Psychological Association and of the American Board of Examiners in Professional Psychology.

The Theory of Personal Constructs

Kelly proposed that a person looks upon and organizes his or her world in the same way that a scientist does—by making various hypotheses about the world and testing them against the reality of his or her own experience. People observe all the events in their world—the facts or data of their experience—and interpret them. This interpreting or *construing* of experience represents the individual's own unique view of these events, a pattern within which he or she fits or places them. Kelly wrote: "Man looks at his world through transparent patterns or templets which he creates and then attempts to fit over the realities of which the world is composed."

As a perhaps overly simplified example, we might compare these patterns or templets to sunglasses that provide a particular tint or coloring to everything the wearer sees. One person's glasses may have a bluish tint, another's a greenish tint. Each person can look at the identical scene and yet perceive it in a different way, as a function of the tint that frames and biases his or her view. So it is with the hypotheses, patterns, or templets each of us constructs. We each see the world through our own special lens. And it is this special view, this unique pattern created by each individual, that defines the word *construct* as Kelly used it. A construct is a person's way of looking at the events in his or her world, a way of construing that world.

Each person advances a hypothesis that a particular construct he or she holds will "fit over the realities" of some event in his or her world. Like a scientist, the person then proceeds to test this hypothesis by acting in accordance with it in relation to the event. For example, take the case of a student who is in danger of failing a course and is trying to influence her professor to give her a passing grade. On the basis of observing the professor for most of the semester, the student concludes that the professor acts in a very authoritarian and superior manner in the classroom and seems to have an inflated picture of himself and his importance.

From this observation, the student forms the hypothesis (the construct) that, if she behaves in a manner that plays up to the professor's exaggerated sense of self-importance, the teacher will respond favorably. The student now tests this hypothesis against reality. She goes to the library and reads an article the professor has written. Then she asks the professor questions about it, praises the professor's insight, comments on the importance of the area in which he is working, and asks when the next article will be published.

If the professor gives the student a passing grade at the end of the semester, then the hypothesis is confirmed. The construct is a useful one and can be called into play again if the student takes another course with the same professor. If the student fails the course, then she must construct a new hypothesis for dealing with that professor in a later course or with other professors who seem similar in nature.

We develop many constructs over the course of our lives—one to deal with every kind of situation or event or person with whom we come in contact. We are always increasing the repertoire of constructs as we meet new people and events. Further, existing constructs may need to be refined, modified, or elaborated on because people and events change over time.

Not only do we form a large number of constructs but, throughout our lives, alternative constructions must always remain available to us. There is nothing absolute or final about any construct, because none can be created that will predict or anticipate every eventuality. Revision, to a greater or lesser extent, is always necessary, and the individual must have alternative constructions to turn to. Otherwise—if constructs were fixed and rigid—the person would, as Kelly stated, "paint himself into a corner."

He firmly believed that this need not happen: "No one needs to be completely hemmed in by circumstances; no one needs to be the victim of his biography." People are not dictated to by the constructs they have developed for use. Kelly's notion of *constructive alternativism* holds that we are free to revise or replace our constructs. However, while they are always capable of being changed, the change must be judicious and based on the facts of experience. Inappropriate constructs can do more harm than good. Kelly noted that the alternative hypotheses chosen must be constructive in nature.

Kelly's theory of constructs and how they work was presented in a straightforward fashion, organized into one fundamental postulate and 11 corollaries.

Postulate and Corollaries of Kelly's Theory

Fundamental Postulate: "A person's processes are psychologically channelized by the ways in which he anticipates events."

By using the word *processes,* Kelly made it clear that he was not suggesting the existence of any kind of inert substance, such as mental energy, in his view of mankind. Rather, the person is seen as a flowing, moving process. The psychological processes are directed (channelized) by the constructs, by the way in which the person construes his or her world. While always subject to change, there is nevertheless a degree of stability in the way a person behaves, because he or she operates through a network of channels. Channels can change, of course, but they are structured, and changes ordinarily occur within the limits or range imposed by this structure.

Another key word in the postulate is *anticipates.* The whole notion of constructs is anticipatory in nature in that a person uses them to predict (anticipate) the future, so that he or she has some idea of what will happen as the result of behaving in one way or another.

The 11 corollaries in Kelly's system both evolve from and build upon the fundamental postulate.

1. *Construction Corollary.* "A person anticipates events by construing their replications."

Kelly believed that no event or experience in a person's life is ever reproduced exactly as it occurred before. Even though an event is repeated, it will not be precisely the same the second time it is experienced. If you listen to the same recording today that you heard yesterday, the experience that you have can differ. Your mood may not be the same, and during the passage of one day you were exposed to diverse experiences that may have influenced you in a variety of ways.

However, even though repeated events are not experienced identically, there will be recurrent features. Certain aspects of the repeated experience will be similar to those found in its earlier occurrences. On the basis of these continuing themes, a person is able to make predictions—to set up anticipations—about how an event will be experienced in the future. The predictions are based on the notion that future events, while not duplicates of past events, are nevertheless going to be at least partial repeats of past events. Certain themes of the past will appear again in the future. Constructs are formulated on the basis of these recurring themes.

2. *Individuality Corollary.* "Persons differ from each other in their construction of events."

With this corollary, Kelly introduced the notion of individual differences into his system. He pointed out the obvious fact that people differ from one another in how they perceive or interpret an event. As the result of construing events in different ways, people formulate quite different constructs. Constructs, then, do not so much reflect the objective reality of the event as they constitute the interpretation the person places on the event.

However, in spite of these individual differences in constructs, Kelly believed, there are recurrent characteristics of constructs common to all persons. In other words, no matter how individual the interpretation of an event may be, there is some degree of sharing of experiences. It is possible to find some common ground among people's construed experiences, particularly when the people have similar cultural and group norms, values, and mores.

Nevertheless, remember that the corollary is labeled *individuality*. Kelly's main emphasis remains on the uniqueness of each person's constructs.

3. *Organization Corollary.* "Each person characteristically evolves, for his convenience in anticipating events, a construction system embracing ordinal relationships between constructs."

What Kelly is suggesting here is that a person tends to organize his or her individual constructs into a system or pattern of constructs according to his or her own view of the relationships (both similarities and contrasts) among them. Because of this organization of the constructs, two people who have highly similar individual constructs may yet differ markedly from each other because the constructs are ordered in different ways.

By using the phrase *ordinal relationships between constructs,* Kelly proposed that constructs are organized in a hierarchical fashion, with some subordinate to others. That is, one construct can include one or more others. The construct *good,* for example, may include among its subordinates the constructs *intelligent, moral,* and *efficient.* The construct *moral* could, in turn, include other subordinate concepts. Also, the construct *good* could be subordinate to yet another construct.

These relationships, while usually longer lasting than the individual constructs, can nevertheless change; they are not rigid. For example, if a person feels that he or she has been harmed in some way by people more intelligent than himself or herself, that individual may switch the construct *intelligent* from a subordinate place under the construct *good* to a place under the construct *bad.* As with individual constructs, the test for a construction system is its predictive efficiency. If a system no longer provides a valid prediction of future events, it will be modified or discarded.

4. *Dichotomy Corollary.* "A person's construction system is composed of a finite number of dichotomous constructs."

All constructs, in Kelly's view, are bipolar or dichotomous. This dichotomous nature is necessary if future events are to be correctly anticipated. Just as it is necessary to note similarities among events or people, dissimilarities must also be noted. It is not enough, according to Kelly, to have a construct about a friend that notes his or her characteristic of honesty. One must also note the opposite of that construct (dishonesty) to show how the honest friend differs from people who are dishonest. If such a contrast did not exist—for example, if all people were honest— then forming the construct of honesty about a person would serve no predictive purpose. One friend can be predicted to be honest in future relations only in contrast to someone else who can be predicted to be dishonest.

The personal construct, then, would be *honest-dishonest.* Friends A and B may be construed as honest, in contrast to Friend C who is construed as dishonest. Of course, the same three people could also be construed in other terms. Friends A and C may be construed as helpful, Friend B as not helpful. The view—the construct—is always in terms of a dichotomy, a pair of qualities.

5. *Choice Corollary.* "A person chooses for himself that alternative in a dichotomized construct through which he anticipates the greater possibility for extension and definition of his system."

The notion that an individual has choice is a theme that runs through all of Kelly's writings. According to the *Dichotomy Corollary,* each construct has two opposing poles. For any particular situation, a person must choose which of the alternatives will work best—that is, which will best help predict future events. Ordinarily, and ideally, the person will choose the alternative that provides the best opportunity for anticipating future events.

However, there is some latitude (or choice) involved in deciding between the alternatives, and that choice is between *security* and *adventure*. To give a modest example, suppose a student must decide which of two courses to take next semester. One course is easy because it is very much like one the student is now completing and is taught by a professor who gives high grades for very little work. There is virtually no risk involved but perhaps not much reward either; the student knows the professor is dull and the similar course that he is now finishing has not taught him much he didn't already know. There is no risk or gamble involved in taking the new course—it is the secure choice. The student can make a highly accurate prediction about the outcome of this choice.

The other course he can choose is filled with unknowns: the professor is new but rumored to be tough, and the content is not like anything the student has studied. However, the material to be covered seems to be interesting and would expose the student to a new field that he would like to know more about. Here there is a risk or gamble. The student cannot make a fully accurate prediction about the outcome of his choice. However, the potential reward and satisfaction could be much higher than with the other course. This is the more adventuresome choice.

The student must choose between the low-risk, minimal-reward secure choice and the high-risk, high-reward adventurous choice. The first has a high predictive efficiency; the second has a much lower predictive efficiency. Kelly believed that we face such choices all our lives—choices between *definition* and *extension* of the personal construct system. The secure choice—that which closely resembles past choices—further defines the individual's construct system by repeating similar experiences and events. The more adventurous choice leads to an extension of the construct system by introducing new experiences and events into it.

Kelly felt that a tendency to take the secure, no-risk alternative may explain why some people persist in behaving in the "wrong" way. Why, for example, does a person continue to behave in a hostile fashion toward others—even when rebuffed for it—instead of being friendly and open? Kelly answered that such a person is simply making the secure, low-risk choice by behaving in that way. For whatever reasons, the person has come to know what to expect, to be able to predict how others will react when he or she is hostile. (Remember that choices are made in terms of how best to anticipate the future, not necessarily in terms of what is best for the individual.)

If such a person were to choose to behave in a friendly and nonhostile fashion, he or she would not be able to anticipate the future as well, not knowing what to expect. The rewards might be greater but so is the uncertainty. And the individual, like the scientist, does his or her best to predict future events with a high degree of certainty.

6. *Range Corollary.* "A construct is convenient for the anticipation of a finite range of events only."

This corollary is largely self-explanatory. Very few, if any, personal constructs are appropriate or relevant for all situations. Kelly offered the example of the construct *tall versus short.* It obviously has a limited *range of convenience;* it is simply not relevant to everything. It can be useful with respect to buildings, trees, or people, but it is of no value in describing a pizza or the weather.

Some constructs can be applied to many situations or people, while others can be applied in an extremely narrow and limited way, perhaps only to one person or situation. What is appropriate or relevant for a construct—what is within its range of convenience—is a matter of individual choice. Let us take the construct *trust versus suspicion,* for example. One person applies it to all people with whom she has contact, another finds it relevant for only some people, and a third person does not find it appropriate for people at all. The last may apply it to his pet dog but not to people. In understanding an individual, Kelly noted, it is just as important to know what is excluded from the range of convenience of a construct as to know what is included.

7. *Experience Corollary.* "A person's construction system varies as he successively construes the replications of events."

We have seen that each construct is like a hypothesis, in that it is generated on the basis of past experience to predict or anticipate future experiences. Each hypothesis is tested against reality by determining how well it predicted a future event. Most people are continually exposed to new events, and so the process of testing the fit of a construct (seeing how well it predicted the event) is going on much of the time.

If a construct has not been a valid predictor, it must be reformulated or replaced in the light of the new experiences. Events and experiences must be reconstrued as a person's world broadens and varies. Constructs that worked at age 16 may be harmful at age 40. In the years between 16 and 40, the individual must constantly reinterpret (reconstrue) the nature of his or her experiences. In other words, learning is taking place, as a result of which one's construction system undergoes continuous revision.

Construct systems cannot remain fixed, unless a person lives a life involving no change, no new experiences. In that case, constructs would not have to change, for such a person would have no new events to anticipate. But those whose lives involve meeting new people and facing new situations must reconstrue these experiences and alter their constructs accordingly.

8. *Modulation Corollary.* "The variation in a person's construction system is limited by the permeability of the constructs within whose range of convenience the variants lie."

Before attempting to explain this corollary, we must define one of its key terms, *permeability.* To permeate means to penetrate or pass through something. And that is the sense in which Kelly used the term. A construct that is capable of being permeated (is permeable) is one that will allow entirely new elements to be admitted into its range of convenience. Such a construct is thus open to new experiences and events.

Therefore, how thoroughly a person's construction system may change as a function of new experiences and new learning depends on how open or permeable the constructs are. An impermeable or concrete construct is not capable of being revised or replaced, no matter what new experiences are available to it. For example, if a person holds the impermeable construct that all black people are of inferior intelligence, he or she will not change that belief, regardless of how many highly intelligent blacks he or she meets. The construct is closed tightly against the intrusion of any new experiences, and the person is closed to new learning.

9. *Fragmentation Corollary.* "A person may successively employ a variety of construction subsystems which are inferentially incompatible with each other."

At first glance, this corollary may appear to be a bit strange. How can individual constructs that are incompatible with one another exist within the pattern of an overall construction system? It would seem that all constructs would have to be consistent with one another.

Yet it must be remembered that ordinarily a construction system is in a continual state of change in the light of new experiences. However, even though it is changing within the framework of an overall pattern or design, new constructs do not necessarily derive from or grow out of old ones. Even when they do, the new construct may not be compatible with the old. In one situation, two constructs may be compatible or consistent, but in a changed situation (even one involving a minor change) the same constructs may be inconsistent.

For example, you meet a person for the first time and immediately like him. He is also a psychology major and his interests in the field are the same as yours. His views and attitudes in that area coincide with yours. He thus fits with your construct of friend—someone to be liked and respected. The next day you meet him again, this time at a political meeting, and you are disappointed to find him expressing views opposite to your own. He now fits a different construct for you—that of extreme conservatism—and this places him in the category of enemy. However, this inconsistency is at a subordinate level. The larger, superordinate construct—liberals are friends, conservatives are enemies, for example—remains undisturbed. A person can tolerate a number of subordinate inconsistencies without discarding or modifying the overall construct.

10. *Commonality Corollary.* "To the extent that one person employs a construction of experience which is similar to that employed by another, his psychological processes are similar to those of the other person."

With this corollary (and the *Sociality Corollary* below), Kelly extended his theory of personal constructs into the area of interpersonal relations. As we saw with the *Individuality Corollary*, people differ from one another in the ways in which they construe events, and unique constructs develop as a result. However, just as people differ because of differences in ways of construing, so they can be similar to one another because of similarities in construing. If two people or 20 million people construe an experience in a similar way, their psychological processes will be highly similar. They will not be identical in their psychological makeup, but they will share certain characteristics and processes.

Consider a large group of people who have in common cultural norms, mores, and ideals. Their anticipations and expectations of one another will be similar, and they will construe their experiences in like ways. Therefore, people in the same culture may behave in the same manner even though they were exposed to entirely different specific events.

11. *Sociality Corollary.* "To the extent that one person construes the construction processes of another, he may play a role in a social process involving the other person."

As we have just seen, people in the same culture will tend to construe events in the same, or at least similar, ways. While this makes for a commonality among people, it does not by itself bring about constructive interpersonal relationships among them. In order for that to take place, it is not enough that one person construe experiences in the same way as another. The person must also construe the other's constructions. In other words, he or she must have an understanding of how the other person thinks and thus be able to anticipate how that person will predict events.

Construing the constructions of others is a task in which we are constantly engaged. Kelly gave the example of driving down a highway. We literally stake our lives on our anticipations of what other drivers will do. It is, Kelly stated, "an amazing example of people predicting each other's behavior through subsuming each other's perception of a situation."

Only when we can anticipate, with at least a reasonable degree of accuracy, what other drivers, friends, wives, husbands, or professors will do, can we adjust ourselves to them. While we are anticipating and adjusting to others, they are doing the same with regard to us. In this mutual adjustment we each come to assume a certain role with respect to every other person. We play one role with a close friend, another with a lover, another with a police officer. Each role is a behavior pattern that evolves from our understanding of the way in which the other person construes events. In a sense, we put ourselves into that person's constructs.

Techniques of Inquiry

Kelly's theory of personal constructs evolved from his clinical experience with public school and college students. These students, while no doubt troubled, were still capable of functioning in an academic setting; they were not locked away in a mental institution. Also, as noted, they were in a situation that values rational functioning and logical discussion of issues. Not surprisingly, then, Kelly's main method of inquiry took advantage of these characteristics.

His primary technique was a straightforward interview. "If you don't know what's wrong with a client," Kelly said, "ask him; he may tell you!" Adopting what he called the *credulous attitude*, Kelly noted that one should accept what the client says at face value, for this is a way of determining what constructs he or she is using. However, the client may deliberately lie and distort his or her version of events. Kelly's major point is that what the client says must be respected, even if not fully believed.

Another technique used to discover a person's view of the world was to have the person write a personal character sketch. Kelly found this a useful technique for learning how a person perceives himself or herself and his or her relations with others.

After having developed the notion of personal constructs more fully, Kelly devised a test to uncover the constructs by which a person construes important people in his or her life. It is called the *Role Construct Repertory Test*, perhaps better known under its abbreviated title, *Rep Test*. First, the client is asked to write the names of people who have performed each of a number of significant roles in his or her life. For instance, the client is asked who played the role of mother, father, spouse, closest present friend of the same sex, person most pitied, person most threatening, most attractive, happiest, and so on.

The client is then asked to sort the listed people. Given three of the names at a time, he or she is asked to select the two who are most alike and to tell how they differ from the third person. For example, the client may be given the names of the threatening person, pitied person, and attractive person. He or she describes how two of them are similar in some aspect of their behavior or character and how they differ from the third. The basic assumption underlying the use of this test is that people always construe events in dichotomies. By forcing the person into repeated judgments of like-unlike and similar-dissimilar, Kelly is able to uncover the dichotomies that are important in the person's life. There are several variations in the administration of the Rep Test, but the rationale and conclusions drawn remain the same: a person construes the world in dichotomies that, when revealed, show the pattern of his or her personal constructs.

Kelly's Image of Human Nature

Kelly's theory of personality presents us with a positive, hopeful, even flattering image of human nature. More than any other theorist, Kelly treated people as eminently rational beings. We are capable not only of forming our own constructs, through which we view the world, but also of formulating our own unique approaches to reality. "Man is the author of his destiny," not its victim.

Such a view endows us with free will—the ability to choose the path our own life will take. More important, we are able to change paths; we are always capable of changing our outlook and forming new constructs, with their related anticipations. A person is not bound to a path chosen in childhood, adolescence, or at any age. The direction is clearly toward the future because our constructs are formulated in terms of predictions. Humanity, Kelly argued, "lives in anticipation"; our lives are governed by what we predict for the future and where we think our choices will lead us.

Clearly, then, Kelly does not consider events of the past to be capable of totally determining present behavior. We are not victims of our biographies, he said—not prisoners of harsh toilet training, early sex experiences, or parental rejection. However, while the actual events of the past do not enslave us, we can be influenced by our interpretation of those events. But such interpretations result from the free and rational choices of the individual, in Kelly's view.

We are prisoners neither of biological instincts nor of unconscious influences. We are not pushed and prodded by any such determinants. As we saw earlier, Kelly invoked none of the usual motivating forces—incentives, needs, drives—not even the concept of motivation. There is no type of energy force that motivates us. It is not needed because we are already motivated—that is, in motion—for the simple reason that we are alive. Life itself is movement, and Kelly saw no need to invoke any other explanation. We do not have to be pushed or pulled by needs or drives, for we are "delivered fresh into the psychological world alive and struggling."

A Final Commentary

It was mentioned in the introduction to this chapter that Kelly developed a unique theory of personality, and that his work is neither a derivative of nor an elaboration on other theories. It emerges from his own interpretation—his own construct—of the data provided from his clinical experience. It is a highly personal view, and the originality of its construction parallels its message—that every individual is capable of developing his or her own view of life. With no other personality theory do we see such a correspondence—in fact, a duplication—between the way the theorist works and the way his theory explains how mankind functions.

Despite its distinctive flavor—or because of it—Kelly's theory of personal constructs has not gained a very wide acceptance, either in academic psychology or in the clinic. Perhaps it is too extremely different from the concepts and theories that those who work in the area of personality are used to dealing with. Whether in research or practice, psychologists who are concerned with personality expect to think in terms of such familiar concepts as motivation and emotion, unconscious influences, drives, needs, and the like. These familiar concepts—the ones we all learn about, beginning with our very first course in psychology—are not part of Kelly's theory.

Perhaps another reason for Kelly's general lack of acceptance by psychology has to do with the fact that he published little, relative to other personality theorists. Most of his time and effort were devoted to clinical work and the training of students. In all, he published only about a dozen articles and two books. Further, the style of his writing is scholarly and academic in tone, clearly not intended for general public consumption or for the psychologist who might be looking for human passion and drama highlighted by interesting and illustrative case histories. This was not the style of the man or his theory.

A third reason for his less than overwhelming acceptance has to do with criticisms directed against the system itself. Many psychologists take issue with a system that omits one of their major conceptual tools—that is, some device or principle that attempts to explain human motivation. As noted above, the omission of such familiar weapons from psychology's arsenal is seen by many as a serious flaw.

An equally important and related point of criticism involves Kelly's concentration on the intellectual and rational aspects of human functioning, to the exclusion of the emotional aspects. Where, the critics ask, are the passions—loves, hates, fears, and dreams? Kelly's image of us rationally constructing our present and future, forming hypotheses, and making predictions does not square with the everyday experiences of psychologists, who face the heights and depths of human passion with so many of their clients. Kelly's rational human being seems to many people to be an ideal, existing only in the abstract and decidedly not in reality.

It has been said that Freud's view of human beings derived from his exposure to middle-class, Viennese, neurotic patients, which gave him a distorted and unrepresentative view of mankind in general. Kelly's view, critics charge, was equally distorted and unrepresentative, limited as it was to midwestern students, adolescents very much involved in the process of trying to construct their individual worlds.

There are a number of questions left unanswered in Kelly's theory. Each person is able to construe events and experiences in his or her own unique way, but how does one person construe a particular event in one way while another person construes the identical event in an entirely different way? What mechanism or process accounts for this difference?

A person is constantly making choices toward definition or extension of his or her construct system. What determines whether, and under what conditions, a person will opt for security or for adventure—will choose the safer or the riskier step forward?

Without belaboring the point, we can simply say that Kelly's view, like the other systems discussed, contains gaps, uncertainties, and unanswered questions. Kelly recognized these limitations and made no pretense of setting forth a finished and final theory of personality. Just as an individual's constructs are constantly changing in the light of new experiences, so too the personal construct theory was seen as subject to constant change. "At best it is an ad interim theory," Kelly wrote; we must consider the theory to be "expendable in the light of tomorrow's outlooks and discoveries." Even in the years since Kelly's death, his theory has not been finished. But some of the students he so thoroughly trained have continued to refine and develop the theory and to train a new generation of students who may take it further.

The theory of personal constructs has not generated a great deal of research. However, Kelly's Role Construct Repertory Test has been widely used in research as well as in clinical settings. Much more research has been conducted with this test than on the construct theory from which it derived.

Kelly's unique contributions have been recognized with honors accorded him by his former students and by the profession. His theory, whatever the ultimate judgment of its merit, is certainly one of the most controversial to appear in a century of theorizing about the nature of the human personality. Whatever the nature of one's own personal constructs, Kelly's singular contribution cannot be ignored.

Suggested Readings

Bannister, D. A new theory of personality. In B. M. Foss (Ed.), *New horizons in psychology*. Baltimore, Md.: Penguin, 1966.

Bannister, D., & Fransella, F. *Inquiring man: The theory of personal constructs*. Baltimore, Md.: Penguin, 1971.

Kelly, G. A. *The psychology of personal constructs*. (2 vols.). New York: Norton, 1955. First three chapters published as *A theory of personality: The psychology of personal constructs*. New York: Norton, 1963.

Sechest, L. The psychology of personal constructs. George Kelly. In J. Wepman & R. Heine (Eds.), *Concepts of personality*. Chicago: Aldine, 1963. Pp. 206–233.

Thompson, G. G. George Alexander Kelly (1905–1967). *Journal of General Psychology*, 1968, *79*, 19–24.

Raymond B. Cattell **14**

*Personality is that which permits a prediction of
what a person will do in a given situation.*

—Raymond B. Cattell

The opening quote provides us with an indication of the general
tone or theme of Cattell's view of the nature of personality and his approach to understanding it. His purpose or goal in studying personality
is the prediction of behavior, of what a person will do in response to
a particular stimulus situation. He expressed this view of personality
mathematically, in the following equation:

$$R = f(P,S)$$

R stands for the response or reaction of the individual (what a person
will do), *S* refers to a given situation or stimulus, and *P* stands for personality. Elements of the stimulus situation can be known and precisely
defined. Indeed, in the laboratory, it is the experimenter who designs
and sets up the stimulus situation. The unknown factor—or the one most
difficult to know—is *P*, the structure and function of the personality.

In Cattell's approach to personality, there is no reference to changing or modifying behavior from undesirable to desirable or from abnormal to normal. That has been the aim of many of the previous theories discussed that were concerned with individuals in a clinical setting. The subjects or patients from which the more clinically oriented theories were derived had sought the services of a psychologist precisely because they were unhappy or disturbed by some aspects of their behavior, which they therefore wanted to change.

This is not the case with Cattell's subjects. They are normal individuals, whose personalities are studied, not treated. Cattell firmly believes that it is impossible (or at least very unwise) to attempt to change a personality before knowing in great detail what is being changed. A valid study of personality, then, must come first, and Cattell has been critical of clinicians who try to modify personality without knowing the exact nature of that which they are trying to modify.

Cattell's theory did not derive, then, from a clinical frame of reference. Rather, his approach has been a rigorously scientific one, using extensive observations of behavior and collecting great masses of data on each individual. It is not unusual, in his studies, for more than 50 kinds of measurement to be made of each of 100 subjects. Cattell's data come from questionnaires, objective tests and observations, and ratings of behavior as it occurs in real-life situations. The key aspect of Cattell's approach to studying behavior, and what makes it so totally different from all other approaches, is what he does with the huge amounts of data thus generated.

The data are subjected to the statistical process of *factor analysis*. In essence, this very complex procedure involves assessing the relationship between each possible pair of measurements taken from a group of subjects. Each pair of measurements (for example, scores on two different psychological tests or on two subscales of the same test) is analyzed to determine how highly the scores correlate with each other. In other words, a correlation coefficient is determined for each pair of measurements.

If two measures show a high correlation with each other, then it is assumed that they must be measuring related aspects of personality. To take a hypothetical case, if the guilt proneness and introversion subscales of a personality test yield a high correlation coefficient, then it is assumed that they both provide information on the same aspect or factor of personality. Thus, large amounts of data are statistically analyzed to determine these common factors (hence the term *factor analysis*).

Cattell calls these factors of personality *traits*, and this is the most important concept in his theory. He views traits as mental structures—the elements or component parts of personality. Only when we know which traits characterize an individual are we in a position to predict what he or she will do in a given situation. Cattell defines *trait* as a reaction tendency of a person that is a relatively permanent part of his or her personality. To fully understand a person, then, we must know in precise terms the entire pattern of traits that defines that person as an individual.

Cattell and his associates have devoted years of concentrated effort to teasing out the factors or traits that underlie personality. It is difficult, detailed, tedious, and time-consuming work. In recent years, the use of computers has eliminated some of the drudgery but not the necessity for detailed attention.

Cattell's use of factor analysis is the strong point in his system as well as the reason that the theory has not received wider recognition in psychology. Psychologists not adequately trained in this highly sophisticated technique find it difficult to evaluate Cattell's approach. Further, this lack of adequate comprehension of factor analysis means that psychologists often neglect Cattell's theory in their teaching.

There is also the matter of the sheer volume of research data produced by Cattell and his associates. The amount is overwhelming, and considerable time and effort are required to pull from it an understanding of the findings. A mere glance at the lengthy list of Cattell's publications can easily instill a sense of the futility of trying to come to grips with it, however meaningful it might ultimately prove in the study of personality. And that is precisely the kind of attitude of which Cattell legitimately complains. Difficult though his system may be, it is much too important to ignore in any presentation of the variety of approaches available for understanding personality.

The Life of Cattell (1905–   )

Cattell was born in England, where he had, by his own account, a happy childhood and youth, both at home and at school. His parents were exacting about the standards of performance they expected from their children but permissive regarding how the children spent their time. Cattell and his brothers and friends spent a great deal of time outdoors, sailing, swimming, exploring caves, and fighting mock battles over terrain in which they "occasionally drowned or fell over cliffs."

When Cattell was 9, England entered World War I, an event that profoundly influenced him. A mansion near his home was converted into a hospital, where Cattell saw trainloads of wounded men coming directly from the battlefields of France. As a result of this experience, he wrote, he became unusually serious for a young boy and aware of the "brevity of life and the need to accomplish while one might." His later amazing dedication to his work and the intensely long hours that he devoted to it may well have had their origins in these times.

And these characteristics of Cattell may also have been reinforced by his competition with his older brother. He wrote of the problems of trying to maintain his own freedom of development in the face of a brother three years his senior who could not be "overcome."

At the age of 16, Cattell entered London University to study what had interested him since boyhood—physics and chemistry. He graduated at 19 with high honors, but his years in London had intensified an already strong interest in social problems. He became increasingly concerned with social ills and realized that his training in the physical sciences did not equip him to deal with such problems. He concluded that the only recourse available to him was to study the human mind itself.

It was something of a courageous decision to take at that time in England (1924), because psychology was regarded as a discipline for "cranks" and there were few professional opportunities in the field. In all of England there were only six professorships in psychology. Against the advice of all his friends, Cattell began graduate studies at the University of London, under the eminent psychologist-statistician C. Spearman, the man who developed the technique of factor analysis.

Awarded his Ph.D. in 1929, Cattell found that his friends had been correct—there were no jobs for psychologists—and so he took several "fringe" jobs, as he called them, in psychology. He lectured at Exeter University and set up a psychological service and clinic in the school system of the city of Leicester, all the while continuing to conduct research and to write. He had resolved to apply the method of factor analysis—which Spearman had used successfully to uncover the structure of human abilities—to the study of the structure of personality, a monumental task never before undertaken.

During the first year after receiving his Ph.D., Cattell became ill with a long-lasting stomach condition, the result of too much work, poor food, and poor living conditions. To compound his difficulties, there was the world-wide economic depression, and a few years later his wife left him because of their poverty-ridden circumstances and his total absorption in his work. Yet, through all this adversity, his single-minded devotion to the task of understanding the structure of personality never wavered.

He also derived, according to his own account, some positive benefits from that long period of hardship: "Those years made me as canny and distrustful as a squirrel who has known a long winter. It bred asceticism, and impatience with irrelevance, to the point of ruthlessness." The experience also caused him to focus on practical issues and problems, rather than on purely theoretical or experimental issues, which he said he might have pursued had he been in more comfortable and secure circumstances.

Finally, in 1937, full-time work in psychology was made available by an invitation from the prominent American psychologist Edward L. Thorndike to spend a year in his laboratory at Columbia University. It was a marvelous opportunity, even though it was difficult for Cattell to leave his native country. He said that he was continually depressed during his year in New York.

In 1938, he became Professor of Psychology at Clark University in Massachusetts and in 1941 moved to Harvard, where, as he put it, "the sap of creativity" rose. Finally, in 1945, when he was 40 years of age, he was able to settle down and organize his life totally around his research. His second wife was a mathematician and shared his research interests, and he moved to the University of Illinois, where he was granted a research professorship.

In the absence of teaching or other responsibilities, Cattell could at last devote his every effort to research. He worked at the laboratory until at least 11:00 every night and was generally so involved in an ongoing research project that he joked that he could easily find his car at night because it was the last one remaining in the parking lot. Since 1945, he has continued to work at almost the same pace, never taking sabbatical leave or spending a significant amount of time away from the laboratory. He has published more than 300 articles and 30 books, a monumental accomplishment reflecting his obvious dedication and perseverance.

As the capstone to his life of research, Cattell established the Institute for Research on Morality and Self-Realization in Boulder, Colorado, in 1973. In this nonprofit organization, Cattell hopes to integrate his interest in science with his interest in social and religious issues. He is definitely not turning away from science, despite the possible incongruence of the word *morality* in the institute's name. He feels that he has developed a reliable framework with which to measure personality and motivation —a technique of measurement that will allow psychology to proceed as a science.

The Trait Approach to Personality

The concept of traits is so much at the core of Cattell's view of personality that his system has been called, justifiably, a trait theory of personality. Other psychologists, most notably Gordon Allport, also developed theories of personality around the concept of traits, but no one else has given us such a detailed analysis and classification of traits.

Traits are the factors of personality culled (by the method of factor analysis) out of the great masses of measurement taken of human subjects. Traits are relatively permanent reaction tendencies of a person, and they form the basic unit of structure of an individual's personality. Only through a thorough knowledge of an individual's traits is it possible to predict what that individual will do in any given situation. A person's personality, then, can be viewed as a pattern of traits.

There are several ways of classifying or grouping traits. For instance, Cattell distinguishes between *common traits* and *unique traits* (a distinction shared by Allport). A common trait is one that is possessed by everyone, to some degree. General mental ability or intelligence is a common trait. Everyone possesses it, although some people have more of it than others. Introversion and gregariousness are other examples of common traits. The reason for the universal existence of common traits is that all people share a more or less similar background of hereditary potential and are subjected to similar patterns of social pressure, at least within the same culture.

People differ from one another, of course, in that they possess different amounts or degrees of these common traits. But they differ even more because of their unique traits—traits shared by few or perhaps no other people. According to Cattell, unique traits are particularly apparent in the areas of interests and attitudes: one person has a consuming interest in an obscure species of butterfly, while another is passionately in favor of banning bare feet in public. Very few people would share these interests and attitudes.

A second way of classifying traits is by dividing them into *ability traits, temperament traits,* and *dynamic traits.* The way that these three kinds of traits differ is in the modality through which they are manifested or expressed. Ability traits determine how efficiently a person will be able to work toward a goal. Temperament traits define the "general style and tempo" of behavior, while the dynamic traits are concerned with the motivations or driving forces of human behavior.

An example of an ability trait is intelligence. One's level of intelligence determines how effectively a goal—say, a college degree—is striven for. Temperament traits include how high-strung, bold, easygoing, or irritable a person is. These traits influence the way in which a person works or acts—the style of his or her behavior. Dynamic traits are concerned with motivations and interests, including factors such as ambition and interest in acquiring knowledge or material possessions. The dynamic traits are emphasized in Cattell's system, and we will discuss them in greater detail later.

A third way to classify traits is in terms of the difference between *surface traits* and *source traits.* A surface trait is a set of personality characteristics that show a correlation with one another but that, nevertheless, do not form a factor because they are not determined by a single source.

In other words, various personality characteristics are seen to be complementary because of the overlap of several influences. In a normal individual, Cattell refers to this overlap of influences as a surface trait. In an abnormal personality, he calls it a *syndrome*.

For example, several elements of behavior—such as anxiety, indecision, and irrational fears—may cluster together to form the surface trait of neuroticism. Thus, the trait of neuroticism is due to a cluster of several elements; it does not derive from any single one. Because they are composed of several elements, surface traits are less stable and permanent in nature and are therefore considered by Cattell to be less important in the understanding of personality.

Of greater importance in Cattell's view, and much more stable and permanent, are the source traits, which are unitary or single factors, each of which is the sole source of some aspect of behavior. Source traits are the individual factors that derive from factor analysis and that, in combination, account for some surface trait. Source traits, therefore, are the basic elements of personality as we defined factors or traits in the beginning of this section. Examples of source traits will be seen in the list of Cattell's personality factors, to be discussed shortly.

Source traits can be divided into two types—*constitutional traits* and *environmental-mold traits*—according to their origins. The labels define the sources. Constitutional traits have their origin in the internal conditions of the organism. These traits are not necessarily innate (although they may be, in some cases) but do depend on the physiology of the organism. For example, the use of alcohol can yield a number of influences on human behavior, such as carelessness, talkativeness, and slurring of words —characteristics that factor analysis would indicate to be source traits.

Environmental-mold traits derive from influences in the social and physical environment. These traits are learned characteristics and ways of behaving and form a pattern, imposed and imprinted on the personality by one's environment. For example, a person who grows up in an inner-city ghetto behaves differently from one raised in upper-class luxury; a career military officer shows a different pattern of behavior from a jazz musician.

Now that we have noted the ways in which traits can be classified, it is time to consider the traits themselves.

The Source Traits of Personality

After more than two decades of intensive factor-analytic research, Cattell identified 16 basic factors or source traits that he was convinced constituted the "building blocks" of personality. These factors are perhaps best known in the form in which they are most often used—in an objective test of personality called *The Sixteen P.F. Test.* (P. F. stands for

Personality Factor.) This test, along with several others Cattell designed, has proved to be very useful and popular in both applied and research settings. The Sixteen P. F. Test has been used to profile such diverse personalities as the creative, the neurotic, and the psychosomatic, to predict the possibility of heart attacks in men, and to measure human sexual response to pornographic pictures. It is also used to predict accident proneness, scholastic performance, and occupational success in a number of kinds of jobs. Cattell's tests, while useful in psychology, are important to their author only as outgrowths of his factor-analytic studies. He makes it clear that he has little personal interest in psychological tests in general.

The traits listed below are in dichotomized or bipolar form. Thus, a low score on a particular factor indicates the presence of some characteristic, just as a high score does.

A person with a low score on this factor is described as:

A person with a high score on this factor is described as:

Factor A

Reserved, detached, critical, aloof

Outgoing, warmhearted, easygoing, participating

Factor B

Less intelligent, concrete thinking

More intelligent, abstract thinking, bright

Factor C

Affected by feelings, emotionally less stable, easily upset

Emotionally stable, faces reality, calm, mature

Factor E

Humble, mild, accommodating, conforming

Assertive, aggressive, stubborn, competitive

Factor F

Sober, prudent, serious, taciturn

Happy-go-lucky, impulsively lively, enthusiastic

Factor G

Expedient, disregards rules, feels few obligations

Conscientious, persevering, staid, moralistic

Factor H

Shy, restrained, timid,
threat sensitive

Venturesome, socially bold,
uninhibited, spontaneous

Factor I

Tough-minded, self-reliant,
realistic, no nonsense

Tender-minded, clinging,
overprotected, sensitive

Factor L

Trusting, adaptable, free of
jealousy, easy to get along with

Suspicious, self-opinionated,
hard to fool

Factor M

Practical, careful, conventional,
regulated by external realities,
proper

Imaginative, wrapped up in inner
urgencies, careless of practical
matters

Factor N

Forthright, natural, artless,
unpretentious

Shrewd, calculating, worldly,
penetrating

Factor O

Self-assured, confident, serene

Apprehensive, self-reproaching,
worrying, troubled

Factor Q_1

Conservative, respecting
established ideas, tolerant of
traditional difficulties

Experimenting, liberal,
analytical, freethinking

Factor Q_2

Group dependent, a "joiner"
and sound follower

Self-sufficient, prefers own
decisions, resourceful

Factor Q_3

Casual, follows own urges,
careless of protocol, poor
self-sentiment formation

Controlled, socially precise,
self-disciplined, high
self-sentiment formation

Factor Q_4

Relaxed, tranquil, unfrustrated,	*Tense*, frustrated, driven,
low ergic tension	overwrought, high ergic tension

The four Q factors were derived from a factor analysis of other factors. Cattell has also developed second-, third-, and even fourth-order factoring, in which groups of factors or traits are factor analyzed. As a result, four composite second-order factors have been derived. The two principal second-order composites are *anxiety* and *extraversion-introversion*.

It is important to remember exactly what these factors or traits are in Cattell's system. They are the components, elements, or basic units of the personality, in the sense that atoms are the basic units of the material world. Cattell argues that we cannot generate laws about personality, nor can we fully understand it, without being able to define, in precise mathematical terms, the nature of these building blocks of the personality.

The Dynamics of Personality

As noted earlier, the dynamic traits are directly concerned with motivation, a topic of central importance in almost every theory of personality. Cattell argues that a personality theory that does not take into account dynamic or motivating forces is incomplete and analogous to a description of an engine that does not take into account fuel.

There are two kinds of dynamic traits in Cattell's system—ergs and sentiments—both of which are manifested in attitudes. The word *erg* comes from the Greek *ergon* which means work or energy, and is used by Cattell in place of the concepts of instinct or drive, which he feels are too vague. An erg is the energy source for all behavior; it is innate and therefore constitutionally derived. It is the basic unit of motivation and is directed toward specific goals. There are, of course, a wide range of behaviors that may lead to a goal, but the erg itself is primary and fundamental. Cattell's factor-analytic research has identified eleven ergs in humans, which are listed in Figure 14.1.

While an erg is a constitutional source trait, a *sentiment* is an environmental-mold source trait, which means that it derives from external social and physical influences. A sentiment is a pattern of attitudes one has learned; it is focused on important objects in one's life—for example, country, spouse, job, religion, hobby. Both ergs and sentiments serve to motivate behavior, but beyond that there is a vital difference between them. An erg, since it is constitutionally based, is a permanent structure, and, while it can weaken or intensify, it cannot disappear altogether. Sentiments, which result from learning, can be unlearned and therefore can disappear, so that a particular sentiment may no longer be of any importance in a person's life.

An *attitude*, in Cattell's view, is a person's interest in some area, object, or person—an interest that will usually manifest itself in some form of overt behavior. As Cattell uses the term, it does not refer exclusively to an opinion for or against something, which is the traditional use of the word *attitude* in psychology. Cattell's definition of attitude is more inclusive, encompassing all of a person's emotions and actions toward an event or object.

Ergs, sentiments, and attitudes are related to one another through the concept of *subsidiation*, which simply means that some elements are subsidiary to others in the system. Attitudes, for example, are subsidiary to sentiments, which, in turn, are subsidiary to ergs. And, at another level, one attitude can be subsidiary to a second (it *subsidiates* the other, to use Cattell's expression), which, in turn, subsidiates a third attitude. We may do one thing in order to do a second thing, with a view to accomplishing a third. Cattell gives the example of a young man who goes to college and studies accounting for the purpose of getting a job and earning a living so that he may have a wife and family.

The interrelationships of ergs, sentiments, and attitudes are expressed schematically in what Cattell called the *dynamic lattice* (Figure 14.1).

The dynamic lattice is not really as forbidding as it might appear at first glance. The basic human motivations—the ergs—are listed at the right-hand side of the diagram. The large circles in the center are sentiments toward several aspects of this person's life. Note that each of the sentiments is subsidiary to one or more ergs. The sentiment toward bank account, for example, expresses two ergs: self-assertion and security. The sentiment toward wife expresses four ergs: sex, gregariousness, protection, and self-assertion. In other words, those four ergs energize this husband's sentiment toward his wife.

The smaller circles, on the left-hand side of Figure 14.1 are the attitudes—a person's emotions and actions toward an object. Each attitude, you will note, is subsidiary to one or more sentiments; that is, one or more sentiments can be expressed in an attitude. For example, this man's attitude toward a business friend is linked to the sentiment toward bank account (perhaps the friend wants to borrow money or is trying to persuade him to invest in his business). Through the bank account sentiment, the attitude toward business friend expresses the ergs of self-assertion,

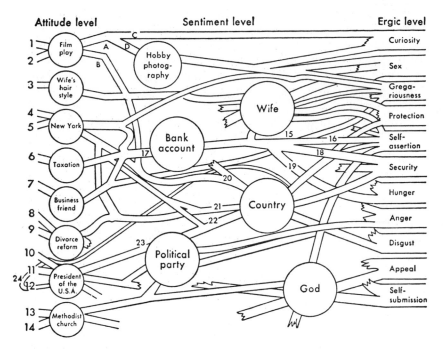

Figure 14.1 Portion of a dynamic lattice illustrating subsidiation. From *Personality,* by Raymond B. Cattell. Copyright 1950 by Raymond B. Cattell. Reprinted by permission.

security, and hunger. You can also see, by following the crisscrossing lines, that the attitude toward business friend directly expresses the erg of gregariousness.

Each person's set or pattern of sentiments is organized consistently through a master sentiment, which Cattell calls the *self-sentiment.* Perhaps the most important sentiment of them all, the self-sentiment refers to a person's conception of himself or herself, which is reflected in virtually all the attitudes he or she holds. It provides stability, coherence, and organization to all the source traits and is directly linked to the expression of the ergs and sentiments. If the self-sentiment were pictured in the dynamic lattice shown in Figure 14.1, it would appear to the far left of all the other sentiments, indicating that it is among the last of the sentiments to reach a full level of development. Because it contributes to the satisfaction of all the ergs and sentiments, the self-sentiment functions to control all the structures in the personality.

Anxiety

Cattell places a strong emphasis on anxiety as an aspect of personality because of the harmful consequences it can exert on both mental and physical functioning. As he views it, anxiety is both a state of being and a trait of personality. That is, we may experience varying degrees of anxiety as a result of circumstances that we find threatening or stressful. In this case we would be in a state of anxiety. However, there are also people who are chronically anxious, in which case anxiety is a trait or factor of their personality.

While previous writings on the topic of anxiety have suggested its existence in a variety of forms, Cattell's factor-analytic research has identified anxiety as a unitary entity that encompasses five other factors. A person with chronic anxiety would be easily affected by feelings, be suspicious of others, be apprehensive and self-reproaching, have an inadequately formed self-concept, and be tense and excitable.

Heredity versus Environment

Cattell has shown a much greater interest than most other personality theorists in the relative influences of heredity and environment in shaping personality. His method of investigating the importance of hereditary and environmental factors is known as multiple abstract variance analysis, a technique that compares the extent of similarity found between twins raised in the same family, twins raised apart, non-twin siblings raised in the same family, and non-twin siblings raised apart. The result is an estimation of the extent to which differences in traits are due to genetic or to environmental differences.

On the basis of extensive research, Cattell has demonstrated a very important role for heredity, at least with some of the traits. For example, his data reveal that 80% of intelligence, 80% of venturesomeness versus shyness, and 30% of the dissatisfied emotionally traits can be accounted for by genetic rather than environmental influences. With some traits, heredity was found to be the dominant influence, a finding that led Cattell to argue strongly for the notion of selective breeding, which, at the very least, he contends, could lead to a more intelligent society.

In his investigations of the influence of the environment on the individual, Cattell has studied not only a person's immediate environment but the larger social or cultural environment as well. In the same way that an individual can be described in terms of his or her traits, so a society can be described in terms of objective factors that comprise it. The "traits" of a society, taken together, constitute what Cattell calls *syntality*, which refers to the relevant characteristics or attributes of a large social group. He argues that we must understand both the personality of the individual and the syntality of the groups that influence him or her (such as religion, peer group, school, and nation). Cattell described a number of factors that comprise the syntality of small groups and also identified eight factors in the syntality of nations, including size, industriousness, enlightened affluence, and morale. No other personality theorist has made such a detailed objective analysis of the characteristics of a society and their effect on individuals.

The Development of Personality

Cattell divides the growth of the human personality into six stages, covering the full range of life, from birth through old age.

Infancy, lasting from birth until the age of 6, is the major formative period in the development of personality. During this stage, the individual is strongly influenced by parents and siblings and by the nature of his or her weaning and toilet-training experiences. As a result of these influences, primary social attitudes are formed, along with the stability and strength of the superego, the feeling of security or insecurity, the attitude toward authority, and the possible tendency to neuroticism.

Between ages 6 and 14, during the *childhood* stage, there are few psychological problems. Cattell calls it a time of *consolidation* after the more critical infancy period. There is the beginning of a trend toward independence from parents and a concomitant increase in identification with peers, but there are no major problems, compared with the next stage.

Cattell sees *adolescence* (which lasts, in his view, from 14 to 23) as the most troublesome and stressful stage of development. The incidence of mental disorders, neuroses, and delinquency rises sharply during this period, and a great deal of conflict is manifested around the drives for independence, self-assertion, and sex.

The fourth phase of development, *maturity*, lasts from ages 23 to 50. In general, it is, at least in its earlier years, a busy, happy, and productive time for most people, as they prepare for and begin a career, marriage, and family. The personality tends to become less fluid and more set, as compared with earlier stages of growth. Indeed, Cattell found little change in interests and attitudes between 23 and 50.

The stage of *middle age* involves shifts and adjustments in the personality in response to physical, social, and psychological changes. Health and vigor often dim at this time, along with attractiveness. Children leave home, and, for the first time, the end of one's life is in view. There is usually a re-examination of the values around which one has centered one's life and a searching of (and for) oneself.

Senility, the final stage, involves adjustment to a number of losses —the deaths of relatives and friends, work lost in retirement, loss of status in a society that worships youth—and the accompanying loneliness and insecurity.

Techniques of Inquiry

The technique by which Cattell derived the traits of personality is the sophisticated statistical procedure of factor analysis. However, before the factor-analytic procedure can be applied, masses of data must be collected from a large number of human subjects. Believing that everything that exists is measurable, in some degree, Cattell has undertaken to measure personality objectively and precisely, using three techniques of measurement. The data provided by these techniques are called L-data, Q-data, and T-data.

The *L-data* technique (*L* stands for life record) involves ratings made by observers on specific kinds of behavior that occur in the people they are observing. The behavior being observed occurs in a real-life situation rather than in a laboratory. Some examples of L-data include: frequency of absence from work, grades in school, conscientiousness in performing duties, emotional stability on the playing field, sociability at work, conventionality, and considerateness. The two important points about this technique are that it involves actual behavior in a naturalistic setting and that it must involve behavior that can be observed by someone else.

The *Q-data* technique utilizes questionnaires that the subject answers personally. While the L-data technique had someone else rating the subject, the Q-data technique requires that the subject rate himself or herself. A variety of questionnaires are used: the standard self-report type of personality inventory as well as scales that measure attitudes, interests, and opinions. Even the interview can be used, as long as the essential ingredient of the technique is kept intact: the subject must introspect and rate himself or herself on whatever aspect of behavior is being examined.

Cattell recognizes that there are limitations in the use of introspection and self-report. First, some subjects may not know themselves very well, and so their answers might not reflect the true nature of their personality. Second, even if subjects do know themselves, they may not want others to know them and so may deliberately bias or falsify their answers. This stems from the fact that the Q-data technique involves tests or questionnaires that most subjects are usually able to see through to judge what aspect of their personality is being measured. For example, if you were asked whether you prefer to be by yourself or with other people, you might reasonably guess that the question relates to gregariousness or shyness and thus respond accordingly. If you were extremely shy, and sensitive about it, you might say that you preferred to be with other people, in order to conceal what you consider a disturbing aspect of your personality. Because of these limitations, Cattell warns that the investigator must not blindly accept Q-data reports as accurate.

The third technique, *T-data*, involves the use of objective tests, which Cattell defines as "miniature situations," in which a person responds without knowing what aspect of his or her performance is being evaluated. These tests circumvent the Q-data problems by making it impossible (or at least extremely difficult) for a subject to know what a test item, or a whole test, is measuring. And if you cannot see through the test, it follows that you cannot distort your responses to conceal something about yourself or to present yourself in a more favorable light. If, for example, you were shown an inkblot from the Rorschach Test, you could not predict the interpretation that would be given to your response. How could you know what your answer might be revealing about you? For the most part, you cannot know, and that is why Cattell calls the Rorschach, along with Murray's Thematic Apperception Test and Jung's word-association test, among others, objective tests. They are objective in that they are resistant to faking.

It is important to note that Cattell's choice of the word *objective* to describe such tests is unfortunate and may be misleading. Traditionally, these tests have been called *subjective* because of the subjectivity that can enter into their scoring and interpretation, as opposed to tests that can be scored by a key so that anyone who grades them will come up with the same score. It is the latter type of test that is usually called *objective.*

In order to understand the total personality in all of its complexity, Cattell insists that these three sets of data, deriving from quite different sources, be integrated. By considering such a broad range of data simultaneously (which is called the *multivariate approach*), it is possible to uncover the interconnections among the aspects of the personality as it exists in an actual-life situation. He argues that the usual laboratory approach in psychology, which studies just one variable at a time (the *univariate approach*), deals with only limited aspects of personality and does not consider significant emotional experiences.

When the data are collected and traits uncovered by factor analysis, Cattell is in a position to accomplish his ultimate goal: to predict what a person will do in a given situation. For that purpose he uses a *behavioral specification equation*, given in the following formula:

$$R = s_1 T_1 + s_2 T_2 + s_3 T_3 + \ldots + s_n T_n$$

With this formula, it is possible to predict R (the response) from knowledge of a person's traits $(T_1 \ldots T_n)$. Each trait is given a weight in accordance with how relevant it is in the present given situation $(s_1 \ldots s_n)$. A trait that is highly relevant to the situation is assigned a higher weight than one that is less relevant. For example, if, in a given situation, R stands for tennis-playing behavior, we could predict a person's ability by a knowledge of certain of his or her traits. The factor of general intelligence would be highly relevant because good tennis playing requires advance planning; in other words, intelligence is equal to *ability to plan*. That factor would therefore be assigned a high weight. Enthusiasm and high ergic tension might also be relevant but somewhat less so than intelligence, and their assigned weights would thus be lower. In like manner, the analysis of all relevant traits proceeds until all the elements in the equation are known. Then it is possible to specify or predict how the person will behave in the situation of playing tennis.

Cattell's Image of Human Nature

Cattell does not present us with as explicit a view of human nature as have our previous theorists. We can, however, get some indication of his image of us by re-examining his definition of personality: "Personality is that which permits a prediction of what a person will do in a given situation." One would assume from this statement that Cattell views human behavior as capable of being predicted. Indeed, the behavioral specification equation states just that quite directly. Once we know the traits of which personality is composed—and Cattell has devoted three decades to uncovering them—we can then predict how an individual will behave. And once we can predict that behavior, we are in a position to control it.

For behavior to be considered predictable, it must be assumed to be lawful and orderly: how would prediction be possible without regularity and consistency? Cattell notes that wives can predict with "considerable accuracy" what their husbands will do when placed in certain situations, because their past behavior has been consistent, lawful, and orderly. There would seem, therefore, to be no room in Cattell's view of human nature for irregularity and spontaneity, since such characteristics would preclude prediction. On the free will versus determinism issue, then, Cattell's view seems to fall on the side of determinism.

While the doctrine of free will, which accords spontaneity and randomness to behavior, cannot be part of a system that has as its goal the complete predictability of human behavior, it must be noted that

Cattell does not totally rule out the possibility of free will. Psychology, he wrote, may someday find that its laws of behavior have misfired, but, until and unless that happens, "psychologists will continue to believe in orderly cause and effect."

Cattell's system does not posit any overall motivating force that dominates an individual's behavior. There is no self-actualization or other form of ultimate fulfillment constantly pulling us forward, nor are there universal instinctual psychosexual conflicts pushing from behind. He does note the determining influence of the period of infancy—"the great formation period." Basic social attitudes, the superego, a sense of security, and the tendency to neuroticism are formed by the time we are 6 years of age. Yet one does not get the impression from Cattell's writings that he views us as forever locked in or imprisoned by these childhood influences, unable to revise or modify them at a later stage of development.

Cattell's *professional* views on human nature are not entirely clear, primarily because he did not discuss the issue directly. As a result, any discussion of his opinions on the general nature of mankind must remain conjectural and inferred from his system (not, it is hoped, projected into it).

Cattell's *personal* view of human nature is a little less obtuse, for he has made direct, though quite brief, reference to it. The biographical sketch earlier in the chapter noted how Cattell became very much interested in social problems. He came to realize that the only way he, or anyone, might be able to ameliorate social ills was to "study the workings" of the human mind. This provided the basic motivation for his switch from the study of chemistry and physics to psychology. In his younger years he was optimistic about humanity's ability to resolve social ills. People, he wrote, will gain greater knowledge and more control over their environment. The intelligence of mankind will rise, he thought, and he expected to see within his lifetime "a more gracious community life of creatively occupied citizens."

Reality, of course, has not lived up to his expectations, and by 1974 he wrote that he had lost some of his earlier optimism about mankind. Not only did people and their societies not progress and improve in line with Cattell's earlier hopes, but they have, he now sees, regressed in some respects.

A Final Commentary

A man who has presented huge volumes of research in over 300 articles and 30 books, who has accumulated monumental amounts of experimental data in an area usually defined by subjective case histories and equally subjective intuitions and speculations, and who has developed new ways of measuring aspects of personality simply cannot be ignored. If for no other reason than the sheer quantity of his research, Cattell's system demands consideration.

However, as we pointed out in the introductory section of this chapter, the amount of his research and the complex method of factor analysis are among the reasons for the general lack of acceptance of his point of view. Cattell wrote in 1974 that he had "a sense of unquestionable failure" in convincing others of the ultimate wisdom of his approach, which he caustically defends as the only method that is of value in the study of personality. His work has been described as being much respected but seldom read; this seems, unfortunately, all too accurate.

His theory is clearly not as popular among psychologists as some of the other personality theories, and it is virtually unknown among the general public (an audience with which Cattell has not attempted to communicate). While part of the reason is, as we have seen, its demanding and technical nature, there have also been specific criticisms, directed against the substance of his approach.

Despite the legitimate claim that factor analysis is a highly objective and precise technique, there is still opportunity for subjectivity to creep into Cattell's overall research methodology. At several stages of the research process, decisions must be made, which, critics argue, may be influenced by personal opinions and preferences. For example, in the initial step of collecting data the psychologist must decide which specific tests to use and what aspects of behavior to measure. Next, the researcher must decide which specific technique of factor analysis to use, and there is not a unanimity of opinion on this question. If factor analysis is so objective, critics ask, why can't factor analysts agree on matters of technique? It must also be decided which level of statistical significance will be accepted as appropriate. Once the factors have been identified, the psychologist must decide what labels to apply to them. If a factor is given a name that may be ambiguously interpreted, it may not express the real meaning of the factor.

This is not to suggest that Cattell's theory is weak from the standpoint of the necessity of making these decisions, but the opportunity for subjective error does find its way into a factor-analytic approach. It is a point of possible vulnerability, not only in Cattell's approach but also in other techniques of inquiry discussed in this book.

It is unfortunate that despite the tremendous efforts of Cattell and his small band of associates to convince the psychological world of the utility of his approach, they have not succeeded, at least not on a large scale. His theory is one of the most firmly grounded in data and one of the most systematically constructed, and it has taught us a great deal about the structure (if not the nature) of personality. His method and goal are in the best tradition of science—to measure the subject matter with utmost precision before attempting to theorize about it.

In spite of the lack of full recognition accorded his position, Cattell remains convinced that his approach will one day enable us to predict human behavior with the same degree of accuracy with which the movement of the planets can be predicted today.

Suggested Readings

Cattell, R. B. *Personality and social psychology.* San Diego: Knapp, 1964.

Cattell, R. B. *The scientific analysis of personality.* Baltimore, Md.: Penguin, 1965.

Cattell, R. B. *A new morality from science: Beyondism.* New York: Pergamon, 1972.

Cattell, R. B. *Personality and mood by questionnaire.* San Francisco: Jossey-Bass, 1973.

Gorsuch, R. L. *Factor analysis.* Philadelphia: Saunders, 1974.

Sells, S. B. Structured measurement of personality and motivation: A review of contributions of Raymond B. Cattell. *Journal of Clinical Psychology,* 1959, *15,* 3–21.

B. F. Skinner

Man is a machine in the sense that he is a complex system behaving in lawful ways. . . .

—B. F. Skinner

It may seem strange, at first glance, to find B. F. Skinner, the foremost exponent of behaviorism, in a book that discusses theories of personality. His position would seem to be out of place here for two reasons: (1) he does not believe psychology is ready, in the sense of having enough factual data, to theorize about anything and (2) he does not deal specifically with the topic of personality, considering it nothing more than a label for certain aspects of behavior. In view of this, it is hardly surprising that he has not offered a theory of personality that can be contrasted and compared with the ones previously discussed. Indeed, he has not offered a theory of personality at all!

Skinner's work is an attempt to account for all behavior, not just that which some theorists call personality, and to account for it in purely factual and descriptive terms. He rejects all attempts to theorize about personality: "You can't get results by sitting around and theorizing about the inner world. . . . I want to say to those people: get down to the facts."

Getting down to facts has been the guiding theme of all of Skinner's work, for more than 40 very productive years. He has argued strongly that psychology must restrict itself to what it can see and what can be manipulated and measured in the laboratory. And that means an exclusive emphasis on the overt responses the subject makes—and on nothing beyond that. Simply stated, Skinner's argument is that psychology is the science of behavior—the study of what the organism does.

You may recognize this approach as similar in nature to that proposed by John B. Watson, whose work in the founding of behaviorism was mentioned in Chapter 1. The spirit of Watson's revolution in psychology, which greatly influenced the young Skinner, lives on in more sophisticated and more fully developed fashion in Skinner's exclusive emphasis on behavior. Skinner's work, like Watson's before him, is the antithesis of the psychoanalytic approach to personality, differing not only in subject matter but in methodology and aims as well. In addition to denying that there is a separate entity or process known as personality, Skinner's approach diverges from other approaches in the following ways.

In their explanations of the nature of personality, most other theorists we have discussed have looked inside the organism. The causes, motives, and drives—the motivating and directing forces—originate, in their view, within the person. Other personality theorists invoke needs—whether innate or learned—such as self-actualization, superiority, safety, or security—all of which serve to direct the person from within. Whether they invoke traits, instincts, or needs, other theorists all use what Skinner calls the "inner man" approach.

Skinner's approach, in contrast, makes absolutely no reference to any presumed internal state in accounting for the behavior of the organism. After all, a basic tenet of the behavioristic position is that psychology must deal only with that which can be observed. Unconscious forces, defense mechanisms, traits, and the like cannot be seen and therefore can have no place in a scientific psychology. Such internal driving forces are no more real, Skinner argues, and have no more value to science than the old philosophical and theological concept of the soul.

The same argument is used by Skinner in relation to physiological events or processes, which, again, are not overtly observable and so have no relevance for science. "As far as I'm concerned," he wrote, "the organism is irrelevant either as the site of physiological processes or as the locus of mentalistic activities." The only aspect of human beings that is real and relevant to psychology, he argues, is overt behavior, and the only way to be able to predict and control behavior is by relating it to antecedent events in the environment. The reference is always to something external to the organism—something in the environment—as the "cause" of behavior. There is no need to look inside the organism for some form of inner activity. As far as Skinner is concerned, a human being is an "empty organism"; there is nothing inside us that can be invoked to explain our behavior scientifically.

Notice that Skinner does not say that internal processes of a physiological or mentalistic nature do not exist. Their possible existence, however, has no meaning for a science of psychology. Even if they do exist, they cannot be seen and thus are of no use in predicting and controlling behavior; they are simply irrelevant.

A second point of difference between Skinner and the previously discussed personality theorists involves the matter of individual differences. Regardless of the variations among them, our previous theorists were all concerned with some aspect of individual differences. Whether they talked in terms of traits, life style, or ego and superego, the theorists recognized the fundamental uniqueness of the individual. Even those theorists who posited universal drives or conflicts pointed out the vast range of differences in the means of satisfying the drives or of defending oneself against the conflicts.

Skinner, in contrast, has shown very little interest in the matter of individual differences, primarily because his search has been for general laws of human behavior. He seeks unchangeable empirical statements of the relationships between stimulus events and responses. If there are differences in behavior among people, it is due to the fact that the events that elicited their responses were different. The laws relating the response to a stimulus are immutable.

A third way in which Skinner diverges radically from the other theorists is in the kind of subject studied. As we have seen, some theorists used as subjects those who are emotionally disturbed. Others have insisted that only normal, average individuals be studied, while at least one (Maslow) has used only the best and the brightest individuals.

Skinner does not take the normal, the subnormal, or the supernormal as his subjects of study. But what is left if you exclude these categories? Animals! While Skinner's approach to behavior has, in more recent years, been applied to humans with apparent success, the research that led to his "theory" of behavior was conducted with rats and pigeons—primarily the latter.

That statement is often met with incredulity and shock. How can anything be learned about human personality by studying pigeons? Well, the first thing to remember is that Skinner is not dealing with personality. Rather, his concern is with all behavior (of which what others call personality is but one aspect). His focus is on the responses the organism makes, not on what a patient reports of his or her childhood or how a subject says he or she feels.

Responding to stimuli is something animals can usually do as well as humans—and sometimes better. Skinner grants that human beings are vastly more complex than animals, but he also notes that the differences between them are in degree, not in kind, and that the basic processes are not very different. He believes that any science must proceed from simple to complex, the basic processes being investigated first. Thus, Skinner studies animal behavior because it is "simpler."

There are additional advantages to the use of animals in laboratory study. Their genetic and experiential backgrounds can be well controlled, and they can be studied for longer periods of time and in more dangerous or uncomfortable situations than humans are usually willing to endure. Also, they don't, as a rule, become hostile to experimenters and behave in ways opposite to the ways they think the experimenter wants them to behave. Nor do they become overly cooperative and behave as they think the experimenter wants them to. (They also don't have to be paid as much as college students, the usual human subjects.) Skinner has extrapolated from his animal data to human behavior, and, as noted earlier, there is much recent practical application of his work to humans in a variety of situations. But, again, the basic data of Skinner's approach were derived from experiments with rats and pigeons.

Since Skinner is decidedly not a personality theorist, and since his approach to the study of people is so vastly different from those described in earlier chapters of this book, it is natural to ask: what is he doing here? Why has he been included among those who attempt to understand the nature of personality?

Actually, it would be more difficult to justify his exclusion than to explain his inclusion. Skinner is simply too important a force and commands too much status in contemporary psychology to be ignored. A textbook that purports, as this one does, to bring into view the diversity of approaches available for the understanding of personality would be incomplete without consideration of Skinner (even though he avoids recognition of personality as a separate entity or structure).

Whether one agrees or disagrees with his views, there is no denying Skinner's monumental importance and influence in American psychology today. In 1958, the American Psychological Association awarded him the Distinguished Scientific Contribution Award and noted that "few American psychologists have had so profound an impact on the development of psychology and on promising younger psychologists." The magazine *Psychology Today* wrote in 1967 that "when history makes its judgment, he may well be known as the major contributor to psychology in this century." In 1968, the United States awarded him the National Medal of Science, the highest public award for scientific contribution, and in 1971 the American Psychological Foundation presented him its Gold Medal.

His work has had wide practical ramifications. He invented an automatic baby-tending device and is largely responsible for the widespread use of teaching machines. He has also published a successful novel spelling out a program of behavioral control of human societies. In addition, Skinner's methodology has found its way into the clinical setting, where it is being used to treat psychotics, the mentally retarded, and autistic children. His approach to the modification of behavior (as distinct from trying to change personalities) has become popular in a variety of settings, including schools, prisons, and hospitals.

Skinner's influence is strong not only in psychology but also among the general public. In 1971, his book *Beyond Freedom and Dignity* won best-seller status, generated much publicity, and prompted Skinner's appearance on several television talk shows. The controversy surrounding his ideas is extensive and usually of a highly emotional nature.

His approach to personality is radical and extreme (compared to those of the previous theorists), but it is also so influential and notorious that to omit it would be to close our eyes to a man whom *The New York Times* has called "the most important influence in psychology"—a statement echoed by large numbers of psychologists.

The Life of Skinner (1904–   )

Skinner views the human organism as a machine, "a complex system behaving in lawful ways." He considers the causes or driving forces of behavior to have their origins in external forces. In this view, a person is a product of past reinforcements; those behaviors that have been rewarded will be repeated, and those that have not been rewarded or that have brought punishment will not be repeated. Our behavior is thus predetermined, lawful, and controlled.

A test of this approach would be to see if it fits what is known of Skinner's life. Were there events (or reinforcements) in Skinner's childhood that have determined his adult view of and approach to the study of mankind? Was Skinner's life predetermined, lawful, and controlled, as he says all human lives are?

Skinner was born in Susquehanna, Pennsylvania, the older of two sons; his brother died at the age of 16. His parents were hard-working people who instilled in him a strong sense of proper behavior. "I was taught to fear God, the police, and what people will think," Skinner wrote. His mother had strict standards of what was right and proper, and she never deviated from them. She evidenced great alarm if her son demonstrated any tendency to stray from the path she had so clearly pointed out. Her method of control (reinforcement), Skinner said, was to say "tut-tut" and "What will people think?" His grandmother made certain that young Skinner understood what hell was all about by pointing out to him the red-hot bed of coals in the parlor stove.

Skinner's father, an ambitious lawyer, longed for praise but bitterly considered himself to be a failure. He too contributed to his son's moral education, continually telling him what would happen if he turned out to be a criminal. He showed Skinner the county jail and on another occasion took him to a lecture (with slides) on life in Sing Sing (a notorious state prison in New York).

Skinner's autobiography contains a number of references to the influence on his adult behavior of the admonitions and instruction given him in childhood. Referring to his father's harping on the punishments that would befall him for breaking the law, Skinner wrote: "As a result I am afraid of the police and buy too many tickets to their annual dances." He tells of visiting a cathedral as an adult and taking great pains to avoid stepping on the gravestones in the floor. As a child, he had played in a cemetery next door to his house and had been cautioned never to step on a grave—it wouldn't be "right." These and other instances made it clear to him that many facets of his adult life were determined by reinforcements in childhood.

Prophetic of his later view of people as machines, Skinner as a youth spent many hours designing and constructing machines—wagons, seesaws, merry-go-rounds, slingshots, water pistols, a steam cannon (used to shoot potato and carrot plugs over neighboring houses), model airplanes, and a flotation system that separated ripe from unripe elderberries. He also worked for years on a perpetual motion machine (which perpetually failed).

Skinner's adult interest in the study of animal behavior also seems to have derived from childhood experiences. He caught and made pets of an assortment of animals, including turtles, snakes, toads, lizards, and chipmunks. He read a great deal about animals and spent time talking with the local livery-stable owner about the behavior of horses. And, at a county fair, he once saw a flock of performing pigeons. They raced on the stage pulling a fire engine up to a "burning" building. Wearing red hats, they put a ladder against the building, and one pigeon climbed to an upper-story window and rescued another pigeon. Skinner was later to train pigeons to perform a variety of amazing feats, including playing ping-pong and guiding a missile to its target.

As a boy, Skinner liked school—so much so that he was always the first to arrive there in the morning. After he graduated from high school (in a class of eight), he went to Hamilton College in upstate New York. As he tells it, he never felt part of the student life, was poor at sports, objected to some of the college requirements (like compulsory chapel), and was disappointed by the lack of intellectual interest shown by his fellow students.

By his senior year he was in "open revolt." He disrupted the college with hoaxes, including one that jammed the campus and the railroad station with swarms of people arriving to hear a lecture by Charlie Chaplin, whose appearance Skinner had falsely announced with posters he had printed and distributed all over town. He also wrote articles highly critical of the faculty and administration. His antics continued up to the last possible moment; the college president warned Skinner and his friends during commencement ceremonies that they would not graduate if they did not behave themselves.

His career plans after graduation were clear and had nothing to do with psychology. He had majored in English and was firmly committed to becoming a writer. Spurred on by favorable comment on some of his work from the eminent poet Robert Frost, Skinner built a study in the attic of his parents' home, now in Scranton, Pennsylvania, and sat down to write. What resulted, he notes, was "disastrous." He read, listened to the radio, played the piano, built ship models, and considered seeing a psychiatrist.

He left Scranton for Greenwich Village, New York, and then went to Europe for a summer. Finally, he decided to give up his attempt at writing, because he had "nothing important to say." He felt he still wanted to understand human behavior, so he turned from a literary investigation of it to a scientific one. While living in Greenwich Village, he read books by Ivan Pavlov and John B. Watson, which influenced him greatly. As a result, he entered graduate school at Harvard in 1928 to study psychology.

Working with tremendous dedication and effort, he was able to earn his Ph.D. in three years. The next time you feel like complaining about having too little time to finish all your assignments, consider Skinner's regimen: "I would rise at six, study until breakfast, go to classes, laboratories, and libraries with no more than fifteen minutes unscheduled during the day, study until exactly nine o'clock at night and go to bed. I saw no movies or plays, seldom went to concerts, had scarcely any dates, and read nothing but psychology and physiology."

Skinner remained at Harvard, with postdoctoral fellowships, until 1936, when he joined the faculty of the University of Minnesota. He stayed there until 1945, spent two years at Indiana University, and then returned to Harvard, where he works with as much enthusiasm and dedication as when he entered the field more than four decades ago. He still regulates his work habits with precision, carefully recording his daily work output and his average time spent per published word (two minutes)—continuing to reflect his own definition of a person as "a complex system behaving in lawful ways."

Reinforcement: The Basis of Behavior

Though based on thousands of hours of well-controlled research, Skinner's approach to behavior is quite simple in its essential concept. It says, in effect, that all behavior can be controlled by its consequences—by what follows the behavior. Skinner believes that an animal or a human can be trained to perform virtually any kind of behavior by the extent and nature of the reinforcement that follows the behavior. Thus, whoever controls the reinforcement available to a person (or a group of people) is in a position to change and control the behavior of that person (or that group of people), in the same way that an experimenter can control the behavior of a laboratory rat.

Skinner's position distinguishes between two kinds of behavior: respondent and operant. *Respondent* behavior, as the name suggests, involves a response made to or elicited by specific and known stimuli in the environment. At the simplest level of behavior, a reflex such as the knee jerk is respondent behavior. A stimulus is applied (a tap on the knee) and the response occurs (the leg jerks forward). The behavior in this example is, of course, unlearned. We don't have to be trained (or conditioned) to make the appropriate response; it is elicited automatically and involuntarily.

At a higher level, there is respondent behavior that is learned. The process of this learning, known as conditioning, involves the substitution of one stimulus for another; the concept originated with the important work of the Russian physiologist Ivan Pavlov. It was Pavlov, as you no doubt remember from other courses, who gave the concept of conditioning to psychology. Working with dogs, Pavlov found (quite by accident) that they would salivate to stimuli that were neutral—for instance, to the sound of their keeper's footsteps. Previously, the response of salivation had been elicited by only one stimulus—the presentation of food.

Intrigued by this observation, Pavlov began to study the phenomenon more systematically. For example, he would sound a bell shortly before feeding a dog. At first the dog salivated only to the food; after all, what "meaning" could the bell have? But after a number of pairings of the bell followed by the food, the dog began to salivate at the sound of the bell. The dog had been conditioned to respond to the bell; the response had shifted to a previously neutral stimulus.

The essential feature of this now classic experiment was the demonstration of the importance of *reinforcement*. The dogs would never learn to respond to the bell unless they were getting something for it—in this case, food. Pavlov thus formulated his first law of learning, which said that a conditioned response cannot be established in the absence of reinforcement.

Nor can an established conditioned response be maintained in the absence of reinforcement. Take a dog already conditioned to respond to the sound of the bell; every time the bell rings, the dog salivates. Now the experimenter suddenly stops presenting food after sounding the bell. The dog hears the bell and then nothing happens—no more food (no more reinforcement). With successive ringings of the bell, the dog's response decreases in frequency and intensity until finally no response is made at all. The response has been *extinguished* because reinforcement for it was no longer forthcoming.

Respondent behavior, then, depends on reinforcement and is made directly to an immediately present physical stimulus. Every response is elicited by a specific stimulus. Skinner feels that this form of conditioning is much less important than what he calls *operant* behavior. He recognizes that we are indeed conditioned to respond directly to many stimuli in our environment, but he also believes that not all of our behavior can be accounted for in this way. Both humans and animals behave in what seem like spontaneous ways; that is, the behavior cannot be traced to specific stimuli. Such behaviors are, in Skinner's terms, *emitted* rather than being elicited by a stimulus. They involve acting in ways that appear to be voluntary rather than reacting involuntarily to a stimulus to which one has been conditioned.

The nature and frequency of operant behavior will be determined and/or modified by the reinforcement that follows it. Respondent behavior has absolutely no effect on the environment. The dog's salivary response to the ringing bell does nothing to change either the bell or the reinforcement (the food) that follows it. Operant behavior, on the other hand, operates on the environment and, as a result, changes it. For example, the cries of an infant may bring attention from its mother or father, thus changing the infant's environment. The changes that are introduced into the environment serve as feedback to the behavior. If the environmental changes brought about by the behavior are reinforcing (provide some reward to the organism or eliminate some noxious stimulation), then the probability is increased that that behavior will be emitted again. If the infant's cries are reinforced with food or caressing, the infant may well emit such behavior again. If, on the other hand, the environmental changes provide no reinforcement (or provide some kind of punishment), that behavior is less likely to recur.

Note that the reinforcement is dependent upon the kind of behavior displayed. Whether any reinforcement will follow the behavior depends on how the behavior changes the environment. The reinforcement, if there is to be any, comes after the behavior and acts to modify the behavior in the future. Perhaps this idea will become less strange as we follow the progress of a rat in Skinner's well-known piece of laboratory equipment, which he prefers to call an *operant conditioning apparatus* but which seems destined to be forever known as the *Skinner box*.

We will describe the use of this box in research in the "Techniques of Inquiry" section, but for now an examination of the rat's behavior in the box is more important. When a rat that has been deprived of food for a period of time is placed in the box, its behavior is initially spontaneous and random. Usually, the rat is very active, poking, sniffing, and prodding its new environment. These behaviors are emitted and not elicited; the rat is not responding to any specific environmental stimuli.

At some time during the course of this random and spontaneous activity, the rat will depress a lever or bar located on one wall of the box, which causes a food pellet to drop into a trough. Note that the rat's behavior has operated on the environment and changed it: the environment now includes a food pellet. That food pellet is a reinforcement for the behavior of depressing the bar. The rat begins to depress the bar more often. What happens? It gets more food (reinforcement) and consequently depresses the bar even more frequently. Its behavior is now under the control of the reinforcement. Its actions in the box have become considerably less random and spontaneous. The rat now spends most of its time pressing the bar (and eating).

If we put the rat back in the box the following day, we can predict with great accuracy what it will do, and we can control its actions by presenting or withholding the reinforcement (or presenting the reinforcement at different schedules or rates, as we will see later). The person who controls reinforcement thus controls behavior. Skinner said: "I had the clue from Pavlov: control your conditions and you will see order." (A popular cartoon shows one rat in a Skinner box saying to another "I really have this experimenter well conditioned. Every time I press that bar, he gives me another food pellet.")

Skinner believes that most human and animal behavior is learned in this way. An infant displays a great deal of random, spontaneous behavior, only some of which is reinforced by its parents. As the infant grows older, the positively reinforced behaviors (those of which the parents approve—approval being a form of reinforcement) are continued, while those of which the parents disapprove may not be continued. The concept is the same as with the rat in the Skinner box: those behaviors that "work" are repeated and those that don't work or that bring punishment are not. The organism's behavior operates on the environment; the environment, in the form of reinforcement, operates in turn on the organism's behavior.

You can see how powerful reinforcement—and those who control an individual's or a society's reinforcement—is in determining behavior. "Operant conditioning," Skinner wrote, "shapes behavior as a sculptor shapes a lump of clay." If the "lump of clay" wants or needs the reinforcer badly enough, there is virtually no limit to how it can be shaped by an experimenter with a food pellet, a puppy owner with a dog biscuit, a mother with a smile, a boss with a pat on the back, or a government with a promise.

From infancy on, we emit a great many behaviors, and those that are reinforced grow stronger and form into networks or patterns. And that is all that Skinner means when he occasionally refers to *personality:* a pattern or collection of operant behaviors, and nothing more. What others have called neurotic or abnormal behavior is, to Skinner, nothing more mysterious than the continued performance of certain behaviors that (for whatever reason) have been reinforced.

Always seeking to perfect a method of modifying and controlling behavior, Skinner asked another question. Having demonstrated how behavior can be modified by *continuous reinforcement*—presenting a reinforcement after every response—he then asked how behavior might be modified by varying the rate at which behavior is reinforced. Actually, what led Skinner to ask this question was a practical, even mundane, matter—a matter more of expediency than of intellectual curiosity. It is worth examining the impetus for this new line of research, for it demonstrates something of the nature of the operation of science, which is often quite different from the idealized picture that textbooks present.

It all started with the food pellets used to reinforce the rats in the Skinner box. Today, such pellets are commercially available and need merely to be taken from a bag to be ready to use. In the 1930s, however, experimenters (or their luckless graduate students) had to make their own food pellets—a time consuming and laborious procedure. In Skinner's laboratory, at that time, at least 800 pellets a day were required to keep the research going.

One Saturday afternoon, Skinner discovered that, unless he were to spend the rest of that day and evening making more pellets, the supply would be exhausted by the following Monday morning. Spending the rest of the day slaving over the pill machine was not, even for a dedicated researcher, the most attractive prospect. It was then that another choice occurred to him. Why, he asked himself, must every response be reinforced? What would happen if the rat were reinforced only one time per minute, regardless of how many responses it was making?

As a result of this line of reasoning, he and his students spent considerably less time making pills, and Skinner embarked on a program of research that has come to be considered by many psychologists as his most important contribution: the investigation of different schedules of reinforcement.

Schedules of Reinforcement

It is obvious that, in everyday life outside the laboratory, behavior is not reinforced each time it occurs. A baby is not picked up by its mother every time it cries. The Little League baseball player doesn't get a home run, or even a hit, every time at bat. The bagger in a supermarket does not receive pay or a cry of "Well done!" from the boss every time he or she packs a bag. There are countless examples of behaviors that, although only intermittently reinforced, persist.

Seeing that his rats continued to press the bar at a fairly constant response rate, even when they were not being reinforced continuously, Skinner proceeded to investigate different schedules or rates of reinforcement to determine which would be most effective in controlling behavior. We will discuss four different schedules: fixed interval, fixed ratio, variable interval, and variable ratio. .

The *fixed-interval* schedule of reinforcement means precisely that: the reinforcement is presented at fixed intervals of time. For example, the reinforcement might be given every one minute or every three minutes. Note that the reinforcement has nothing to do with how many responses are being made. Whether the rat responds once a minute or 20 times a minute, the reinforcement still arrives only after the passage of a fixed interval of time.

There are many real-life situations that operate in accordance with this schedule of reinforcement. In your own case, if your instructor gives a midterm and a final examination, he or she is operating on a fixed-interval schedule. A job in which a salary is paid once a week or once a month also operates on the fixed-interval schedule. Under such a system, a worker is not paid by the number of items he or she produces (the number of responses made) but by the number of hours, days, or weeks that elapse.

The research results are what you would probably predict. The shorter the interval between reinforcements, the greater the frequency of the organism's response. The response rate declines as the interval between reinforcements is lengthened. How frequently the reinforcements appear also affects how quickly a response will be extinguished. The response will stop sooner if the rat has been continuously reinforced (and the reinforcement then stopped) than if it has been reinforced intermittently.

In the *fixed-ratio* schedule of reinforcement, the reinforcement is presented only after the organism has made a specified number of responses. The experimenter could reinforce, for example, at every tenth or at every twentieth response. In this schedule, then, unlike the fixed-interval schedule, the reinforcement depends on how frequently the animal responds, for the animal won't receive a food pellet until it emits the required number of responses. As a result, this reinforcement schedule brings about a faster rate of response than the fixed-interval one.

The higher response rate of the fixed-ratio schedule has been found to hold true in a variety of situations for rats, pigeons, and humans. In a job in which the pay is determined on a piece-rate basis, how much a worker makes depends on how much he or she produces. The more items produced, the higher the pay. Thus, the person's reinforcement depends directly upon his or her rate of responding. The same holds for a salesperson working solely on a commission basis. His or her income depends on the number of units of the product sold; the more sold, the more earned. A salesperson on a weekly salary, in contrast, will earn the same each week, whether he or she sells five or 50 units of the product.

It often happens in real life that reinforcement does not follow a fixed interval or fixed ratio but rather appears on a variable basis. In the *variable-interval* schedule, the reinforcement might appear after two hours one time, after an hour and 30 minutes the next time, after two hours and 15 minutes the third time, and so on, averaging approximately two hours between reinforcements. A person spending a day fishing might be rewarded (if at all) on such a variable-interval basis, the rate of reinforcement being determined by the random appearance of fish.

A *variable-ratio* schedule of reinforcement is based on an average number of responses between reinforcements, but there is great variability around that average. Skinner has found that the variable-ratio schedule is extremely effective in bringing about high and stable response rates, as those who operate gambling casinos can happily attest. Slot machines, roulette wheels, horse races, and the like pay off on this variable-ratio reinforcement schedule and, as any addicted gambler can tell you, it is an extremely effective means of controlling behavior.

What all of this research on different schedules of reinforcement means is an increased efficiency in controlling, modifying, and shaping behavior. If you're in charge of rats, salespeople or assembly-line workers, or are trying to train your dog, cat, or child, you can see how such operant conditioning techniques can be useful in inducing the kind of behavior you would like to see. The same techniques have also been used in the clinical setting—the kind of setting around which the work of most of the previously discussed theorists was oriented.

Applications of Operant Conditioning

In one example of a real-world application of Skinner's conditioning principles, an entire ward of more than 40 female psychotic patients in a state mental institution was treated as a Skinner box.[1] All the patients were considered beyond treatment (and hope), had been institutionalized for very long periods of time, were generally unable to take care of themselves, and spent their days in aimless isolation.

In this setting, the patients were offered opportunities to work at certain jobs (jobs usually performed by paid hospital attendants) for which they would receive tokens. These tokens could be used like money to buy extra privileges and possessions. For example, with a certain number of tokens the patients could purchase candy, cigarettes, lipstick, gloves, newspapers, or a variety of other consumer goods. Also by paying tokens they could attend a movie (on the ward), take a 20-minute walk around the hospital grounds, or get a more private room. The most expensive privileges (those that required the greatest number of tokens—100) were a trip into town with an escort and a private meeting with a social worker. (A private meeting with the ward psychologist was only one-fifth the price of the social worker, which is an interesting comment on something.)

Like people on the outside, the patients could buy items and privileges to improve the quality of their lives. Their tokens functioned like money. What did they have to do to earn these tokens? What kinds of behaviors did they have to emit in order to be reinforced? If they bathed at the time designated, brushed their teeth, made their bed, combed their hair, and dressed properly, they earned one token for each activity. More tokens (up to ten per activity) were earned by working for short periods in the hospital kitchen or laundry, helping to clean the ward, running errands, or helping to care for other patients (taking them for walks, for example). You might think that these tasks are simple and low level, and so they are. But remember that these patients were hopeless psychotics, most of whom could not even take care of their own bodily needs, at least not before given a reinforcement for doing so.

The system worked dramatically. Not only did the patients begin to groom themselves and clean and improve their ward, but they also began to be busy at a variety of jobs. They interacted much more, both with one another and with the staff. Some degree of responsibility for patient care shifted from the staff to the patients themselves, and their sense of self-esteem and self-worth improved markedly.

[1]T. Ayllon & N. Azrin. *The Token Economy.* (New York: Appleton-Century-Crofts, 1968.)

The reinforcement offered in return for certain behaviors altered their overall behavior. The patients changed from dependent, incompetent, hopeless psychotics to less dependent and more responsible individuals. The overall technique is known as *behavior modification* or *behavior therapy* and has become a highly prominent—even revolutionary—technique in clinical psychology. (We will discuss this technique further in Chapter 16.) The process has been successfully applied in several institutional or group settings: prisons, school classrooms, reform schools, and with groups of mentally disturbed and mentally retarded children. It has also been used to treat a variety of individual behavior problems, including hyperactivity, bedwetting, temper tantrums, stuttering, and constipation.

There are two points of interest about behavior modification. First, no attempt is made to deal with any presumed underlying conflict, repressed trauma, or unconscious motivating force. The focus in the practical application of the behavior modification technique is strictly on overt behavior. There was no more concern for what might be happening "inside" the psychotic patients than for what might be going on inside a rat in the Skinner box. The concern is solely with behavior and with the kind and rate of presentation of reinforcement that will change behavior.

Second, most operant-conditioning applications involve positive reinforcement and not punishment. The patients in the hospital study were not punished for failing to behave in more desirable ways. Rather, they were reinforced only when their behavior did change in positive ways. Skinner feels that punishment is not very effective, in general, in changing behavior from undesirable to desirable or from abnormal to normal. Positive reinforcement applied to behaviors that are considered desirable is much more effective. (It is interesting to note that Skinner reported that he was never physically punished as a child by his father and only once by his mother; she washed out his mouth with soap and water for saying a naughty word. He did not report whether that worked to change his behavior.)

Mention should be made here of *negative reinforcement*, which is not the same as punishment. A negative reinforcement is an aversive or noxious stimulus, the removal of which is rewarding. An operant conditioning situation can be set up, in the laboratory or an applied setting, in which the aversive stimulus (such as a loud noise or an electric shock) will continue until the subject makes the desired response. As with positive reinforcement, the environment will change (the noxious stimulus will disappear) as a consequence of behavior. Certainly it is reinforcing to escape something odious or harmful, and thus negative reinforcement can be a powerful way of modifying behavior.

We see examples of negative reinforcement in many situations. You study for this course and attend most of the class meetings at least in part to avoid the aversive stimulus of a failing grade. A child behaves in certain ways to avoid or escape the disapproval or loss of affection of its parents. Negative reinforcement is also used in the clinical setting, where a noxious stimulus is continued when the undesirable behavior is displayed and discontinued only when the desirable behavior is displayed.

Skinner is strongly opposed to the use of noxious stimuli in trying to modify behavior, because he feels the consequences are not as firmly predictable as they are with positive reinforcement—in other words, negative reinforcement doesn't always work. In general, positive reinforcement is more consistently effective.

It is easy to see in the case of Skinner how research with rats and pigeons can lead to important and practical ramifications for what others call personality. (Whether these consequences will ultimately prove harmful or helpful to mankind is another matter.)

Techniques of Inquiry

We have seen that Skinner's methods of inquiry are radically different from those discussed in earlier chapters. In addition, it is important to note that his methods differ from the rest of experimental psychology in at least one important respect.

The usual procedure followed by non-Skinnerian experimental psychologists is to study large groups of subjects (animal or human) and statistically compare the average responses of these subjects. In contrast, Skinner chooses to intensively study a single subject. He argues that knowledge of how an average subject performs is of very little value in dealing with an individual. A science that deals with averages, he contends, provides little information in understanding the unique case.

The rat or pigeon to be studied is placed inside the Skinner box. A sophisticated piece of laboratory apparatus, the Skinner box contains a variety of equipment that can be used for operant conditioning. We have mentioned the bar or lever that a rat can depress in order to obtain reinforcement. A model for use with pigeons contains a translucent disk mounted on one wall, about ten inches from the floor. The disk can be illuminated from behind and is usually red in color. When the pigeon pecks at the disk, food is delivered into the box.

The Skinner box is well lighted, and its walls are soundproof and opaque to eliminate all stimulation from outside the box. The only stimuli to which the animal is exposed are those directly under the experimenter's control. More important, in terms of the sophistication and refinement of the experimental procedure, is the automatic, precision recording of every operant response the subject emits. The box is wired to additional equipment so that every press of the bar or peck of the disk is recorded and the food delivered automatically. Once the proper reinforcement rate has been determined by the experimenter, the experiment will run by itself, with only a periodic clicking sound as evidence that the complex system is behaving in a lawful way.

Skinner has also introduced a precise and yet simple means of recording responses—a device called a *cumulative recorder*. Recording paper revolves sideways on a drum at a constant speed, and a recording stylus or pen moves upward each time a response is made. The steeper the line, the faster the animal is responding. When the experiment is finished, a cumulative record of every response and its rate is available. This technique also indicates changes in the rate of responding.

Skinner's Image of Human Nature

There is no ambiguity concerning where Skinner stands on this issue. Humans function in the same way machines function—in lawful, orderly, predetermined fashion. As noted in the introduction, Skinner firmly rejects all notions of an inner person—an autonomous self—determining a course and choosing to act spontaneously and freely. We are operated by forces in the external world, not by forces within ourselves. Not since Freud have we met a theorist who is so completely deterministic in his viewpoint, allowing for not even the slightest hint of freedom of will and spontaneity of behavior.

From Skinner's highly technical writing, to his popular novel about a utopian society based on operant conditioning principles, to a recent book that received much public attention, the message is the same: "If we are to use the methods of science in the field of human affairs, we must assume that behavior is lawful and determined . . . ." "The issue of personal freedom must not be allowed to interfere with a scientific analysis of human behavior."

All aspects of human behavior are controlled from without. A person's behavior is beyond that person's control, which means that it is pointless to blame or punish people for their actions. In this view, Adolf Hitler can no more be held responsible for what he did than can a driverless car that plunged down a hill—both operate in lawful, predictable ways and are controlled only by variables outside themselves.

We are left, it seems, with a pessimistic view of ourselves as helpless and passive robots, unable to play an active role in the determination of our own behavior. Surprisingly, however, that does not represent Skinner's ultimate view. He does not see us as victims, or even as mere passive spectators, in spite of the fact that our behavior is so thoroughly controlled. "I take an optimistic view," Skinner wrote. "Man can control his future even though his behavior is wholly determined."

But how can this be? How can one who is totally controlled also control? Skinner deals with this apparent paradox in the following manner. It is true, he said, beyond doubt, that people are controlled by their environment—but who designs the environment? People! Skinner points out the obvious fact that our physical environment is, for the most part, designed and built by humans. Clothing, buildings, tools, vehicles—virtually everything we see, hear, and work and play with—are the result of human fabrication. So too is our social environment. Our language, customs, and mores are human products.

And we are constantly changing our environment, usually to our own advantage. When we do bring about changes in the social and physical environment, we are at once controller and controlled; we design a controlling culture and are the product of the culture. The fact that we are products of a culture may somewhat limit or inhibit our freedom to change it; we will be guided, in making changes, by those characteristics in the environment that have provided positive reinforcement in the past. In changing our culture, we seek ever greater opportunities for positive reinforcement, and in the process we can change our own behavior.

"Man," Skinner argues, "controls himself, but he does so by controlling his environment." We are left with the paradoxical image of person-as-machine, constantly changing the environmental conditions that guide the machine's behavior.

A Final Commentary

It is easy for people to retain an emotional neutrality about some of the theorists in this book but difficult to do so in the case of B. F. Skinner. His is an extreme stance in behaviorism, just as Freud's was an extreme stance in quite the opposite direction. As radical positions, these approaches to the understanding of human personality or behavior invite a polarity of opinion, with highly emotionally charged disagreement between opponents and proponents.

Spirited and verbally violent controversy has raged around Skinner's position almost since its beginnings. He has been dismissed as one of the greatest minds of the 19th century, and "intellectually bankrupt," and he has been accused of committing "crucial errors of fact" and of offering vague generalities and "naïve misinformation." One of his recent books was condemned publicly by a high government official as attacking "the very precepts on which our society is based." Whatever one may say about Skinner, his position has clearly not suffered the fate of being ignored.

His approach has been criticized on a number of points. Obviously, those persons who oppose a deterministic view of human nature must oppose Skinner. Some of the more vocal attacks against him have come from those who believe that humans are more than machines directed by external forces. These critics object to Skinner's image of us as over-grown white rats and argue that the exclusive emphasis on overt behavior ignores those human characteristics that set us apart from rats or pigeons. People, these critics contend, are not merely empty organisms or robots but conscious beings who can act with free will and spontaneity.

These and other critics also express concern over Skinner's belief that we can be totally controlled and manipulated, arguing that such a point of view lends support to fascist thinking—to the idea that a demagogue could mold and shape a culture in any desired direction. These critics argue that if Skinner's view of humanity were to become totally accepted, it would ease the way for a government to institute a society in which every aspect of behavior, from infancy on, would be controlled and directed.

At a more specific level, we find criticism directed at the low level of subject and the simplicity of the situations studied. As noted, Skinner has made many assertions and predictions about human behavior and human societies. His writings have ranged from social and economic to religious and cultural speculations, all of which he puts forth with great confidence (even arrogance, some have said). How, it is asked, can Skinner extrapolate from a pigeon pecking at a disk in a Skinner box to a highly complex person functioning in a world consisting of a vast range of stimuli? The gap between human and pigeon, these critics charge, is too vast to permit Skinner's broad generalizations. Most of the other personality theorists discussed dealt with the whole person functioning in the real world. Even those who are more experimentally oriented, such as Cattell, have at least studied human beings. Many aspects of human behavior, it is charged, cannot be reduced meaningfully to the level at which behavior is investigated by Skinner.

Additionally criticisms have been directed against technical aspects of Skinner's research methodology and the statistical analyses he uses, but these criticisms are beyond the scope of a book dealing with personality theories.

For the most part, Skinner's reaction to his critics has been to ignore them. "I read a bit of it," he said, referring to a negative review of one of his books, "and saw that he missed the point, so I never read the rest. I never answer any of my critics. . . . There are better things to do with my time than clear up their misunderstandings."

Skinner, despite these criticisms, is undoubtedly one of the most potent forces in 20th-century psychology. American psychology in general has been shaped and influenced more by his work than by the work of any other individual. Huge quantities of research have been performed by Skinner and those who follow his point of view. Clearly, no other viewpoint discussed in this book has been more productive of research.

His radical behavioristic position remains strong and vital in both the laboratory and the applied setting and shows no sign of diminishing in either influence or enthusiasm. The Skinnerian-oriented *Journal of the Experimental Analysis of Behavior* has flourished since 1958, as has the Division for the Experimental Analysis of Behavior of the American Psychological Association. Many university psychology departments take Skinner's position as their basic orientation in training their graduate students. Behavior modification as a technique of controlling behavior has gained increasing popularity, providing more empirical support for his approach.

Whether we agree or disagree with Skinner's position, its presence can be felt in many areas—from classrooms to assembly lines, from Skinner boxes to prisons and mental institutions. In Skinner's view, he has presented and refined a technique that will vastly improve human nature and the societies humans design.

Suggested Readings

Evans, R. I. *B. F. Skinner: The man and his ideas.* New York: Dutton, 1969.

Ferster, C. B., & Skinner, B. F. *Schedules of reinforcement.* New York: Appleton-Century-Crofts, 1957.

Rice, B. Skinner agrees he is the most important influence in psychology. *New York Times Magazine*, March 17, 1968, pp. 27 ff.

Skinner, B. F. *Walden two.* New York: Macmillan, 1948.

Skinner, B. F. *Science and human behavior.* New York: Macmillan, 1953.

Skinner, B. F. *Contingencies of reinforcement.* New York: Appleton-Century-Crofts, 1954.

Skinner, B. F. Autobiography. In E. G. Boring & G. Lindzey (Eds.), *A history of psychology in autobiography* (Vol. 5). New York: Appleton-Century-Crofts, 1967, pp. 385–413.

Skinner, B. F. The machine that is man. *Psychology Today*, April 1969, pp. 20–25; 60–63.

Skinner, B. F. *Beyond freedom and dignity.* New York: Knopf, 1971.

Skinner, B. F. Will success spoil B. F. Skinner? *Psychology Today*, June 1972, pp. 65–72; 130.

Albert Bandura and Richard Walters
Observational-Learning Theory

16

Virtually every phenomenon that occurs by direct experience can occur vicariously as well—by observing other people and the consequences for them.

—Albert Bandura

As learning theorists, Bandura and Walters agree with Skinner that behavior, in its normal as well as abnormal manifestations, is learned. With that point, however, the similarity ends. Bandura and Walters have criticized Skinner's emphasis on studying individual subjects—and mainly rats—rather than on studying human subjects in interaction with others. Their approach is a truly social kind of learning theory, which investigates behavior as it is formed and modified in a social context. They argue that one cannot expect findings of experiments that involve no social interaction to be relevant to the everyday world, in which few people function in social isolation.

Skinner's approach stresses that reinforcement is a necessary condition for the acquisition, maintenance, and modification of behavior. A
person's behavior changes as a result of the consequences of that behavior—the reinforcement experienced directly by the individual. While
Bandura and Walters recognize that much learning does take place as
a result of reinforcement, they also stress that virtually all forms of behavior can be learned in the absence of directly experienced reinforcement. Their approach is sometimes labeled *observational learning*, to
indicate the role in learning of observing the behavior of other people.
Rather than having to experience reinforcement oneself, Bandura and
Walters argue, one can learn through a kind of vicarious reinforcement,
by observing the behavior of other people and the consequences of those
behaviors. This emphasis on learning by observation or example, rather
than always by direct reinforcement, is the most distinctive feature of
Bandura and Walters' theory.

Another distinctive feature of the observational-learning approach,
relative to Skinnerian theory, has to do with its treatment of inner aspects
of the person. Bandura and Walters do not completely rule out the existence of internal influencing variables (as does Skinner). They believe
cognition or thought processes are capable of influencing observational
learning. A person does not automatically copy or reproduce the behavior
he or she sees in other people. Rather, the individual makes a deliberate
decision to behave in the same way.

To be able to learn through example and vicarious reinforcement
necessitates an ability to anticipate and appreciate consequences that a
person has only observed in others and not yet experienced. Bandura
and Walters assume that a person can, in this fashion, regulate and guide
his or her own behavior—by visualizing or imagining the unexperienced
consequences of that behavior. There is not a direct link or coupling
between stimulus and response or between behavior and reinforcement.
There is, instead, a mediating mechanism interposed between the two,
and that mechanism is the person—or, more specifically, the person's
cognitive processes.

For example, Bandura and Walters argue that it is not the schedule
of reinforcement itself that is so powerful in changing behavior but rather
what the person thinks or perceives that schedule to be. Similarly, an
aversive or painful stimulus need not actually be applied in order to
modify behavior. The person's belief that it will be applied is sufficient
to get that person to change his or her behavior.

We have, then, with Bandura and Walters, a less extreme form of
behaviorism, which stresses the role of observation of others as a means
of learning and considers learning to be mediated by cognitive factors.
We also have a theory soundly based on rigorous laboratory research

with normal human subjects in social-interaction situations rather than one based on rats in cages or neurotics on couches. Bandura and Walters call it a *socio-behavioristic* approach.

The Lives of Bandura and Walters

Albert Bandura (1925–   ) was born in a small town in the province of Alberta, Canada. Little published information is available on his child-hood. He was one of 20 students in a high school that had only two teachers. As a result, he and the others had to largely educate themselves —a process that was obviously successful, since Bandura and almost all of his classmates have undertaken successful professional careers.

Bandura attended the University of British Columbia as an under-graduate and received his Ph.D. from the University of Iowa in 1952. He spent a year at the Wichita Kansas Guidance Center and then joined the faculty at Stanford University, where he has remained ever since. In 1969, he spent a year as a Fellow of the Center for Advanced Study in the Behavioral Sciences (at Stanford) and has been a consultant to several government organizations, including the Veterans' Administra-tion. Throughout his career, he has maintained a very vigorous record of publications, and, in 1973, he was elected President of the American Psychological Association.

Richard Walters (1918–1967) was born in Wales and received an undergraduate degree in philosophy from Oxford University, in England, in 1948. His entry into psychology came late in his professional career. He taught philosophy at Auckland University College, in New Zealand, from 1949 to 1953 and then came to the United States to study psychology at Stanford University, where he was Bandura's first Ph.D. student. He received his degree in 1957 and then moved to Canada to teach, first at the University of Toronto and later at the University of Waterloo. Walters conducted a great deal of research on various aspects of social learning and co-authored, with Bandura, many articles, monographs, and books reporting on the development of the theory.

Modeling: The Basis of Observational Learning

The notion that learning can occur through observation or example, rather than by direct reinforcement, is the most distinctive aspect of

Bandura and Walters' social-learning theory. It is important to note that Bandura and Walters do not deny the importance of direct reinforcement as a technique of influencing behavior. What they are denying is the proposition that behavior can be learned or changed *only* through direct reinforcement. Also, they argue that reinforcement is a highly inefficient way of changing behavior. It is time consuming and potentially dangerous; the world would be extremely hazardous indeed if people needed direct reinforcement in order to learn such things as not to cross an intersection on foot against a red light at the height of rush-hour traffic. This is not the kind of situation in which one would want to try out a number of behaviors before finding the one that brings reinforcement.

Operant conditioning, in which trial-and-error behavior continues until the correct response is found, is an inefficient way of teaching skills such as swimming or driving, because the person could drown or crash before finding the sequence of behaviors that leads to positive reinforcement. Most human behavior, Bandura and Walters argue, is learned through example, either intentionally or accidentally. We learn by observing other people and modeling our behavior after theirs. Some behaviors can be learned only through the influence of models; language is perhaps the best example of this. How could a child learn to speak if he or she never had the opportunity to hear words, phrases, and sentences? If learning to speak could be accomplished by operant conditioning alone, it would mean that the infant would not be reinforced for saying words (or approximations of them) until *after* he or she had said them spontaneously, having never heard them before.

Through the observation of a model, it is possible to acquire responses never before performed or displayed and to strengthen or weaken responses that already exist in one's repertoire of behavior. In this regard, perhaps the most famous study conducted by Bandura and Walters involved the Bobo doll, an inflated plastic figure three to four feet tall. The subjects, preschool children, watched an adult hit and kick Bobo. The adult model shouted angrily as he attacked the doll "Sock him in the nose!" "Throw him in the air!" and so on. When the children were left alone with the doll, they modeled their behavior after the example they had just seen. When their behavior was compared with that of a control group of children who had not seen the model, it was shown to be twice as aggressive.

Would it make a difference if the model were viewed on television instead of in person? No. The intensity of the aggressive behavior was the same. The intensity of aggression was also the same when the model was a filmed cartoon character. The effect of the model in all three forms was to elicit the same kind of behavior—behavior that was not displayed

Figure 16.1   Children reproducing aggressive behavior of model.

at the same intensity by other children of the same age who had not viewed the same model.

In another example of the impact of modeling on learning, Bandura and Walters compared the behavior of parents of two groups of children. One group was made up of very aggressive children and the other of more inhibited children. According to the modeling theory, children's behavior imitates their parents' behavior. Thus, the parents of the inhibited children should be inhibited and the parents of the aggressive children should be aggressive. The study revealed this to be the case.

Other experiments have shown that an already existing form of behavior that is usually suppressed or inhibited may be performed more readily under the influence of an appropriate model. This phenomenon, called *disinhibition* by Bandura and Walters, refers to the weakening of an inhibition through exposure to a model. There are many examples of disinhibition in everyday life. A person in a crowd (a lynch mob or a protest demonstration, for example) often performs acts that he or she would never have been able to perform if alone. A person is much more likely to violate prohibitions if he or she sees others violating them.

One clever experiment demonstrated that sexual responses can be disinhibited by models. A group of male college undergraduates was shown a film that contained a series of erotic pictures of nude females and males. They were told that a spot of light that moved over the film indicated the eye movements of a previous subject, showing which parts of the pictures that subject had looked at. This represented the model. For half of the subjects, the light roamed over the bodies of the nudes, concentrating on the breasts and genitals. For the other half of the subjects, the light remained on the background of the picture, as though the subject had avoided looking at the nude bodies.

After watching this film, each subject was shown slides made from the movie sequences. By means of a special camera, the subjects' eye movements were recorded as they looked at each picture. Those subjects whose model was uninhibited (looking directly at the nude bodies) did the same thing. Those subjects whose model had avoided looking at the nudes spent significantly more time looking at the backgrounds of the pictures than at the figures.

Thus, it seems that modeling can influence not only overt behavior with respect to an object but also perceptual responses to an object. Modeling can determine not only what we do but also what we look at and what we perceive.

Incidentally, these studies indicate something of the techniques of inquiry of Bandura and Walters and their general approach to the theory. Through a series of well controlled and imaginative research studies, involving human subjects in interaction, they derived principles of how behavior is learned and modified through the imitation of models.

On the basis of their extensive research, Bandura and Walters were convinced that much human behavior, both "good" and "bad," normal and abnormal, is learned by imitation. From infancy on, we develop our behavioral repertoire in response to the many models society offers us. Beginning with parents as models, we learn a language and become socialized in line with the mores and customs of our culture.

The individual who deviates from the cultural norms—the delinquent, neurotic, criminal, or psychopath—has learned his or her behavior in the same way that everyone else has. The difference is that the deviant person has followed a different model—one not considered desirable by the rest of society. Bandura has been greatly concerned about the "wrong" models our culture provides to children, particularly the models of violent behavior that are regular fare on television, including on children's cartoon programs. He has spoken and written forcefully against these models since his research (and that of others) has clearly shown how effective they are in influencing behavior. If what we see is what we become, the distance between watching Bobo being attacked on television and then committing an act of violence ourselves is not very great.

There is no limit to the new behaviors children can acquire through modeling, including nonrational fears. A child who sees his or her father become fearful every time there is a thunderstorm or sees his or her mother become nervous every time she is around strangers will easily acquire these same fears and carry them through to adult life with no awareness of their origin. Of course, strength and courage in the face of difficulties and hope and optimism in the face of new experiences can be just as easily learned. In Skinner's system, we saw that the person who controls the reinforcers can control behavior. In Bandura and Walters' view, the person who controls the models controls behavior.

The Nature of Observational Learning

In a typical modeling experiment, the subject (usually a preschool child) observes another person (the model) in the performance of some behavior or sequence of behaviors. Some time after this observation, the subject is observed, to determine if his or her behavior imitates the behavior of the model. The subject's behavior, as compared to that of a control group of subjects who did not observe the model, indicates how fully or completely modeling has occurred.

In this kind of experiment, several variables can be investigated to determine their influence on the extent of modeling. For example, one can change various characteristics or properties of the model (such as age or sex), the behavior performed by the model, the reinforcement consequences of the model's behavior, and the incentive or motivation of the subject to imitate the model.

Bandura and Walters, and others, have conducted research to investigate these various components of the modeling situation. We shall discuss a few of these findings to illustrate the kinds of factors that are capable of influencing the modeling process. As you might suspect, characteristics of the model can greatly influence imitation. In real life, we may be more prone to be influenced by someone who appears to be very like ourselves than by someone who differs from us in obvious and significant ways. So it is in the laboratory. For example, although children imitate the behavior of a child model in the same room, of a child in a film, and of a filmed cartoon character, the extent of the modeling decreases as the similarity between the model and the subject decreases. There is greater imitation of a live model than of a cartoon character (although in both cases the modeling behavior is significantly greater than that of control subjects).

Other characteristics of the model that influence the extent of imitation include the model's age, sex, and status relative to the subject. For example, we are more likely to model our behavior after a person of the same sex than after a person of the opposite sex. An adult model might well induce more imitation in a 4-year-old than in a 16-year-old who is struggling for independence from adults.

The kind of behavior performed by the model will also influence the extent of imitation. Highly complex behaviors are not imitated as quickly or readily as are simpler behaviors. Hostile and aggressive responses consistently tend to be strongly imitated, at least by children. Another influencing factor is the consequence of the model's behavior—whether the behavior is rewarded, punished, or ignored. Those behaviors that are rewarded are the ones most likely to be imitated.

In addition to investigating the variables that influence modeling, Bandura and Walters have carefully analyzed the nature of observational learning and found it to be governed by four interrelated processes or mechanisms: attentional processes, retention processes, motor reproduction processes, and incentive and motivational processes.

Attentional processes govern observational learning by virtue of the fact that modeling will not occur unless the subject attends to the model. Merely exposing the subject to the model does not guarantee that the subject will be attentive to the relevant cues, will select the most relevant stimulus events, or will even perceive the stimulus situation accurately. It is not sufficient for the subject merely to see the model and what it is doing; the subject must attend to the model with enough perceptual accuracy to acquire the necessary information to use in imitating the model. A number of variables (including some discussed earlier) can influence how closely the subject attends to the behavior of the model. In the real world, as in the laboratory, we are more attentive and responsive to some people (and some situations) than to others.

We have mentioned such characteristics as age and sex of the model and degree of similarity between the model and the subject. These factors can determine how closely a subject will attend. It has also been found that models who appear high in competence, who are alleged to be experts, or who are celebrities, command greater attention than models who lack these attributes. In general, any set of characteristics that causes a model to be perceived as more attractive increases the probability of more careful attention to the model and, consequently, the probability of imitation.

A second mechanism in observational learning involves the *retention processes.* Unless the subject is imitating a model's behavior as that behavior is taking place, the subject must retain or remember all significant aspects of the behavior. If the subject cannot remember the behavior, he or she will not be able to imitate it five days or five minutes after observing it.

In order to retain what has been attended to, it is necessary, in some fashion, to encode and represent symbolically what has been seen. This internal process of symbolic representation is, as has been noted, a basic point of difference between the approach of Bandura and Walters and that of Skinner. The admission of cognitive processes (image formation and problem solving, for example) into their system means that Bandura and Walters recognize certain inner aspects of the person to be operative in the development and modification of behavior. Thus, their focus is not exclusively on overt behavior, as is the case with Skinner.

Bandura and Walters propose two internal representational systems —*imaginal* and *verbal*—as means by which the behavior of the model is retained by the subject. While observing the model, the subject forms permanent and easily retrievable images of what he or she has seen. The images are formed through a process of conditioning, so that any reference to events previously observed immediately calls forth a vivid image or picture of the physical stimuli involved, even though they are no longer present. This is a common phenomenon and accounts for your being able to "see" an image of the person you had a date with last week or an image of a particular place you visited last summer. We can form an image of the event or the model and then use that image as a basis for imitating the model's behavior quite some time after we actually experienced it.

The other representational system, the verbal, is similar to image formation and involves a verbal coding of something we have previously observed. During the original observation, a subject might verbally describe to himself or herself what the model is doing. These verbal descriptions (codes) can later be rehearsed internally, without an overt display of the behavior; for example, a person might "talk through" to himself or herself the steps in a complicated skill. In that situation, the person is silently rehearsing a sequence of behavior to be performed at a later time, and, when he or she does wish to perform the skill, the verbal code will provide cues. Together these symbolic representations—images and verbal symbols—provide the means by which we store or retain the observed events and rehearse them for later performance.

Translating these symbolic representations into overt behavior is what is involved in the third mechanism of observational learning, the *motor reproduction processes*. Even though a person may have carefully formed and retained symbolic representations of a model's behavior and silently rehearsed that behavior many times, he or she still may not be able to perform the behavior correctly. This is particularly applicable to highly skilled acts that require many individual component behaviors for their skillful performance. Consider the highly complex skill of driving a car. The fundamental movements involved may be learned by watching someone else drive, and the symbolic representation of the model's behavior may be repeated internally a number of times, but the translation into actual behavior will be rough and clumsy at first. Mere observation in this case is not sufficient to achieve a smooth and skillful performance of the act. Actual practice in performing the motor movements (and feedback on their correctness) is needed to refine the behavior. However, as indicated, observing and silently rehearsing some behaviors is of definite help in learning, for the person is at least able to begin to perform the necessary movements on the basis of his or her retention of what had been earlier observed. This internal rehearsal is helpful with skills such as driving but may not be as useful with more sophisticated skills, such as playing the violin.

The fourth mechanism of observational learning involves *incentive and motivational processes*. No matter how well we attend to and retain the behavior of a model or how much ability we possess to perform that behavior, we will not perform it without sufficient incentive or motivation to do so. When sufficient incentives are available, modeling or observational learning is quickly translated into action. Not only does proper incentive bring about the actual performance of the behavior; it also influences the attentional and retention processes. We do not pay as much attention to something when no incentive impels us to; and when little attention has been paid, there is little or nothing to retain.

One way in which incentive to attend, retain, and perform a certain behavior may be influenced is through the anticipation of reinforcement or punishment for so doing. The observation that the model's behavior produced some positive reward, or avoided some negative reinforcement, can be a strong incentive to attend to, retain, and later (when in a similar situation) perform that behavior. The reinforcement is thus experienced vicariously during the observation, after which the subject can anticipate that his or her performance of the same behavior will lead to the same consequences.

Bandura and Walters are careful to point out that while reinforcement, in their system, can indeed facilitate learning, it is not necessary in order that learning take place. There are many factors, they note, other than the reward consequences of behavior that can determine what people will attend to. We attend to loud sounds, bright lights, interesting displays, and unusual stimuli, without receiving reinforcement for doing so.

In their experiments, Bandura and Walters have shown that children watching a model on television have imitated the model's behavior regardless of whether they had been told in advance that such imitation would lead to reinforcement. Reinforcement, therefore, can aid in modeling, but it is not vital to it.

When reinforcement does occur, it can be experienced vicariously, given directly by another, or given by the self. Bandura and Walters believe that self-administered reinforcement can be at least as important as reinforcement administered by others, particularly for older children and adults. People often set standards of behavior or achievement for themselves and then reward or punish themselves for meeting, exceeding, or falling short of their own expectations. This self-administered reward may be simply a feeling of pride or satisfaction; self-administered punishment may consist of shame or guilt or depression about not having behaved the way one wanted to. Such self-reinforcement would seem to indicate the presence of something not unlike the Freudian superego—an internalized set of standards for one's own behavior.

Such internalized standards are usually learned from the behavior of models, particularly parents and other significant people in a child's life. Once having adopted the model's standard or style of behavior, one continues to evaluate one's own behavior against that standard. Thus, one's self-esteem and self-concept develop through the principles of observational learning.

Behavior Therapy

Bandura and Walters had a very practical goal in the development of their theory of social learning: to learn how best to modify or change behavior that is considered undesirable or abnormal. If behavior is initially learned through the principles of observational learning, it should be possible to change or relearn behavior—to eliminate undesirable acts and replace them with new ones. As we discussed in Chapter 15, Skinner uses behavior-modification techniques based on operant conditioning. Like Skinner's approach to therapy, that of Bandura and Walters focuses on external aspects of abnormality—inappropriate or destructive behaviors—in the belief that these, like all other behaviors, are learned. They do not refer to underlying unconscious conflicts that must be uncovered and then relieved. It is the behavior or symptom, rather than any presumed inner cause for a neurosis, that is the target of the social-learning approach to abnormality. In essence, Bandura and Walters believe that to treat the symptom is to treat the disorder; they are one and the same.

If modeling is the basic procedure by which we learn our behaviors originally, it should be an equally effective way of changing behavior. Modeling has been used as a device to eliminate fears and other intense emotional reactions. In one case, young children who were afraid of dogs observed a child of the same age playing with a dog. While the subjects watched from a safe distance, the model made progressively bolder movements with respect to the dog. Initially, the model petted the dog through the bars of a playpen in which the dog had been placed. Finally, the child model went inside the pen and played openly and cheerfully with the dog. The observers' fears of dogs were considerably reduced as a result of this observational learning.

In a famous study with snakes, Bandura and his associates were able to eliminate an intense fear of snakes in adult subjects. The subjects watched a film in which children, adolescents, and adults displayed progressively closer contact with a snake. At first the models handled plastic snakes, then real ones, and finally they let a large snake crawl freely over their bodies. A subject was allowed to stop the film whenever the scenes became too threatening and to move the film back to less threatening scenes. The fear of snakes was gradually overcome.

A more effective modeling procedure involved first watching a live model and then actively participating with the model. Initially, the subject watched a model who was boldly handling a snake on the opposite side of an observation window. Then the subject entered the same room with the model and observed the handling of the snake at close range. Next, wearing gloves, the subject was coaxed into touching the middle of the snake while the model held the tail and head. The subject then touched the snake without gloves and made progressively bolder approach movements.

Bandura and Walters point out that modeling, particularly when it makes use of films, offers several practical advantages in therapy. Complex behaviors can be seen as a whole, and extraneous behaviors can be edited out, so that time is spent viewing only that which is relevant to the behavior problem being treated. Second, once a film is made, it can be less expensive than the continued use of live models, since it can be repeated easily and used by many therapists simultaneously. The modeling technique, on film or live, can be used with groups of patients, circumventing the more expensive and time-consuming practice of treating people who have the same problem individually.

There are a great many variations, integrations, and combinations of behavior therapy techniques—too many to cover fully in a text devoted to theories of personality. The important point here is to show that very practical and, apparently, successful therapeutic techniques have resulted from a conception of personality formulated in social-learning terms. Since the 1960s, hundreds of articles have been published on behavior-modification techniques. Such techniques have become increasingly popular as alternatives to psychoanalysis and to other psychotherapeutic approaches. Rather than trying to bring about changes in personality, behavior therapy tries to change the overt manifestation of personality; it tries to change behavior.

Techniques of Inquiry

We have already offered a number of examples of the way in which Bandura and Walters collect data for the social-learning theory. Their studies of observational learning, in which a subject observes a model's behavior and is then tested to see if he or she displays the same behavior in a similar situation, are well-controlled investigations, conducted in the tradition of experimental psychology. Since Bandura and Walters are not concerned with any presumed internal motivational forces of a conscious or unconscious nature, they have not attempted to probe the inner person through free association, dream analysis, or any of the traditional psychotherapeutic techniques. Their subjects have exhibited a wide range of disorders, from phobias to alcoholism and from fetishism to frigidity, as well as many non-neurotic behaviors. Further, the ages of the subjects have ranged from preschool to adult. Of all the theories covered in this book, the social-learning theory of Bandura and Walters is probably based on the broadest range of human subjects, a fact that serves to increase the generalizability of their findings.

Bandura and Walters' Image of Human Nature

Bandura and Walters make it clear that they view people as at least partial products of past learning experiences. All human behavior develops from past social-stimulus events, which include the nature and characteristics of the child's social models. Bandura and Walters do not focus on internal motivating forces. In their view, people are neither pushed by inner drives or needs nor pulled by any desire for self-actualization, perfection, or fulfillment. This would seem to indicate a somewhat passive view, in which people are shaped solely by external forces, over which they may have no control.

However, this is decidedly not the case. While human behavior is seen as influenced by external social stimuli, the individual is not considered a helpless robot with respect to outside events. Responses are not triggered automatically by external stimuli. Rather, the reactions to these stimuli are *self-activated* in accordance with learned anticipations. The individual is able to observe and interpret the effects of his or her own behavior and, in that way, determine which behaviors are appropriate in which situations. People are able to encode and symbolize environmental events and to anticipate that a certain behavior will bring a certain response. Thus, we choose and shape many of our behaviors in order to gain anticipated rewards or avoid anticipated pain.

Acknowledged, in this view, are self-awareness, self-reinforcement, and other forms of internal regulation of behavior. Reinforcement does not automatically change human behavior. When it does bring about a change, it does so because the individual is aware of what is being reinforced and anticipates the same reinforcement for behaving in the same way again. Thus, some degree of self-direction interacts with past and present social-stimulus events. We are influenced by external forces, but we are also able to regulate and guide the extent and direction of such influences.

The introduction of the notion of inner- or self-direction of behavior (in combination with external stimuli) changes what at first appeared to be a pessimistic view of human nature. Indeed, Bandura refers to himself as a "devoted optimist" because of his belief that individuals can, in part, create their own environments and because he believes abnormal behavior is nothing more than "bad habits." Inappropriate or destructive behavior results from learning and, therefore, is amenable to change by the same techniques and principles by which it was originally acquired. If bad behavior is learned from the social environment, then good behavior can be learned just as easily.

We can see, then, that the image of human nature projected by the observational learning theory of Bandura and Walters is couched in optimistic terms. However, the technique of changing behavior that is associated with their theory (as well as with Skinner's) has drawn widespread professional and public criticism because it is alleged to be based on an inhuman and manipulative approach to human beings. Behavior modification arouses passionate attacks in newspapers and magazines by educators, government officials, and other interested individuals because, they charge, it is sometimes used to manipulate individuals without their awareness.

Bandura has reacted sharply to these charges. It is not, he says, behavior modification that should be called inhuman. Rather, other therapeutic techniques that are not effective deserve that label. What is inhuman, he argues, is to refuse to use the most efficient technique available to help a person who is having difficulties. To do nothing for such a person, or to string him or her along for years in a doubtful program of therapy, is inhuman, not only for the individual but also for his or her family and friends and, ultimately, for all of society.

Bandura believes that the accusation of manipulative control of an individual through behavior modification is a totally false and misleading charge. For one thing, such "control" does not take place without the knowledge of the subject. As we have seen, Bandura and Walters have posited self-awareness and self-regulation as operative in the behavior-change process. Modification of behavior does not occur, Bandura argues, unless the person is able to understand what is being reinforced. Second, Bandura suggests that it is wrong to talk about control, since it is the individuals who decide what it is about themselves they want changed. It is the client who comes to the therapist because he or she wants to eliminate a fear of snakes, a girdle fetish, or an inability to walk on a sidewalk with other people. Bandura suggests that this is analogous to going to a dentist with a toothache; the client has a problem that he or she would like to have relieved. The client-therapist relationship is therefore a contract between two consenting individuals, not a master-slave relationship.

Finally, Bandura feels that, far from manipulating or enslaving an individual, behavior modification actually increases the person's freedom. A woman who cannot leave the house, a man who can go out only if he wears a girdle, or a person who must wash his or her hands 20 times each hour is not fully free. Such people are living within the constraints imposed by their own behavior. And sometimes those constraints are very binding, allowing the person little, if any, free choice about how to behave. By removing these constraining symptoms, Bandura argues, behavior modification greatly increases the individual's true freedom and allows more opportunity for personal growth.

A Final Commentary

The learning-theory approach to personality (as represented in Chapter 15 as well as in this chapter) is seen by many research psychologists and clinicians as one of the most exciting and productive innovations in the study and treatment of personality in the 20th century. The great number of books, articles, and research studies attests to its current popularity, both as a means of studying behavior in the laboratory and as a way of changing behavior in the clinic.

Observational-learning theory has too recently become a forceful movement to allow the wisdom of temporal perspective (better known as hindsight). However, increasing numbers of psychologists are being trained in the theory and technique of observational learning, and the vigor—indeed passion—with which the adherents of this approach defend and extend the theory seems to guarantee the continued growth of interest in it.

The approach enjoys additional advantages. First, it is highly objective and directly amenable to precise laboratory methods of investigation, making it congruent with the strong emphasis on experimental research that characterizes the mainstream of psychology in the United States. Most psychologists of an experimental persuasion reject other theoretical work in the area of personality because it posits unseen unconscious forces, which cannot be manipulated or measured under laboratory conditions. Second, observational learning and the derivative behavior modification seem directly compatible with the functional, pragmatic spirit that defines so much of American psychology. Much more readily than other approaches, observational-learning techniques can be taken from the laboratory and applied directly to problems in the real world. And there is more immediate reinforcement for the efforts of the practitioner than with more traditional approaches. He or she is able to see dramatic changes in a client's behavior within weeks or even days.

Critics of this approach argue that social learning, like Skinner's more extreme behaviorism, deals with only the peripheral aspects of personality—a person's overt behavior. This emphasis on overt behavior, critics suggest, misses or ignores our distinctly human aspects—conscious and unconscious motivating forces. It is perhaps analogous to a physician trying to treat a patient who complains of stomach pains by dealing only with what the patient says and does—by trying to get the patient to stop doubling over, pressing on his stomach, and saying "It hurts." What is necessary in this case, critics say, is medicine or surgery; the physician must get to the underlying source of the behavior—the afflicted internal organ. A somewhat related charge is that, if only the symptom is treated and not the cause of the disorder, substitute symptoms are bound to appear, since the cause remains unaffected. This charge has not been supported by the research available to date.

Whatever the eventual status of social-learning theory in the study of personality, there is no doubt that it is a potent force in psychology. Growing numbers of psychologists are modeling their behavior after that of Bandura and Walters and are evidently finding sufficient reinforcement for so doing.

Suggested Readings

Bandura, A. What TV violence can do to your child. *Look Magazine*, October 22, 1963, pp. 46–52.

Bandura, A. *Principles of behavior modification*. New York: Holt, Rinehart and Winston, 1969.

Bandura, A. *Aggression: A social learning analysis*. Englewood Cliffs, N.J.: Prentice-Hall, 1973.

Bandura, A. *Psychological modeling: Conflicting theories*. Chicago: Atherton, 1974.

Bandura, A. Behavior theory and the models of man. *American Psychologist*, 1974, *29*, 859–869.

Bandura, A., & Walters, R. *Social learning and personality development*. New York: Holt, Rinehart and Winston, 1963.

Rotter, J., Chance, J., & Phares, E. *Applications of a social learning theory of personality*. New York: Holt, Rinehart and Winston, 1972.

Stolz, S., Wienckowski, L., & Brown, B. Behavior modification: A perspective on critical issues. *American Psychologist*, 1975, *30*, 1027–1048.

Festinger   McClelland   Witkin

Limited-Domain
Theories

17

I. Need for Achievement (David McClelland)
II. Psychological Differentiation (Herman Witkin)
III. Cognitive Dissonance (Leon Festinger)

The proposing of personality theories is increasingly an experimentally oriented venture. Therefore, the specialized or limited-domain approach may assume greater importance in the years to come.

Personality theorists, in general, have considered the achievement of comprehensiveness or completeness to be a major theoretical goal. Some theories come closer to achieving this goal than others, but more and more writers in the area of personality are concluding that no existing theory can legitimately be called comprehensive, regardless of the theorist's stated aims. Further, it has been suggested that such a goal may be unrealistic.

Some psychologists argue that few (and perhaps none) of the available theories adequately account for all aspects of personality, no matter how broadly they try to stretch their formulations. Rather, each theory is seen to operate within a *range of convenience* (to use Kelly's term); each covers only certain aspects of personality, leaving other facets relatively unexplored. For example, Erikson focuses on the developmental aspects of personality, Kelly on cognitive processes, Bandura and Walters on modeling, Cattell on traits, Murray on needs, and so on. To be sure, the range of convenience of some theories is broader than that of others, but is any theory sufficiently broad to be called comprehensive?

Because of their feeling that no theory is comprehensive—and that perhaps no theory can be—some psychologists who study personality suggest that to achieve a fuller understanding of personality we may need to develop a number of separate theories, each having a narrow range of convenience. These *limited-domain* theories would each focus on a narrow or limited aspect of personality. Restriction of the target or focus of investigation would allow the domain selected to be investigated more thoroughly, it is suggested, than occurs when the total personality is dealt with.

There are indications that this fragmentation is taking place. If so, then the field of personality is following the example of other areas of psychology that have replaced their attempts to develop large-scale, all-encompassing theories with what have been called *miniature theories*. As researchers in other areas of psychology—such as learning and motivation—realized the impossibility of including all aspects of their subject matter in one theory, they turned to theories of limited domain and narrow range of convenience. In the field of learning, for example, we find theoretical formulations that focus on specific types of learning, such as verbal learning, conditioning, or maze learning—circumscribed areas of behavior. Theories that try to account for all aspects of learning over all situations with all types of subjects are no longer in vogue.

It is easy to see why the global-theory approach has characterized the field of personality for so long. The early personality theorists—Freud, Adler, Jung—dealt with individual patients in the clinical setting. They tried to change or "cure" abnormalities of behavior and were thus forced to deal with whole human beings trying to function in the real world. They attempted to treat the whole person, not just a part, not just one aspect of the personality.

The focus shifted from the whole person only when the topic of personality began to be brought out of the clinic and into the research laboratory. Experimental psychologists began to (and continue to) study one variable at a time (all other variables being controlled or held constant); thus, they focus on a limited domain. Also, their approach is characterized by the collection of large amounts of empirical data, which are derived from the investigation of how the variable relates to its antecedents and to its behavioral consequences. Therefore, limited-domain theories are characterized by a different type of supporting data from those used in the clinical approach.

Limited-domain theories also place less emphasis on the therapeutic value of the theoretical formulations. Their proponents are usually not clinicians but researchers, and so their focus is more on investigating personality than on trying to change it. This does not mean, of course, that there is no therapeutic utility to these theories. It merely indicates that the theories are not developed specifically for use in the clinic, as was the case with many of our earlier theorists.

Since the study of personality and the proposing of personality theories is increasingly an experimentally oriented venture and less a clinical one, it follows that the limited-domain approach may assume greater importance in the years to come.

We will discuss three limited-domain theories: need for achievement, psychological differentiation, and cognitive dissonance. While these are certainly not the only ones available, nor perhaps even the best ones, they do illustrate the nature of the limited-domain approach and are sufficiently well developed to serve as examples of what may be a growing trend in personality study.[1]

I. Need for Achievement

One of the needs Henry Murray posited was the need for achievement—the need to overcome obstacles, to excel, to live up to a high standard. Since 1947, Harvard psychologist David McClelland (1917–   ) has conducted a broad and intensive research program to investigate this need. The amount of his research (and of the additional research it has inspired) is staggering and has important theoretical as well as practical implications.

McClelland's work on achievement motivation provides an excellent example of how much can be learned when the domain of research is restricted to one aspect of personality. It also provides an example of the importance of the limited-domain approach to understanding the domain of the total personality. While the focus of study is narrow, the ramifications are broad. McClelland believes that concentration on a limited area is not at all narrowing. "By concentrating on one problem, on *one motive*, we have found in the course of our study that we have learned not only a lot about the achievement motive but other areas of personality as well."

[1]Since these three theories are being presented as examples of the limited-domain approach, and not as comprehensive theories of personality, they will not be discussed in as much detail as the previous theories. The intent is to give the flavor of each approach. The theorists' lives and images of human nature will not be discussed, and critical commentary has purposely been kept to a minimum.

Through diligent, thorough, and imaginative research, McClelland and his associates have developed a technique with which to measure an individual's achievement motivation and have determined how behavior varies in a number of situations as a function of the level of the need for achievement. They have also uncovered sources responsible for the development of the need for achievement (or for its lack of development) in an individual.

Finally, in an exciting, far-reaching, and unusual research program, McClelland has presented an empirical account of the economic growth and decline of ancient and contemporary cultures in terms of their general level of need for achievement. As a result of this research, it is possible to predict a country's future economic growth or decline by measuring its current level of the need. He has also developed techniques for increasing the need for achievement in developing nations, with striking results. As you can see, there is nothing narrow or limited about what McClelland has been able to achieve by studying only one aspect of personality.

Measuring the Need for Achievement

In developing a technique for measuring achievement motivation (need achievement), McClelland was guided by certain insights of Sigmund Freud as well as by the methodological requirements of experimental psychology. From Freud he borrowed the basic approach of uncovering and measuring the motive in question through the fantasy reports of subjects. However, while Freud searched for fantasy in dreams and free association, McClelland used a specific psychological test, developed by Murray and already widely used in research: the Thematic Apperception Test (TAT). In this test, the subject is presented with a series of pictures, each of which can be interpreted in more than one way. In other words, different people see different things in the pictures presented to them. The theory behind this projective technique is that a person, in interpreting a picture, will do so in terms of his or her own needs, fears, values, or fantasies, which are projected onto the ambiguous stimulus picture.

McClelland asked groups of male college students to write brief stories about some of the TAT pictures after having been exposed to different experimental conditions. For example, through the use of different test-taking instructions, weak achievement need was induced in one group and strong achievement need in another. Then the content of their stories was compared to see if the two groups differed significantly in the amount of achievement-oriented material found in their stories. The research question was: what effect does an experimentally

Figure 17.1 Sample picture administered for the measurement of
achievement motivation. From *The Achievement Motive,* by D. C.
McClelland, J. W. Atkinson, R. A. Clark, & E. L. Lowell (Eds.), 1953.
Reprinted by permission of Irvington Publishers.

induced state of achievement motivation have on a subject's fantasy production? If the experimental treatments worked (if the group exhorted
to high achievement actually showed higher achievement in their stories
than the group not so exhorted), and if these different levels of fantasy
production could be detected in the TAT-produced stories, then the test
could be used as a valid measure of need for achievement.

And that was precisely what happened. The stories written under
the high-achievement conditions contained many more references to attaining standards of excellence and to wanting to do well or actually
doing well. For example, one of the pictures showed a young man sitting
at a desk with a book open in front of him. Stories from the low need
achievement group dealt with sedentary and passive activities: daydreaming, thinking, recalling past events. They contained minimal reference
to doing things involving excelling, striving, or achieving. The stories
told by the high need achievement subjects involved many references
to doing one's best, working instead of daydreaming, striving, and so on.

Through this initial research, McClelland concluded that TAT-
produced stories can be used as a valid measure of the need to achieve,
and this became the basic tool for selecting high and low need achievement subjects for his extensive research program.

Achievement Motivation and Behavior

A large number of studies have been conducted to discover in what ways people who score high in need achievement behave differently from those who score low in this area of motivation. We will summarize these findings briefly. The findings deal with males, since males made up the primary subject group studied. High need achievement males more often are members of the middle class and much less often of the lower or upper classes. They demonstrate a better memory than low need achievement males for tasks uncompleted, are much more active in college and community activities, and are more likely to volunteer to serve as subjects for psychological research (including research on need achievement). In addition, they are more resistant to social pressure; that is, they are significantly less conforming than low need achievement males.

Of potentially greater practical significance are studies comparing the performances of those with high and low need for achievement in experimentally designed work situations. In the first of these experiments, the subjects had to unscramble the letters of a large number of scrambled words. Though both groups began the task at the same level of performance, the high achievers showed a progressive improvement in their performance. McClelland concluded that these high achievers were motivated so strongly to do the job well (to achieve) that they learned how to do it better as they continued with the task.

The high achievers worked harder and did the job better. Does it follow that persons high in achievement need perform better on any kind of task? To answer that question, other experiments were conducted, in which the task and certain conditions surrounding it were studied. In one such experiment, the task to be performed was highly repetitive and routine: to cross out the Es and Os in a long series of random letters. In this kind of task there is really no room for improvement; there is no way to learn to do the task better, only faster. High and low need achievement subjects performed at the same level in this task.

In another study, high need achievement subjects were given instructions prior to the task that eliminated all achievement significance from the work. As a result, they performed no better than low need achievement subjects. Other studies investigated the effects of extrinsic rewards (rewards other than achievement itself) for performance. In one case, subjects were told that those who performed best could leave immediately. This kind of reward held no motivation for the high achievers. They actually performed slightly worse than the low achievers.

These experiments suggest that subjects high in need for achievement do not perform better than subjects low in need for achievement unless the achievement motive itself is activated. Only when the high-need individual is challenged to excel will he do so. This point was again demonstrated in studies involving a ringtoss game in which subjects were allowed to choose how far or how close to the target they would stand. Obviously, standing very close would assure success at the task, while standing very far away would tend to assure failure. By taking either extreme position, the subject could ensure that the outcome would depend little on skill or excellence and that there would be minimal challenge to the task. Subjects low in need achievement tended to stand either very close or very far away, while subjects high in need achievement stood at distances where it was possible to demonstrate or develop skill and excellence at the task. That is, they stood neither too close (where skill was not required) nor too far away (where skill would have made little difference in the outcome). They preferred to take a moderate risk rather than no risk or an impossible risk.

From these findings, McClelland concluded that people with high achievement needs will, in their everyday activities (and particularly in their work) seek situations that will allow them to satisfy these achievement needs. They will set certain achievement standards for themselves and then work hard to reach those standards.

McClelland assumed that if sufficient numbers of high need achievement people existed in a given culture or country at the same time, the general level of economic development of the country would rise. In an ingenious and lengthy program of investigation, he set out to find evidence that would link the level of need for achievement among the members of a given country's population and its level of economic growth and prosperity. This is a rare kind of research—that designed to investigate how personality (or at least one aspect of it) may act to influence the nature of society. In the other theories discussed, we sometimes dealt with the reverse process: how society influences an individual. In other cases, we discussed the assertion that people are capable of changing society, although we saw that how that happens and which specific aspects of society the individual might influence remain unanswered questions. McClelland's research represents probably the only instance in which such questions have been empirically investigated.

Achievement Motivation and Culture

The theoretical rationale for considering the possibility of a link between need for achievement and a culture's level of economic growth grew out of the work of the German sociologist Max Weber. Writing in the early years of this century, Weber offered the suggestion that the

Protestant Reformation had produced a new character orientation in Protestant countries, which in turn produced the Industrial Revolution and the spirit of capitalism. This orientation stressed a continuing effort to improve oneself, to progress, strive, seek, pursue—in a word, to achieve. McClelland suggested that these values of hard work and striving for excellence became the norm in Protestant cultures and were taught to each succeeding generation, as a result of which the new values became increasingly widespread. The stress on individual achievement was then manifested in ways that advanced the economic growth of the culture.

As an initial test of this proposed relationship between need achievement and economic growth, McClelland compared the average per capita consumption of electric power (a measure of level of economic development) of 12 Protestant and 13 Catholic countries. The data showed that the Protestant countries were the more economically advanced.

In a more direct study performed by Berlew,[2] the relationship between achievement motivation and economic growth was studied in three time periods of ancient Greek civilization—a period of growth, of climax, and of decline. If there is a causal relationship between need achievement and economic growth, then the general level of achievement motivation should have been highest during the period of growth and dropped during the climax, leading to the later decline.

But how does one measure need achievement in a culture long dead? You cannot ask individuals to write stories into which they project their need for achievement, but stories written at the time can be analyzed for evidence of need achievement themes, on the assumption that the writers reflected the values of their society. This is an indirect but clever way to assess a culture's level of achievement motivation. When Berlew compared these empirical measures of need achievement with measures of the economic level during the three time periods, the results were as predicted. There was a high level of need achievement during the period of growth, which presumably led to the period of climax in economic development. During the climax period, the level of need achievement fell, which, it was suggested, resulted in the economic decline that followed.

Because the measures were indirect, one might question these findings had they not been strikingly confirmed in similar studies with other cultures. For example, a study of Spain during the Middle Ages and another of England from 1400 to the Industrial Revolution (around 1830) showed the same high level of need achievement preceding a period of heightened economic growth and a declining need achievement level

[2]D. Berlew. The achievement motive and the growth of Greek civilization. Unpublished bachelor's thesis. Middletown, Conn., Wesleyan University, 1956. Discussed in D. McClelland, *The Achieving Society* (Princeton, N.J.: Van Nostrand, 1961).

preceding a time of economic decline. These studies support the notion that an individual motive, when manifested generally in a culture, is able to drastically change the nature of that culture.

To apply this idea to more contemporary cultures, McClelland undertook a complex and sophisticated investigation of more than 20 countries, comparing their economic and achievement-need levels in 1925 and in 1950. He analyzed, as a measure of need achievement, the content of children's stories found in second- to fourth-grade school books. Children's stories were chosen because they reflect the motives and values a culture wants its children to learn; the stories represent the popular culture that is to be inculcated into the next generation. The morals of these stories are presented directly, "in such simple terms that even a behavioral scientist can understand them."

The results showed that the higher a country's need achievement level in 1925, the greater its rate of economic growth was between 1925 and 1950. It is important to note that the need achievement came first. That is, it was not an increased level of economic development that led to an increased achievement need. Thus, examining a country's 1925 achievement need enabled McClelland to predict that country's economic level only 25 years later.

Having provided such impressive evidence of the importance of the need for achievement, McClelland turned to a related and potentially more important issue: can the level of achievement motivation be increased in adults? Particularly in developing countries, if sufficient numbers of persons could become highly motivated to achieve, the consequences might significantly raise the economic levels of those countries.

Developing the Need for Achievement in Adults

In the last section, we discussed the possibility of a change in one aspect of personality producing a meaningful change in society. In order for societal change to take place quickly, the acquisition of new motives in adulthood must be possible—and much of psychology believes that it is not. As we have seen, Freud and other theorists have argued that personality is formed and rather solidly crystallized in the very early years of life and is difficult, if not impossible, to change after that.

McClelland was encouraged in his efforts by the examples of two different groups of "change agents": operant conditioners and missionaries. In operant conditioning, if you want a person to exhibit a new kind of behavior, all you have to do is arrange for that behavior to be elicited and then reinforce it. Missionaries have also changed behavior successfully, McClelland noted, through forceful programs of education and the vigorous belief that it is possible to change the behavior of adults.

Drawing on principles of learning obtained from human and animal studies, the findings of attitude-change research, and principles of psychotherapy, McClelland developed formal courses that teach achievement motivation to adult men. Performed in the United States, Mexico, and India, the courses were conducted with groups of 9 to 25 people. The training sessions were short but intensive, lasting up to 14 days, 12 to 18 hours a day. From the initial training sessions, McClelland derived a series of principles or guidelines, the use of which he believes can induce a change in the level of need achievement (or of any other motive).

The first objective of the training is to instill confidence in the participants that the program will work. Training techniques are more likely to be effective if the person believes that he will (and should) develop this new motive. The techniques are also more effective if the person is able to see their relevance to the real world—that is, how the person can use what he is learning. As a first step, the individual is taught to use, in a series of games, what he is learning about achievement motivation. In this way, he is able to translate theory into action. Participants are also taught to examine personal and cultural values with respect to achievement motivation and to understand how a greater level of need for achievement can work to improve both themselves and their culture. The trainees must commit themselves to a specific course of action designed to achieve definite goals in their lives, and they must record the extent of their progress in attaining those goals.

Two additional points deserve mention. First, the course leaders behaved in warm and rewarding ways and were nondirective in their relationships with the trainees. McClelland believes that motivational changes are much more likely to occur if a person feels warmly and honestly supported as well as respected by both teachers and peers. These people should reaffirm the person's belief in his ability to direct the course of his own future behavior. Second, McClelland feels that changes in motivation are more likely to occur when the training is conducted in a retreat, in which participants study and live together away from the routine of their everyday lives.

The results of these training programs show significant changes in behavior for large numbers of trainees. The behavioral index of increased achievement motivation was any activity that led to an "unusual promotion or salary raise or starting a new business venture of some kind." Such behavior was evaluated for two years prior to the course and two years after it and showed significant increases in activities related to the need for achievement.

Origins of Achievement Motivation

While McClelland has demonstrated that adults can be formally taught to develop a need for achievement, this is not the only way in which it can originate. No more than a few hundred people have taken McClelland's course, yet many times that number demonstrate the need for achievement. In his search for the source of need for achievement, McClelland has concentrated on the family environment—specifically, certain child-rearing practices that seem to account for the emergence of achievement motivation.

In an early study, it was demonstrated that differences in need achievement level can be detected in children as young as 5 and that these differences can be traced to specific attitudes held by their mothers. In another study, 8- to 10-year-old boys were divided into high and low need achievement groups, and the mothers were interviewed about the demands and restrictions they placed on their children. Interesting differences were found between the mothers of the two groups of boys. For example, mothers of high need achievement boys expected more *self-reliant mastery* (doing things on their own, taking responsibility, doing well, trying hard, and so on) than did mothers of boys with low need achievement. Mothers of the high need achievement boys also placed fewer restrictions on their sons than did the other mothers. However, those restrictions that were imposed by the "high" mothers were expected to be followed at an earlier age. The high need achievement boys were encouraged to become more independent, and to do so at a younger age, than were the other boys.

In another set of experiments, fathers and mothers of high and low need achievement boys observed their children performing tasks such as building towers out of blocks, playing ringtoss, and copying patterns with blocks. During the tasks, the parents were allowed to say whatever they wished to their sons, and some interesting parent-child interactions were observed. For example, parents of high need achievement children set higher standards of excellence than did the other parents, expecting their sons to build higher towers and to stand farther away from the peg in the ringtoss game. McClelland concluded that one way to develop a high need for achievement is to have parents who expect a high level of performance.

Another difference between the two sets of parents was in the general degree of warmth of their comments to their sons during the tasks. While exhorting their sons to do well, the "high" parents were pleasant, anxiety relieving, and joking—much more so than the parents of low need achievement sons. Another finding relates to the level of authoritarian behavior of the parents. The "high" mothers tended to be more authoritarian (pushing or dominating the child) than the "low" mothers. On the other hand, the "high" fathers were less authoritarian than the "low" fathers. That finding, together with the results of other studies, led McClelland to conclude that strong rigidity or authoritarianism, particularly from the father, will tend to lower the need for achievement.

What emerges from this research is a clear picture of the parental behavior likely to produce a high need for achievement: setting realistically high standards of performance at an age when such standards can be reached, not overprotecting or indulging, not interfering with the child's efforts to achieve, and demonstrating genuine pleasure in the child's achievements.

Comment

As McClelland's work demonstrates, it is possible for a limited-domain approach to personality to have a wide domain of influence and application. In fact, some psychologists argue that McClelland's massive investigation of this one facet of personality is far more useful than large-scale theories that attempt to account for all aspects of personality. It would be difficult not to agree that the theory of need achievement has a more solid foundation of empirical support than many of the other theories discussed. The data derive exclusively from experimental research. While other theorists speculate on the relationship between personality and environment, McClelland has empirically investigated that relationship.

His work has generated additional research within a large network of scholars, although McClelland has remained the most prolific. The fact that his initial research has been so widely extended is effective tribute to its importance both as a theoretical and as an applied endeavor. The theory is still evolving under the impact of new findings. It provides an instructive example of how much can be accomplished when the focus of investigation is restricted to a limited domain.

II. Psychological Differentiation

The second limited-domain approach to personality is the product of many years of research by Herman Witkin (1916-   ), long associated with the State University of New York Downstate Medical Center (New York City) as director of the Psychological Laboratory. As the title of his major work, *Personality through Perception*, suggests, Witkin's approach to personality is through the investigation of the relationship between an individual's personal characteristics and the way in which he or she perceives the world. Specifically, this approach attempts to study the ways in which the personality of an individual may influence his or her perception. This may seem an indirect method of studying personality—and it is—but the idea behind it has been recognized for years.

The basic idea is that a person's emotional and motivational attributes will influence his or her perception. We have already noted that this influence is the theoretical basis of projective techniques, such as the Rorschach Inkblot Test and Murray's Thematic Apperception Test. In both cases, a subject is presented with an unstructured object and is asked to give it a structure—that is, to tell what he or she sees in it. This is a clear example of how personality influences perception; the interpretations that people give to these unstructured stimuli are a function of their own needs, fears, and values—their personality.

However, while the idea of a relationship between personality and perception has been around for quite some time, it was never investigated thoroughly and systematically until Witkin began his research, during the 1940s. The initial project took ten years to complete, which indicates the complexity of the problem and the dedication of Witkin and his associates.

To accomplish his task, Witkin had to develop a set of situations that would provide, under laboratory conditions, reliable tests of perception and that would reveal important aspects of human perceptual ability. The range of perceptual issues studied was vast: individual differences in the manner of perceiving, stability of perception over time, consistency of perception under different circumstances, perceptual changes from childhood to adulthood, and sex differences in perception. Not only were different perceptual tasks studied, but also different kinds of subjects: normals and psychotics, children and adults, males and females. Finally, the subjects' performance on different measures of personality was investigated.

Perhaps you are wondering what this has to do with personality. The focus of Witkin's research is perception, yet the title of his book, *Personality through Perception*, gives a different impression. The analysis of the relationship between perceptual performance and personality measurements reveals personality-related individual differences in perception.To relate these two sets of data—that is, to relate personality and perception—Witkin invokes the concept of psychological differentiation, which has to do with the degree of complexity of the relevant structures or systems.

The more highly differentiated is a system, the more heterogeneous and specialized are its subsystems. And the more heterogeneous and specialized the subsystems, the greater the number of specific functions that can be mediated by the system as a whole. *Psychological differentiation* refers to the extent to which the areas of psychological operation in an individual (such as feeling, perceiving, and thinking) are separate from one another and capable of functioning with a degree of specificity. In other words, the more highly differentiated a person's psychological functioning, the more capable the person is of making a specific response to a specific stimulus, instead of just a diffuse response to many stimuli. In perception, a high degree of differentiation means that a person can more readily experience and respond to individual parts of a perceptual field, instead of just to the field as a whole. The individual's perception is differentiated rather than diffuse, specific rather than general and broad.

The same reasoning applies to functioning in the sphere of personality. The highly differentiated individual functions in a more specific and sophisticated fashion than one who is less differentiated. For example, Witkin hypothesized that subjects characterized by a low degree of differentiation will be more easily influenced by other people because they are less able to rely on their own judgments. Such a prediction proceeds from the notion of psychological differentiation in the following way. Poorly differentiated individuals, since they respond in a diffuse fashion, are unable to separate the ideas and suggestions of others from their own. As a result, they tend to assimilate all ideas, regardless of their sources, with their own. Highly differentiated people, on the other hand, are able to respond specifically to ideas and their sources and can thus clearly separate their own ideas from those of others.

Witkin assumes that there is a positive correlation between the level of differentiation within one sphere of behavior and the levels of differentiation within other spheres. In other words, the way you perceive will be the way you function in other areas.

We will now discuss how this linkage of perception and personality has been investigated by Witkin.

Witkin's Program of Research

Witkin's theory initially developed from his observations of subjects' behavior in a perceptual task known as the *rod-and-frame test*. The subject, seated in a darkened room, faces a luminous vertical rod surrounded by a luminous square frame. The rod has been tilted to some degree away from the true vertical position, and the surrounding frame is also tilted, sometimes in the same direction as the rod and sometimes in the opposite direction. The subject's task is to adjust the position of the rod back to the true vertical, a difficult task to perform, considering the context in which it must be done. The only visual stimuli available to the subject are the rod and the frame; there are no other cues to help determine the vertical position. Thus, the frame of reference within which this perceptual task must be performed is the frame surrounding the rod. But the frame is also tilted away from the vertical, and it cannot be moved by the subject.

There are two ways of responding in this situation. Either subjects use the cues supplied by the surrounding frame of reference or they operate independently of it. If they use the frame as a reference point, then they tilt the rod in the same direction as the frame. Thus, their perception has been determined by the surrounding visual field; they are not able to overcome its influence. Subjects who responded in this manner (on this and similar tasks) were called *field dependent* in Witkin's early work.

Those subjects who can bring the rod close to true vertical are, in contrast, capable of functioning independently of the surrounding field. They have the ability to overcome an *embedding context*. That is, they are unaffected by misleading or irrelevant aspects of a situation (here, the surrounding frame). These subjects are able to concentrate solely on whatever provides the true basis for correct performance. In the rod-and-frame test, they are able to concentrate on the rod and its relation to their own body position. Such subjects were called *field independent*.

The terms field dependent and field independent were later subsumed under the general term *psychological differentiation*, which can be represented as a continuum, ranging from full dependence on the surrounding field to full independence of that field. Witkin found a wide range of individual differences in the ability of subjects to perform perceptual tasks—differences that were later correlated with a variety of measures of personality.

Witkin used other perceptual tasks to measure a subject's ability to overcome an embedding context. One such task, the *body-adjustment test*, required the subject to adjust his or her own body to a position of true vertical. The subject is seated in a chair that can be tilted, inside a room that can also be tilted. The subject is blindfolded while being placed in the chair and, when the blindfold is removed, finds himself or herself in a tilted position relative to the room. Sometimes chair and room tilt in the same direction and sometimes in opposite directions. It is the same conceptual arrangement as the rod-and-frame test; in a sense, the person becomes the rod that must be adjusted to the vertical position. The visual cue or frame of reference is the tilt of the room. The basic question remains: will the person perform the task independently of the visual field, or will he or she use that field (the room) as the point of reference? As with the rod-and-frame test, the results

Figure 17.2   The body-adjustment test. Photo by David Linton from *Psychological Differentiation: Studies of Development,* by H. A. Witkin, R. B. Dyk, H. F. Faterson, D. R. Goodenough, & S. A. Karp. Copyright © 1962 by John Wiley & Sons, Inc. Reprinted by permission.

showed a wide range of individual differences in ability to perform the task.

A variation of the body-adjustment test is the *rotating-room test,* which also involves a tilting chair inside a tilting room. However, the entire room rotates on a track at almost 19 revolutions per minute. This adds the pull of gravity to the subject's frame of reference. Again, the task is to overcome the embedding context, to differentiate among the cues available.

To perform successfully in any of these experimental situations requires the ability to deal separately with the individual items in the total field. The subject, to achieve true verticality (of the body or of a rod), must disregard or ignore the tilted frame or the tilted room.

To determine whether the ability to deal with an item independently of its context or surroundings is a persistent characteristic of an individual's perception, Witkin devised a less expensive and time-consuming measure called the *embedded-figures test*. This paper-and-pencil test is composed of 24 complex geometrical figures. Somewhere within each figure a simple figure is hidden, incorporated into the pattern of the more complex figure. The subject is first shown the complex figure and then the simple figure. When the subject is again shown the complex figure, his or her task is to find the simple figure that is embedded in it. Witkin's data show that these various tests of perception produce stable scores that are highly correlated with one another.

Thus far, we have discussed the perception side of Witkin's personality-perception relationship. To measure personality, he used the Rorschach Inkblot Test, the Thematic Apperception Test, a personality questionnaire made up of items extracted from the Minnesota Multiphasic Personality Inventory (MMPI), plus sentence-completion, figure-drawing, and word-association tests. In addition, each subject was interviewed and biographical information taken. The correlation between these personality measures and performance on the perceptual tasks was such that Witkin considered each of them to be measuring some aspect of psychological differentiation.

Research Findings

In the perceptual tasks, Witkin found, in general, that the visual field or surrounding frame of reference significantly influenced the subjects' performance. In the rod-and-frame test, for example, subjects tended to adjust the rod in the direction in which the frame was tilted rather than to true vertical. Male subjects were considerably less influenced by the surrounding context than female subjects. The influence of the visual field was greater when the subject had to adjust the field as a whole than when he or she had to adjust only one item in the field. For example, in the body-adjustment test, the subject had much more difficulty adjusting the room to vertical than adjusting the position of his or her own body within the room. Also, adjusting the body was less influenced by the visual field than adjusting an object external to the body (the rod).

These results were from normal adult subjects; Witkin also studied children and disturbed adults. Psychotic adults made many more deviant adjustments than normal adults. Psychotics as a whole tended to score at the extremes of the psychological differentiation continuum. That is, many more psychotics than normals tended to be either highly dependent or highly independent of the visual field. Very few fell in the intermediate range. In contrast, normal subjects tended to be dependent on the visual field. Most were in the intermediate range, with very few at the extremes of very high dependence or independence.

The studies with children revealed interesting developmental changes in psychological differentiation, showing that it tends to increase with age. In one study, a group of boys and girls were studied at age 8 and later at age 13. A second group was studied at ages 10, 14, and 17. In both groups, performance on the perceptual tasks improved with age. The subjects were increasingly able to overcome the influence of the embedding context. The sex difference mentioned above with regard to adult subjects also held for children. Girls were more influenced by the visual field than were boys. Other studies have demonstrated that the rate of increase in the growth of psychological differentiation declines after the age of 17.

What do these differences in perceptual functioning tell us about personality? There are a number of dimensions of personality in which those high in psychological differentiation (field-independent) differ from those low in differentiation (field-dependent). In the clinical interview, poorly differentiated subjects displayed a lack of self-insight, tended to experience inferiority feelings, and were prone to repress their feelings and impulses. In the figure-drawing test, they tended to draw immature figures; highly differentiated subjects drew more mature-looking figures. In the performance on the Rorschach, poorly differentiated subjects revealed a low ability to cope with the environment and with life in general.

The way in which people interact with all aspects of their environment, including other people, seems to be influenced by their level of psychological differentiation. In their attitudes and behavior, poorly differentiated subjects tend to be passive with respect to their environment. For example, they are unable to function independently of their environment, find it difficult to initiate activity on their own, and are prone to submit to authority and be conforming. Highly differentiated subjects are more active, in that they are able to function independently of their environment, initiate, organize, and direct activities, and work to achieve mastery or control over their environments.

The degree of differentiation also seems to be related to anxiety and to self-esteem. Poorly differentiated subjects feel inferior and tend to repress their impulses, particularly sexual and aggressive ones. In addition, they experience considerable anxiety, which they are unable to control or regulate. Allied with these feelings is a low sense of self-esteem and difficulty in accepting themselves. Those high in psychological differentiation are in better control of their impulses, have a lower level of anxiety, and have a higher sense of self-esteem. These findings, which were derived initially from the study of normal adults, were confirmed in the investigation of children and psychotics. It seems clear, then, that there is a relationship between individual differences in perceiving and individual differences in personality. Knowledge of either set of differences can be used to predict the other.

In later research, Witkin studied the Freudian concept of defense mechanisms. On the basis of his psychological differentiation theory, he hypothesized that poorly differentiated people will tend to use more primitive (less differentiated) defense mechanisms, such as repression and denial, than well-differentiated people. The rationale is as follows.

In Freud's view, repression and denial are used in an undifferentiated or diffuse manner. They involve the repression or denial of a large area of impulses, not the isolation of a single item out of the total context, and they are also associated with the earlier stages of development. Highly differentiated people, Witkin hypothesized, will use defenses of a more intellectual or sophisticated nature, which involve the separation of the intellectual content of an impulse from its emotional content. Several studies support the hypothesis, showing the wide range of behaviors with which perceptual functioning appears to be associated—from self-esteem to interaction with others to unconscious defense mechanisms.

Comment

Witkin concludes from his research that particular modes of perceiving the world are consistently related to particular ways of adjusting to the world. The relationship between these two processes—perception and personality—seems to be one of mutual influence. On the one hand, perceptual capacities form part of the fund of resources a person uses to cope with and adjust to the world. On the other hand, a person's pattern of adjusting and coping acts to determine the nature of his or her perceptual capacities. Perception thus contributes to adjustment and at the same time reflects that adjustment. Therefore, knowledge of one process tells us something about the other process.

What does this mean for the understanding of personality? According to Witkin, it points up the necessity of considering an individual as a fully integrated system. We can understand each of the parts, he argues, only by understanding the setting or context of the whole. The reverse also holds: we cannot understand the whole without knowledge of each of the parts. Since Witkin regards personality as the *overall psychological organization* of a person, personality becomes the whole or the context, of which such processes as learning, thinking, and perception are the parts. Thus, personality cannot be adequately understood without information about all of these parts. We can understand the personality of an individual only if we know his or her motivational and emotional characteristics and the ways in which he or she perceives, learns, and thinks. Personality, then, must be approached in a highly differentiated way, with proper isolation of and attention to all of its part processes. Thus, while Witkin's concept of differentiation is of limited domain with respect to approach (studying only one part—perception), it is not limited in overall aim; the goal is to develop an understanding of the whole personality.

III. Cognitive Dissonance

Our third limited-domain theory takes yet another approach to the study of personality. As the first word in its name indicates, its concern is with the cognitive processes of the individual: thoughts, attitudes, ideas, and the like. Ordinarily, there is consistency and congruence among these various aspects of our inner cognitions. As a rule, we do not simultaneously hold beliefs or values or ideas that are incompatible or behave in ways contradictory to our beliefs. The self is usually consistent, with all its aspects in basic agreement.

But what happens when a discrepancy, an inconsistency, appears in our cognitive processes? What is the effect on our personality if we are confronted with the realization that two beliefs or ideas we hold do not fit together—that one is antagonistic to the other? This was the basic question asked by Leon Festinger (1919–   ), beginning in the mid-1950s. Since then, he and many others have conducted research on what Festinger calls *cognitive dissonance*—a "nonfitting relation among cognitions." Though Festinger's original concern in putting forth his theory was with the problem of attitude change, it has come to be realized that the theory has considerable application to the understanding of personality.

The Nature of Cognitive Dissonance

We have seen what *cognitive* means, and you no doubt have an idea of the meaning of *dissonance*. We know the feeling a dissonant musical chord produces; its harshness and lack of harmony grates on us. This sensation is the same as the feeling produced by dissonance within ourselves. Festinger describes the experience as one of being "psychologically uncomfortable." Suppose you have always firmly believed yourself to be highly intelligent and competent. Your parents, teachers, and grades confirm this belief year after year. Yet, when you graduate from college and begin a job, you find yourself consistently failing. There is in this situation an inconsistency, an incongruity in evidence, and the phrase "psychologically uncomfortable" may seem much too mild to describe the confusion and uncertainty you feel. As another example, suppose you believe the research that links smoking and lung cancer, yet you continue to smoke. There is a dissonance between your belief and your behavior.

The notion is really quite simple. The complexity becomes apparent when we consider the effect on people when they realize the existence of dissonance among their otherwise orderly and well-balanced cognitions. Festinger believes that cognitive dissonance produces a state of tension within the organism, and tension, as we have seen with other theorists, becomes a motivating force. Festinger feels that cognitive dissonance can become just as effective a motivating force as, for example, hunger. As happens with any tension-induced motivation, behavior is activated and directed toward reducing the tension, which means, in this case, reducing the dissonance and bringing the cognitions back into a balanced or consistent relationship.

Cognitive dissonance varies in its intensity. One determinant of this intensity is, obviously, the importance to the individual of the cognitive elements involved. For example, a person who believes that smoking causes cancer and yet smokes four packs of cigarettes a day may well experience greater dissonance than someone who holds the same belief but smokes only an occasional cigarette. Another determinant of the intensity of cognitive dissonance is the number of cognitive elements involved. Regardless of its source or magnitude, cognitive dissonance motivates the person to do something to eliminate this unpleasant condition.

Techniques of Reducing Dissonance

Let us continue with the example of the heavy cigarette smoker and the dissonance between his behavior (smoking) and his awareness of the link between smoking and cancer. What can he do to reduce the friction and inconsistency between his knowledge and his behavior? He can change his behavior—stop entirely or cut down drastically on the number of cigarettes he smokes. However, this is often more easily said than done and may create more complications than the dissonance caused in the first place. That is, the withdrawal symptoms may be more psychologically (and physically) uncomfortable than the dissonance-produced tension. However, in those situations in which a change in behavior can reduce the dissonance, without at the same time causing additional problems, it is an effective way of reducing the tension and bringing the system back into balance.

If our smoker cannot change his behavior, perhaps he can modify his attitude or awareness. He might accomplish this by refusing to read articles dealing with harmful effects of smoking, thereby closing off any further awareness of the problem. A more effective approach would be for him to add new cognitive elements that would be compatible with continued smoking. For example, the person could seek out articles that criticize the research that links cancer to smoking or stories about healthy elderly people who have smoked all their lives, and thus the person could conclude that there is nothing to worry about after all. Then there would no longer be any reason to experience dissonance about smoking.

Still another way to reduce dissonance is to make one alternative more attractive or desirable than the other one. Our smoker could, for instance, decide that smoking relaxes him, makes him feel less tense and anxious, and allows him to be more creative and alert in his work. He could convince himself that it is more desirable and useful to smoke for its present benefits than to stop for any potentially harmful consequences, which, if they occur, will occur far in the future. The smoker is therefore free to light up, undisturbed by cognitive dissonance.

The motivation to reduce the dissonance-induced tension can be strong—so strong that the person is driven to totally distort reality in an effort to restore cognitive balance. In this sense, there is a similarity between Festinger and Freud, both of whom posited defensive mechanisms that distort reality as they attempt to protect the person from anxiety. There is often, then, an irrational component in cognition.

Cognitive dissonance has ramifications for personality because it can influence not only behavior but also thoughts, perceptions, values, and ideas, which form part of the personality. In addition, Festinger and others have applied the theory to a wide range of phenomena that affect personality or are a part of it.

Applications of the Theory of Cognitive Dissonance

Festinger discussed and performed research on four topics in which he feels cognitive dissonance plays an important role: the consequences of decisions, forced compliance, voluntary and involuntary exposure to information, and social support.

A great deal of research in psychology has been performed on the nature of the decision-making process, but few psychologists have addressed themselves to the *consequences of a decision*. Festinger believes that conflict between two or more alternatives is involved in making a decision. Once the decision is reached, the conflict is reduced, but then dissonance appears. Suppose you have finally reached a decision about which of two cars to buy. Festinger says that some degree of dissonance almost always exists after such a decision because you are aware of the good features of the car you did not buy and the negative features of the car you did buy. Such dissonance may be mild, as in this example, or strong, as in the case of whether one married the right person. Whether mild or strong, the dissonance must be reduced. How is it to be done?

An obvious but not very satisfactory way is to revoke the decision. This may not always be possible (the dealer won't take back your car or your spouse won't agree to a divorce two days after the wedding), and it would also result in the substitution of one dissonance for another. Having made the decision to revoke the earlier decision, you would be in another post-decision dissonance situation, anxiously wondering if you chose the correct alternative this time.

Perhaps a more effective way to reduce post-decision dissonance is to establish what Festinger calls *cognitive overlap*. This involves looking for (or deliberately creating) so many points of similarity between the two alternatives that you become convinced that there really had been no decision to make. After all, you can tell yourself, the cars are very similar, so it makes no difference which one I chose.

Another way to reduce post-decision dissonance is to convince yourself that the decision was correct by seeking out information that justifies the decision. You could read advertisements only for the car you chose or seek out people who have had trouble with the car you rejected.

The second area in which the notion of cognitive dissonance has been applied is *forced compliance,* a situation in which a person is compelled to behave in a way in which he or she would not voluntarily behave. A classic example is the brainwashing of American prisoners during the Korean war, in which, as a result of being forced to comply with certain patterns of behavior, the prisoners sometimes adopted the enemy ideology underlying those behaviors. In a classroom or a job you may be compelled to agree overtly with positions or points of view you privately oppose. In these situations of forced compliance, dissonance occurs between your original beliefs or ideas and the behaviors you are forced to perform; there is a discrepancy between what you are required to do and what you believe you should do. Festinger found that the less the threat for not complying, or the less the reward for complying, the greater is the dissonance.

In one experiment, a group of students worked for an hour on a boring task and then were asked to tell incoming subjects that the task was interesting and a lot of fun. Dissonance was thus created by the discrepancy between what the subjects were being asked to say and what they really believed. Rewards were offered, to induce compliance. Some subjects received $1.00 and others $20.00; thus, the rewards for complying differed in intensity. Later, the subjects were asked to rate their degree of interest in the boring task. Those who received the smaller justification

($1.00) for their dissonant behavior rated the task as significantly more interesting than those who received a larger reward for complying.

Festinger interpreted the results in this way. Those whose justification for lying was small had greater dissonance between behavior and belief. This pressured them into believing that the task was really enjoyable after all. Those who had received $20.00 presumably had been sufficiently rewarded for their discrepant behavior, so that less dissonance had been aroused. They felt more justified in their behavior.

In an experiment that used punishment instead of reward, children were told not to play with very appealing toys after the experimenter left the room. Two levels of threat for playing with the toys (mild and severe) were invoked. Measures of the toys' attractiveness revealed that toys in the mild-threat condition were rated as considerably less attractive than toys in the severe-threat condition. Why should this be? According to Festinger, if you restrain yourself from a pleasant activity—something you would really like to do—because of a severe threat, then the dissonance (between wanting to do something and not doing it) is reduced. But when you restrain yourself from a pleasant activity when the threat is only a mild one, then you have to find another justification for denying yourself the pleasure. And one excellent justification is to tell yourself that you really didn't want to do whatever it is you're denying yourself. In that way you reduce the dissonance, as the children did by convincing themselves that the toys under the mild-threat condition weren't so attractive after all.

The third area of application of cognitive dissonance is that of voluntary and involuntary *self-exposure to information*. According to Festinger, the voluntary seeking of information represents an attempt to add new cognitive elements, which, as noted, can be effective in reducing dissonance. One study found that owners of new cars more often read advertisements for their cars (and avoided ads for other makes of car) than did owners of older cars of the same make. The new-car owner, in an effort to reduce post-decision dissonance, tries to support the decision by exposing himself or herself only to favorable information and avoiding information that may be unfavorable (ads for competing cars that might show them to be better than the one bought). Owners of older cars, on the other hand, presumably no longer have any dissonance about their decision and do not have to seek out supporting information or suppress nonsupporting information.

If we cannot avoid seeing information that does not support our decision, we may well act negatively toward the information, discounting its validity or reinterpreting it to fit our own point of view. Thus, the effort to reduce dissonance (or prevent its appearance) can influence perception by determining what we see, what we deliberately avoid seeing, and how we interpret what we do see.

The final area of application, *social support,* has to do with the role played by other people in identifying and maintaining our opinions, beliefs, and ideals. Clearly, we learn attitudes and beliefs from other people and maintain them largely because of the support for those beliefs we receive from those around us. Our attitudes usually echo the ones favored by the culture or by smaller groups of which we are members—for example, family, club, peer group, and church. But what happens if we hold an opinion that is at variance with those held by the group—when there is no longer social support for our opinion? This can happen if the modal opinion of our group shifts while ours does not. In that case, we experience dissonance, just as we do when there is a discrepancy within ourselves between two beliefs.

There are two aspects of the group that influence the intensity of this socially created dissonance. First, how relevant the group is to the opinion, belief, or issue is of importance. For example, if a man does not hold the same opinion about televised football as the rest of his church group, he is not likely to experience dissonance, because the issue is not one of importance in that group. However, if an individual's fundamental ideas about God are in disagreement with the church group, then dissonance will likely occur because that is a major issue with which the group deals.

A second important feature of the group is its degree of cohesiveness. Dissonance will be greater if the members of the group have a high level of mutual attraction than if the group is not closely knit. Further, and perhaps even more important, dissonance will be greater for an individual who is strongly attracted to the members of the group than for someone who really cares little for the group members. The discord between your opinion and that of a group will cause greater dissonance if you value your membership in the group and want to continue as a member. If you are not strongly attracted to the group, you will probably not be bothered by your disagreement with the group.

When socially created dissonance does exist, what can we do to reduce it? An obvious technique is to change our opinion to match that of the group. This is not altogether satisfactory unless we did not feel strongly about the issue in the first place. Another technique is to try to change the opinions of those with whom our views are discrepant. Finally, we can try in some way to convince ourself that those who disagree with us are so unlike us on some other dimension that there is no meaningful basis for comparison of the two points of view. We could conclude, for example, that the others are not as intelligent as we are, or have not studied the issue as extensively as we have, or are viewing the issue from a different (and obviously wrong) perspective.

Festinger points out that it is usually difficult for a person to maintain an opinion or belief that is strongly at variance with the opinion of a highly cohesive group to which the person is attracted. You can probably testify to the truth of this if you have ever held a strongly differing attitude or opinion in a fraternity or sorority, or in your family, or simply in an informal group of close friends. The pressure can be strong to change your opinion, and it comes from yourself, in your attempt to reduce the dissonance, as well as from the group. Being the sole holder of an unpopular view is uncomfortable and a difficult position to maintain for very long.

Comment

The great amount of research generated by the theory of cognitive dissonance provides a quantitative estimate of how influential the position has been. Research continues at an active pace today, often serving to modify and extend the basic elements of the theory and to increase the range of behavior that it can encompass. In general, the research continues to focus on attitude change (Festinger's original concern), but it also ranges into other aspects of social psychology and into the study of personality. By stressing cognition, it approaches personality in a limited-domain fashion. Like the other theories in this chapter, cognitive dissonance makes no attempt to deal with all aspects of personality. Yet it, too, serves to increase our understanding of the total personality by focusing in detail on one aspect.

The notion of cognitive dissonance has not gone unchallenged. Indeed, it has been severely criticized with respect to its research methodology and the interpretation it places on the behavior under observation. Whatever the outcome of this controversy, however, the approach is consonant with psychology's present emphasis on controlled experimentation and observation of one construct or variable at a time.

Suggested Readings

Festinger, L. *A theory of cognitive dissonance.* Stanford, Calif.: Stanford University Press, 1957.

McClelland, D. C. *Personality.* New York: Dryden, 1951.

McClelland, D. C. *The achieving society.* Princeton, N.J.: Van Nostrand, 1961.

Witkin, H. A., Lewis, H. B., Hertzman, M., Machover, K., Meissner, P. B., & Wapner, S. *Personality through perception.* New York: Harper & Row, 1954.

Witkin, H. A., et al. *Psychological differentiation.* New York: Halstead Press, 1974.

Appendix
Contemporary
German-Language
Personology

We have traced the historical development of personality theories from their origins on the psychoanalytic couch in the closing years of 19th-century Vienna to the laboratories and clinics of late 20th-century America. For a period of three to four decades, the study of personality was almost exclusively a European phenomenon, as we have seen, and was further restricted to that portion of Europe in which the German language predominates. Work published during this period in any modern language other than German was not included in this book for there was none in the field of personality that was of comparable stature. Look again at the early chapters, devoted to the pioneering work in personality: Freud and Adler in Austria, Fromm and Horney in Germany, Jung in the German-speaking part of Switzerland.

This dominance of the field by German-language theorists continued until the 1930s, when they fled their homelands, with many of their disciples and students, to escape Nazi persecution (with the exception of Jung, safe in Switzerland). As noted in Chapter 1, it was during that period—the 1930s—that American psychologists first began to formally investigate personality. Between the repressive measures then imposed on psychoanalysis in Germany and Austria and the characteristic enterprise and initiative of American psychology as a whole, the language of personality shifted from German to American-accented English.

Since that time, the bulk of all theoretical and research work on personality has remained centered in the United States, a phenomenon that has come to characterize all areas of psychology. Indeed, it has been estimated that as much as 90% of the world's psychological literature is American in design, direction and scope. Until the 1930s, many Americans journeyed to Germany and Austria to study; now scientists from all over the world come to the United States to be exposed to the latest developments in the field.

This concentration of psychology as a whole, and personality specifically, in the United States, has served to make many American psychologists chauvinistic and parochial in their outlook. There is a tendency to ignore work done in other countries or to consider it irrelevant and unimportant. A constant complaint of psychologists from Europe and other parts of the world is that their work is not sufficiently recognized or cited in American books and articles—a charge that is frequently well founded.

Because of such criticism, this chapter is appended; its purpose is to acquaint you with current developments in personality theory and research outside the United States. However, as the title indicates, we are once again dealing with German-language developments. Interest in personality in Germany and German-speaking areas seems both more pronounced and less strongly influenced by American positions than is the case in other countries. We are, in a sense, returning to where the study of personality began. And, as we shall see, contemporary German work on personality bears little resemblance to its Freudian, Jungian, and Adlerian origins. Just as American personality theorists have ranged far and wide from those origins, so have their German counterparts.

The following material was written by Lewis W. Brandt.

Contemporary German-Language Personology by Lewis W. Brandt[1]

With the rise of National Socialism in Germany in the 1930s, many scientists (mostly of Jewish origin) emigrated to English-speaking countries. Among them were the physicists Albert Einstein and Niels Bohr, their personal friends the psychologists Wolfgang Köhler and Max Wertheimer, and some of the personality theorists mentioned earlier in

[1]Brandt's *Weltanschauung* (world view) was formed by European and North American experiences. After four years of Montessori school and five years of Gymnasium in Berlin, three years in a German-French bilingual coeducational boarding school, and three years in refugee labor camps in Switzerland, Brandt studied English, French, and Spanish at the University of Geneva, from which he received a diploma in translation. He moved to New York, first studying French literature at Columbia University and then training to become a psychoanalyst. At the age of 33, he began studying academic psychology. He received an M.A. from the New School for Social Research and a Ph.D. from New York University.

Brandt is in psychoanalytic practice and is a professor of psychology at the University of Regina, Canada. He considers himself to be a "theoretical psychologist." In his numerous journal articles, he explores mainly questions of methodology and the basic assumptions underlying psychological research. His own research investigates the validity of such research tools as the Semantic Differential and the Eysenck Personality Inventory, which he found to lack a sound scientific basis. He maintains close contacts with leading psychologists in Austria, Switzerland, and both Germanies.

this book. Gradually, their theories became known among their new colleagues. At the same time, however, there began a trend among graduate schools in North America toward abolishing foreign-language requirements for Ph.D.s in psychology; and many schools that did not abolish them did not take them very seriously. Thus, the work of foreign psychologists who have remained in their respective countries remains largely unknown in the English-speaking parts of the world.

At the 1963 International Congress of Psychology in Washington, D.C., Wolfgang Metzger, who had been invited to report on German psychology, stated: "From my many years' occupation with psychological literature I got the impression that there is at least one outstanding characteristic of German psychological thinking . . . the widespread inclination towards personality theory." Metzger's impression of the focus of German-language psychology seems supported by the fact that the volume on personality of the 14-volume *Handbuch der Psychologie* (Handbook of Psychology) was the third in the series to appear and has been reprinted four times in 15 years.

Another characteristic of German-language psychology is its Gestalt-phenomenological approach. The basic question of this approach with respect to personality is not "What is an individual's personality like?" but "How do people go about forming ideas about themselves and others?"[2] This viewpoint also stresses individuality (as with Allport) rather than the establishment of types and corresponding ideals, like self-actualization or genital maturity, against which to measure each of us.

Among the German-language personologists whose approaches are generally unknown in North America are Lersch, Rothacker, and Welleck, who offer different stratification theories of personality,[3] and Klages, whose theory is based on the analysis of handwriting, which he views as a spontaneous expression of the individual. Klages' distinction between *structure of the character* and *qualities of the personality*, and his categories of both, were considered to be "outstanding" by Karl Jaspers. Klages' classifications have been widely used in German-speaking universities in the teaching of graphology as a basic diagnostic tool. However, given the limitations of space, I have chosen to present briefly only the approaches of Hans Thomae, Gerhard Kaminski, Erwin Roth, and Karl Jaspers.

[2]To some extent you are already familiar with this question from the chapter on Kelly.

[3]The concept of stratification appeared already in Freud's theories of unconscious, preconscious, and conscious and of id, ego, and superego.

Hans Thomae (1915–   )[4]

In his *Das Individuum und seine Welt* (The Individual and His World), Thomae attempts to develop an empirical personality theory. Rather than starting out with a theory and then attempting to support it by experimental or field research, Thomae and his assistants collected material for 15 years from about 3000 West Germans of all social classes between the ages of 5 and 75 and then distilled a theory out of those data. Since no one can collect data without some preliminary ideas to serve as a guide to what to look for or disregard, Thomae worked with a clearly defined strategy. He wanted to "work out a psychological analysis of human behavior during the natural course of life which can serve as a basis for grasping the 'authentic' units for describing personality."

He decided that, in order to find categories of personality that were relevant for and representative of personality-systems, he would consider only those categories that appeared in small, medium, and large temporal units. He chose as the smallest units *acts*, as medium-sized units descriptions of *a typical day*, and as large units *autobiographies*. The acts were measured by various tests, and the ways in which the individual dealt with the test situations were recorded and analyzed. The description of the typical day and the autobiography were obtained in open-ended interviews. The interviewer tried to avoid taking the role of a knowledgeable expert in order to explore as fully as possible with the subject his or her life. These explorations were recorded and repeated with the same individuals over 8- to 12-year periods.

The analysis of the protocols of acts, typical days, and autobiographies led to the discovery of a number of *themes*. For example, in the description of a typical day—from the moment of getting up to the moment of going to bed—some individuals emphasized their work and others their leisure activities. In discussing their work, some people talked about a sense of duty and others about self-fulfillment. When speaking about duties, some felt they had fulfilled them and others felt they had not. When work was experienced as routine, one individual considered this highly negative and another positive.

Some themes were called *regulative* because they dealt with the regulation of disturbances such as dissatisfactions, physical shortcomings or suffering, disappointments, threats, and fears. Some of these regulations are *anticipatory* because they serve to forestall disturbances or are designed to lead from one disturbance-free state to a new disturbance-free state.

[4]Professor of Psychology, University of Bonn, West Germany.

Another theme found by Thomae in the protocols was the attempt to broaden one's existence through either more experiences or more intense experiences or activities. This was seen as a reaction to boredom or feelings of emptiness, as an attempt at social integration with others or social differentiation from others, as planning for the future, or as meeting social expectations and norms.

As the title of his book indicates, Thomae is interested in how an individual experiences his or her world, and not how a person *adapts* to a world that is considered to be the same for everyone. He points out that, when we speak of adaptation, we are considering the environment to be the independent variable and the individual to be the dependent variable. However, the nature of the environment depends partially on the individual. What may be objectively the same environment for everyone is different for the sighted and for the blind, for the hearing and for the deaf, for the rich and for the poor, for the educated and for the uneducated, for the strong and for the weak, for the friendly and for the hostile, for the good looking and for the deformed individual. Thus, a given situation can be experienced by one individual as permissive, by someone else as threatening, and by a third person as an invitation to take a specific action. Correspondingly, one individual may experience himself as competent, another as popular, and a third as rejected.

From the analysis of large numbers of protocols of individual acts, typical days, and autobiographies, various dimensions were derived on which various facets of an individual's experiences and actions can be measured and compared.

Thomae calls one set of these dimensions *formal qualities.* They include: level of activity, moods (more or less positive or negative), the readiness to react to anything, empathy (the readiness to react to emotional changes in others), adaptiveness (the agreement between behavior and the experienced demands of a given situation), steering (the degree to which actions are in line with one's overall goal), psychological stability, and involvement with one's activities and environment. By assigning points on a nine-point scale to these dimensions on the basis of the protocols, the researcher can study intra-individual as well as inter-individual variations.

Thomae makes no attempt to classify personality in terms of either traits or types. Instead, his empirically derived dimensions serve as a first step in a new direction, which can be expanded to include further dimensions of individual functioning.

While most personality theories assume that an individual's personality is something stable, Thomae is particularly interested in the question of personality change. In his longitudinal studies he found that individuals vary greatly in the amount of change their personalities undergo over time, as well as in the areas of the personality that are amenable to change. Changes can occur in one's formal qualities, in one's themes (and the techniques for implementing the various themes), in one's self-concept, and in the various regions of one's subjective life space.

Personality change does not usually consist of alterations in all aspects of a personality, nor is it usually drastic, such as a change from a popular to a hated self-concept, or from extreme integration with society's norms to extreme defiance of them. This has frequently led to a complete neglect of the issue of personality change in the "average" individual.

Gerhard Kaminski (1925–   )[5]

According to Kaminski, a personality theory is a cognitive system for making sense out of one's observations of other people. The attempt to "understand" people is related to one's own personality theory; one "understands" people in terms of some implicit or explicit personality theory, and that theory may change as a result of these attempts to understand people. A person's theory may change, but it need not. Through *exhaustion* (stretching a theory), one may keep it unchanged in the face of new and different observations. For example, one may conclude that the observations were not precise enough or that some unaccounted-for circumstances intervened and therefore that these observations do not require any revision of one's own personality theory.

The observations we make that are related to our personality theory consist of impressions formed about other people. Kaminski calls the formation of such impressions in a scientific or applied psychological setting *psychodiagnosis*. In his *Das Bild vom anderen* (The Image of the Other), Kaminski analyzed impression formation in relation to psychological diagnoses. His method is *phenomenal analysis,* which consists of describing, in minute detail and by means of concrete examples, what must take place within a person's mind in forming an impression of someone else. The external factors that may contribute to impression formation are also considered. These *objective* factors include the length of time over which one has observed the other person, the number of different situations in which one has encountered the other, and the different roles in which one has seen the other.

For example, the impression one has of one's dentist will differ depending on whether one has met him or her only in the role of dentist

---

[5]Professor of Psychology, University of Tübingen, West Germany.

or also in the role of husband or wife, father or mother, political candidate, and so on, and whether one has met the dentist only at the office or also at parties, at a football game, or at a dentistry convention.

Many other factors enter into impression formation that can also be discussed objectively, although they may be considered *subjective* because they lie within the person who forms the impression. Among these subjective factors are the prejudices and attitudes of the person who forms the impression, the momentary mood, the kind of relationship between the impression former and the other person, the cultural background of the impression former, the basis for comparing the other person to people the observer has known in the past, the purpose for forming an impression and the corresponding characteristics the observer is looking for, and the personality theory held by the observer.

Applying these factors to the example of forming an impression of one's dentist, we could say that Mr. Smith's picture of his dentist depends on the following: Mr. Smith's general ideas about dentists, his feelings toward dentists, his mood at the moment he asks himself what kind of an individual his dentist is, his relationship with his dentist (for example, whether he is only a patient or is also a neighbor and a fraternity brother of the dentist), Mr. Smith's social class and ethnic background and whether these are similar to or different from those of the dentist, whether Mr. Smith mentally compares his dentist to other dentists, to other professionals in general, or just to other men, whether he compares the dentist to people of the same age and background, and, finally, whether Mr. Smith asks himself what kind of a person his dentist is because he considers recommending him as a dentist to his brother-in-law or his boss or because he considers introducing the dentist to his sister for a date.

In his second major work, *Verhaltenstheorie und Verhaltensmodifikation* (Behavior Theory and Behavior Modification),[6] Kaminski attempts a *micropsychological* phenomenal analysis of the diagnostic process as it must occur within the psychologist when he or she is presented with a case and called upon to suggest some form of treatment to bring about some change in a client.

When you try to understand why your father wants you to get high marks in school, you make some assumptions about his motivations, goals, role, expectations, etc. These assumptions form your theory—a *naïve behavior theory*—about how your father functions. When I, then (as a psychologist), try to understand how you (as a client) try to understand your father—when I try to figure out what your implicit, underlying personality

---

[6]The word *behavior* is used in this title in the most general sense of the word and has nothing to do with behaviorism.

theory is about your father—then I, myself, am using some personality theory to conceptualize your personality theory.

Kaminski's analysis of the psychodiagnostic process thus also implies some personality theory or model. His model deals primarily with *cognitions*, which are stored in a number of different memories, depending on whether they represent knowledge derived from science, from the psychologist's training and professional experience, or from everyday life experience. Furthermore, different kinds of knowledge are stored according to content. These stored cognitions can be *actualized*, or called back from storage, and information for decision making can be *read off* from them. These decisions may lead to actions. Thus, Kaminski developed an *action model*, in which *codings* of behavior (cognitions) play a central part, though much of the coding, the reading off from actualized memories, and other steps in the decision-making process need not become conscious, in the usual meaning of that term.

In order to get from the *action model* to a *personality model*, one must ask what is expected of the latter. Kaminski assumes that a personality model should (1) enable one to describe the total organization of an individual, (2) enable one to show how that organization came about and how it may possibly be altered, and (3) enable one to show that knowledge of the "cognitive and behavioral systems" that constitute the personality organization ought to allow for approximate predictions of that individual's behavior within a given situation. Kaminski recognizes that we are far from having such a personality model or theory and he does not even attempt to reach such an ambitious goal. He discusses, however, in great detail, the possible personality theories and models a psychologist may use in a concrete diagnostic situation.

We may imagine, for example, a situation in which a mother goes to a psychologist with the complaint that her son does not get along with other children. The personality model held by the psychologist (plus a number of other factors) determines what he or she will do—for example, what questions the psychologist will ask the mother, what tests (if any) he or she will give to the mother and/or the son, whether he or she will consult other sources (the boy's father, teachers, physicians), and what kind of treatment the psychologist will suggest to change the mother's expectations or the son's behavior.

In other words, the next step by the psychologist, in his or her interaction with the mother, depends upon, among other things, the extent to which the psychologist considers the son's behavior (as reported by the mother) hereditary or resulting from the environment, fixed in the son's character or due to situational stimulus conditions, or under the boy's conscious control, and whether the psychologist relates that behavior to roles, traits, types, levels of psychosexual maturity, body build, mental illness, social class, or racial background.

Kaminski demands of any psychological theory that it give a basis for explaining how psychologists develop such theories. Since he conceptualizes human beings as consisting of complex cognitive and behavior systems partially (but not fully) integrated with one another, he avoids the paradox into which some personality models fall by being inapplicable to their inventors. Kaminski's own theory can be conceptualized as resulting from his own cognitive and behavioral systems, and this in no way diminishes its usefulness or logical consistency.

In his doctoral dissertation, *Naive Verhaltenstheorie* (Naïve Behavior Theory), Kaminski's student Uwe Laucken (1941–   ) shows, on the basis of a phenomenal analysis of how people explain the everyday actions of others, that the personality theories that people use to judge one another do not meet the scientific criterion of *falsifiability*. There seem to be no limitations to their possible exhaustion. In practical terms, this means that our common-sense theories about how people function are constructed in such a way that whatever someone does can be explained within our theories, even if the other person acts contrary to our expectations and predictions. It follows, of course, that our common-sense personality theories (our naïve behavior theories) are useless as far as prediction of behavior is concerned. Since we hold such theories, however, Laucken concludes that they must serve some purpose. He suggests that this purpose is to impose some kind of order and structure on our experiences—to make sense out of our observations of human behavior.

Erwin Roth (1926–   )[7]

Progress in science requires critique. This view, held by such leading philosophers of science as Sir Karl Popper and Hans Kuhn, is shared by Roth. His critical analysis of past approaches to the study of personality finds all of the approaches wanting.

Roth considers the idea of traits or dispositions to imply consistencies of behavior under varying circumstances; this independence of behavior from situations does not, however, correspond to our observations. The notion of habits, formed through learning on the basis of responses to stimuli, overemphasizes environmental determinants of behavior at the expense of internal determinants. Another useless approach to the study of personality, according to Roth, is the factor-analytic one. Factor analysis is based on too many assumptions derived from mathematics, which cannot be justified in psychology. The shortcomings of motives as a central concept in personality theories are that motives are usually poorly

[7]Professor of Psychology, University of Salzburg, Austria.

defined and that they often necessitate the introduction of some form of psychic energy, a notion that conflicts with the rest of science. Role theories of personality deal exclusively with the social aspects of personality (which other theories completely disregard) and do not allow sufficiently for individual differences in role playing. Finally, the self-concept can be investigated by others only to a limited extent and thus raises methodological problems when used as a central concept.

Roth defines personality as "the sum total of the conditions for individual behavior." He finds that useful aspects of the traditional concepts in personality theory are preserved (and their disadvantages avoided) by introducing the concept of *attitudes* from social psychology. He regards attitudes as hypothetical constructs based on the consistency of observed behavior. Attitudes are systems consisting of cognitive and affective subsystems, and they form higher-order systems with the objects toward which they are directed. Both momentary and lasting attitudes are acquired through experience and interaction with the environment. Thus, they are systems that involve feedback.

Research on attitudes has usually been limited to studying their direction (positive or negative) and intensity. The phenomenal analysis of attitudes indicates that additional dimensions are (1) specificity or generality with respect to given objects, (2) universality or singularity—that is, the number of individuals who hold certain attitudes—and (3) the subjective importance of the attitude-object in the life of an individual. Furthermore, one can distinguish among momentary, occasional, frequent, and habitual attitudes, between stable and easily changing attitudes, and between more or less complex, differentiated, and internally consistent attitudes. Attitudes also differ in terms of their internal structure, although tools for the measurement of this dimension have yet to be developed.

Roth thus uses a *systems* approach to personality. This approach combines the useful aspects of the structural approach of psychoanalytic theory, the process or dynamic approach used in psychoanalytic theory and by Allport, and the field-theoretical approach used by Kurt Lewin.[8] According to Roth, personality can be understood as a system of attitudes, which are themselves systems.

The concept of attitudes enables one to express both the interactions of the organism with its environment and that organism's individuality. Since attitudes are directed toward aspects of the environment and formed

---

[8]The work of Kurt Lewin (1890–1947) is grounded in Gestalt psychology and centers on needs, personality, and social factors. Field theory is the methodology that he applied to psychology, which considers a person's psychological activities to occur in a kind of psychological field or life space. See Kurt Lewin, *Principles of Topological Psychology* (New York: McGraw-Hill, 1936).

by experience with the environment, they present a unique basis for the study of people and their interactions with the environment. Since attitudes also result, in part, from unique individual endowments and experiences (and from the interaction of these two factors), it is possible to study each individual in his or her uniqueness through a study of attitudes. Furthermore, by using the systems approach, the unity of the individual is preserved. Rather than being a bundle of unrelated attitudes, personality is presented as their integration. Considering personality as a system permits such integration without destroying its complexity.

Karl Jaspers (1883–1969)

Although Karl Jaspers died in 1969 at the age of 86 and his main psychological work, *Allgemeine Psychopathologie* (General Psychopathology), was first published in 1913, his approach to the study of humanity is included here because he was the first psychologist to clearly present the phenomenological method that later characterized much of German-language psychology. He remains almost unknown among English-speaking psychologists, including many humanistic and existential psychologists.

Since the nature of a researcher's understanding of people depends on his or her background, a summary of Jaspers' life is appropriate. Jaspers had studied three semesters of law, received his M.D., and worked as a psychiatric intern before becoming a lecturer in psychology at age 30 at the University of Heidelberg, Germany. In the same year he published the first edition of his *General Psychopathology*. At 38, he became a professor of philosophy, which position the Nazis took from him in 1937. He subsequently revised his work on psychopathology and wrote several philosophical (largely existentialist) books. In 1945, he was reinstated as a professor of philosophy at Heidelberg. He moved to the University of Basel, Switzerland, in 1948.

According to Jaspers, human beings are (1) existence in the world, (2) consciousness, and (3) mind. As consciousness, we can become aware; only what I am aware of exists for me. As mind, we can develop ideas about our experiences and thus "explain" them by thinking beyond what we can actually experience.

Mere existence does not give us any knowledge about others. To study human beings, we must use our consciousness and our mind. As consciousness, we can "understand" others through shared experiences. This understanding is empathic, intuitive, the result of identification—we understand others, in Jaspers' terms, "from inside." We phenomenologically describe others' psychic states and qualities—that is, in terms of how they are experienced—and also understand the emergence of psychic connections—for example, the connection between a person being attacked and his or her anger. In order to understand a person, we must study his or her expressions, gestures, and communications—including self-descriptions and life story—as well as reports by others who have known the person. This is called the case-study method.

Human functioning, however, has some biological bases that cannot be understood from within—that is, by putting oneself into someone else's shoes. While biological factors thus limit understanding, they can be explained by means of theories. Such causal explanation is, therefore, "from outside." The methods used for causal explanation are experimentation and statistics. Psychology as a science must use both the case-study method, for understanding, and experiments and statistics, for explaining.

There remains an area of human functioning that can neither be understood nor explained by these methods: individual freedom. It can be grasped through one's feeling of freedom of choice and through an appreciation of the impossibility of predicting an individual act with certainty. Freedom thus lies outside psychology as a science, just as it lies outside physics (in terms of the uncertainty principle).[9]

Understanding obviously depends on the researcher's ability to understand. What is not understandable to the researcher he or she tries to grasp as biological; for example, the researcher may posit the existence of *dispositions (Anlagen)*. Since dispositions do not refer to "what is" but to "what can be," the concept becomes an appeal to freedom. Thus, for Jaspers, personality is open-ended, as in Allport's concept of *becoming* and Freud's "Where it [id] was I [ego] shall become." We can always discover something new about a person.

We understand human beings through an understanding of certain aspects of them—through an understanding of the urges that can result from accumulated tension or from feelings of emptiness and boredom, through an understanding of people's active reactions to individually experienced situations, through an understanding of their knowledge and of what someone else's knowledge means to them (how they acquired it and what effect it has upon their actions), and through an understanding of their basic beliefs.[10] Urges, which Jaspers called *drives*, may appear periodically (like hunger) or at any time. Some, like hunger, can be temporarily satisfied completely; others, like curiosity, increase with satisfaction. We can also understand logically contradictory psychic tensions,

---

[9]It corresponds to what general systems theory calls *flexible strategies* as opposed to *fixed rules*.

[10]"What kind of god he has sums up the man."

such as internal conflicts, as well as dialectical movements, such as sudden changes in feelings. We understand the feedback loops directing thinking, feeling, and acting, as well as the self-understanding of the other person—his or her reflection, which distinguishes intentional action from unintentional occurrences, which merely happen to someone.

It is characteristic of the phenomenological method that the researcher uses no theory but tries out different assumptions, to see where they lead. The researcher is continuously conscious of his or her assumptions and critically reflects upon them. This requires clear and specific definitions of terms. For this reason, Jaspers used the term *personality* only to refer to "the whole or Gestalt resulting from all psychic processes and expressions in as far as these point beyond themselves at an individual, entirely understandable connection which is experienced by an individual with the consciousness of having a particular self." This definition excludes our fascination with something new, which, though understandable, does not point beyond itself at the totality of connections. An expression of fear in a mentally defective person is excluded by this definition because an idiot has no consciousness of having a particular self. Also excluded from Jaspers' definition of personality are abilities and dispositions because they cannot be understood from within.

As a whole, an individual personality stands in a logical relationship to its elements; it is composed of elements that themselves are meaningful only in their relationship to the whole. However, we can never grasp a personality in its entirety; we can only analyze its parts. When we analyze a personality in terms of traits, we assume that there is some kind of consistency and, accordingly, that some traits exclude others. But, in reality, contradictory traits form dialectic relations: if someone is entirely free of fear, it makes no sense to call him or her courageous. Someone who is free of possessiveness cannot be considered generous. Another problem arises when human beings are described in terms of types; each individual is a representative of every type to a varying degree. Thus, the study of personality is ambiguous, as is all "understanding" psychology. Jaspers recognized these limits of psychology even before Heisenberg discovered those of physics and Goedel those of mathematics.

Bibliography

Sources in German

Kaminski, G. *Das Bild vom anderen.* Berlin: Dr. G. Lüttke Verlag, 1959.

Kaminski, G. *Verhaltenstheorie und Verhaltensmodifikation.* Stuttgart: Ernst Klett Verlag, 1970.

Laucken, U. *Naive Verhaltenstheorie*. Stuttgart: Ernst Klett Verlag, 1973.

Lersch, Ph., & Thomae, H. (Eds.). *Handbuch der Psychologie. 4. Band*. Persönlichkeits-forschung und Persönlichkeitstheorie. Göttingen: Verlag f. Psychologie—Dr. C. J. Hogrefe, 1960.

Roth, E. *Persönlichkeitspsychologie*. Stuttgart: Verlag W. Kohlhammer, 1969.

Thomae, H. *Persönlichkeit. Eine dynamische Interpretation*. Bonn: Bouvier, 1951.

Thomae, H. *Der Mensch in der Entscheidung* [Human decision making]. München: J. A. Barth Verlag, 1960.

Thomae, H. *Das Individuum und seine Welt*. Göttingen: Verlag f. Psychologie—Dr. C. J. Hogrefe, 1968.

Thomae, H., & Feger, H. (Eds.). *Einführung in die Psychologie. 7. Band* Hauptstromün-gen der neueren Psychologie. [Introduction to psychology. Mainstreams in contemporary psychology.] Frankfurt: Akademische Verlagsgesellschaft, 1969.

Sources in English

Brandt, L. W., & Brandt, E. P. Second-hand personication: A new model for "person perception" research. *Canadian Psychologist*, 1972, *13*, 217–238.

Brandt, L. W. Personication and psychotherapy. *Psychoanalytic Review*, 1973, *60*, 439–442. These two articles are built on Kaminski's approach.

David, H. P., & von Bracken, H. (Eds.). *Perspectives in personality theory*. New York: Basic Books, 1957. Contains an overview by Allport—"European and American Theories of Personality"—and chapters by nine European personologists, including Thomae.

David, H. P., & Brengelmann, J. C. (Eds.). *Perspectives in personality research*. New York: Springer, 1960.

Jaspers, K. [*General psychopathology*.] (J. Hoenig & M. W. Hamilton, trans.). England: Manchester University Press, 1963.

Metzger, W. The historical background for national trends in psychology: German psychology. *Journal of the History of the Behavioral Sciences*, 1965–1966, *1-2*, 109–115.

Schilpp, P. A. *The philosophy of Karl Jaspers*. New York: Tudor, 1957. Contains a complete bibliography of Jaspers' writings to 1957.

Thomae, H. Cognition and motivation: Modern aspects of an ancient problem. *Psychologia*, 1973, *16*(4), 179–190.

Bibliography

Adler, A. Individual psychology. In C. Murchison (Ed.), *Psychologies of 1930.* Worcester, Mass.: Clark University Press, 1930. Pp. 395–405.

Adler, A. The fundamental views of individual psychology. *International Journal of Individual Psychology,* 1935, *1,* 5–8.

Adler, A. *Social interest.* New York: Putnam, 1939.

Allport, G. *Personality: A psychological interpretation.* New York: Holt, Rinehart and Winston, 1937.

Allport, G. *Becoming: Basic considerations for a psychology of personality.* New Haven, Conn.: Yale University Press, 1955.

Allport, G. *Pattern and growth in personality.* New York: Holt, Rinehart and Winston, 1961.

Allport, G. W. (Ed.). *Letters from Jenny.* New York: Harcourt Brace Jovanovich, 1965.

Allport, G. Autobiography. In E. G. Boring & G. Lindzey (Eds.), *A history of psychology in autobiography* (Vol. 5). New York: Appleton-Century-Crofts, 1967. Pp. 1–25.

Allport, G. Personality: Contemporary viewpoints. I. A unique and open system. In D. Sills (Ed.), *International encyclopedia of the social sciences* (Vol. 12). New York: Macmillan, 1968. Pp. 1–5.

Allport, G., Vernon, P. E., & Lindzey, G. *A study of values.* Boston: Houghton Mifflin, 1951.

Ansbacher, H. L., & Ansbacher, R. R. *The individual psychology of Alfred Adler.* New York: Basic Books, 1956.

Arndt, W. B. *Theories of personality.* New York: Macmillan, 1974.

Bandura, A. *Principles of behavior modification.* New York: Holt, Rinehart and Winston, 1969.

Bandura, A., & Walters, R. *Social learning and personality development.* New York: Holt, Rinehart and Winston, 1963.

Bannister, D. A new theory of personality. In B. M. Foss (Ed.), *New horizons in psychology.* Baltimore, Md.: Penguin, 1966.

Baughman, E. E., & Welsh, G. S. *Personality: A behavioral science.* Englewood Cliffs, N.J.: Prentice-Hall, 1962.

Bischof, L. J. *Interpreting personality theories* (2nd ed.). New York: Harper & Row, 1970.

Borgatta, E. F., & Lambert, W. W. (Eds.). *Handbook of personality and research.* Chicago: Rand McNally, 1968.

Bottome, P. *Alfred Adler.* New York: Vanguard, 1957.

Brams, J. From Freud to Fromm. *Psychology Today,* February 1968, pp. 32–35; 64–65.

Brody, N. *Personality: Research and theory.* New York: Academic Press, 1972.

Brown, J. A. C. *Freud and the post-Freudians.* Baltimore, Md.: Penguin, 1961.

Cattell, R. B. *The scientific analysis of personality.* Chicago: Aldine, 1965.

Cattell, R. B. Personality pinned down. *Psychology Today,* July 1973, pp. 40–46.

Cattell, R. B. Travels in psychological hyperspace. In T. S. Krawiec (Ed.), *The psychologists,* (Vol. 2). New York: Oxford University Press, 1974. Pp. 85–133.

Cattell, R. B. Autobiography. In G. Lindzey (Ed.), *A history of psychology in autobiography* (Vol. 6). Englewood Cliffs, N.J.: Prentice-Hall, 1974. Pp. 59–100.

Chaplin, J., & Krawiec, T. S. *Systems and theories of psychology* (2nd ed.). New York: Holt, Rinehart and Winston, 1968.

Cherry, R., & Cherry, L. The Horney heresy. *New York Times Magazine,* August 26, 1973, pp. 12 ff.

Cofer, C., & Appley, M. *Motivation: Theory and research.* New York: Wiley, 1964.

Coles, R. *Erik H. Erikson: The growth of his work.* Boston: Little, Brown, 1970.

DiCaprio, N. S. *Personality theories: Guides to living.* Philadelphia: Saunders, 1974.

Elkind, D. Erik Erikson's eight ages of man. *New York Times Magazine,* April 5, 1970, pp. 25 ff.

Elkind, D. "Good me" or "bad me"—the Sullivan approach to personality. *New York Times Magazine,* September 24, 1972, pp. 18 ff.

Erikson, E. H. *Childhood and society* (2nd ed.). New York: Norton, 1963.

Erikson, E. H. *Insight and responsibility.* New York: Norton, 1964.

Erikson, E. H. *Identity: Youth and crisis.* New York: Norton, 1968.

Evans, R. I. *Conversations with Carl Jung and reactions from Ernest Jones.* Princeton, N.J.: Van Nostrand, 1964.

Evans, R. I. *Dialogue with Erich Fromm.* New York: Harper & Row, 1966.

Evans, R. I. *Dialogue with Erik Erikson.* New York: Harper & Row, 1967.

Evans, R. I. *B. F. Skinner: The man and his ideas.* New York: Dutton, 1969.

Fordham, F. *An introduction to Jung's psychology.* Baltimore, Md.: Penguin, 1953.

Freud, S. *On the history of the psychoanalytic movement.* London: Hogarth Press, 1914.

Frick, W. B. *Humanistic psychology: Interviews with Maslow, Murphy, & Rogers.* Columbus, Ohio: Charles E. Merrill, 1971.

Fromm, E. *Escape from freedom.* New York: Holt, Rinehart and Winston, 1941.

Fromm, E. *Man for himself.* New York: Holt, Rinehart and Winston, 1947.

Fromm, E. *The heart of man.* New York: Harper & Row, 1964.

Fromm, E. *The revolution of hope.* New York: Harper & Row, 1968.

Geiwitz, P. J. *Non-Freudian personality theories.* Monterey, Calif.: Brooks/Cole, 1969.

Goble, F. G. *The third force: The psychology of Abraham Maslow.* New York: Grossman, 1970.

Hall, C. S. *A primer of Freudian psychology.* New York: World, 1954.

Hall, C. S., & Lindzey, G. *Theories of personality* (2nd ed.). New York: Wiley, 1970.

Hall, C. S., & Nordby, V. J. *A primer of Jungian psychology.* New York: New American Library, 1973.

Hall, M. H. An interview with "Mr. Behaviorist" B. F. Skinner. *Psychology Today,* September 1967, pp. 20–23; 68–71.

Hall, M. H. A conversation with Carl Rogers. *Psychology Today*, December 1967, pp. 18–21; 62–66.

Hall, M. H. A conversation with Abraham H. Maslow. *Psychology Today*, July 1968, pp. 34–37; 54–57.

Hall, M. H. A conversation with Henry A. Murray. *Psychology Today*, September 1968, pp. 56–63.

Hausdorff, D. Erich Fromm. Boston: Twayne, 1972.

Heidbreder, E. *Seven psychologies.* New York: Appleton-Century-Crofts, 1933.

Hilgard, E. R., & Bower, G. H. *Theories of learning* (4th ed.). Englewood Cliffs, N.J.: Prentice-Hall, 1975.

Horney, K. *The neurotic personality of our time.* New York: Norton, 1937.

Horney, K. *New ways in psychoanalysis.* New York: Norton, 1939.

Horney, K. *Self-analysis.* New York: Norton, 1942.

Horney, K. *Our inner conflicts.* New York: Norton, 1945.

Horney, K. *Neurosis and human growth.* New York: Norton, 1950.

Horney, K. *Feminine psychology.* New York: Norton, 1967.

Jaffé, A. *From the life and work of C. G. Jung.* New York: Harper & Row, 1971.

Janis, I. L., Mahl, G. F., Kagan, J., & Holt, R. R. *Personality: Dynamics, development, and assessment.* New York: Harcourt Brace Jovanovich, 1969.

Jones, E. *The life and work of Sigmund Freud* (3 vols.). New York: Basic Books, 1953–1957.

Jung, C. G. *The undiscovered self.* Boston: Little, Brown, 1957.

Jung, C. G. *Memories, dreams, reflections.* New York: Pantheon, 1961.

Kelly, G. A. *The psychology of personal constructs* (2 vols.). New York: Norton, 1955.

Kiester, E., & Cudhea, D. Albert Bandura: A very modern model. *Human behavior*, September 1974, pp. 27–31.

Kluckhohn, C., Murray, H. A., & Schneider, D. M. (Eds.). *Personality in nature, society, and culture* (2nd ed.). New York: Knopf, 1956.

Liebert, R. M., & Spiegler, M. D. *Personality: An introduction to theory and research.* Homewood, Ill.: Dorsey Press, 1970.

Lindzey, G., Hall, C. S., & Manosevitz, M. *Theories of personality: Primary sources and research* (2nd ed.). New York: Wiley, 1973.

McClelland, D. C. *Personality.* New York: Dryden Press, 1951.

McClelland, D. C. *The achieving society.* New York: Van Nostrand, 1961.

McClelland, D. C., Atkinson, J. W., Clark, R. A., & Lowell, E. L. *The achievement motive.* New York: Appleton-Century-Crofts, 1953.

McGuire, W. (Ed.). *The Freud/Jung letters.* Princeton, N.J.: Princeton University Press, 1974.

Maddi, S. R. Humanistic psychology: Allport & Murray. In J. Wepman & R. Heine (Eds.), *Concepts of personality.* Chicago: Aldine, 1963. Pp. 162–205.

Maddi, S. R. *Personality theories: A comparative analysis* (Rev. ed.). Homewood, Ill.: Dorsey Press, 1972.

Maddi, S. R., & Costa, P. T. *Humanism in personology.* Chicago: Aldine, 1972.

Maher, B. A. (Ed.). *Progress in experimental personality research* (Vol. 2). New York: Academic Press, 1965.

Marx, M. H., & Hillix, W. A. *Systems and theories in psychology* (2nd ed.). New York: McGraw-Hill, 1973.

Maslow, A. H. A philosophy of psychology: The need for a mature science of human nature. *Main Currents in Modern Thought*, 1957, *13*, 27–32.

Maslow, A. H. *The psychology of science*. New York: Harper & Row, 1966.

Maslow, A. H. *Toward a psychology of being* (2nd ed.). New York: Van Nostrand, 1968.

Maslow, A. H. *Motivation and personality* (2nd ed.). New York: Harper & Row, 1970.

Maslow, A. H. *The farther reaches of human nature*. New York: Viking, 1971.

Matson, F. W. *The broken image*. New York: George Braziller, 1964.

Mehrabian, A. *An analysis of personality theories*. Englewood Cliffs, N.J.: Prentice-Hall, 1968.

Miller, G. A., & Buckhout, R. *Psychology: The science of mental life* (2nd ed.). New York: Harper & Row, 1973.

Mischel, W. *Introduction to personality*. New York: Holt, Rinehart and Winston, 1971.

Munroe, R. L. *Schools of psychoanalytic thought*. New York: Holt, Rinehart and Winston, 1955.

Murray, H. A., et al. *Explorations in personality*. New York: Oxford University Press, 1938.

Murray, H. A. Autobiography. In E. G. Boring & G. Lindzey (Eds.), *A history of psychology in autobiography* (Vol. 5.). New York: Appleton-Century-Crofts, 1967. Pp. 283–310.

Murray, H. A. Personality: Contemporary viewpoints. II. Components of an evolving personological system. In D. Sills (Ed.), *International encyclopedia of the social sciences* (Vol. 12). New York: Macmillan, 1968. Pp. 5–13.

Neel, A. F. *Theories of psychology: A handbook*. Cambridge, Mass.: Schenkman, 1969.

Orgler, H. *Alfred Adler: The man and his work*. New York: Liveright, 1963.

Progoff, I. *The death and rebirth of psychology*. New York: Julian Press, 1956.

Rachlin, H. *Introduction to modern behaviorism*. San Francisco: W. H. Freeman, 1970.

Roazen, P. *Freud and his followers*. New York: Knopf, 1975.

Rogers, C. R. *On becoming a person*. Boston: Houghton Mifflin, 1961.

Rogers, C. R. Toward a science of the person. In T. Wann (Ed.), *Behaviorism and phenomenology*. Chicago: University of Chicago Press, 1964. Pp. 109–133.

Rogers, C. R. Autobiography. In E. G. Boring & G. Lindzey (Eds.), *A history of psychology in autobiography* (Vol. 5). New York: Appleton-Century-Crofts, 1967. Pp. 341–384.

Rychlak, J. F. *Introduction to personality and psychotherapy*. Boston: Houghton Mifflin, 1973.

Sahakian, W. S. (Ed.). *Psychology of personality: Readings in theory* (2nd ed.). Chicago: Rand McNally, 1974.

Sanford, N. Personality: Its place in psychology. In S. Koch (Ed.), *Psychology: A study of a science* (Vol. 5). New York: McGraw-Hill, 1963.

Scarf, M. The man who gave us "inferiority complex," "compensation," "aggressive drive" and "style of life." *New York Times Magazine,* February 28, 1971, pp. 10 ff.

Schultz, D. *A history of modern psychology* (2nd ed.). New York: Academic Press, 1975.

Singer, J. *Boundaries of the soul: The practice of Jung's psychology.* Garden City, New York: Doubleday, 1972.

Skinner, B. F. *Walden two.* New York: Macmillan, 1948.

Skinner, B. F. *Science and human behavior.* New York: Macmillan, 1953.

Skinner, B. F. Autobiography. In E. G. Boring & G. Lindzey (Eds.), *A history of psychology in autobiography* (Vol. 5). New York: Appleton-Century-Crofts, 1967. Pp. 385–413.

Skinner, B. F. The machine that is man. *Psychology Today,* April 1969, pp. 20–25; 60–63.

Skinner, B. F. *Beyond freedom and dignity.* New York: Knopf, 1971.

Southwell, E. A., & Merbaum, M. *Personality: Readings in theory and research* (2nd ed.). Monterey, Calif.: Brooks/Cole, 1971.

Storr, A. *C. G. Jung.* New York: Viking Press, 1973.

Thompson, G. G. George Alexander Kelly. *Journal of General Psychology,* 1968, *79,* 19–24.

Wepman, J., & Heine, R. (Eds.). *Concepts of personality.* Chicago: Aldine, 1963.

Whitmont, E. Jungian analysis today. *Psychology Today,* December 1972, pp. 63–72.

Wiggins, J. S., Renner, K. E., Clore, G. L., & Rose, R. J. *The psychology of personality.* Reading, Mass.: Addison-Wesley, 1971.

Witkin, H. A., et al. *Personality through perception.* New York: Harper & Row, 1954.

Witkin, H. A., et al. *Psychological differentiation.* New York: Halstead, 1974.

Wollheim, R. *Sigmund Freud.* New York: Viking, 1971.

Woodworth, R. S., & Sheehan, M. *Contemporary schools of psychology* (3rd ed.). New York: Ronald Press, 1964.

Index